THE NEW
TESTAMENT
WORLD

THE NEW TESTAMENT WORLD

JOHN AND KATHLEEN COURT

PRENTICE-HALL
Englewood Cliffs, N.J. 07632

DEDICATION

This book is dedicated to Kingsley Barrett, a beloved theological guide and counsellor to both of us. We hope he will accept this, and not grade our essays too strictly!

ACKNOWLEDGEMENTS

We also wish to express our thanks to our many colleagues and friends, particularly in the New Testament society (*Studiorum Novi Testamenti Societas*), and at Simon Langton Girls' School in Canterbury. We owe a great debt to them in terms of ideas, encouragement and practical help. The constraints of this volume prevent us from acknowledging every indebtedness; but we hope they will recognize their contribution and accept our gratitude.

In particular we must thank by name: Professor C.K. Barrett for his critique on the chapter on John; Professor R.McL. Wilson for his valuable assistance on the subject of Gnosticism; Dr. G. Meaden for drawing the range of maps so splendidly; and finally the whole staff of John Calmann and King Ltd. without whose aid this project would not have been either started or completed. "Let the reader understand" (Mark 13.14).

North and South American Edition first published in 1990 by Prentice-Hall, Inc.
Englewood Cliffs
NJ 07632

A John Calmann and King book

ISBN 0–13–538992–5

This book was designed and produced by
JOHN CALMANN AND KING LTD, LONDON

Designed by Karen Osborne
Picture Research by Sara Waterson
Typeset by Fakenham Photosetting Ltd
Printed and bound in Hong Kong

CREDITS

The authors and publishers wish to acknowledge, with thanks, the following photographic sources:

Rev. J.C. Allen: 84, 189, 203, 240, 315 (top); Ancient Art and Architecture Collection: 54 (top, right), 103; Andes Press/Carlos Reyes: 368; Art Institute of Chicago; Gift of Alfred S. Anschuler: 137; Ashmolean Museum, Oxford: 219; Barnaby's Picture Library: 32, 54 (bottom), 65, 255, 264, 363; Bib. Medicea Laurenziana, Florence/Photo Sansoni: 141; Bib. Nationale, Paris: 71 (right), 167; Bodleian Library, Oxford: 300, 369; British Library: 16, 73, 178, 188, 331 (left); British Museum: 18, 30 (left), 30 (right), 31 (left), 75, 132, 141, 204 (bottom), 217 (top), 293, 305, 321, 357; Bridgeman Art Library: 71 (left), 205, 262, 297; BAL/Akademie der Bildendenkunst, Vienna: 298; BAL/British Library: 2, 85, 249; BAL/Lambeth Palace Library: 19 (left); BAL/Mus. des Beaux Arts, Ghent: 74; BAL/York City Art Gallery: 180, 350; Cephas/Mick Rock: 69, 261; J & K Court: 19 (left), 20 (bottom), 88, 92, 104, 117, 139 (left), 140 (left), 140, 149 (top), 168 (bottom), 171, 197, 224, 253; Courtauld Institute London: 226; C.M. Dixon: 349 (top, left); Fitzwilliam Museum, Cambridge: 190; Fotomas Index: 91, 206 (top), 206 (bottom); The Guardian: 128; German Archaeological Institute Rome: 110, 152; Sonia Halliday Collection: 1, 20 (top, left), 20 (top, right), 72 (top), 72 (bottom), 138 (top), 149 (bottom), 150 (top, left), 150 (top, right), 150 (bottom), 168 (top), 177, 179, 195 (left), 195 (right), 215, 229, 233, 250, 252, 256, 279 (top), 315 (bottom, left), 316, 349 (bottom), 367 (bottom); Hirmer Verlag: 209; Michael Holford: 248, 341; Hunterian Collection of the University Library, Glasgow: 318; Institute for Antiquity and Christianity, Claremont, Calif: 338, 343; Israel Museum, Jerusalem: 153, 202 (top), 204 (top); JCK Archives: 111, 123, 353; AF Kersting: 186, 299, 360; Kunsthaus, Zurich: 53; Landesmuseum, Trier: 21; Mansell Collection: 24, 29, 157, 247 (right), 313, 325, 339; Mansell/Alinari: 15, 46, 67, 119, 246, 269, 296, 317; Mansell/Anderson: 52, 86, 145, 247 (left); Metropolitan Museum of Art, New York/Rogers Fund: 20 (top, left)/Gift of Philip Hofer: 32/Gift of J. Pierpoint Morgan: 108/Bequest of Michael Friedsam: 355; National Gallery of Art Washington; Chester Gall Collection: 280; Richard Nowitz: 54 (top, left), 59, 89, 101 (bottom), 367 (top); Pont. Comm. di Arch. Sacra, Rome: 131, 133, 222; Popperfoto: 28, 61, 94, 163; Robert Hunt Library: 154, 320; Scala Fotografica: 101 (top), 223, 279 (bottom), 315 (bottom, right); Staatliche Museen Preussischer Kulturbesitz, E. Berlin: 340; University of Manchester, John Rylands Library: 238; Victoria and Albert Museum, Crown Copyright: 331 (top, right); Williamson Art Gallery, Wirral: 138; Jerry Wooldridge: 102; Yale University Art Collection: 198; Estate of Yigael Yadin: 202 (bottom, left). The "split orange" diagram of Gnostic spheres on page 335 was taken from *Gnosis* by Kurt Rudolph, 1983. Reproduced by permission of the publishers T & T Clark.

Half title: The parable of the sower (13th century CE stained glass detail from a Bible window in the North choir aisle, Canterbury cathedral).

Frontispiece: Christ in Majesty from the Stavelot Bible (1093–7). The traditional symbols of the four evangelists are seen in the roundels at the corners.

Contents

CHAPTER 4
THE MATTHEAN CHURCH AND JUDAISM 187

CHAPTER 5
JOHN AND THE COMMUNITY APART 238

Introduction

The Jewish author Isaac Bashevis Singer gave this advice to writers: "They should write a story with a beginning, a middle and an end, so that the reader doesn't say, 'I was confused'. There is no great art in confusing the reader."

Such advice, fully in accord with the classical definition of the plot in literature, is equally relevant for authors embarking on the task of introducing the New Testament documents in their diversity, within the context of the Mediterranean world of the first century. So we shall tell the story straight, in three parts. The first provides background information, showing how we may reasonably claim to know about the rudiments of the Christian faith in its original historical setting of the lifetime of Jesus. The middle section shows how the various communities of early Christians developed their understanding of these basic facts and related them to their ways of living, for example in their work and their worship, where some of the pressures and the enthusiasms are comparable to those of the modern world. The final section indicates how in the first hundred years or more of Christianity many of these groups came together or became more conscious of their interrelationships. In this way, institutional structures and concepts of authority emerged in the early Church.

The evidence for these developments is to be found in the pages of the New Testament documents, considered in the light of critical scholarship in such fields as archaeology, history, sociology and literature. And it is precisely this broad range of critical options, this mixture of possibilities within the cultural contexts of the ancient world, that we must consider when reading the New Testament. We have no business to settle exclusively on one option and impose this single method on all the evidence. This would have the neatness of a monochrome picture and the satisfaction of monolithic unity. But it would be a scholar's fiction.

In contrast the current volume was deliberately conceived as a multi-coloured picture on a broad canvas. We aim to provide a balanced presentation in words and pictures of the New Testament world. The use of illustration has several functions: not only does it facilitate direct understanding of the results of archaeology, the reconstruction of the social situation, and the descriptions of historical and geographical background; it can also be used to help make important distinctions clear in the more abstract areas of thought about early church doctrine and practice. So, for example, Salvador Dali's painting of *Christ of St. John of the Cross* can be compared and contrasted with Graham Sutherland's tapestry of *Christ in Majesty* from Coventry Cathedral in order to show the different emphases, and Christological statements, which are being made in pictures of Jesus. Such distinctions are as valid in early word pictures in the Gospels as they are in modern works of art. In the same way pictures and images which illustrate varieties of church practice and worship in the modern world can provide helpful analogies to the behaviour of ancient religious communities.

Because the subject matter of religion is of general interest, whether the reader is committed to Christianity or not, one might well go on to ask a question with a philosophical perspective: what is the essential relationship between practising a religion (that is declaring faith in Jesus Christ) and creating a body of writings (the literature that belongs to Christianity)? We possess some of these writings in what is widely known as the Bible (the Old and New Testaments); we may know of other materials of this kind from Church worship, materials such as the creeds and the formulations of liturgy. How essential are these writings to the living faith of Christianity? What purposes did they serve historically? What purposes do they still serve? Are they the inspiration or have they become the straitjacket of the Christian religion? Such questions come to a focus in the concluding chapter of the book.

This book begins by exploring the relation between the faith and practice of the earliest Christians and the creation of the New Testament books called "gospels". What is a gospel?

The preaching of the cross

A dictionary definition of gospel is as follows:

> *noun*: the teaching of Christ; a narrative of the life of Christ, esp. one of those included in the New Testament, Matthew, Mark, Luke, and John: good news [Old English *godspel(l)*, a translation of the Latin *evangelium* which is in turn from the Greek *euaggelion*, meaning *gôd* = good + *spel(l)* = story]

Simple dictionary definitions, however – "a life/a biography of Jesus" – are inadequate and may even be misleading. Two of the gospels (Mark and John) see no reason to begin with the birth of Jesus; and of the others only Luke tells us (Luke 2.41–53) anything of Jesus' life between the time of his presentation in the Temple at a few weeks old, and the baptism in the river Jordan at about the age of thirty. Biographies rarely have this sort of gap in the chronology. Although the focus of interest seems to be the ministry of Jesus, it is difficult to ascertain whether this lasted for one or for three years. Furthermore, it is almost impossible to determine the correct chronological order of the events within the ministry. Mark's was probably the earliest of the gospels to be written down, and he concentrates on the last week of Jesus' ministry for one third of the space of his gospel. This would be quite out of proportion in any normal chronological biography.

Perhaps the modern idea of biography is not a helpful approach to the question of defining a gospel. Were the early Christians really concerned with producing an objective, scientific, historical account of Jesus' life – or were they attempting something else? Acts 2.22–24, for example, reads like a summary of the gospel in the form of preaching:

> *Men of Israel, hear these words: Jesus of Nazareth, a man attested to you by God with mighty works and wonders and signs which God did through him in your midst, as you yourselves know – this Jesus, delivered up according to the definite plan and foreknowledge of God, you crucified and killed by the hands of lawless men. But God raised him up, having loosed the pangs of death, because it was not possible for him to be held by it.*

This suggests what a gospel is intended to be: a proclamation of faith in Jesus, based on the historical events of his life and death. It is not a "straight" biography or history; it is a preaching. The original Greek word used in the New Testament for "preaching" is *kerygma*. Modern theologians and commentators often use this Greek word as shorthand for the gospel as preached. It is a telling of the story of Jesus from the standpoint of faith, in order to evoke faith in others. The belief is that God has acted within history on behalf of humanity. This means there is an overriding religious and theological dimension to the gospel of Jesus which we think is untraceable in the other, contemporary or earlier, Greek lives cited as parallels by recent scholars. And there is no parallel in Judaism to the Christian gospel's concentration upon the significance of a single person. The gospels are a unique form of literature, produced by a unique belief, in response to a unique situation.

The growth of a tradition

How do we reconstruct the information to fill the gaps in the sequence between the words of Jesus himself; the church preaching about Jesus (e.g. Peter's preaching in the Temple, in Acts 2); and the pages of the New Testament? The sequence can be broken down into three stages: oral tradition, written tradition, and the conferring of authority on selected material.

1 Oral tradition The apostles and eyewitnesses who had been with Jesus and are the original source had had their lives changed by the encounter. They would therefore have remembered both the events that had taken place and the words of Jesus. The way in which stories and legends were handed on in the ancient world was by word of mouth from one generation to the next; modern research among non-literate societies shows that such tradition is sacred, protected, and unvarying. Within such a framework of oral tradition, Jesus may well have trained his disciples, as Jewish rabbis trained theirs, to learn by rote.

2 Written tradition Jesus' teaching in pithy sayings and memorable parables may well have existed as isolated individual units at first, but then came to be collected as "sayings of Jesus", strung together like beads on a thread, and then written down. Papias, an early church bishop, says that "Matthew composed the Sayings ..."; traces of this are certainly visible in the gospel which bears his name (e.g. Matthew 13). Jesus' teaching about the end of the world – a very pressing and urgent topic in the first century – may well have been collected, interpreted and written down quite early (e.g. Mark 13).

The death of the eyewitness generation – whether through natural causes or martyrdom – brought about the need for a permanent and trustworthy record of what had happened, for those in the church and outside it. Mark fitted the various items of preaching and collections of sayings etc. into an outline scheme of the life of Jesus. This was added to and altered by Matthew and Luke, with the interests of their own particular Christian communities in mind. John probably followed a largely independent tradition.

3 Authoritative tradition The growth of an authoritative tradition is a long and complex process. Over a period of time a number of gospels were written, some of which can now be read only in collections entitled "The Apocryphal New Testament". Some were charming, some bizarre, and some (according to the teachings increasingly finding acceptance within the church) were downright dangerous and heretical. In a period when Christianity was beset by intermittent persecution from the civil authorities, and by conflicting teachings from within, the churches sifted out the best of the gospels, and eventually gave these four and no others the stamp of authority. The canon of the New Testament was forged *c.* 200 CE. The final selection was by no means a foregone conclusion; the gospel of John, for example, nearly did not survive it.

The gospel grew backwards

The way in which the gospel grew reflects the priorities of the early church. Aspects of the life and teachings of Jesus were included in the church's teaching in the reverse of the order in which they happened. The early Christians were preaching Christ crucified and resurrected; they needed accounts with witnesses to prove this; they selected from the best available for this purpose. The church also came to view all other events to do with Jesus in the light of the *Resurrection*; this automatically required an account of Jesus' death and burial, and also of the events leading up to his trial and execution. The set of *Passion stories* must also have been assembled early on. As we have seen, these events covering one week (called by Christians "Holy Week") occupy one third of Mark.

The church needed to show, by the way it told these stories, that Jesus was in fact innocent and that what happened to him was no unfortunate accident but was in accordance with what the Old Testament prophets had foretold. These two motives are called apologetic tendencies. "Apologetic" is used in the technical sense of providing an explanation for something. These motives shape the way the stories are told.

A second group of stories is concerned with the *controversies* that surrounded Jesus. They accounted for the growth of enmity and aggression between the religious authorities and Jesus, attitudes which culminated in his execution (see Mark 2.1–3.6). These stories not only set the historical record straight (as the Christians saw it), but also gave some guidance to those Christians who were still engaged in debate with the Jewish synagogues.

The underlying questions in the controversy stories are: "Who is Jesus?" and "What right has he to do/say these things?" These questions are answered by the inclusion of a number of status stories, varying from the accounts of Jesus' baptism and his Transfiguration (where God himself is heard to confirm Jesus' status), to the temptation stories (where Jesus forges his own interpretation of what being the Messiah is all about), and to those occasions where Jesus tries to put this over to the disciples (e.g. Mark 8.27–33).

Jesus' status is further enhanced by *miracle stories* about his actions (faith healings, exorcisms or expulsion of demonic powers, feeding the crowds and rescuing the disciples) which attract attention and indicate special powers. Claiming to work miracles and performing magic were not uncommon in the ancient world. This was the way many people thought about the healing of physical and psychological illness. But the gospels are not trying to set Jesus up as a bigger and better magician than his rivals. The stories are told about him with some reticence; they create a sense of awe and mystery as well as a picture of caring compassion.

It is unlikely that we have a full and complete set of Jesus' *teaching*, either in proverbial sayings or in parables (illustrative stories); nor do the constructed sequences of discourse or sermon preserve the original logic of Jesus' argument. Christians preserved Christ's teaching either because of what it said about him or for the ethical guidance it gave them in living the Christian life. Various heretical sects thrived for a while on the basis that they were peddling "authentic" teachings of Jesus which had been committed in secret to the innermost circle of his disciples, and were not therefore for public consumption. Some remains of these (which would be called bizarre from the perspective of the gospels of the New Testament canon) are to be seen in the Gnostic tradition of "secret" or "alternative" gospels (see Chapter 7).

Much of the teaching that is preserved in the New Testament gives indications of its usefulness for church purposes, for example in how the words of Jesus were used to resolve moral dilemmas (e.g. 1 Corinthians 7.10). Other aspects of the teaching defined the role of the church in the world, e.g. the parable of the sower in Mark 4.2ff and its sequel in Mark 4.11–12 and 13–20, where Christians are exhorted to go out and preach but are warned that their preaching will not always be successful. It is therefore likely that what we find preserved is what was useful for the making and instruction of new Christians.

Teachings about the imminence of the *end of the world* catered for an all-consuming interest of many Jewish and early Christian believers. In particular Mark 13 seems to be a special collection of this material, a kind of "Apocalypse" in miniature. Its purpose is very practical, to interpret a crisis, and to deliver a warning to those inside and outside of the church community. The moral is "Take heed ... watch!" as the parable of the master's absence found at 13.33–37 shows.

Finally, with the *birth stories* the gospel tradition reaches the theoretical starting-point. But these stories could equally well be regarded as *status stories*, validating Jesus' claims about himself. The view of many modern theologians is that the birth stories are charming legends which were used by Matthew and Luke, not only to give Jesus a logical human beginning as a baby, but also to say various important things about him, e.g. that Jesus was of proper descent from King David; that the messianic promises could rightly be claimed as referring to him; and that it is possible that a human being could also be a Son of God. The writer of the fourth gospel apparently knew these stories (see John 7.41–42; 8.41) but, for some reason, did not wish to use them. He preferred to root the existence of Jesus not in babyhood, but in the pre-existent Word, before creation itself.

Out of all this raw material each of the evangelists was able to select what suited his purpose, in order to write the gospel for his community and their particular situation. The gospels were not pious works of fiction, but were carefully constructed on the basis of solid, accumulated evidence. They were the end product of an extended process of reflection in a religious context. The whole was thoughtfully interpreted to meet local needs and concerns.

Each gospel therefore affords us a different interpretation of Jesus and what he said and did. This is not to say that there are not many similarities; indeed, for example, the same parables are shared by Mark with Matthew and Luke, and the feeding of the five thousand occurs in all four gospels. But each evangelist contributes something distinctive, as he considers the basic *kerygma* from his situation. Similarly, each of the gospels has a particular approach to Jesus, and its material is shaped accordingly. We shall look at the main characteristics of each gospel in Chapters 1, 3, 4, and 5.

The evidence

The New Testament is an established collection of twenty-seven books. However definitive the collection, the books themselves vary in kinds of writing and in length and have emerged from a range of distinctive situations. The books can be read as classics of literature, to appreciate what each book is saying, and why and how it is saying so. For this purpose it is important, therefore, to bring literary criteria to bear on the text, and consider the source material, the methods of editing or constructing the text, the style of writing, and the various indicators of the work's structure.

It is important to remember, however, that the New Testament is not just a set of literary classics, but was written as the guide book to living the Christian life. The nature of the story and the style of the literature should be considered in the light of their purpose as preaching and teaching. So we must be fully aware of the contexts in the Christian communities in which these books were created. The story was told in a certain style because the community wanted to communicate its belief, or needed to set down guidelines for its own life as a church.

The New Testament is the source for the body of teaching and preaching at the same time as providing evidence of the social and historical context within which the teaching was promulgated. The historical situation can be understood better by bringing together the evidence from the New Testament itself, with documentary and archaeological evidence for its environmental setting in the Mediterranean world, and the social and political movements within the Roman Empire at this period. The data include imperial and provincial archives, the statements of classical writers, the evidence from inscriptions and coinage, and the conclusions about societies that can be drawn from archaeological excavations of ancient sites.

On its own the application of each category of evidence is strictly limited. Because archaeology, for example, is concerned with material remains, there are practical constraints on what an archaeologist can reasonably claim to tell us. But some inferences can be drawn from an excavation about the social structure, organization, and values of the people concerned. Archaeology can treat only certain aspects of the evidence; studies of a text are concerned with other kinds of evidence. In combination they can provide a more complete picture of the material, social, and intellectual culture. By studying the enlarged range of accumulated evidence with insights derived from the disciplines of sociology and social anthropology, we can achieve a multi-dimensional view, and some explanation of the particular regions of the Mediterranean world with which we are concerned in New Testament studies. Books exist within communities; they exist in the acts of writing and being read aloud; and they exist in the processes of circulation and use.

The critical methods

This section looks at some of the methods used in New Testament study today. From what has already been said, it should be clear that a complementary use of a variety of methods will give a more rounded view than exclusive reliance on one method of criticism.

Historical method

This seeks to assess the relative reliability of different kinds of evidence and to determine the ordering of events. Historical evidence is not restricted to the annals, lists, and records of civil servants in ancient societies, and the narratives of professional historians in the ancient world. All materials can be used, provided the types of evidence are distinguished, the appropriate questions are asked, and the weight of the evidence is judged accordingly. An ancient piece of fiction can be useful to an historian in showing the interests and presuppositions of a society, but it should not be confused with an ancient factual chronicle.

A report is more likely to be reliable if it is written down soon after the event to which it refers. Details mentioned in a narrative may be historical clues to the date. For example, a detailed description of the fall of Jerusalem in a narrative would indicate that the document achieved its final form sometime after 70 CE. Trustworthy reports of the same event can be expected to agree with one another in many (but not all) respects. Disagreements and

The Fall of Jerusalem as depicted on the Arch of Titus in Rome. Victorious Romans carry the spoils, including the Menorah (seven-branched candlestick), from the Temple.

differences of emphasis can be explained by the standpoints of their authors. Where disagreements or inconsistencies occur in a single narrative, this may indicate an unreliable account, or one that is a composite, i.e. a result of the blending of traditions from more than one source. It is important for a historian to make allowances for any strong or consistent bias which the original author has imposed upon his material. This would include the interpretation of events in the light of religious belief. A modern historian may have to be particularly careful in the assessment of miracle stories or elements of the supernatural or of fantasy within the narrative. These are not to be dismissed automatically, but they may say more about the beliefs of the original readers or writer than about events of historical fact.

Next, a chronology is constructed from the various pieces of historical evidence that have been assessed as useful and reliable. At this stage the different kinds of "literary" evidence are interrelated with other material evidence from archaeology. This can be dated by coins, or by the pottery levels with which it is associated, or by the radiocarbon method of dating (where the decay of the radioactive isotope of carbon, ^{14}C, is measured, to indicate the age of the material analysed). What results is an approximate historical framework in which a miscellaneous variety of elements are grouped in chronological sequence.

With any sequence of disparate material, discovered at random, there are bound to be serious gaps. Historians achieve a reconstruction of the main framework into which much of the wealth of supporting detail can be fitted.

The task resembles completing a jigsaw puzzle with no picture to follow, and many pieces missing. With careful application, drawing on analogous experience, and with some speculation, some of the gaps can provisionally be filled.

Christians often claim that the events of the New Testament stand quite outside the ordinary run of historical happenings. But the understanding of historical events is culturally relative, i.e., the understanding of historical events can never be unbiased. Observers – of whatever century – carry with them a complex set of assumptions about how the world works, a "world view" that is specific to their own cultures. Thus the evidence written down by the evangelists is coloured by the attitudes and ideas of the times and place in which they lived; similarly, the interpretation of modern historians is conditioned by the scientific methods and assumptions of the modern world. So honest historians may assess the reliability or otherwise of the evidence for Christianity, but are unable to accept claims for the absoluteness of Christianity. Historians are in a position to investigate, to the best of their knowledge and ability (relative to their own situation), those elements of Christianity which appear different and distinctive within the ancient world,

A page from St. John's gospel in the later codex (book) form of New Testament manuscripts. Compare this with the fragmentary papyrus on page 238.

to distinguish those features in which Christianity, on present knowledge, appears to stand out from its environment, as well as those which are deeply rooted in their time and place.

Literary criticism

At least to begin with, the methods of the literary critic are also historical, just as the historian also studies literary products. The study of ancient literature must involve an understanding of the practicalities of writing, the availability of writing materials, and the social implications of communicating in writing rather than orally, and of using Greek rather than Aramaic or Hebrew.

> *All the New Testament books were written within a period of one hundred years from the death of Jesus Christ, and they were all written in Greek, for Greek-speaking readers, by men who for the most part themselves lived in a Greek-speaking society. There can, then, be no accurate reconstruction of primitive Christian thought which does not rest upon an accurate study of the grammar and syntax of the Greek language during the first century AD [CE], and upon an accurate knowledge of the meaning which the Greek words used by Christian writers had for their readers.*
>
> (Hoskyns and Davey, *Riddle of the New Testament*, p. 16)

In the early years of the twentieth century, large numbers of ancient Greek papyri were discovered in Egypt, preserved in the desert. The Greek language represented here was the *Koine* (common) Hellenistic form that was the vernacular of the New Testament period. It was the ordinary spoken language of the time, but, as these papyri show, it was also used for written correspondence and business records. These texts greatly enlarged the "dictionary" which scholars could consult in interpreting the meaning of the New Testament, and they led to the conclusion that the New Testament was simply written in the ordinary vernacular of its day. This was the obvious language to use, for ease of communication.

This is not the whole story of New Testament Greek. The language also belongs within the tradition of Biblical Greek, established by the Greek translations (notably the SEPTUAGINT) of the Old Testament in Hebrew. It is Greek with a Semitic background, for those brought up on the Old Testament. So any Greek word in the New Testament could possibly set up a chain of resonances for a reader/hearer of that time. It could have a Biblical aura, reminiscent of the Old Testament; in that sense the language had "scriptural" connotations. At the same time, it could set up echoes of the ordinary speech of the day. Just as the gospel message speaks of God's son being made incarnate, so the language of the gospel is cast in everyday speech.

Here are two examples to illustrate the association of ideas that is available to readers of the New Testament:

Coins from Greek and Roman sources to assist archaeological dating.

1 *hypostasis* in Hebrews 11.1:
In the Greek papyri the word means "title-deeds"; the central idea is of something underlying the visible conditions which guarantees the future; it is concretely represented in documentary evidence of ownership. So the text would mean: "Faith is the title-deed/guarantee of what is hoped for". By contrast, in the Septuagint this word translates the Hebrew *toheleth* meaning "hope"; it indicates the attitude of patient expectation and waiting in confidence.

2 *parousia*: used frequently in the New Testament of Christ's coming or second coming/return.
In the papyri the word denotes a royal visit, the "coming" or the "presence" of a king. In contrast, the Jewish writer Josephus uses the same word, in the light of the Old Testament tradition, specifically of the holy cloud and mist surrounding the wilderness Tabernacle (e.g. Exodus 33.10). It therefore refers to the presence of God himself in a THEOPHANY.

Establishing the authentic text of the New Testament

An authentic version of the text is the first requirement for the study of the New Testament. There are no authors' manuscripts or "first editions" that have survived from the first century CE. Prior to the CODICES produced in the fourth century and later, the surviving texts are partial and fragmentary. Texts can be dated by the kind of writing or the material used, or by external facts such as where they were found or when a particular wording is quoted by the church fathers. This means that scholars must attempt to reconstruct the "original" text of the New Testament on the basis of the most rigorous and systematic comparison of available manuscripts and early translations (e.g. into Syriac or Latin). Scholars are familiar with the kind of changes, additions, and alterations which happen to manuscripts in the processes of copying and use. They can make allowance for these in their desire to preserve the most accurate readings and to try to reconstruct the original text.

The text of the New Testament has undergone a long historical process which may also reflect regional variations. It is the history of the way the New Testament has been used by religious people in many different times and places. It involves not only many sequences of texts reproduced in the original language, but also the complicating processes of translation from Greek into new languages, which may not possess exactly equivalent expressions for what was originally said. There are two main concerns which apply to the transmission of such a text in any age: the *contemporary* concern and the *scriptural* concern. Firstly, because a text is felt to be relevant to the present day, great attention is paid to clarifying what it says – by notes in the margin or by extended commentaries – in order to provide answers to religious problems of the day, and confirm the Christian faith. Secondly, a religious community which depends for its existence upon sacred scripture will do all that it can to safeguard the correct, original content and meaning

below Tree of Jesse from the Vaux Psalter. From the sleeping figure of Jesse (Isaiah 11.1) at the foot of the initial letter, comes the tree of Davidic descent bearing the figures of Child and Virgin, Christ crucified, and Christ enthroned.

above Mary the mother of Jesus, and king Josiah – details from the Jesse window, North Corona, Canterbury cathedral.

Old and New Testament figures in parallel, from the North porch of Chartres cathedral. **left** Isaiah, Jeremiah, Simeon, John the Baptist, Peter (+ Elijah). **right** Melchizedek, Abraham, Moses, Samuel (+ Peter).

Noah's Ark as depicted in the Vienna manuscript of Genesis.

Transport by cart and mule, such as the Ethiopian (Acts 8.27f) may have used (Roman, 1st century CE).

of that scripture. Recognizing the power of these twin concerns, and the tension between them, we can appreciate developments brought about by the history of the church, while remaining confident that the tradition reflects a conscientious desire to reproduce the original text.

Comparisons of different texts are best made in the original language. Modern editions of the Greek Testament have full sets of notes to indicate variations between manuscripts. Although English translations are less satisfactory for this purpose, footnotes in the text, the comparison of different translations, and the use of commentaries can help one to appreciate textual questions. Here is one example of an interesting and significant variation:

Acts 8.37 does not appear in the main text of the Revised Standard Version (RSV), although there is a full reference to the Ethiopian's confession in the text of the old Authorized (King James) Version. In the RSV you will find it in a footnote: "Other ancient authorities add all or most of verse 37: *And Philip said, 'If you believe with all your heart, you may.' And he replied, 'I believe that Jesus Christ is the Son of God.'*" In the ancient manuscripts the pattern of evidence for including these words strongly suggests that they were added to the original because of an anxiety in the church that proper baptismal initiation must be preceded by a confession of faith.

Identifying the literary sources

Over many centuries there has been curiosity about the literary relationships between the first three gospels. Since J. J. Griesbach arranged the text of Matthew, Mark, and Luke in parallel columns in 1776 they have been termed "SYNOPTIC GOSPELS". Direct comparisons reveal many close similarities (and significant differences) between them, affecting subject matter, order of events, and even actual wording.

1 In subject matter, nearly all of Mark is found in Matthew and Luke taken together. Matthew especially contains nearly all of Mark, with other material as well.
2 Mark's order of events is normally followed by Matthew and Luke.
3 The evidence of vocabulary from a sample paragraph (Matthew 21.23–27; Mark 11, 27–33; Luke 20. 1–8) is as follows:
   Matthew has 116 words, 105 have parallels, 95 paralleled in Mark;
   Mark has 125 words, 109 have parallels;
   Luke has 118 words, 88 have parallels, 79 paralleled in Mark.

Scholars have agreed that the only adequate explanation for all three kinds of "agreement", especially when they occur together, is that there is a literary relationship between these three gospels. The majority of scholars agree that it is Mark which stands in some special relationship over against the other two, in short that Mark is the source which Matthew and Luke have each used independently. This conclusion is based on the evidence of "disagreements" as well as "agreements". For example, the order of events in Matthew and Mark agrees in some instances where Luke follows a different sequence. Similarly, Luke and Mark sometimes agree where Matthew diverges but it is quite rare for Matthew and Luke to agree and for Mark to differ. There are some signs of growing support for the explanation, first proffered by the church father Augustine, that Matthew came first (as the source for the others). But there are problems with this theory: if Mark used Matthew, what reason did Mark have for omitting so much of Matthew? If he was summarizing Matthew, why did he actually tell Matthew's stories in a longer form? It is more probable that the relationship was the other way round.

Apart from Mark, it is argued that Matthew and Luke had another source in common. This source has not survived, and so scholars call their reconstructions of it "Q" (the initial letter of the German word *Quelle* for "source"). The theory has it that both Matthew and Luke made use of this collection, principally of teaching material. One of the best examples of "Q" material is the preaching of John the Baptist (Matthew 3.7–10; Luke 3.7–9). But other relationships are much more speculative. Agreements are in terms of vocabulary, or of shared ideas; but the underlying order is derived from Mark. So there is not the corroboration of three kinds of agreement which is the strength of the argument for Mark as a source. However, it is clear that Matthew and Luke both used other sources than Mark. Much of this was independent material, unknown to, or unused by, the other. "Q" may be not so much a document as an area of overlap in their sources.

Oral tradition behind the written gospel

Scholars were eager to press further back, earlier than the written gospels, earlier than rediscovered documentary sources, to oral tradition of early

Material common to Matthew and Luke which may belong to a written source "Q"

Luke		Matthew
3.7–9, 16f	Preaching of John the Baptist	3.7–12
4.1–13	Temptations of Jesus	4.1–11
6.20–49	Preaching of Jesus	various (chs. 5, 7, 10, 12, 15)
7.1–10	Centurion at Capernaum	8.5–10, 12
7.18–35	John's question; Jesus' reply	11.2–11, 16–19
9.57–62	Nature of discipleship	8.19–22
10.2; 8–16	The mission charge	9.37f; 10.15f, 40; 11.20–24
10.21–24; 11.9–13	Privileges of discipleship	11.25–27; 13.16f; 7.7–11
11.14–26	Beelzebub controversy	12.22–37, 43–45
11.29–36	Against those seeking signs	12.38–42; 5.15; 6.22f
11.42–52; 12.2f	Against Pharisaism	Ch. 23
12.4–12; 22–34	Disciples under persecution	10.28–33; 12.32; 6.25–33
12.35–39; 13.18–21	The time of crisis	24.43–51; 10.34–36; 5.25f; 13.31–33
13.22–30, 34f; 14.15–24	The fate of the unrepentant	8.11f; 23.37f; 22.1–10
14.26f, 34f; 16.13, 16–18	Discipleship in a time of crisis	10.37f; 5.12, 18; 6.24; 11.12f
17.22–37	The Day of the Son of Man	24.26f, 37f, 40f; 28

OBSERVATIONS:

1 Almost all of this material is to be described as sayings and teaching rather than narrative. Is "Q" then a sayings-source rather than a gospel?

2 The material is listed in the sequence of Luke; notice how rarely the related material occurs in the same order in Matthew's sequence. Agreement in order was an important aspect of the case for Mark's relationship to the other synoptic gospels.

3 There is immense variation in the degrees of agreement between Luke and Matthew, for example:

agreement in wording	Lk. 3.7–9; Mt. 3.7–10
agreement in underlying ideas	Lk. 12.22–31; Mt. 6.28–34
different images and ideas (with basis in common original saying?)	Lk. 11.44; Mt. 23.27
totally different subject (but linked by possible confusion between two very similar Aramaic words in an original saying)	Lk. 11.41; Mt. 23.26

Christian preaching and teaching which might link up with Jesus himself. A method known as "Form Criticism" uses the concept of the gospels as beads (story-units) threaded on a string by the evangelists. Scholars wished to study the individual stories (beads) to test the theory that these were free-floating pieces of oral tradition, which had been fashioned by retelling, and ultimately by being written down.

New Testament scholars had borrowed the techniques for analysing oral tradition from their colleagues in the Old Testament field. It had long been clear that the Hebrew Bible was the final written deposit of a living process of retelling the stories. The process was strictly controlled by methods of recitation which had imposed conventional forms and patterns upon the

Bronze statue of a classical orator (Museo Archeologica, Florence).

material. Similar processes had been at work in the creation of the Greek epic poems, attributed to Homer, which reflected the conditions in Mycenaean society centuries before the poems were written down in the eighth century BCE. The forms which are examined in this way within the New Testament gospels include tales, pronouncement stories (which conclude with a moral or theological "punch-line"), dialogues, parables, proverbs, and verse (using the structures of Hebrew poetry even in Greek). Other forms, including rhetorical structures, apply to the rest of the New Testament.

The fact that examples of these forms appear in the New Testament documents as concise, rounded-off, units (well-polished beads) suggests the existence of a significant stage of controlled oral tradition in the production of the New Testament. These units can be recovered from the subsequent literary structures in which they are now found. They reflect a sustained period of retelling in which they acquired their final forms. Their use was in preaching, the training of converts, and the practice of worship. They reflect the needs and concerns of the earliest church communities and their setting is the local church; they were produced by the church and for the church. But they do not necessarily lead us back directly to the words of Jesus himself. The modern STRUCTURALIST understanding of language helps to reinforce this conclusion of Form Criticism. The oral forms correspond to the system of language, the range of language as experienced within a social community, while subsequent written forms, in contrast, are imprinted with a greater sense of individuality, and they are applied in accordance with the understanding and usage of the individual author.

Gospel writer as editor?

Form Criticism has thus helped to make the practical situations of the early Christians come alive. But it has also had a reductionist effect by concentrating on the separate units of tradition; the original gospel material seem to lack any unifying structure of a comprehensive literary kind. This makes any attempt to understand the gospels as totalities very difficult, if not impossible. The evangelist appears to have been demoted to the status of an uninspired compiler, a filing clerk who had put the material away at random. However, Form Criticism is only one aspect of the literary methods of criticism that have been applied to the gospel material. There are at least three equally important stages in the procedure. The first is to discover the main literary sources behind the gospels; the second step is to analyse the oral forms behind the written sources; a third step is a consideration of what the final editor of the gospel intended to do with the material, both oral and written, which he had collected.

This third process is called "Redaction Criticism" – redaction being another word for the editing activity. The critical concern is to identify the special interests, ideas, and purposes of the evangelist, as these are reflected in the way the gospel material has been selected and arranged. It is possible to do this by presupposing that literary relationships had been established, particularly between the three "synoptic" gospels. When Matthew or Luke does not follow Mark in order of material, wording, or ideas there is likely to be a reason for this. Distinctive arrangements or emphases are taken to express the particular purpose of that evangelist. It is obviously risky to draw conclusions too rapidly; some changes may be coincidence, or due to chance. But the larger matters, such as the point at which a gospel begins (John the Baptist, the birth of Jesus, or creation), may well be a good indicator of the evangelist's purpose and theological ideas.

If the gospels are like a full string of beads, then it is Redaction Criticism's task to understand the nature of the string. It is not simply a matter of gathering up the bits of string which can be cut away from the beads (such as introductory formulae and connecting paragraphs). The critic takes a view of the string as it runs through the beads, and also makes an assessment of the whole necklace. It is noticeable that higher value is now accorded to the process of editing, and the evangelists are called "creative" redactors, even "authors" and "theologians". This is the result of a more careful examination of the process of composition. The relationships identified by these literary methods of criticism, applied to the gospels, are not simply the parts of a pyramid (broad base of oral tradition, central concentration of written sources, and a topping of the final editor's work). A better model would be the close interrelationship of three interlocking rings.

Gospel writer as author?

Many modern critics are confident that it is accurate to speak of the evangelists as authors. Understanding the process of editing is now seen to offer all kinds of clues to the meaning of the whole gospel text, viewed as a literary work. It is therefore appropriate to apply a range of critical methods of analysis for the work of authors, such as the psychological assessment of one person's creativity, or an aesthetic judgement on skills of communication. There are as many kinds of structuralist analysis as there are theories. Perhaps most appropriate here are the studies of ancient techniques of communication, where the New Testament writings are compared with ancient (and modern) theories of rhetoric. The general question being asked is about the way any composition succeeds in communicating, or the way it wishes to be heard. The answer may be in terms of dramatic intention (even thinking of the gospel as a drama), or the skill of an orator in arguing a case (e.g. the argument of a Pauline letter), or the literary arrangement of a narrative in terms of the actions and interactions of its participants. The great expansion in these kinds of interpretation of the Biblical text in recent years is an indication of a trend towards thinking of the New Testament writers as individual authors and of characterizing the methods and course of their communications with their audience and readers.

The individual author and the social setting

This great wealth of both historical and literary methods of criticism enables the student of the New Testament to examine the contents of these writings, and to ask the right kind of question about each stage of the processes by which they were produced. The first units of teaching and stories are understood as oral communications. From these develop an organic growth which produces eventually the final literary structures. However, both the early preachers and the final writers can also be studied in relation to the society in which they lived and worked. Techniques for studying the setting have been borrowed from the disciplines of the social sciences.

The aim is to reconstruct a more comprehensive picture of the social experience of early Christians and the ways they formed groups. So, for example, J. Z. Smith has called for a "social description of early Christianity". Forms of religious self-expression are seen as activities which order and organize life, and which develop structures, practices, and patterns of symbols. In this way religion is seen as intimately related to groupings and structures, existing locally or created within society, while religious symbols may seek to go beyond daily experience. Ideas about the holy and the sacred are related to secular society, yet are distanced from it as hope and aspiration. In reconstructing any religious situation, including that of the early Christians, it may be necessary to take account of the difference between what people *say* they do and what they *actually* do.

These critical methods of a broadly sociological kind have not always been welcomed by scholars in New Testament studies. Among the anxieties

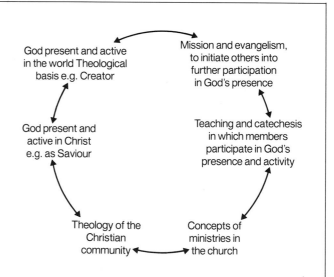

Theological presuppositions
Nature of God's relation with the world
Nature of God's activity
History of salvation – continuous with the Old
    Testament

Christology: the person of Christ
Particular mode of Christ's activity
Picture of Christ: special emphasis?
Summing up the way Christ is understood

The Christian community
Nature of the church: looking inward or outward?
Particular relations with Judaism
Strategies for mission, if any

Church organization and practice
Structure of the church: organization of ministry
Patterns of worship: liturgy?
Ethical behaviour and charitable practice

Doctrines and beliefs of the community
Nature of inspiration and revelation: Holy Spirit
Particular contributions of community to world
The future

God present and active in the world Theological basis e.g. Creator

Mission and evangelism, to initiate others into further participation in God's presence

God present and active in Christ e.g. as Saviour

Teaching and catechesis in which members participate in God's presence and activity

Theology of the Christian community

Concepts of ministries in the church

Notes
1 There can be no inflexible order in which these topics are treated. Instead the order in any one chapter tries to reflect the priorities of that community, as part of the process of characterization. Nor are all topics necessarily considered, or discussed in the same proportions, in every chapter, for the same reason.

2 The relationships among these topics is suggested by the accompanying diagram of a two-directional circle ("a coherent circle of interconnections"). This relationship is only theoretical; in practice any one community might see things differently, and distort the circle, because of its special emphases.

expressed are that those applying such methods often tend to be innately sceptical about the religious claims which are made in these historical situations. They also tend to be reductionist, in explaining everything purely as movements in society, and perhaps discounting the influence of individual innovators. They may also seem to be doctrinaire in elevating what is actually only the theory of a sociologist to the status of a decisive and universally applicable principle. Despite these genuine worries, there are real benefits and insights to be gained by a careful and selective application of such methods.

The approach of this book is not tied to any one theoretical model from sociology. But it seeks to use the overall idea of social descriptions to clarify both the variety of social settings and the variety of theologies which they have produced. Interest in the social setting is common to both historical/ sociological enquiry and to literary criticism (such as Form Criticism). This provides common ground on which the wide variety of critical methods may be applied to the New Testament in an appropriate and complementary manner. A number of standard questions will be asked in relation to each Christian community or church, as revealed by a section of the New Testament. The range of questions, and their interrelationship, is indicated by the table or "grid" on page 26.

The clash of cultures

The background to the New Testament world

The world of the New Testament is a distant world, but one that can be brought nearer by the study of archaeology and history; it is also a complex world because of the variety of different peoples and civilizations which mingle within it. Jesus was a Jew, and the Jewish people (with their long perspective of religious history recorded in the scriptures Christians call the Old Testament) occupy an important place in the New Testament world. While the Jews are centred on Jerusalem, there are also many Jews more widely scattered in a Diaspora (a dispersion) which took them to Rome and Egypt and Asia Minor. Some of these Jews played a central role in the societies to which they belonged, but there were other groups of Jews who retreated to the margins of society (like the probably Essene community at Qumran on the shore of the Dead Sea). The Jews became very numerous — between four and seven million, perhaps as many as seven per cent of the total population of the Roman Empire.

The political structure of this world around the Mediterranean Sea was provided by the Roman Empire. The power of Rome had been steadily extending eastwards, in Asia Minor, Syria, and Egypt. Judea was conquered by Pompey in 63 BCE, putting an end to Jewish independence. The Romans administered their Empire by provincial governors appointed by the Senate, or, in more troublesome areas, by the Emperor himself. Roman legions of soldiers would be stationed in the frontier provinces to maintain order, but there were still parts of the Empire which were ruled by client kings, local monarchs who were indebted to Rome. One example of a line of such local kings was the Herod family from Idumea. Whether Judea was administered by a client king, or by a Roman procurator, is an indicator of how politically sensitive the area was at any one time; but in either case it was firmly under Roman control.

To understand the New Testament world we need to understand not only the Jews and the Romans, but also the Greeks. The Greeks were not so obvious in this world, but in many ways they were more influential. The eastern part of the Roman Empire was built on foundations laid by Alexander the Great, who conquered the eastern end of the Mediterranean and the Persian empire and beyond (as far as India). The Greek rulers had administered these lands and introduced Greek culture and philosophy, which the Romans had appreciated and absorbed. Greek thinking on science and religion, derived from Aristotle and Plato, and Greek civilization in terms of city life, drama, and athletic attainment (the legacy of the Olympic Games) were widespread and influential in the New Testament world and had inevitably come into conflict with other views of life, such as that of the orthodox Jew.

The Greek language had also become a common means of communication, a lingua franca, much as English is in the modern world. Greek language, along with Greek culture, had been widely diffused in the east in the last few centuries BCE. The "common" dialect (*Koine* Greek) was still extensively used in the eastern part of the Roman Empire. But, as language can be an expression of independence and power, so the Greek language came into conflict with the Latin of the conquerors to the west and the Semitic language of Aramaic to the east. There was also a linguistic tension which was related to social class. While *Koine* (common) Greek was domi-

The Ark of the Covenant was a chest to hold the law books of the Hebrew Bible. This first intact example, decorated with lions and a shell and made of limestone, was found in Israel by American researchers in 1980.

A Greek family worship (and offer sacrifice to) Zeus and Hera at a country shrine near Corinth. On the pillar by the tree are statues of Apollo and Artemis.

nant during the Hellenistic period and the rise of Christianity, and while the first New Testament documents were being written, yet there was growing pressure among educated groups to restore a better class of Greek, the purer forms of Classical Greek used in Athens in the great days of Pericles (fifth century BCE). There are even signs of this in the New Testament, where Luke corrected the Greek he found in Mark.

The specific historical context of the New Testament world – its larger issues, conflicts, and tensions – is vital to an understanding of the gospels. At the same time, there are elements such as alliances and conflicts, the tensions created by racial, cultural, economic, and religious differences, which are common to all periods of history and can be studied as general phenomena. It is of course dangerous to make sweeping generalizations and transpose from one situation, into another. But it can be argued that an understanding of today's problems in northern and southern Ireland can help us to understand the political tensions and potential terrorism of first-century Galilee.

The following illustrations demonstrate the relation between the study of the New Testament and an understanding of its background in the New Testament world. The first example is on a large scale because it comprises the two books, the gospel of Luke and the Acts of the Apostles, the work of a single author who thereby ranks as a major contributor to the New Testament. This work stands comparison with the history writings in the Classical Greek tradition and with the history of the Jewish War by the Jewish historian Josephus. The author of Luke–Acts, more than most writers of the

New Testament, appears to have been conscious of writing history in the established literary tradition of those times. Specifically he wishes to relate the events of the life of Jesus, and the account of the beginnings of the Christian church, to what was happening in the Roman Empire at that time, to relate them closely to the cultural world with its interaction of Roman, Greek, and Jewish interests which have been described above.

This point can be illustrated by looking at chapter three of Luke. As in Mark's gospel, the beginning of the story focusses on John the Baptist and the baptism of Jesus; as in Matthew's account, the ancestry of Jesus is traced back through the generations of Old Testament history; but distinctively in Luke these events have a precise time reference which locates them in the world of Roman imperial administration:

> *In the fifteenth year of the reign of Tiberius Caesar, Pontius Pilate being governor of Judea, and Herod being tetrarch of Galilee, and his brother Philip being tetrarch of the region of Iturea and Trachonitis, and Lysanias tetrarch of Abilene, in the high priesthood of Annas and Caiaphas.* (3.1–2)

Towards the end of the gospel, in Luke 23.7ff, another distinctive aspect of this gospel is the involvement of Herod, as tetrarch of Galilee, within the sequence of the trial of Jesus in front of the Jewish chief priests and of Pilate the Roman procurator.

The Acts of the Apostles reveals, in addition, a sensitivity to the geographical context of the development of the Christian church. The church is seen to grow from Jerusalem (at the end of the gospel and the beginning of Acts), through "Judea and Samaria and to the end of the earth". In fact the movement represented particularly by the missionary journeys of Paul is a movement through the provinces of the Roman Empire, which reaches its

Roman emperors: Tiberius, Augustus, Claudius, Gaius (Caligula).

climax as Paul, despite shipwreck, imprisonment, and other hardships, comes to the city of Rome itself, at the heart of the Empire. For Paul to preach openly in Rome is the triumphant conclusion of Luke's view of Christianity in the Roman world. This is how Luke underlines the meaning of the story he has told. And we should also be aware of how carefully he has told that story in relation to the social and political realities of Jew and Greek in the Roman Empire. Episodes such as the visit of Peter to Cornelius in Acts 10 and the preaching of Paul at Athens in Acts 17 are important examples of the cosmopolitan nature of Luke's material.

Our first illustration of the importance of understanding the New Testament world was the large picture of the two-volume work Luke–Acts. The second illustration is by contrast very compact. It is the story of the woman who anointed Jesus' feet in the house of Simon the Pharisee, as told by Luke in chapter 7.36–50. It reveals a great deal about the social situation and attitudes of the times. The Pharisees were growing more numerous and wealthy in the New Testament period. It is likely that Simon's house was a substantial one, in contrast to the close-packed houses that can be seen in the excavations at Capernaum. There is likely to have been an open courtyard with rooms around it (like a small cloister). The village people could come and go through the courtyard, and might stand and watch, but not interrupt. As a wealthy local figure, Simon would entertain visitors on behalf of the locality. One point of the story is that Simon has wasted his opportunity to show hospitality. The owner's son should have provided water (and oil) at the entrance to the courtyard for anyone taking part in the banquet.

Jesus is invited, perhaps as a stranger who is causing something of a stir; he is not necessarily the chief guest at the banquet. How the Pharisee greeted Jesus would determine his local status. And this may have been part of the problem. The Pharisee could not perform any of the conventional greeting

rituals: a kiss on the lips would be for family; on the cheek would indicate equal status; on the hand would mean subservience; and to clasp or kiss the feet would be a greeting for royalty. The woman, who is a prostitute, or perhaps a debtor, stands in the courtyard and observes the banquet. She does not share the Pharisee's inhibitions about acknowledging the status of Jesus.

As Jesus reclined, on a rush mat (or a couch) in the raised dining area off the courtyard, he might be facing the Pharisee across the table. Jesus' feet might well be closest to the woman standing in the courtyard. She seizes her opportunity and effectively disrupts the proceedings. She provides the basic requirement of foot washing and in addition she anoints the feet with oil. In so doing she saves the community from the consequences of the insult the Pharisee has perpetrated on his guest. And by kissing Jesus' feet she greets him in the appropriate way to acknowledge a royal, messianic figure. In the story the economic status of rich and poor is instantly reversed when this is seen in terms of the resources of love and forgiveness. This is particularly a theme for Luke. A knowledge of the social conventions of such a situation enables us to see what is being affirmed in this story about the status and importance of Jesus in relation to the Pharisee.

Women in the New Testament world

The position of women in the New Testament world illustrates many aspects of the social and cultural background. Here, of course, space permits us only to touch on this important topic, which will also be considered in discussing

A typical village in the Palestinian countryside (actually in Jordan near Petra).

MAP 1 Political map of
the Mediterranean
world.

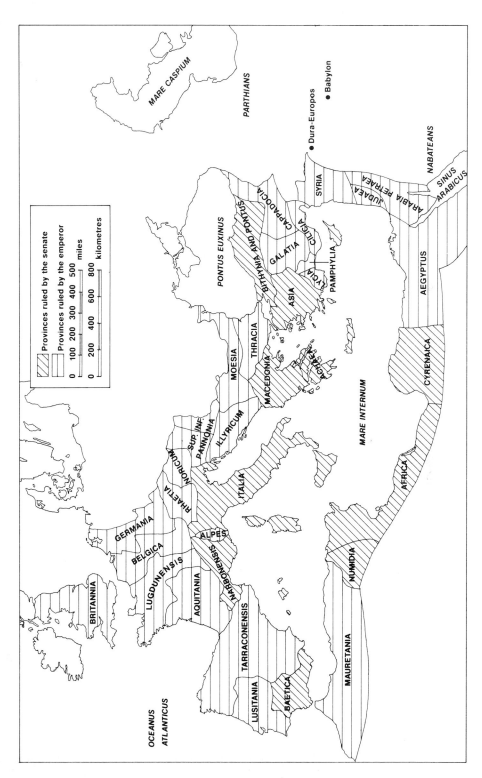

A Roman matrona (lady) of the Flavian period (69–96 CE). Her sepulchral altar in marble is inscribed "for holiest Cominia Tyche, wife most chaste and loving"

the individual gospels and their social background. The New Testament shows clearly how different cultures and different social purposes affected the way women were regarded in the contemporary world. As we will see from the following examples, it may be quite a tricky and controversial matter to interpret the detailed context accurately.

Luke's story, about a particular woman who "offended" in the most polite circle, raises the general question of the position of women in the social world around the Mediterranean Sea, in Greece and Rome and Judea, and in the places where the first Christian communities sprang up. This appears to be a straightforward question of social history with a simple factual answer, but it is more complicated, partly because of the wide range of social context involved, and also because this kind of historical evidence reflects the social assumptions of class and gender made by those who write and read the history.

The stance of women themselves would clearly be modified by their status and situation, for example:

* a Roman matron from a high-born patrician family
* a slave girl from Britain working in a Roman household
* a country woman working a small farm with her husband
* a Jewish mother from a Pharisaic family
* a female convert to Christianity in the church at Corinth

Further modifications arise according to the issue under discussion, whether the concern is primarily with legal status, with guarantees of direct physical descent, with the nature of the partnership between the sexes, and in religious matters with traditional established religion or with ecstatic cults. The following is a classical statement of Roman law:

> Our ancestors established the rule that all women, because of their weakness of intellect, should be under the power of guardians. Guardians are appointed for males as well as for females: for males only when under age, on account of their tender age; but for females, when under and of age, on account of the weakness of their sex and their ignorance of business matters.

By contrast, a Jewish tradition from the Old Testament, in Proverbs 31.10–31, suggests a more positive view of a woman's intelligence and business acumen:

> She opens her mouth with wisdom, and the teaching of kindness is on her tongue. She looks well to the ways of her household, and does not eat the bread of idleness. (31.26f)

A "good wife and mother" is a key structural element in Jewish society.

The particular questions one might ask in relation to Christian women in the New Testament world include:

* What did women in this social world gain from becoming Christians?

* Was Christianity's appeal to women an important factor in the success of the religion?
* Was it all due to the rising status of women in the Greek world and the general questioning of male/female roles in the early Empire?

There are three major views of the relationship of women to early Christianity. Firstly, women who converted to Christianity in the first century CE found patterns of worship and religious expectation which differed radically from those of traditional Greek and Roman religion; but the differences were much less between Christianity and the small groups of the mystery cults which had supplemented traditional religion for the previous three centuries. Christian worship aroused suspicion only in so far as women were here behaving in ways associated with the unconventional practices of the ecstastic cults.

Secondly, if one thinks of the Jesus movement as characterized by the equality of men and women in discipleship, then this is only plausible historically in so far as such notions of equality are conceivable in the context of Jewish life and faith. The actions and visionary ideals of Jesus and his movement are best understood as those of a renewal movement within Judaism. This would have proposed an *alternative* to the dominant patriarchal structures of Judaism in the past, rather than being a revolutionary party totally at odds with the values and practice of Judaism.

Thirdly, Christianity benefited from this pool of available women converts just as much as rival creeds, and the speed with which converts were won suggests less a rising status for them in their social world, or a real new role now offered to them, than their own previous lack of public position, which took them to the mysteries, to Isis, and to Judaism as well as to Christianity. But once converted to Christianity, they brought to it the same energy and organizational skill that many of them employed in their commercial lives. The paradox was, of course, that women, like slaves, those other underprivileged early Christians, were joining a sect which, on any interpretation of Pauline teaching, officially urged them to stay in their subordinate role, and indeed added a new justification for their subordination (1 Corinthians 11.3).

Women in the New Testament

Within the books of the New Testament, the number of women who are mentioned *by name* is no less than twenty-nine. The ratio of named women to named men in Paul's letter to the Romans, for example, is fifteen to eighteen. There are also many more general references to the influence and leadership of women in the Early Church:

e.g. "the devout women of high standing" in Pisidian Antioch (Acts 13.50);

"not a few of the leading women" believed at Thessalonica (Acts 17.4);

"not a few Greek women of high standing" at Beroea (Acts 17.12).

Particular examples of named women are:

Chloe 1 Corinthians 1.11 refers to "the people of Chloe", in all probability a group of uneducated slaves and foreign dockworkers, representatives of the lower strata of society, who are led by a woman. She emerges as a striking figure from Walter Hollenweger's reconstruction in *Conflict in Corinth* (1978).

Damaris An Athenian woman converted to Christianity at the same time as Dionysius the Areopagite (Acts 17.34).

Lydia A wealthy business woman, a dealer in purple dye (much in demand); she came from Thyatira in Lydia, but was living in Philippi at the time of her conversion to Christianity. Sympathetic to Judaism, she is converted to the Christian faith and is baptized and her household with her, during Paul's second missionary journey. She offers Paul hospitality; when Paul is released from prison, he returns to her house to say farewell to the Christian community of the city (Acts 16.14–15, 40).

Mary The mother of Mark, at whose house in Jerusalem the first disciples gather, and where Peter seeks refuge when he is rescued from prison (Acts 12.12–17). Her servant Rhoda is also mentioned in the account. There is also the Mary "who has worked hard among you" (that is, the Christian community at Rome, according to Romans 16.6), not to mention the other well-known members of the Christian Church called Mary.

Phoebe Paul calls her "our sister, a deaconess of the church at Cenchreae … she has looked after a good many people, myself included" and he commends her, perhaps as the bearer of the letter to the Romans (16.1–2).

Priscilla Described as a tentmaker like her husband Aquila (Acts 18.3), she was expelled with him from Rome when the Emperor Claudius expelled the Jews. Priscilla and Aquila moved to Corinth, where they started a church in their house like the one they had had in Rome (1 Corinthians 16.19; Romans 16.3).

Tabitha An Aramaic name (Greek equivalent Dorcas, meaning "gazelle"). She is a Christian woman of Joppa, "full of good works and acts of charity". When she dies, Peter is called to her bedside and restores her to life (Acts 9.36–41).

New and old
New Testament Christianity and the Jewish scriptures

Christianity is unique among the religions of the world because it was born with a Bible in its cradle. This was the Bible the Christians inherited from Judaism. They recognized its authority without question, although, towards the end of the second century CE, they started to refer to it with a critical air as the "*Old* Testament". The exact limits of the content of the Old Testament may well not have been fixed finally by the start of the New Testament period, but there was already sufficient clarity of definition for the books to be referred to collectively as "scripture" or "the scriptures", or by their separate sections as "the law of Moses, and the prophets, and the psalms" (Luke 24.44).

The effects of this scripture on the first Christians were far-reaching. For most of them it was their only literature; and, partly because it was the Bible Jesus used, it was their principal frame of reference. Inevitably it evoked and directed their religious thinking, as an authoritative work by which the religious issues of the day could be decided. For some at least of the early Christians, Biblical study (the reading and interpreting of the Old Testament) was an essential activity. It was claimed that the good news of Jesus was "in accordance with the scriptures", or, what amounts to the same thing, that it was "according to the definite plan and foreknowledge of God". A wide range of interpretations of the Old Testament was available in Judaism: there were the expositions of rabbis as well as a variety of interpretations from sectarian groups such as that of Qumran, with its library of Dead Sea Scrolls.

But for the Christians their new faith was not necessarily a straightforward continuation of the Jewish past. There were certain features of the tradition which grew up within Christianity itself that gave rise to new approaches to the Old Testament, fresh ways of handling it. For example, there was criticism of the Pharisees, and of the interpretation of some of the Old Testament laws, in the teaching which Jesus had given. And an apparently hot-tempered man called Paul had expressed himself forcibly, to the Galatian church in particular, about what was wrong with the Jewish Law, and with the way the "foolish Galatians" harked back to it. Furthermore, the major period in Judaism for interpreting the Law had begun when the voice of spontaneous prophecy had died out. Now, with the birth of the Christian movement, there was a rebirth of inspired prophetic activity, and this could not be ignored.

However much the Jewish Bible was esteemed by Christians, there was a shift in the centre of gravity. Christianity claimed to be not simply a "religion of the Book", but the religion of Christ, who was alive through resurrection. While for the Jewish leaders scripture was essentially a matter of Torah (Law), for Christian interpreters scripture was essentially prophecy. This means that the primary emphasis was placed on the second rather than the first section of the Hebrew Bible. For the rabbinic teachers of Judaism scripture was instruction in the way of life that was willed for man by God. In the hands of Christians, scripture was treated as a quarry for predictions which found fulfilment in Christ and his church. It is hardly surprising that the Christians upset the rabbis: they were making use of material from the same Bible, but the Christians were defying established priorities, and insisting on using their own (sectarian) methods of interpretation, while rejecting the traditional methods of the rabbis. A traditional Christian who has tried to debate with Jehovah's Witnesses on the doorstep about the meaning of scripture might well sympathize with the rabbis!

However, it was a fact that Jesus himself had used and interpreted the Old

Testament as scripture. And with a ready-made authoritative work of scripture in existence, the product of so many generations of Israel, this naturally had the effect of inhibiting any thought of producing new books of scripture, if and when this thought occurred. Although the early Christians were sure they had vitally important "good news" about Jesus to proclaim, there is more than a suggestion of a reluctance in the early church to write it down. Except for the letters of Paul on the needs of the moment, the writings of the New Testament were quite slow to appear. And when they did appear, a high proportion were anonymous or pseudonymous, not signed works of authority. Their obvious characteristics are not those of great literature, but of a personal mode of address, the direct qualities of the spoken word.

As there was already in existence a collection of written scriptures, even radical teachers like the Pharisees did not try to rewrite scripture. Instead they placed great emphasis on oral teaching and exposition, as a method of applying scripture relevantly to the problems of the day. Similarly neither John the Baptist nor Jesus himself appears to have recorded any teaching in the permanent form of writing. In this Jesus Christ was unlike Muhammad and other founders or reformers of religion. John the Baptist and Jesus shared an extreme sense of urgency in their message and mission to "this generation". The appropriate medium for urgent communication was the short oracular utterance of prophecy; the more impersonal and protracted medium of formal writing seems almost to have been precluded by the situation.

The preaching of Jesus was controlled by the expectation of the Reign or Kingdom of God, and a belief that it was on the point of happening. In this Jesus did indeed stand in a line of continuity with Jewish expectations, without necessarily being committed to their more nationalistic expressions. He never spoke of a political Messiah who would destroy the enemies of Israel, or of the establishment of a Jewish world-empire. But Jesus' expectations were cosmic in dimension, and world-wide in their effectiveness, without sharing in the more fantastic speculations of the apocalyptic writers. Jesus' message was the proclamation that the fulfilment of past promises was at hand, that the Reign of God was beginning. The time of the long-expected climax was near:

> *Happy are the eyes that see what you see!*
> *For I tell you that many prophets and kings have desired to see what*
> *you see, and have not seen it;*
> *To hear what you hear, and have not heard it.* (Luke 10.23f)

From scriptural prophecy to a new scripture

The sequence of events can be summarized in this way:

* Jesus proclaims the Reign/Kingdom of God (the prophecies of the Old Testament scripture are being fulfilled);

* The early Christians proclaim Jesus (the prophecies of the Old Testament

scripture are applied to Jesus himself – this is a *new* interpretation);
* The Christian proclamation becomes scripture (the Old Testament scripture is clearly regarded as the *Old* Testament).

This must be described in more detail, before we indicate the main ways in which Christian preachers applied the prophecies of the Old Testament.

The traditional picture of the earliest Christians is of a small group of eleven men, who believed that they had been commissioned by Jesus to carry on his work, and bring his message to the whole world. They were not distinguished people, not well educated, and they had no influential backers. In their own nation they were nobodies. In any case their own nation was a mere second-class province on the eastern extremity of the Roman map. If they had stopped to weigh up the probabilities of any kind of success in their task, even granted their conviction that Jesus was alive and that his spirit accompanied them and equipped them for what they had to do, their hearts must surely have sunk, so heavily were all the odds weighted against them.

But they were convinced that they had a message to proclaim about Jesus. While the content of Jesus' message had been about God's kingdom, the focus of the first Christians' message was Jesus himself. This was the good news they felt compelled to share; this was the person to whom they were bound to bear witness. The message was not simply about a carpenter/teacher who had been executed under the Roman procurator. It was a joyful announcement of the long-awaited salvation of the Jews. For in the person of Jesus – identified as Christ, the Messiah – God had come to the rescue of a world in need. Because this *was* good news, it is not surprising that the content of the early Christian message gradually became known as "the good news" (= the gospel = [Greek] *to euaggelion*). Only later did this term come to be used of the documents in which the stories of Jesus were eventually recorded, that is the written gospels. Primarily the term "good news" was applied to the events concerning Jesus, and to the action of the early Christians in announcing those events (see Mark 1.1; 1 Corinthians 15.1).

When, much later, in the second century CE, the term gospel or good news was apparently first applied to a book or books, such as the "memoirs of the apostles" (as Justin Martyr calls them), it was felt necessary to lay stress on the identity of the written with the preached gospel, the essential continuity between these two modes of communication. It was the evidence of the historical record in these books which confirmed the truth of what the earliest Christians had preached. Such a valuation placed upon the written work shows that the gospel preaching was now well on the way to becoming scripture. It was not only to be scripture in its own right, but also scripture attested by proofs from the authority of earlier scripture.

The process of change

The content of Jesus' message was the Kingdom of God: the content of the church's message was Jesus himself. But this contrast may appear to be more extreme than it actually is. For in Jesus' own preaching the Kingdom of God was regarded as being very much bound up with his own person (e.g. Mark 1.14; 4.11; Luke 17.20f). It was with Jesus that the Kingdom of God came near. But while the church saw itself as carrying on the mission and work of Jesus himself, there was no way in which the church could simply project Jesus' own self-understanding and self-consciousness. It belonged to Jesus rather than to the church. And so the solution to the problem for the church was to focus on Jesus as the heart of the church's message. Through teaching about Jesus, the relation of Jesus to the Kingdom of God could become apparent to a wider audience. And so the task of the different churches was to show how they understood Jesus and his significance for their situations.

What began as preaching in Jerusalem – the spoken message about who Jesus was and what he had done – eventually became solidified in the various forms of letters exchanged between Christian churches, and of accounts of Jesus' life and death, his work and significance, all of which was ultimately written down. And these written documents became, after many more years and changing circumstances, the New Testament, that is, a set of scriptures which demoted the Jewish Bible to the status of the Old Testament. What was proclaimed was written down, and what was written down came to be regarded as scripture for three main reasons.

First, there was an overpowering sense of urgency about early Christian preaching. (As Paul says: "Woe to me if I do not preach the gospel!") The importance of the preaching was not diminished by the passing of years, even if God's delay in bringing a climax to world history was puzzling. But the lapse of time brought new situations in which to preach, and the particular problem that the first preachers would soon be no longer available. The first eyewitnesses to Jesus had either been executed by the authorities or were near the end of their natural lives. Their evidence could only be preserved for the next generations by committing it to writing. So the urgent message of oral preaching became the important and revered witness in writing (see the statement in John 21.20–24).

Secondly, in its Jewish environment the earliest Christian community looked like a Jewish sect. It did not begin by splitting off from Judaism, as if conscious of itself as a new religious society. But the Christian communities developed their identities with the passage of time, and in contact with new situations and cultural contexts. New organization, attitudes, and philosophies developed as a result of these contacts. A decisive step was taken when the gospel of Jesus was taken beyond the confines of Palestinian Judaism, and Christian congregations appeared in the wider Greco-Roman world. The gospel had to be presented in other ways, and in different material forms. An educated Greek audience could not make sense of a wandering Palestinian preacher. (See the way in which Luke depicts Paul preaching in Athens in Acts 17.16ff.) These new audiences appreciated the essentials of the gospel proclamation in their own ways. Christianity developed a variety of ideas and patterns of presentation, not least in relation to the strange world of Gnostic ideas.

Thirdly, the continuing history of the Christian movement was soon marked by the beginnings of controversy. There were arguments about what was to be preached and taught, and how it should be interpreted and understood. The recognition accorded to written works, which came to be seen as scriptural and normative, provided an important regulator of church debates, and a means of erecting barriers to exclude the heretics. The authority of a recognized tradition within the Christian church can be seen in this reference to Polycarp, a second-century bishop of Smyrna. He was "a far more reliable and more steadfast witness of truth than Valentinus and Marcion and the rest of the evil minded. He it was who, coming to Rome, caused many to turn away from the aforesaid heretics to the church of God, *proclaiming that he had received this one and sole truth from the apostles — that namely which is handed down by the church.*"

What eventually took place was precisely what could hardly have been conceived in the earliest days of the church, namely the creation of a second Bible to go alongside that already in existence; ultimately it would relegate the first (prophetic) scripture to the status of "old" within a Bible composed of two testaments. The story of the development of the New Testament is the history of the process by which books, written mostly for other purposes and with different motives, came to be accorded this unique status. And later hands imposed upon the New Testament a doctrinal unity and a fixity which originally it could not be imagined to possess.

Christian interpretation of the Old Testament

In the second century Justin Martyr claims, in his *Dialogue with Trypho* (a Jew) 29.2, that his words

> *have neither been prepared by me, nor embellished by the art of man; but David sang them, Isaiah preached them, Zechariah proclaimed them, Moses wrote them. Are you acquainted with them, Trypho? They are contained in your scriptures, or rather, not yours, but ours. For we believe them; but you, though you read them, do not catch the spirit that is in them.*

The following are examples of the relationship with the Old Testament that is set up in New Testament writings:

> *Behold a virgin shall conceive and bear a son, and his name shall be called Emmanuel (which means, God with us).*
> (Isaiah 7.14/Matthew 1.23)
> *Out of Egypt have I called my son.* (Hosea 11.1/Matthew 2.15)
> *He who through faith is righteous shall live.*
> (Habakkuk 2.4/Romans 1.17)
> *What is man that thou art mindful of him,*
> *or the son of man that thou carest for him?*
> (Psalm 8.4/Hebrews 2.6)
> *As a sheep led to the slaughter or a lamb before its shearer is dumb, so he opens not his mouth.*

> *In his humiliation justice was denied him. Who can describe his generation? For his life is taken up from the earth.*
> (Isaiah 53.7–8/Acts 8.32–33)

Some differences may be noted between the Old and the New Testament wording. See if you can discover (from a concordance) how many times a particular Old Testament text is quoted in the New Testament. Look up both references and observe the ideas in their contexts. It is surprising how rarely there are references (such as the last example, referring to the suffering servant figure from the prophecy of Isaiah). The Old Testament texts are cited in a number of ways:

* sometimes quotations are made directly (and accurately) from the original Hebrew text or a Greek translation;
* sometimes quotations are made from memory and are therefore approximate;
* sometimes there is an allusion to an Old Testament idea rather than an exact quotation;
* sometimes the quotation is not accurately attributed (as would be expected with a modern reference);
* sometimes the Old Testament is misquoted, or its emphasis modified deliberately, in order to make the Christian meaning clearer;
* sometimes a modern reader would feel that the quotation is invalidated because it has been taken out of context, or misapplied.

But there are various reasons why Christian writers have made quotations from, or allusions to, the Old Testament. It may be

* to derive traditional rules for Christian living
* to support an argument for Jesus as the fulfilment of prophecy
* to make the case for the church as the new Israel
* to use the Old Testament as a quarry for ultimate truths.

Depending on the reason for quoting it, and on the nature of the Christian group for which the quotation is made, there are different ways of making a Christian interpretation of the Old Testament text. The presupposition underlying all of them is that there is a correspondence, a typological relationship, between the Old and the New. Here are four methods which are found frequently in the New Testament:

1 The use of the Old Testament text as the historical prototype – so that any part of the Old Testament can be a prophecy which the Christian writer saw as fulfilled in his own day. The Qumran community used a similar method of interpretation (called *pesher*). The prophecy could be effectively rewritten in terms of the modern situation; it was not thought that this was taking liberties, but rather that the ultimate meaning of the prophecy was being understood for the first time. An example is the use of Hosea 11.1 in Matthew 2.15. Hosea was describing the loving fatherhood of God, as demonstrated in Israel's historically formative experience at the Exodus from Egypt (see Exodus 4.22f). Matthew uses the prophecy of Hosea in the story of Jesus' birth, to describe the flight into Egypt and temporary refuge there. Matthew has hijacked this prophecy out of its original context for two reasons. It is a radical restatement, to show the importance of the rescue of the child Jesus from Herod; it is a saving event on the same scale as Israel's Exodus. It is also an assertion about Jesus as "Son of God"; this is the perfect fulfilment of the Father/Son relationship which was prefigured in the ideal commitment of Israel to God.

2 The construction of an argument from several Old Testament texts, in the way the Jewish rabbis did. This worked by strict rules which permitted the making of analogies, drawing an inference from a lesser situation to a greater, or making a general application from an immediately preceding particular case. An example is the extended argument in 2 Corinthians 3, which is based on the narrative of Exodus 24 in combination principally with Jeremiah 31.31. Moses had to wear a veil so as not to terrify the Israelites; but it also concealed the fact that the radiance waned. Moses' splendour waxed when he was in contact with God on the mountain top; when he came away it waned. The glory of the Mosaic covenant, based on letters carved in stone, was an alternating (a waxing and waning) glory. Some Jews are similarly blindfolded and fail to recognize this. But the glory of the New Covenant grows steadily, and no veils are necessary. The apostle can constantly reflect the glory with ever-increasing brilliance, since (through Jesus Christ) God is constantly present as spirit.

3 The Old Testament example functions as a salutary story, from which warning lessons can be drawn. A similar principle operates in the parables which Jesus told: the story is a striking way to focus attention on the moral which is drawn. So in 1 Corinthians 10.1–11 the stories of Israel's Exodus from Egypt, the crossing of the Red Sea and the feeding in the wilderness are applied to the Christian church. "Now these things happened to them as a warning, but they were written down for our instruction, upon whom the end of the ages has come" (10.11). Ultimately these stories serve as a warning for the church of the last days, and emphasize the proper use of the sacraments of baptism and eucharist in the church. The people of God can rely only on the security which their faith gives them. In the same way the story of Noah's ark is used in 1 Peter 3.20–21. Just as a few persons in the time of Noah were saved by means of the ark, so in the church (the ark of God?) the believing people of God experience the process of salvation, initiated by means of the rite of baptism.

4 Other readers of the Old Testament do not rest at the historical level (of precedents in the story of Israel) or at the level of moral teaching (edificatory stories): they see a yet deeper spiritual meaning even in incidental features of the Old Testament. Elements are abstracted from the narrative and become timeless, spiritual truths. Like dry tinder they catch alight with the spark of the allegorical method and blaze up as freely imaginative interpretations. The church fathers of Alexandria were the first to produce a system of levels of meaning in scripture (literal, moral, and spiritual) by analogy with human

ROMAN EMPIRE	JEWISH EVENTS	RISE OF CHRISTIANITY
BCE	*BCE* 168 Maccabean Revolt against Seleucids (Syria) 142 Judean independence Rule of Hasmonean dynasty	*BCE*
63 Birth of Octavian (Augustus) Closing years of Roman Republic	63 Roman commander, Pompey, occupies Syria and captures Jerusalem	
	57/55 Sepphoris adopted as administrative capital of Galilee	
49–8 Civil War: Julius Caesar crosses the Rubicon, and ultimately defeats Pompey at Pharsalus 47–4 Dictatorship of Julius Caesar 44 Assassination of Julius Caesar (15 March) 43 Government by triumvirate (Antony, Octavian, Lepidus) 42 Brutus and Cassius (Caesar's murderers) defeated at Philippi		
	40–37 Palestine invaded by Parthians 37 Herod conquers Jerusalem 37–4 Palestine ruled by Herod the Great (under Roman patronage)	
31 Mark Antony (and Cleopatra) defeated at battle of Actium Octavian assumes power 27 Rule of "Augustus" (Octavian) – establishment of the Roman Empire	10 Inauguration of Caesarea by Herod	
9 Dedication of the altar to the Augustan Peace in Rome		
		6/4? Birth of Jesus

	4 Herod dies and his territory is divided among his sons:
	      Antipas (Galilee and Peraea)
	      Philip (Northern Transjordan)
	      Archelaus (Judea, Idumea, Samaria)	

CE	*CE* 6 Archelaus removed and Judea annexed by Romans Census of Quirinius	*CE*
14 Accession of Emperor Tiberius on death of Augustus	*c.* 20 Herod Antipas founds Tiberias in honour of the Emperor	
26 Tiberius withdraws to Capri; Sejanus effectively in charge	26–36 Pontius Pilate procurator of Judea	
		30/33 Crucifixion of Jesus

	34 Death of Philip, the tetrarch of Transjordan
	     Philo (Jewish Theologian)
	     c. 15 BCE–45 CE	

37 Accession of Emperor Gaius (Caligula) on death of Tiberius Dedication of temple to divine Augustus		
	38 Jewish pogroms in Alexandria	
40 Jews from Alexandria send embassy to Rome	40 Removal of Herod Antipas	
41 Assassination of Caligula Accession of Emperor Claudius Claudius settles dispute in Alexandria	41 Threat to desecrate Jerusalem temple averted	
	41–44 Jewish kingdom of Herod Agrippa I (grandson of Herod the Great)	
	44 Death of Agrippa I Roman rule of Jewish province by procurators reintroduced	48 Council in Jerusalem
49 Expulsion of Jews from Rome Seneca appointed tutor to Nero		51 Paul appears before Gallio in Corinth
54 Accession of Emperor Nero after Claudius is poisoned Claudius deified	52–62 Felix governor in Palestine Succeeded by Porcius Festus	
64 Great Fire of Rome		64 Persecutions of Roman Christians
	66 Outbreak of Jewish War against Rome	
68 Year of the Four Emperors (Nero, Galba, Otho, Vitellius): Civil War		
69 Accession of Emperor Vespasian	70 Destruction of Jerusalem by Titus. Temple tax diverted to Rome	
	73 Fall of Masada (suicide of defenders)	
	75/79 Josephus' account of *Jewish War* published	
79 Accession of Emperor Titus on death of Vespasian Vesuvius erupts; Pompeii and Herculaneum destroyed		
80 Fire at Rome: destruction of Capitoline temple		
81 Accession of Emperor Domitian on death of Titus	85 Rabbinic council at Jamnia	
95 Flavius Clemens put to death		Traditionally period of Christian persecution under Domitian John's exile to Patmos
96 Accession of Emperor Nerva on assassination of Domitian		
97 Tacitus consul		
98 Accession of Emperor Trajan on death of Nerva Tacitus writes *Histories* and *Annals*		*c.* 112 Pliny consults Trajan about method of dealing with Christians in Bithynia (Asia Minor)
114–117 Trajan's Parthian war: Armenia and Mesopotamia annexed	115–117 Jewish revolts begin in Cyrene, Egypt and Cyprus	
117 Accession of Emperor Hadrian on death of Trajan	132–135 Bar Kochba leads Jewish revolt against Rome Foundation of Aelia Capitolina and reorganization of Syria–Palestine	

The payment of taxes (a Roman provincial bas-relief from Trier, 3rd century CE).

psychology (body, soul, and spirit). And they found proof texts in the Bible (e.g. the Greek version of Proverbs 22.20: "Describe these things in a threefold way") to justify their method. As a result, any Old Testament reference to Jerusalem could mean (literally) the city of Judah; (morally) a faithful Christian soul; or, most significant of all, (spiritually) the church of Christ – ultimately the heavenly city, New Jerusalem. But this is not just a matter of the later interpretations of the church fathers. It is found even in the New Testament, as in Galatians 4.22–26. In this allegorical reading (and reversal) of Old Testament history, Hagar stands for the old Israel and Jerusalem while Sarah stands for the new Israel, the church.

By many such methods Christian preachers and writers interpreted the Old Testament. In doing so they bore witness to its continuing importance as authoritative scripture. When the two testaments were established alongside one another, there was a clear recognition of the unity and consistency of the idea of revelation through these books, whether it was seen as an historical sequence of prophecy and fulfilment, or a range of symbols of ultimate truth. Christians were motivated to interpret the Old Testament because they believed that it spoke of Jesus as Christ. They were not conscious of taking liberties, because they were convinced that the Christian gospel was the true ultimate meaning of these prophecies. To the Jew they *might be* prophecies; but even if they spoke of the Messiah (the Christ), they did not necessarily mean Jesus.

Such interpretation was needed because the reference was not self-evident. The Ethiopian who reads the prophet Isaiah does not understand the application. To Philip's question, "Do you understand what you are reading?" he replies: "How can I, unless some one guides me?" So Philip rides in his chariot with him, and beginning with the text of Isaiah 53, "he told him the good news of Jesus" (Acts 8.30–35). The techniques of Christian interpretation, which relate the teaching of the Old Testament and the preaching of the Christian gospel, are illustrated especially in Matthew. And this evangelist records the saying about the Christian interpreter:

> *Therefore every scribe who has been trained for the kingdom of heaven is like a householder who brings out of his treasure* what is new and what is old. (13.52)

CHAPTER 1

The Marcan prototype

How does this apparently early Gospel compare with the basic statement of the cross and resurrection – "The Preaching of the Cross" – that has been reconstructed here? Does the authority of Mark's gospel depend upon its character as a first statement of the gospel type, or upon any traditional link with Simon Peter? What can be said about the gospel's special features, its emphasis on the claim for a hidden messiah, and the problematic ending of the text? Does this illuminate the context of the gospel and its role in early Christian controversy?

Perceptions of Mark's gospel

Not so long ago most students would have been surprised to see any idea of a sharp distinction being made between the basic "good news" (the fundamentals of the original proclamation) and the gospel of Mark, because the gospel of Mark, or perhaps its original form (*Ur-Markus*), was thought to present the earliest form of Christian preaching. For the same reason the Quest for the historical Jesus would have begun with Mark's gospel. But in the last thirty years or so there has been an explosion of a different kind of scholarly interest in the gospel of Mark. This gospel used to be seen, in a simplistic and perhaps patronizing way, as the straight and objective reporting of what Jesus said and did. The new look places a different emphasis – on what the evangelist himself intended, when he presented the materials which he had collected in a particular way. Scholars see a creative editorial process by which a theologian (referred to as "Mark") produced what may well be the first example of a literary form of Christian communication, the first instance of the genre of the written "gospel".

The traditional view was that Mark's gospel was written in Rome in the sixties of the first century, after the death of Peter. It represented a straightforward transmission of Peter's reminiscences by John Mark, who is known elsewhere in the New Testament from the narrative of Acts and references in the Epistle.[1] This claim owes much to the statement by a church father called Papias that Mark was the *hermeneutes* (translator or interpreter) of Peter. Many commentators have tried to identify conclusively the material which could only have come from Peter. Through much of the present century this confidence in Mark's reliability has been supported by conservative and historically positive views of the relationship between the synoptic gospels, and of Matthew's and Luke's dependence upon Mark. But church traditions

Summary of Mark's teaching:

Jesus came to destroy
  the demons;
  The demons destroy
  men.
Jesus came to fulfil
  Judaism;
  Judaism rejects Jesus.
The demons and
  Judaism together
  destroy Jesus;
By his destruction
  Jesus saves men from
  the demons, and
  fulfils and supersedes
  Judaism.
The way of salvation
  through destruction
  is the way of the
  kingdom in this age;
The way of life
  through death is the
  way of the follower
  of Jesus in this age.

J. C. Fenton, *J.T.S.*
n.s.3 (1952), p. 58.

do not always agree with one another. It is ironical that, while the authority of Mark is apparently derived from Peter, for centuries the church has accorded theological and liturgical primacy to Matthew. So, for example, Augustine stated that Mark follows Matthew closely "and looks as if he were his lackey/servant (*pedisequus*) and epitomist/abbreviator (*breviator*)".

The new look was anticipated at the turn of this century by a member of the *Religionsgeschichtliche* (History of Religions) School in Göttingen in Germany called William Wrede. His was a theological challenge to the traditional view of the gospel as pure history: instead "the Gospel of Mark belongs to the history of dogma".[2] The first reactions to Wrede were distinctly cool; his approach was described as a dead end. As a result, Wrede's book, which was first published in 1901, was not translated into English for seventy years. But now it is recognized as the main route of scholarship which leads to the new look, the fresh appreciation of Mark as evangelist and theologian. This redrawing of the map was made possible by the rise of the approach known as Redaction Criticism (see page 24f) in the years following the Second World War. This theological emphasis, much concerned with the person of Christ, is not now regarded simply as the act of the evangelist in imposing theology on the facts. But the creative activity in the writing of the gospel is more accurately described as the *development* of an understanding of Christ which was implicit in the earliest preaching.

The character of Mark's gospel

Let us pursue the possibilities of the new look, and seek to describe the characteristics and special features of Mark's gospel which encouraged the Redaction critics to evaluate the gospel as a theological work, alongside and distinct from those of Matthew and Luke. It is clear that for practical reasons it is not quite so easy to start to describe Mark in this way. For Matthew and Luke we can identify their individual features by comparing them with each other and with Mark, especially if we work on the general assumption that both these evangelists used Mark as their basic source. Without a speculative reconstruction of Mark's sources, his special interests relative to the materials he used cannot be determined. But there are various techniques that can be used, from the most sophisticated linguistic criteria and analyses of literary structure to the much more immediate, if subjective, impressions formed from reading the text. We should ask ourselves particular questions about how Mark's gospel begins and how it ends; what are the principal and recurring themes and how they are presented; whether there are patterns in the organization of the material, and significant turning-points in the gospel story. If you have never sat down with the gospel of Mark and read it from beginning to end in one session, then do so now, with these questions in your mind.

∗ What does Mark want to communicate about Jesus?

* How does he shape his narrative?
* How does he tell his story?

You may well have noted the emphasis of the gospel on the death of Christ, the space devoted to the Passion narrative, the preparations for this and the prophecies of the suffering. Did you mention the confession of Peter at Caesarea Philippi (8.27–30) or the Transfiguration (9.2–8) as a turning-point in the whole story? Were you worried by the limited reference to the Resurrection in 16.1–8 and the abrupt and disquieting conclusion to the gospel. At the beginning of the gospel I expect that you will have noted the brief but impressive transition from John the Baptist to Jesus by means of John's water-baptism and the voice from heaven. There is no space here for the birth and infancy narratives of Matthew and Luke.

The Kingdom of God and the person of Jesus

The discussion of the basic Christian preaching in the Introduction stressed the importance of the concept of the Kingdom of God for the first Christians and for Jesus himself. We can now see how Mark uses this theme as he moves rapidly from John the Baptist to Jesus. The proximity of the Kingdom is emphasized in this statement, which sounds like a programme for action at the start of Jesus' ministry:

> *The time is fulfilled, and the kingdom of God is at hand; repent, and believe in the gospel.* (1.15)

In the parable chapter which begins with the story of the sower, the proclamation of the Kingdom is inextricably bound up with the presence and teaching of Jesus himself:

> *To you* [the disciples] *has been given the secret of the Kingdom of God, but for those outside everything is in parables.* (4.11)

The transition from the preaching of the Kingdom of God to Mark's preaching about Jesus himself is directly and effectively made.

Among the complex themes of what Mark has to say about the person of Jesus, this theme of mystery ("the secret of the Kingdom") is the most pervasive and problematic feature. It was this which Wrede noticed and which formed the basis of his revolutionary argument. It is important to realize that Wrede's concern was not so much with secrecy and obscurantism; that might have been just how things were in the ministry of Jesus. He was much more concerned with the doctrinal implications of a church that preached a mystery and the hidden identity of its Lord. Other aspects of Mark's Christology must be examined in addition to the challenge of working out Christ's identity: the particular designations, Son of God and Son of Man, which he uses; the relation to the predictions of the passion; the understanding of Christ as an ESCHATOLOGICAL figure and worker of miracles; and the function of Christology in the polemics against opposition groups. We shall now look at these in turn, and see how the first three of the headings in our analytical "grid" (see p. 26) are brought immediately into close relationship with each other. And as the evidence is probed, there should be significant pointers to the nature of the community for which Mark wrote.

The identity of Jesus

Statements about Jesus, both within and outside the church, were essentially controversial. This had been true ever since those who wished to proclaim Jesus Christ as risen had been opposed by those who had been involved in his crucifixion. It seems clear that in Mark's day the overall issue of the significance of Jesus was highly charged and vigorously debated. The material arranged in chapter 12 of his gospel represents a broad sample of controversy: the parable of the wicked tenants, the issue of paying tribute to Rome, the doctrine of resurrection, the question as to the first commandment, the designation of the Messiah as David's son or David's Lord, the warning against the scribes. Many other references to controversy material earlier in the gospel add up to a substantial proportion of the work.

This material of course covers a wide variety of topics, but underneath all are the fundamental questions, "Who was Jesus?" and "By what authority did he act and teach as he did?" There are passages which reveal specific answers to these questions:

> *Thou art my beloved Son; with thee I am well pleased.* (1.11)
> *He taught them as one who had authority, and not as the scribes.* (1.22)
> *What have you to do with us, Jesus of Nazareth? Have you come to destroy us? I know who you are, the Holy One of God.* (1.24)
> *Peter answered him, "You are the Christ."* (8.29)
> *The Son of Man also came not to be served but to serve, and to give his life as a ransom for many.* (10.45)

Christ's hidden identity

This process of questioning and answering in itself implies the idea of a hidden identity of Christ; otherwise there would be no need to ask. But Mark's theme is also expressed fairly consistently throughout the gospel in a rather stylized way, employing several different devices and formulae:

* Jesus commands silence
  – from the demons (1.25, 34; 3.12)
  – from witnesses of the miracles (1.43f; 5.43; 7.36; 8.26)
  – from the disciples (8.30; 9.9)
* Others try to silence Bartimaeus (10.47f)
* Attempts to conceal where Jesus is (7.24; 9.30f)
* Cryptic speech – private teaching to a few (7.17; 10.10)
* Cryptic action – miracles with few witnesses (1.29ff; 5.40)

* Jesus as a solitary (1.35ff)
* The theory of parables as concealing meaning (4.10ff, 33f)
* The disciples fail to understand Jesus (4.13, 40f; 6.50ff; 7.18; 8.16ff; 9.5f)

It is of course possible to understand each of these features in the gospel separately, and to construct an explanation for the particular historical circumstances. "Jesus did not wish to have a reputation as a dramatic miracle worker." "Jesus did not want to be associated with popular ideas about the Messiah." "Demons were excluded because it was believed that they were not on God's side." Nevertheless, the fact that all these motifs come together in the gospel, that they appear rather stylized, and that some at least of the historical "explanations" are problematic and implausible, would suggest that here is no set of coincidences. We are seeing the working out in the details of the story of an important theological theme.

The origin of the idea may go back to Jesus himself. However, it is not a straightforward set of historical statements, more a complex development of the implications. What appears to be "hidden" in the identity of Jesus may be presented in this way because Christians were by this time making claims for the Christ that had not actually been made by Jesus himself. It is in the nature of an apologetic, because the truth of a post-Resurrection revelation is now being superimposed on the original story, and the Christian missionaries have to explain themselves. But this suggestion (which Wrede originally made) now appears as too much of a *tour de force*. It is more likely that the implications of a latent theological theme have been teased out within the stories, because this idea was uppermost in the minds of Mark's community, than that it should have been imposed on the text as some totally new and self-justificatory doctrine.

The Jesus of Mark is a figure with an aura of mystery. The Christological insight into his hidden identity is reiterated by literary means throughout the gospel. The effect is to make the readers of the gospel sharers in the secret of who Jesus really is. This secret is shared by relatively few in Mark's gospel. The demons who are exorcized, these supernatural figures, know the truth which is concealed from most of the human participants in the story. Despite their general incomprehension, some of the disciples glimpse the truth. Peter sees it at Caesarea Philippi (8.29) but his understanding is partial (8.32f). The witnesses of the Transfiguration, James and John as well as Peter, share the insight but are forbidden to reveal it until after the Resurrection (9.9). The importance of this text is that it shows the appropriateness of the revelation after Christ's death.

The timing of secrecy and revelation

This is the time scale of a new era beginning after the crucifixion which could be taken to apply quite broadly to the whole complex of mystery. It could even be applied to the parables, the true meaning of which would be revealed after the Resurrection; the particular imagery of 4.21f could be understood

The Transfiguration (right) (Mark 9.2–8) represented in the mosaic at the cathedral of Monreale in Sicily. Jesus' hidden identity is revealed to the recumbent disciples as he is accompanied by Elijah and Moses.

as a symbol of this general truth ("there is nothing hid, except to be made manifest"). So it is not a matter of the gradual and progressive dawning of perception by disciples who had originally been uncomprehending. This would have been quite a plausible consequence of the disciples' keeping company with Jesus, but it is not supported by Mark's treatment of the motif. The disciples still fail to understand both immediately after the revelation and subsequently (9.19; 10.24; 14.37ff). So it must be concluded that what made the difference in Christian understanding, at least according to Mark, was the experience of Christ's Resurrection.

There is another person in Mark's gospel who shares the secret with the supernatural beings and the occasionally comprehending disciples. This is the Roman centurion who is the witness to the death of Christ:

> And when the centurion, who stood facing him, saw that Jesus thus breathed his last, he said, "Truly this man was the Son of God!" (15.39)

One of the two major titles which Mark uses for Jesus is here employed most dramatically, as a Gentile penetrates the secret of Christ's identity. The timing of the revelation is significant; we have moved back behind the experience of Resurrection, to the crucifixion, to the experience of the death itself. Doctrinally this is very important. It is most closely paralleled in the understanding of the death of Christ in the writing of Paul. In Romans 6.5, the readers are said to share with Paul himself an experience of being "united with Christ in a death like his". Here in Mark the readers share with the centurion the secret revealed through Christ's dying.

The title "Son of God"

Against this general background of mystery and hidden identity, it is important to look at the indications provided by Mark's use of the two titles "Son of God" and "Son of Man". It would be possible to achieve a highly dramatic effect (which might even amount to rewriting the history of Christian doctrine) by taking "Son of God" in the very first verse of Mark's gospel and understanding this in terms of the second person of the Trinity as described in the classic Christian creeds of Nicea and Chalcedon. But this would probably be a mistake, on two counts. Firstly it is uncertain whether the title should be read at all in the text of Mark 1.1; for the manuscript evidence is divided. And secondly it is false to fuse gospel and creed in this way, because the worlds of thought of the first and fourth centuries of Christianity were very different. On the former ground alone we should not start to explain Mark's Christology by his first verse, however attractive it might be that Mark should present the whole truth at the outset, almost in the manner of subliminal advertising, and then instantly veil it again for long-term revelation. But in any event we should notice that the possibility of setting "Christ" and "Son of God" in parallel was acceptable at some stages in the manuscript transmission.

There are other well-attested instances of the title "Son of God":

Marc Chagall's large painting *War* (1964–66) makes dramatic use of the symbol of Jesus on the cross and relates it to the suffering of humanity. The general conflagration involves many innocent individuals.

above left Caesarea Philippi as it appears today: the source of the river Jordan at Banias. In Mark's gospel Peter's confession of Jesus' identity at Caesarea Philippi may be seen as a theological watershed.

above right The tombstone of M. Caelius of the Roman 22nd legion, at Bonn (9 CE). Such a Roman officer resembles the centurion who witnessed the death of Christ.

right A storm on the sea of Galilee: waves on Lake Tiberias.

1.11; 9.7 – in the voice from heaven at the Baptism and Transfiguration

3.11; 5.7 – the confession of the unclean spirits

12.6 – in the parable of the wicked tenants (allegory)

13.32 – the eschatological knowledge of the Father, contrasted with the Son's

14.61f – "the Son of the Blessed" in the High Priest's question together with Jesus' positive response

15.39 – the insight of the Roman centurion

Opinion is divided as to how the title should be understood. Is it a Jewish term which indicates the loyal and suffering servant of God, or pre-eminently the royal messianic figure? These are designations with a long Old Testament history and in Jewish terms refer to the loyalty of the agent of God and not to any essential divine status. Alternatively, against a Greek background, is reference being made to a supernatural being, a "divine man" or a manifestation of God in human form? It is difficult to be sure of a single category and a unified concept within the multiple possibilities of the ancient world. But it is at least intelligible as a general description of someone who inspires a feeling of great awe by what he says or does.

In the Jewish context of the voice from heaven (*bath qol*) and of the High Priest's reverential utterance ("Son of the Blessed") the Jewish title sounds more convincing. But this is not to rule out of Mark's perspective the Hellenistic verdict on supernatural abilities in exorcism and other kinds of wonder working. Such a judgement about divinity represents a first tentative step in the direction of later Christian doctrine (as opposed to Jewish monotheism). But it may not have been a step that Mark's community was prepared to take. In terms of historical accuracy, if the Roman centurion spoke as Mark's account relates (15.39), he is more likely to have meant that Jesus was a "divine man" (*theios aner*) who inspired awe. But in Mark's gospel as it stands, this acclamation has more to do with the ultimate triumph of theological revelation, as we have seen, than with the realism of historical record.

The title "Son of Man"

The origin of the second term, "Son of Man", is even more problematic than that of "Son of God", but at least as helpful in clarifying the range of Mark's thought. It can no longer be assumed automatically that the term "Son of Man" was freely available within Judaism as a suitable title to apply to a messianic figure or heavenly mediator between God and man. Instead it is clear that the term was developed considerably, and took on a new lease of life, as a result of the way early Christians (rather than Jews) read and understood Daniel 7. The Christians moved away from the original Old Testament sense of a collective term for the saints of the Most High (or people of God) and towards an individual interpretation of the term "Son of Man" as the title of a person. This specific individual development may have

MARK'S GOSPEL

1.1	Title
2–8	Beginnings with John the Baptist
9–13	Baptism and Temptation of Jesus
14–15	Jesus' proclamation
16–20	First disciples
21–45	A day in Capernaum; first charge to secrecy

2.1–3.6 Debates with the scribes

2.1–12	Cure of paralysed man
13–22	Jesus and Judaism
23–28	Cornfield on the sabbath
3.1–6	Man with withered hand

3.7–6.13 Public controversies of the Galilean ministry

3.7–19	Crowds and the Twelve
20–35	Controversy over Jesus' authority and relationship
4.1–34	Parable teaching (including the Sower parable)
4.35–5.43	Four miracles (the storm; the demoniac; resurrection; and including a healing)
6.1–6	Rejection at Nazareth
7–13	The mission of the Twelve

6.14–8.26 Ministry within and beyond Galilee

6.14–29	John the Baptist
30–44	Feeding of five thousand
45–56	Walking on the lake; landing at Gennesaret
7.1–23	Clean and unclean
24–30	The Syro-Phoenician woman
31–37	Healing of deaf-stammerer
8.1–10	Feeding of four thousand
11–21	Quest for signs; teaching on loaves and leaven
22–26	Healing of blind man of Bethsaida

8.27–10.52 Caesarea Philippi – the turning-point and the journey to Jerusalem

8.27–9.1	Peter's confession; prediction of the Passion
9.2–13	The Transfiguration
14–29	Healing of epileptic boy
30–32	Second prediction of the Passion
33–50	Discourse to disciples, on greatness and exorcism
10.1–31	Journey to Jerusalem; teaching on marriage, children, and riches
32–34	Third Passion prediction
35–45	Request for the sons of Zebedee
46–52	Healing of blind man at Jericho

11.1–13.37 Jesus in Jerusalem

11.1–11	Messianic entry into city
12–14, 20–25	Cursing the fig tree (including 15–19 Cleansing the temple)
11–27–12.40	Controversies (authority; parable of wicked husbandmen; tribute-money; doctrine of resurrection; first commandment; Messiah as David's son; warning against scribes)
12.41–44	The widow's mite
13.1–37	Discourse on the last things

14.1–16.8 The Passion Narrative

14.1–2, 10–11	Conspiracy and Judas' betrayal (including 3–9 Anointing in Bethany)
10–11	Judas' betrayal
12–25	The Last Supper
26–31	Peter's denial predicted
32–52	Gethsemane and the Arrest
53–65	Jesus before the Sanhedrin
66–72	Peter's denial
15.1–15	Jesus before Pilate
16–41	Mockery and Crucifixion
42–47	Burial
16.1–8	The Empty Tomb

(There is no evidence that Mark's gospel continued beyond this point.)

owed much to Jesus' own teaching, if he used the words; and to other Old Testament instances of "son of man" as a generic term for humanity, or the designation of a particular representative human being such as a prophet (as found in the prophecy of Ezekiel – see chapter 37.3 for example – or in the influential Psalm 8.4). One of the earlier descriptions of Jesus was, then, as a prophet of a rather special kind.

It is useful to classify the actual occurrences in Mark of the term "Son of Man" in three groupings:

8.38; 13.26; 14.62 – the triumphant coming (return?) of the Son of Man, in accordance with the Daniel 7.13 prophecy;

2.10; 2.28 – the present, earthly authority of a charismatic figure;

8.31; 9.9, 12, 31; 10.33f, 45: 14.21, 41 – predictions of suffering, death, and resurrection after three days.

These three groups represent an enormous range of time and mood, present and future, glory and suffering. Do they all refer to the same person? And is that person Jesus? The ideas may have different origins, but the connecting link and common denominator is Jesus himself: all these dimensions are applicable to him within the context of the gospel story. It may well be that the fuller articulation of the connections is the work of the evangelist Mark, for whom these theological elements are essential to the structure of his gospel.

"Whoever shall be ashamed of me and of my words in this adulterous and sinful generation, the Son of Man shall be ashamed of him, when he comes in the glory of his Father with the holy angels" (8.38). This verse is particularly illuminating. Originally it need have done no more than draw attention to some relationship between how people reacted to Jesus' teaching and how they would fare in the Last Judgement. But the structural pattern of Hebrew poetry (with clauses in parallel to one another), which this verse imitates in Greek, essentially establishes an intrinsic relationship. An example of the Hebrew method is Psalm 8.4:

> *What is man that thou art mindful of him,*
> *and the son of man that thou dost care for him?*

Just as this psalm establishes the identity of man and son of man (in relation to God), so the parallel structure in Mark 8.38 could serve to underline the identification of Jesus with the "Son of Man". This identification might have been made first of all in the experience reflected in sayings of the second group, concerned with an earthly authority of a special kind.

There is yet more in 8.38, because this one verse combines, by implication, elements from all three groups in the classification. "That men may possibly be ashamed of Jesus and his words implies his teaching ministry, with the rejection of his words by those authorities who might be supposed to be in a position to judge their truth, and that he himself will be placed in a position of obloquy, disgrace, and, we may reasonably add, suffering – suffering such as a few verses earlier. [8.31] is predicted for him under the title of Son of man." Suffering and obscurity meet glory and authority and are constituted in an organic relationship in the person of Jesus. The interrelationship of these varied elements in Jesus as Son of Man is strictly paralleled by the relationship between the secret operations and the triumph of the Kingdom of God (cf. 9.1).

Predictions of suffering and death

The actual predictions of the Passion, applied to the Son of Man, may be part of the traditional theological insights from Mark's sources or they may be Mark's own contribution. What is clear is that these three predictions play a vital part in Mark's deliberate arrangement. The very repetition, with specific variations of detail, has the effect of building to a climax. It is counterbalanced later by another literary structure, with a similar threefold repetition, in Peter's denial (14.66ff – the effect of Mark's insertion of this story within the account of the trial "is to make the disciple's denial and the master's sole public claim to messiahship as nearly simultaneous as narrative allows").[3]

Mark is insistent that Jesus goes the way of the cross; it is only in this way that his lordship could be realized and recognized. At the first instance of a full prediction of the Passion the evangelist makes this clear by his comment (8.32): "And Jesus said this plainly". This is not in flat contradiction of the mystery, the messianic secret (8.30); he is not saying that Jesus speaks openly or publicly. Rather this prophecy is plain speaking, whether or not it is misunderstood, just as Peter misunderstands (8.32). Only by the way of suffering can the hidden identity of Jesus be realized. It may be the very reason why Mark has developed the theological motif of mystery.

Another prediction of the Passion may be found much earlier in Mark, at 2.20. The term "Son of Man" is not used here, but the reference is to "the bridegroom", a similar third-person designation which could point to Jesus himself and evoke the context of the wedding feast and messianic banquet. "The days will come, when the bridegroom is taken away from them, and then they will fast in that day." The term "taken away" is appropriate for a violent death, especially if Isaiah 53.8 ("By oppression and judgement he was taken away") could be in mind. Fasting is a sign of mourning and this idea is uppermost, even if the context also has practical implications for the Christian ascetic ritual of fasting. The evangelist gives an early – and concealed – prediction which is the more effective because of the paradoxical notion of wedding guests fasting.

The necessity of Christ's death on the cross

That Jesus goes the way of the cross is a mysterious truth for Mark. It is also a matter of divine necessity that events take this course. The use made in the gospel of the phrase, "it is necessary", especially in contexts such as 8.31; 9.11 and 13.10, emphasizes the centrality of this doctrine to Mark's theology. This is not to be understood in the sense of constraints imposed by

Christian pilgrims re-enact the journey of Jesus to crucifixion along the Via Dolorosa in Jerusalem.

governments or other human agencies. The thought pattern in the gospel relates to the world of APOCALYPTIC with its complex calendrical calculations of events which appear predestined. These are events within the purposes of God. Hence "the Son of Man *must* suffer" (8.31). The heart of Mark's understanding of Christ and salvation is to be found in the contrasts and the apparent paradoxes of the hidden Son of God and the suffering Son of Man. This emphasis on the inevitability of suffering for the special agent of God would have been equally surprising to most Jewish and Gentile readers.

To try to have Jesus as Lord without the cross is to miss Mark's particular understanding of Jesus' work. And it may well be that Mark is so emphatic and uncompromising on this point precisely because some of Mark's contemporaries wished to avoid the idea of the cross. In a time of competing Christologies, or alternative attempts to understand the achievement of Christ, Mark presents two pictures which appear to be in dramatic contrast with each other. The figure of the powerful exorcist or worker of wonders is set over against the hidden figure who goes the way of the cross. There seems to be a polarization between a theology of glory and a theology of the cross. However, these are not mutually exclusive options.

Mark tells his readers that the two apparently contrasted figures of the wonder worker and the one who must be crucified are actually set in mutual relationship, within a single organism that is the person of Christ.

Christ as king and servant

The first indication of the concept of Christ as both king and servant in Mark's theology is presented in the words of the heavenly voice at Jesus' baptism (1.11): "Thou art my beloved Son; with thee I am well pleased". The words are derived and combined from two different strands of the Old Testament tradition. The first clause comes from the language of the royal Psalms (e.g. 2.7); the reference is to a kingly figure anointed as the messianic agent of God, from whom mighty works can be expected. The second clause comes from the prophetic language of the second part of Isaiah (e.g. 42.1), where the context is that of the servant of God, whether Israel as servant or the mysterious figure who is destined to suffer. While the text of Matthew 3.17 can be said to follow Mark in this combination of Christological images, it should be noted that a major textual tradition in Luke 3.22 has changed the emphasis and concentrated attention on the royal Psalm ("Thou art my beloved Son; today I have begotten thee").

The Christ of the miracle stories

An illustration of the debate between two pictures of Christ and its resolution can be found in the miracle stories which form a substantial proportion of this gospel, particularly in its earlier chapters. Like the controversy material, examined previously, these stories implicitly raise the questions: "Who is Jesus?", "What kind of a man is this?". The point is made explicit, for example, at the close of the story of the stilling of the storm (4.35–41). "Who then is this, that even wind and sea obey him?" (4.41). Opinions are divided as to how Mark would have understood a story like this, whether he would have taken it literally, as the account of an historical event in Jesus' life or whether he would have understood it as myth, that is, as a powerful symbol of God's protective care. It may be that the very distinction between

A 9-metre long wooden boat dating from the time of Christ, found in the mud of the sea of Galilee in February 1986. The archaeologists have wrapped the hull prior to conservation.

history and myth is modern and arbitrary, and a first-century theologian would have held the two together and said "both/and" rather than "either/or".

It is important to grasp the force of the language in this and similar miracle stories: Jesus is seen as in conflict with the powers of darkness, of evil, of Satan. This is something extraordinary, the power of the one stronger than the strong man (3.27 in the context of 3.21ff). The reader is taken back to Mark's initial theme of the Kingdom of God. The miracles represent God's kingdom in operation, and are part of the process of subduing opposition to God's purpose. The fact that the story is told as an eschatological drama of cosmic dimensions, the struggle between God and Satan, should also leave room to derive a smaller-scale, more parochial, message of encouragement for the members of Mark's community in their vulnerability. If God's power is seen to be victorious on the cosmic scale, should this not also be reflected in the local dimension? "Besides the primary teaching in the sea miracles concerning the mystery of Who Jesus is, there is a secondary or PARACLETIC theme, which brings a message of comfort to a storm-tossed Church in a hostile world, and which would speak a word of special encouragement to St. Mark's first readers."[4] Jesus' attack (literally conceived) on the demons of the sea (an embodiment of evil for those like the Hebrews, who distrusted that element) can become a symbolic talisman against any demon of the storm.

Competing Christologies in Mark's community?

There can be no doubt of the power in this conflict of Jesus with the forces of darkness. But there may also be a conflict, a POLEMIC, between the two pictures of Jesus represented in the heavenly voice at the baptism. The figure of power and worker of wonders is ranged against the one who goes the way of the cross. This inner debate, this dialectic with its challenging Christology, could actually be an historical controversy from Mark's time. This suggestion has been made in a strongly argued interpretation of Mark's gospel.

> *Mark decides to dramatise the christological dispute raging between himself and his opponents, through the interrelation of Jesus with his disciples during the course of the public ministry. That is, he stages the christological debate of his community in a "historical" drama in which Jesus serves as a surrogate for Mark and the disciples serve as surrogates for Mark's opponents. Jesus preaches and acts out the Markan suffering-servant theology. The disciples promulgate and act out* theios aner [divine man] *theology.*[5]

This is a striking way of making sense of the contrast in the gospel between the figure of wonder and the figure of suffering. If they are incompatible, they must represent opposing points of view. But where in the gospel is the actual debate conducted between these positions? The disciples are uncomprehending and even reproachful but hardly argumentative in philosophical debate (as Mark's actual opponents would have been, according to the theory). To say that "they were utterly astounded, for they did not understand about the loaves, but their hearts were hardened" (6.52) suggests a failure to grasp the secret of Christ's identity, the relationship of the powerful with the suffering, rather than an articulate opposition. And when Jesus "sighed deeply in his spirit, and said, 'Why does this generation seek a sign? Truly, I say to you, no sign shall be given to this generation'" (8.12), this response was provoked by an argument with the Pharisees and not with the disciples.

The mystery and the paradox of these pictures of Christ remain; they cannot be explained as easily as this theory suggests. The evidence of the gospel is more of two aspects which belong together and need to be harmonized than of two mutually exclusive opposites which confront one another. It would also seem a little strange to cast disciples from Galilee (who might at best represent the Jerusalem church) as the spokesmen for a Hellenistic picture of Christ as "divine man". An apocalyptic style of language, such as that used for the miracle stories about the confrontation of God's kingdom and Satan, would have described the false teachers whom the author wished to oppose in wholly other terms. See, for example, the succinct expression of 1 John 2.18f. The most reasonable conclusion is that the miracle stories have a positive rather than a negative function in the gospel of Mark, to relate the theology of glory to the mysterious theology of suffering.

From glory to suffering

The movement in Mark's gospel is from the earlier emphasis on miracles (with the important qualifications that have been observed) to the later emphasis on the inevitability of suffering and death (with the glimpse that is offered of the Transfiguration). As has been seen, the Passion predictions prepare the way for this climax. "The recognition by Peter of Jesus' messiahship ... produces the first of the three Passion predictions, and begins a new movement, spiritually and geographically, towards Jerusalem."[3] What began as a prediction in terms of the Son of Man ends with an affirmation about the death itself in terms of the Son of God (15.39). This dominant theological motif of the death of Christ in Mark has much in common with Paul's writings, as has already been suggested. But while Paul demonstrates it in theme and argument, Mark uses the power of the narrative.

The narrative of Christ's death

Mark's narrative resources are the substantial materials of the Passion story in the tradition, to which he perhaps adds the episode of the anointing at Bethany (14.3–9), and the chapter often referred to as the Little Apocalypse (13.1–36). The woman at Bethany "has done what she could; she has anointed my body beforehand for burial" (14.8). In Mark it is the only anointing Jesus receives, and burial without these last rites would have been a disgrace. Furthermore, as it is Jesus' head which is anointed this would suggest that he is being anointed as Messiah; but as he actually fulfils this messianic purpose by dying the two aspects are essentially related. This unit of the story can be separated from the Passion narrative, and has varying parallels in the other gospels. What then becomes significant is the way Mark has used it and underlined its theological importance. The same is true of chapter 13; there can be little doubt that here is a separate apocalyptic document, or a composite of such traditional material. The most significant features for Mark are the elements of prophecy derived from Daniel (especially in verses 14 and 26), and the context of the destruction of the temple (13.2) to which they are applied. These prophecies, and the eschatological world-view related to the cataclysm, are transplanted from their original surroundings and applied to events in Jerusalem, the future of the temple and the apparent end of Jesus. Such is the effect of the traditional association of ideas. At a stroke, Mark has applied the cosmic dimension to the death of Jesus, and, indeed, to the whole sequence of events to which the Passion predictions had pointed, by way of the triumphal entry, the cleansing of the temple, the cursing of the fig tree, and the chapter of controversies which begins with the parable of the destruction of the vineyard's tenants.

The eschatological terminology is not confined to chapter 13. The violence of divine judgement can be seen as the gospel moves to its climax. Since the author writes of necessary suffering and death, brought about directly by hostile forces combining against Jesus, the tone of the narrative, the sense of storm clouds imminent and lowering, is understandable as a literary device. Equally understandable, from the point of view of the partisans for Jesus' cause, is the note of divine vengeance often associated with heightened eschatology. But that too should be seen as a device, a theological device to redress the balance, and not to be transmuted into human vengeance. Looked at in literary and theological terms, the intense darkness of Mark's picture is ultimately relieved, firstly as "the curtain of the temple was torn in two, from top to bottom" (15.38), and secondly in the words of the young man in the tomb on Easter morning: "Do not be amazed; you seek Jesus of Nazareth who was crucified. He has risen, he is not here" (16.6).

It is possible to compare Mark's narrative with other literary works where the working out of a pattern of doom seems inescapable, for example in a play such as *Ghosts* by Henrik Ibsen or in a novel like Thomas Hardy's *Jude the Obscure*. By the plan of his gospel, and by the use of a theological motif of mysterious identity, Mark prepares a way for living through this death which the readers can share. He does not need to elaborate the bare fact of Resurrection by accounts of subsequent appearances. He can even risk the ending on a note of terrified silence and apparent failure (16.8). The sequel is the presupposition of Mark's book, that the gospel is good news and not simply a note of warning.

Predestination as explanation

Two features that have been noted, the inevitability of suffering and a possible parallel with the Pauline understanding of the death of Christ, need further inspection in relation to each other. In the 1930s C. H. Dodd, writing about the parables, referred to Mark 4.11–12, which is the primary text for the theory of parables as concealing meaning.

> *According to these verses they* [the parables] *were spoken in order to prevent those who were not predestined to salvation from understanding the teaching of Jesus. This is surely connected with the doctrine of the primitive Church, accepted with modifications by Paul, that the Jewish people to whom Jesus came were by divine providence blinded to the significance of His Coming, in order that the mysterious purpose of God might be fulfilled through their rejection of the Messiah. That is to say, this explanation of the purpose of the parables is an answer to a question which arose after the death of Jesus, and the failure of His followers to win the Jewish people.*[6]

Paul experienced in the Christian mission field what the prophets of Israel had experienced in Old Testament times, namely a sense that Israel was being prevented from receiving their message, and that by these means the ultimate purposes of God were being fulfilled (see Romans 10.14–21 in the context of the argument of chapters 9–11).

Such theological explanations are clear examples of cultural relativism. Theories of predestination are unacceptable in the current climate, with its emphasis on individual freedom and the loving nature of God, whatever the consequences of limiting the range of God's activity. But in the right philosophical mood we can also talk of an individual's activity being constrained by parents or a disadvantaged upbringing, by custom and cultural conditioning, or by the influence of the environment. It may be that the modern world has simply secularized the old doctrine of predestination and restated the general themes in other terms.

Predestination as a doctrine in Mark's community

In the contexts of Mark and Paul, the doctrine of predestination may have fulfilled a more immediate function in binding the group together. It has been suggested that Mark's theme of secrecy and mystery is a coherent theological statement within a complex of available options. It is also possible to argue that it is coherent as a sociological statement: it is concerned with a doctrine of predestination that is intelligible in terms of its social function within Mark's community. What this could mean for Mark, and also for Paul, is that the early Christian reforming movement was in the process of being transformed into a SECTARIAN group or separate body. We could explain that this happened at a point when the pressures of the outside world were particularly severe and hostile. The language of predestination had an immediately useful function in reinforcing the sect's view of itself as an elite. "*We* understand; we possess the secret; we belong to the special community; those outside are beyond the pale; they are not saved or

Caves in the rock at Qumran. The central opening is cave 4 where one of the richest hoards of Dead Sea Scrolls was found; the cave was close-packed with about 400 manuscripts.

enlightened by God." In this way a sectarian group can use its ideology to legitimate its state of separation and separate identity.

But it is necessary to be careful here, for the sociologist is only making suggestions. His argument can be dangerously reductionist, as if his "explanation" were the only thing worth considering. The theme of predestination recurs in many prophetic and apocalyptic texts. In some contexts it can have great value as a statement of theology or of religious experiences (or even of humanist philosophy). And the argument used by the sociologist is not strictly reversible. If we know from other evidence that the Qumran covenanters or the Johannine community were sectarian – in the case of Qumran from archaeology, in the case of the fourth gospel from the words of John 17 – then we can fairly look at the ways they might use predestinarian and other ideological language to reinforce their identities. Not all who use prophetic and eschatological language are necessarily sectarian. So we must take another heading on our grid and look for other evidence bearing on the nature of Mark's community and its understanding of the church.

Community organization and practice

It is difficult to know where to go for data on the church. Where does it even say anything at all about the Church in Mark? We must look for traces of the community's organization and practice, for implicit if not explicit evidence of the church's self-understanding. This might include references to the Holy Spirit and the SACRAMENTS, the ideas about mission and Jewish and Gentile relations, any theories of church organization or of ethics that might be modelled on the practice of Jesus. At best, such indicators are exceedingly fragmentary in Mark.

The Holy Spirit in the church

Of the sparse references to the Holy Spirit three passages are particularly relevant. "I have baptized you with water; but he will baptize you with the Holy Spirit." These words of John the Baptist in 1.8 would have been understood by Mark's readers as referring to the gift of the Spirit to the church, not necessarily to a rite of Christian baptism exclusively. "Jesus, who was himself about to receive the Holy Spirit when he was baptized by John, would in turn bestow the same gift upon his followers."[7] There is a further reference to the gift of the Spirit, specifically in a time of persecution, in 13.11 (within the apocalyptic chapter). "But say whatever is given you in that hour, for it is not you that speak, but the Holy Spirit." Notice that Mark's context of persecution (to which we must return) is different from those in Matthew (see p. 220) and Luke (see p. 139), which are concerned with mission and more general church considerations. Mark points to inspired utterance at the time of crisis. The final passage is on a theme related to the Spirit, namely exorcism in the name of Jesus. Mark 9.38ff reveals that the church had a difference of opinion over the free use of the name of Jesus

A Eucharist or community meal depicted in a wall painting from the catacomb of Callistus in Rome (*c*.200 CE). The fish and the baskets echo the feeding miracles of the four and five thousand.

in Christian exorcism and suggests that one group sought to establish a monopoly of such spiritual powers.

The Eucharist in the church

The Last Supper (14.12–25), which in Mark is scheduled as a Passover meal (14.12), is the natural focus for EUCHARISTIC references. Mark's is probably the first gospel to provide an account of the institution of the Eucharist and the words which interpret the meaning of the event. We can compare this with the account which may well be earlier, but outside the gospels, in Paul's first letter to the Corinthian church (11.23–26). There is significant agreement in these texts between Paul and Mark: firstly in that this event relates to the death of Christ, and is a theological interpretation of it; and secondly the commemoration of this event looks forward to the fullest realization of the Kingdom of God.

The two accounts of miracles of feeding – of the five thousand in 6.30–44, and of the four thousand in 8.1–10 – should also be considered within the context of the Eucharist. Ideas of food and eating are prominent in Mark and may be particularly significant (see 2.26; 5.43; 7.27f; 8.14ff). It is necessary to ask whether the Christian reader in Mark's community would understand the two feeding miracles as prefiguring the Eucharist, and whether, in addition, such a special eucharistic significance could help to alleviate the problem of the apparent near-duplication of these two stories of feedings. If they stand deliberately in parallel, they could be making a theological point, relating the local community and the wider church together in a larger perspective. As an early ECUMENICAL symbol, Mark's narratives then represent the feeding by Jesus first of Jews and then of Gentiles. One difficulty in the interpretation of the two feeding miracles is in whether Mark's geographical references are to be understood literally or as having a symbolic significance. Another problem lies in the probably self-contained nature of the original stories. It is at least possible to conclude, even if both feedings were actually on Gentile soil, that they represent a more generally open and universalist theological ideal. This could well have been Mark's intention: "Mark ... regarded the miracles of the loaves as witnessing to Jesus as the giver of the bread of life, and presenting him as the one who has enough of this spiritual food for all nations."[8] There is an interesting – if speculative – theory that Mark has adopted the parallel miracles of feeding, along with those of the sea and of healings (a double cycle in chapters 4–6 and 6–8) from a eucharistic LITURGY which celebrated Jesus, revealed in the form of a "divine man". If this were so, and there are difficulties with it, we would have to say that the evangelist, who made major modifications to the Christology of his source, may also have altered its eucharistic emphasis.

Community structure: the model of discipleship

Mark's gospel offers almost no evidence about the organization of the community for whom he was writing. We may presume that it possessed some form of ministry, but the gospel does not reveal any details or indicate any leadership roles or special responsibilities. The most positive impression is given by studies of what the gospel says about the theme of discipleship, of what it meant to be following Jesus. The community is depicted as a "family, in which the members are brothers and sisters and share in one another's possessions [3.31ff; 10.28ff]. This image puts members on the same level; no one is isolated as 'father' and therefore the bearer of authority within the family; equally no one is picked out as 'pastor' or 'shepherd' in relation to the metaphor of the flock [6.34; 14.27f] and no one as 'pilot' in relation to the ship [4.35ff; 6.45ff]".[9] The relation to Jesus is primary; beyond, or rather through, this there is a relational interdependence.

At first glance the episode of Mark 3.31–35 might appear highly critical of the idea of the family as a model. Jesus' response – "Who are my mother and my brothers?" (3.33) – has a critical edge to it, as of one renouncing such a context and turning his back on home and family. It seems likely that in the background of this story is the early Palestinian picture of Jesus as a wandering teacher; like many other "wandering charismatics" then and since, he had actually left home, and in his homelessness depended on charity. The piety of such wandering ascetics was admired and supported, in much the same way as local communities support Buddhist monks in their *takuhatsu* or practice of begging. In a relatively settled community such a renunciation of the world could be regarded as invested with special authority and respect.

In the later situation in the church at Rome this idea would still not be totally strange, for there too itinerant philosophers and teachers were found, although many were disparaged as charlatans. It seems likely that the original picture of Jesus, embodied in this story, has been transformed to become the newly established model for the community in Rome. Discipleship is seen as the new family: "Whoever does the will of God is my brother, and sister, and mother" (3.35). But a clear critical edge remains in the teaching; it is not simply the old social structure, but a total transformation.

The alternative family

From the sociological perspective we can begin from the widely received understanding of the family as one form of basic social unit and pattern. As we have suggested, it is possible that the Jesus-movement, in particular Mark's community, may have seen itself as an alternative social structure modelled on the family. But we do not know whether it was one of a number of such alternatives and whether those structures competed with one another. We could say that the gospel of Mark stands as a charter for social and religious belief and action, particularly in relation to a stable community life and the opportunities for mission.

The episode of the calling of the disciples in 1.16–20 can be seen as creating expectations of these kinds. "Follow me and I will make you become fishers of men" (1.17). And the later passage, 10.28–31, with its echoed language of "leaving" and "following", represents a commentary on the call of the disciples. Discipleship provides a model for the process of conversion in the mission field. Mark 10.28–31 can also be seen as a reinterpretation of the rich man's question in 10.17–22: "Good Teacher, what must I do to inherit eternal life?" (10.17). In a context which is particularly concerned with questions of wealth (cf. 10.23) the issue is

A meeting of a modern house church.

generalized and reconsidered in relation to household ties, assets, and responsibilities. To abandon primary household ties might appear to render one effectively "last" and out of account, but actually "first" in the new order of things (10.31).

> *Peter began to say to Jesus, "Lo, we have left everything and followed you". Jesus said, "Truly, I say to you, there is no one who has left house or brothers or sisters or mother or father or children or lands, for my sake and for the gospel, who will not receive a hundredfold now in this time, houses and brothers and sisters and mothers and children and lands,* with persecutions, *and in the age to come eternal life. But many that are first will be last, and the last first."* (10.28–31)

This text can be investigated further, to shed more light on how the ideas of household and family relations may be regarded. The idiom of reward for those who "have left everything" (10.28) suggests radical, alternative household or family units rather than the total and revolutionary replacement of the very structure. Preference for this kind of language may even be a clue to the existence of house churches in Mark's community. But these household ties, past and present, are made only relative by the final clause of the reward: "and in the age to come eternal life" (10.30). One wonders whether meanwhile any redistribution of property was envisaged, in the interests of care for the poor, with again the relativization "and you will have treasure in heaven" (10.21).

Whatever the communal sharing of property, there is no question of widely shared sexual relations, that blight of, or accusation faced by, many communes. Mark preserves strict and uncompromising sayings of Jesus about the ideal of marriage and the prohibition of divorce (10.2–12). We should probably recognize the appeal of the rewards passage to those outside the community, remembering the spirit of universalism we have detected in Mark. These outsiders may perhaps be identified as principally the social outcasts and the "homeless" to whom the appeal would be strongest. In Marcan Christianity can then be identified the ideals and patterns of social integration. The church may have wished to provide such a structure for society but nonetheless found itself having dealings on the margins of society. This picture carries conviction, even if one must recognize that these images rooted in social facts are in the process of becoming symbols.

Persecution by outsiders

A final element to notice in Mark 10.30 is that the reward is accompanied "with persecutions". This apparent jarring note in the sequence of rewards underlines the fact that persecution was a regular feature of life for this community. The reference to persecution is unique to Mark, while of the synoptic parallels only Luke 18.30 preserves the balance between rewards now and in the future. Mark therefore has the fullest picture of reality now. The disciples are promised that they will not suffer real loss, but will be

The head of John the Baptist is presented to Salome in the presence of Herod Antipas and his guest (Mark 6.17–28) – illustration from the Sinope Gospel (6th century CE).

A portrait of a young girl holding a perfume bottle, from El Faiyum in Egypt. The woman who anoints Jesus with perfume (Mark 14.3–9) anticipates his burial.

The Resurrection: a rock tomb of the time of Jesus with the entrance stone rolled away.

An aerial view of the Qumran settlement showing its setting on the coastal strip between the cliffs and the Dead Sea. It may have been designed as a defensive fort rather than as a monastic retreat.

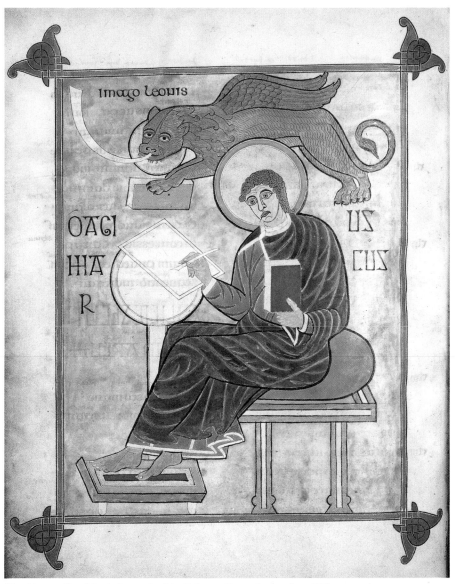

The Evangelist Mark from the Lindisfarne Gospels, made *c*.698 CE on the Northumbrian island.

Christ carrying the Cross – a painting by Hieronymus Bosch (*c.*1450–1516) from Ghent. Bosch used grotesque exaggeration to depict the evils of humanity which he saw as the causes of suffering (especially Christ's suffering).

rewarded one hundredfold within their Christian family life, never mind how devastating the assaults of organized persecution may appear to be at the time. Here as elsewhere in Mark – and not only in chapter 13 – there is a strong eschatological orientation. It must be related essentially to the heightened language used to describe the threats and the state of emergency. It is significant that the last words of formal teaching given by Jesus to his disciples, according to Mark, are: "What I say to you, I say to all: Watch" (13.37).

Discipleship and suffering

One of the most striking features of the structure of Mark's gospel is the threefold prediction of the Passion. Attention has already been drawn to this, in relation to the picture of Christ as Son of Man (p. 58). Within the gospel framework, these three statements about Christ are also intimately related to three statements about discipleship. By these means the evangelist makes a repeated emphasis: the Christ who calls to discipleship is the Christ who must suffer; the inescapable consequence is that the discipleship will likewise involve a reversal of normal values and expectations. It must be expected that discipleship will involve suffering as well.

* Thus the prophecy of 8.31 relates directly to 8.34 ("If any man would come after me, let him take up his cross and follow me"). The disciples' way is also the way of the cross.
* The prophecy of 9.31 relates directly to 9.35 ("If any one would be first, he must be last of all and servant of all"). As the Son of Man is servant so the disciple is servant.
* The prophecy of 10.33 relates directly to 10.39f, 43ff ("The cup that I drink you will drink; and with the baptism with which I am baptized, you will be baptized"). Jesus and his disciples share the same cup and baptism (twin images for the same experience of suffering).

This cumulative definition of discipleship takes clear account of the contemporary realities in the situation for which Mark's gospel was intended. The Christian community might well feel very isolated. The promised return of Christ had not obviously taken place, and instead a terrible persecution had been unleashed, such as that documented by the Roman historian Tacitus as occurring in Rome under the emperor Nero. God must have seemed distant and Jesus altogether hidden; faith must have been difficult to sustain and despair must have been very near. Mark's gospel was an attempt to bring faith out of despair, trust out of perplexity, hope out of hopelessness. Mark did this for his community by the emphasis on the death of Christ. Just as the way of the cross was destined for the hidden Messiah, so the experience of suffering was the appropriate reward for those who took up the cross of Christ. Discipleship and hope of future rewards were defined in relation to one another and to a realistic acceptance of the contemporary sufferings.

Ethics in Mark's community

There is relatively little straight ethical material in Mark and no systematic presentation of an ethical scheme. Some collection of Jesus' words, relevant to the moral problems of the day, was nevertheless felt to be an appropriate resource, in early Christian experience. In Mark the collected fragments appear haphazard, but seem to have their focus in chapter 10. We have already examined some of this text in connection with the definition of discipleship in Mark's community. The traditional ethical demands of the Decalogue (the Ten Commandments) are cited and echoed in the words of Mark 7 (see particularly verses 10 and 21f). These demands are then apparently given a new value within Mark 10 by being made relative to the demand to follow Jesus by giving all to the poor (10.19–21). For Jewish readers this would have seemed a surprising reversal of traditional ethical values, to supplant the foundation of Torah with the peripheral practice of charitable giving. But, as was noted earlier, a reversal of normal values is associated with the call of discipleship.

A statuette of the emperor Nero.

MAP 2 Palestine in the
time of Jesus.

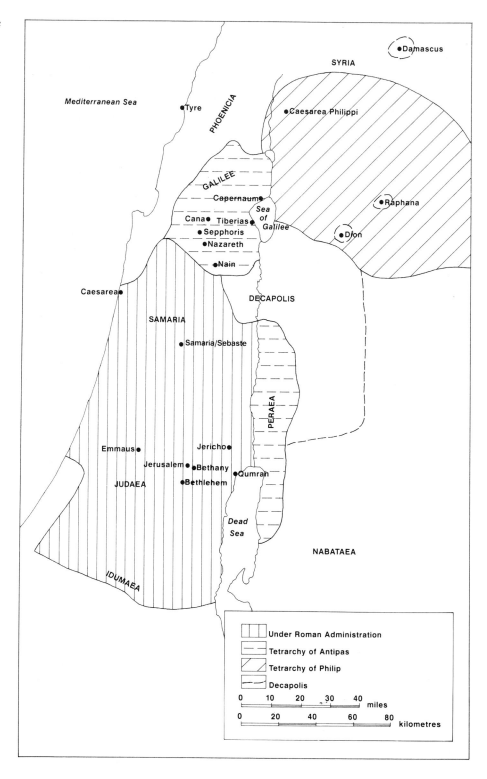

The ethical demand of Mark 10.21 seems absolute: "Go, sell what you have, and give to the poor, and you will have treasure in heaven; and come, follow me." This, in turn, is itself made relative in the episode of the woman who anoints Jesus for burial (14.3–9). The ointment used was very costly and might reasonably have been sold for the benefit of the poor (14.5). But the significance of her action in relation to Jesus, the "beautiful thing" which she has done in acknowledging him as Messiah and avoiding the disgrace of a burial without the last rites, is seen to override the newly established ethical priorities. "For you always have the poor with you, and whenever you will, you can do good to them; but you will not always have me" (14.7). The Christian disciples now increasingly recognize this by experience, as they feel distanced from Christ.

What Mark seeks to provide is a social, and above all a theological, substitute in this deprivation. He urges that any ethical principle tends to fade into insignificance – or at best to be strictly subordinated – in comparison with the vital theological focus and orientation of the disciples on Jesus himself. These ethical demands, as we have seen, are not absolute rules but are rather what Derrida calls "traces" left by the will of God. And in relation to the eschatological context of discipleship (10.29–31), Mark maintains a strict balance between two ages (present and future) in his view of existence, which may seem paradoxical to some. There is a double understanding of time, which takes account of the new eschatological reality. Ethical principles are bound to be subordinated to this new reality because they belong to *this* world.

Locating Mark's community

In conclusion we must look for clues to the possible geographical location of Mark's community. However coherent an account we can give of the church's theological beliefs and understanding of itself and its role, something is lacking if it does not seem to belong anywhere, or relate to anything. Ralph Martin described Mark as "a gospel in search of a life setting".[10] This is a recurrent problem in studies of the gospel, unless one simply takes refuge in the traditional linkage with Peter and Rome. So far there is one clue which might suggest a stronger link with Paul than Peter but the place is hardly limited by that observation.

The opponents of the community

It is often said that the way the gospel describes the opponents of Jesus may actually reflect those hostilities felt by the later church community. In Mark three groups stand out: the chief priests, elders, and scribes who wish to put Jesus to death (14.1; 15.1); the Pharisees and the Herodians who earlier begin plotting against him (3.6; 12.13); and the family of Jesus, the discarded social unit ("Your mother and brothers are outside" – 3.32). The existence of this last group, perhaps linked with the uncomprehending disciples, has been taken to reflect a conflict between Mark and the Jewish Christians or the Jerusalem church (whose spokesmen caused problems for Paul). This seems an unlikely interpretation of the references in Mark, which are best understood (as noted on p. 68) in relation to the social model of the family for discipleship. Mark teaches the essence of the idea by a set of contrasts; the language is forceful in order to encourage self-criticism and a deeper understanding of the theological implications.

The other two groups may be general indications of a Gentile-Christian perspective. By themselves they cannot tell us much, although they have sometimes been regarded as the negative (critical) factor linked to the positive factor of a "divine man" Christology reflected in the miracle stories. But this is a very one-sided view of Mark who, as has been seen, balances his pictures of Christ to emphasize both the glory and the cross.

The Herodians and the tribute money

Among the named opponents there is, however, one designation which seems to be a usage distinctive to Mark: "the Herodians" referred to in 3.6 and 12.13 (reproduced in Matthew 22.16). Unfortunately for us their identity is not entirely clear. If they were the partisans or supporters of Herod Antipas in Galilee, then their involvement in the politically sensitive question about Roman tribute (12.14f) is historically intelligible in the time of Jesus. Such party titles usually related to a situation of conflict; it could be that their ambition "was again to remove Judaea from direct Roman procuratorial rule and make it subject to the rule of a Herod ... Their political aim called for absolute loyalty to Rome".[11]

It seems unlikely that this will help substantially in the characterization of Mark's antagonists. His use of the tribute question reflects the relativity of his ethical position. Tribute is no problem to Jesus as a Galilean without an income. Jesus' statement does not legitimate Roman power as such. Human beings "in the image of God" should give themselves wholly to God, and the disciples of Jesus should be giving up money. Such ethical and theological priorities could of course apply anywhere in the Roman Empire, but might have had a particular ironic force within Rome itself. Here, of all places, Jesus' call involves a reversal of those values prevailing in the surrounding society.

The missionary outreach of the community

Another pointer to Mark's location could be his attitude to mission. We have already seen evidence of some universalist emphases in the interpretation of the feeding miracles, and in the understanding of discipleship. Within those constraints necessarily imposed by a sense of eschatological crisis, the attitude of this gospel is remarkably open. The text speaks of God's "sending" and of the call to discipleship. Among possible proof texts for the community's attitude are:

> *Let us go on to the next towns, that I may preach there also; for that is why I came out.* (1.38).
> *And the gospel must first be preached to all nations.* (13.10).

The interpretation of the parable of the sower (4.13–20) is concerned with the sowing of the word in different kinds of soil. It suggests that the disciples might expect a return for preaching in which seventy-five per cent would lead to no fruitful result (they must be prepared for that) but the remaining twenty-five per cent would produce fruit, "thirtyfold and sixtyfold and a hundredfold".

   This variety of soils and results corresponds broadly with the sense of various backgrounds that are part of the problem in locating Mark's gospel. We would expect the gospel to reflect in some way the situations of Jesus, of the earliest Christians, and of Mark's community. But it is actually more complex than this, because it is not a matter of generalizing and tracing common factors and connecting links, but rather of appreciating several contexts and sets of particularities. One suggestion is that the gospel seeks to leap over the historical and cultural divides between a largely Gentile readership in 68–70 CE, and a largely Galilean happening in 30–33 CE, by seeing things primarily through the eyes of a Jewish–Gentile Christianity on the borderlands of Israel, that is, the view of a Syrian Church of 50–70 CE.

From Galilee to the Syrian church

The Syrian church would represent an important transitional stage in this complex process. It had affinities with the original situation of Jesus, preserving the images of a less sophisticated lifestyle that emerge in parts of Mark's gospel. The missionary situation could reflect the activity of radical Jewish sectarians, or Jewish-Christian wandering teachers, or itinerant Christian charismatics. This more primitive style of Christianity retained its perspective on the Kingdom of God as a future eschatological event. The emphasis on Galilee as the place where the disciples would see Jesus again (and not just as a post-Resurrection experience, but as the fulfilment of the promised PAROUSIA or second coming) is in striking contrast to Luke's orientation on Jerusalem. "But after I am raised up I will go before you to Galilee" (14.28); "But go, tell his disciples and Peter that he is going before you to Galilee; there you will see him, as he told you" (16.7). With such climactic references it is hard to dismiss altogether any sense of place and to assert that Galilee is only a theological symbol for the Gentile mission. Instead we can say that the community which was interested in the Little Apocalypse of Mark 13 was also able to read the Galilee promise as a literal summons to await Jesus' Parousia there at the time of the Jewish War.

From Syria to Rome

From the Syrian community with its literal expectations, the gospel was transposed to a more sophisticated and thoroughly Gentile environment, conceivably in Rome itself. This gospel's earlier traditions were preserved as essential stages in theological understanding. And so Mark 13 and the Galilee promises are still intrinsic to a gospel which now expressed more fully the openness of the Gentile mission (13.10). The particular application of the gospel at this stage was to the situation of persecution, in order to redefine the nature of discipleship in the time of crisis. The language of discipleship (with its Palestinian and Syrian affinities) was in no way alien to this new environment. Greek and Roman teachers also had their bands of disciples/companions with whom readers might identify in this more sophisticated society. There is a particular appropriateness in thinking of Mark's readers in Rome itself. Christians in Rome were neither Jew nor Gentile in a culture where everything was clear for those belonging to one group or the other. Even at the centre of the social world of the Roman Empire, then, there was a small community that was in danger of being forced to the margins of society. There could be no more suitable context in which to preach a message about a reversal of the world's values, a creed which expects suffering, a power which demonstrates itself in weakness, and an order in which the first shall be last, and the last first.

Note: This chapter is not like the kind of novel (such as John Fowles' *The French Lieutenant's Woman*) where there are two endings because the author cannot decide which conclusion is preferred. Mark's gospel contains substantial evidence appropriate to each reconstruction which cannot be accommodated satisfactorily by any other 'situation'. So one argues for both/and rather than either/or, and this enhances the sense of the gospel which we now see as both the prototype and the end-product of traditional processes.

CHAPTER 2

Paul and his churches

The New Testament writings attributed to Paul are in the form of letters, not of a gospel. These letters must have been collected together by Paul's followers, after his death; the present collection also includes other letters, in the Pauline tradition, but not actually written by Paul (see Chapter 6 for these). Because letters (then as now) are designed to be a much more direct means of communication, the consequences are that Paul's personality emerges more clearly than those of the gospel writers, as do the situations of the early Christian communities to whom he wrote. The Corinthian correspondence especially provides a sustained view of the social and economic situation, and some insights into the theological and practical problems faced by one of the earliest Christian groups. All the letters would need to be studied in detail before any assessment could be made concerning whether Paul changed his theology or his missionary strategy, in the course of his work. Paul's methods of argument are difficult to understand and appreciate today (there is also some doubt as to whether he was correctly understood by earlier generations, from the New Testament letter of James, through to the church father Augustine and Luther at the Reformation).

Attitudes to Paul

Reactions to Paul are very mixed. For some he is the arch-misogynist and male chauvinist, politically conservative yet theologically revolutionary, and the one who tainted pure Christianity with Greek influences. For others he is the radical thinker, sensitive to the problems of society, even an advocate of feminist theology, by virtue of his insistence on the equality of the sexes. By his vision of the future he transcends current political dilemmas and preaches a universal Christianity accessible to all, which is yet faithful to its Palestinian origins and supremely to Jesus himself. We must examine the direct evidence of Paul's own writings within the New Testament before we make up our minds whether any of these labels are accurate.

Within the Christian churches today there is a further division in attitudes to Paul. For some people Paul expresses the fundamental ideas of the religion, in a tradition which was carried on by Augustine (bishop of Hippo in North Africa in the fourth/fifth century CE) and by Martin Luther at the time of the Reformation in the sixteenth century. For others, Paul is a largely unknown figure, apart from the dramatic stories of his encounter with the risen Christ on the road to Damascus and of the missionary journeys around the Eastern Mediterranean. Such information is derived from the Acts of the

DATING PAUL'S LIFE AND WORK		
CE Externally fixed points (related to the account in Acts)	*CE* Reconstruction of events in Paul's life	*CE* Approximate dates of widely accepted letters by Paul
	[Born at Tarsus (a cosmopolitan city) Educated as an orthodox Jew Studied at Jerusalem under Gamaliel Involved in actions against Christians and in the death of Stephen]	
30 Crucifixion of Jesus	33 Call/conversion of Paul 35 First journey to Jerusalem (Acts 9.26ff; Gal 1.18) Activity in Syria and Cilicia	
46 Famine in the reign of the Emperor Claudius (Josephus *Antiquities* 20.101)	46 Second journey to Jerusalem – famine relief (Acts 11.30)	
	47–8 Expedition from Antioch to Cyprus, Pamphylia and South Galatia (First Missionary Journey)	
	late 48 Council of Jerusalem (Acts 15; Gal 2.1)	
	early 49 Expedition from Antioch through North Galatia to Troas, Philippi, Thessalonica, Beroea, Athens (Second Missionary Journey)	
49 Edict of Emperor Claudius expelling Jews from Rome	late 49 Arrival in Corinth Meeting with Aquila and Priscilla 18-month stay in Corinth	50 1 Thessalonians
51 Gallio proconsul of Achea (Delphi inscription) 52 Felix as procurator of Judea	Hearing before Gallio (Acts 18.12) 52 Expedition from Antioch to Galatia and Phrygia, overland to Ephesus	53 Galatians
	55 Ephesus (Imprisonment?)	54 1 Corinthians 55 Philippians 55 Philemon 55 2 Corinthians 1–9 56 2 Corinthians 10–13
	56 Macedonia Winter in Corinth	
	57 Return to Jerusalem (Acts 21) Imprisonment in Caesarea under Felix	57 Romans
?59 P. Festus succeeds Felix as procurator of Judea	59 Hearing before P. Festus and Agrippa Journey to Rome Shipwreck (winter in Malta) 60 Arrival and imprisonment in Rome	?58 Colossians
	62 Execution in Rome (sometime between 62 and 64)	

Notes

1   Because of the problems of ancient chronology all dates have the usual margin of error (at least one or two years either way)

2   Scholars are not entirely agreed about the historical worth of the accounts in Acts or their relationship to Paul's own statements in his letters (particularly Galatians)

3   On the other letters, attributed to Paul, but not firmly included above, please see Chapter 7 on *The Other Writings*. As letters in the tradition of Paul they may still be important as evidence for the perpetuation of his theological ideas.

Apostles, possibly without reference to the letters of Paul. The reason for this may lie in the difficulty of Paul's writings. This was felt early on, as can be seen from the New Testament itself: "our beloved brother Paul wrote to you according to the wisdom given him, speaking of this as he does in all his letters. There are some things in them hard to understand, which the ignorant and unstable twist to their own destruction" (2 Peter 3.15f). There is even an indication of this view within Paul's own writings in 2 Corinthians 10.10 ("His letters are weighty and strong"). These two adjectives may be intentionally double-edged; they can have pejorative meanings, such as "indigestible". In contrast, the enthusiasm for Paul is tangible in these words, which have a modern ring, but were actually written in the fourth century CE by a church father called John Chrysostom: "Whenever I hear the epistles of Paul read out in the liturgy, I am filled with joy. I thrill every time I hear his call ringing out. My heart beats faster every time I recognise his voice. He seems to come into our very midst, and to be speaking in this church. What distresses me is that some people hardly know Paul at all. Some know him so little that they can't even tell you how many epistles he wrote! They plead their lack of education, when they ought to admit that they've never bothered to take up his writings and read them. If I'm regarded as a learned man, it's not because I'm brainy. It's simply because I have such a love for Paul that I've never left off reading him. He has taught me all I know. And I want you to listen carefully to what he has to teach you. You don't need to do anything else: just search and you will find, just knock and the door will be opened."[1]

Assessing the letters of Paul

An early Christian group receives a letter

One particular contribution which has been made by modern sociological methods, combined with the techniques of narrative theology, is to reconstruct what it would have been like to attend a meeting of an early Christian group and to hear a letter from Paul read out for the first time:

> Chloe had a house near the baptismal pool. It was known locally as "The Inn of the Christians for Socialism". That is where we were invited to take Sunday breakfast after the service of Baptism. It was a festive and happy meal. We were offered fruit, wine, bread and grilled fish. When everybody was well fed, Crispus stood in front of the people and announced that Erastus was going to read a further passage from Paul's letter.
>
> He read: "I may speak in Tongues of men or of angels, but if I am without love, I am like a circus gong or the hand drum of a popular musician. I may have the insights of the Jewish prophets, the astute knowledge of Greek scientists and all spiritual wisdom; I may have faith strong enough to move mountains; but if I have no love, I am nothing. And I may spend all I possess in order to feed the dock

Corinth: a general view of the remains of the Roman city and, in the background, the earlier Greek citadel (acropolis).

workers, the poor slaves and the foreign workers, and I may burn my body in a public place in protest against an unjust order of society, but if I have no love, I am none the better.

"Paul concludes this passage," Erastus said, "with the hymn which all of us know – And Now Abideth." The Christians joined in the hymn, transforming Chloe's inn into a beautiful temple. "And now abideth faith," some sang. Others added, "And now abideth hope." And a third group joined in singing, "And now abideth love." And all three groups sang together the final stanza, "But the greatest of these is love."[2]

The situation is that of the church at Corinth and the passage read is 1 Corinthians 13.1–13. It can be recognized how directly Paul speaks to the Corinthian church, which he knows with all its faults. He is aware of the social and class differences which prejudice the members of this Christian group. Some are intellectuals and wise in the ways of the world. Some are poor and some are slaves totally dependent on a master's will. But in understanding themselves and their differences, they can recognize the Christian faith and love which is all that binds them together as a community, and which is stronger than any other ties. We see a community understanding and orientating itself under Paul's guidance and inspiration. The guidance is real, even though delivered from a distance. And we see the community taking up Paul's teaching into its own Sunday worship, since Paul's letter becomes lesson, sermon, and hymn within the service and the fellowship meal.

The letters as occasional writings

It is important to remember that the letters of Paul are *real letters* written to particular churches, at a certain time, to meet a particular situation, by someone who clearly possessed specific and passionate beliefs. The letters are primarily "occasional documents", that is, they had a specific purpose arising from Paul's concerns for the churches in his interest and care. For comparison, we have a plentiful supply of real letters of the period, in common Greek on papyrus, discovered by archaeologists in Egypt, where the sands have preserved them. These letters share a basic pattern with Paul's writings, although his are much longer than most of them. They start with address and greetings, then an expression of thanksgiving, followed by the main body of the letter with its special contents (often in detail and of course quite obscure to us), and finally personal salutations and a formal conclusion by the sender. The papyrus letters provide parallels not only in their basic form but also in some of the conventional Greek phrases in which they are expressed: "we beseech and exhort you"; "I would not have you ignorant"/ "I want you to know". A large reference work by Moulton and Milligan charts the correspondences between the actual language of the papyri and that of the New Testament.

An example of a papyrus letter:

The papyrus letter from Isias to Hephaestion, translated in the text. Although this letter dates from 168 BCE, found at Memphis in Egypt, it is written in the "common" Greek found in the New Testament.

Isias to her "brother" Hephaestion greeting.

If you are well and other things are going right, it would accord with the prayer which I make continually to the gods. I myself and the child and all the household are in good health and think of you always.

When I received your letter from Horus, in which you announce that you are in detention in the Serapeum at Memphis, for the news that you are well I straightway thanked the gods, but about your not coming home, when all the others who had been secluded there have come, I am ill-pleased, because after having piloted myself and your child through such bad times and been driven to every extremity (owing to the price of corn) I thought that now at least, with you at home, I should enjoy some respite, whereas you have not even thought of coming home nor given any regard to our circumstances, remembering how I was in want in everything while you were still here, not to mention this long lapse of time and these critical days, during which you have sent us nothing. As, moreover, Horus who delivered the letter has brought news of your having been released from detention, I am thoroughly ill-pleased. Notwithstanding, as your mother also is annoyed, for her sake as well as for mine please return to the city, if nothing more pressing holds you back.

You will do me a favour by taking care of your bodily health.

Goodbye.

(P.Lond. 42 [H.E.97] 168 BCE)

The Roman philosopher Seneca (a bronze bust found at Herculaneum).

The letters as literature

To speak in this way of basic correspondences between the papyri and Paul's letters, to emphasize their shared sense of immediacy and particular application, should not be taken to mean that Paul's letters lack any sense of literary character. Classical authors, such as Aristotle and Cicero, wrote real letters, but with literary style. A distinguished contemporary of Paul, the Roman writer Seneca, wrote one hundred and twenty-four "*epistulae morales*" (moral epistles) which were, in form, letters addressed to his friend Lucilius, but were actually literary constructions to express, as essays, his moral and philosophical reflections upon life. Paul could himself use the literary devices of an educated man (for example, the stylistic form of disputation or diatribe) but he did not allow himself to lose sight of the reality of the situation addressed. Within *Koine* (common) Greek since the time of Augustus there had been a classicizing movement, which sought to re-establish features of literary style, as well as a flourishing popular employment of rhetoric, and the normal practical uses of such means of communication as were available. Allowance also has to be made for the impact within this situation of the most fundamental of social divisions, that between the peasant world (reflected for the most part in the papyri) and the urbanized elite (to which Paul naturally belonged). The latter group would wish to refine common Greek and make use of the "professional prose" styles now available for more technical communications.

Paul, the man and his personality

To understand communications such as letters, however literary or unsophisticated they may be, we should always try to discover something about the writer, and something about the recipients, and also to identify the special problems and concerns with which the letter is dealing. This is true of ancient and modern writings, and it is also true of Paul's letters. They must not be approached as generalized philosophical statements, but always as particular living writings addressed to real situations. That is the starting point and the central focus of this study, although we could go on to ask the further question as to how writings of particular (and therefore transitory) reference came to be regarded as authoritative and scriptural, with the built-in claim that they are valid for all times and therefore of timeless worth.

There is a traditional image of Paul, in Greek icons and manuscript illuminations, which might be traced back to a second-century description in the apocryphal Acts of Paul: "Small of stature, balding, bow legs, large eyes, eyebrows meeting, nose slightly hooked". It is possible to argue that this description is authentic because it is so uncomplimentary when the work itself is in praise of Paul. The rest of the description runs: "His appearance was full of grace; sometimes he looked more like an angel than a man". Certainly Paul was a man of many contrasts, perhaps including physical contrasts. His own writings refer to one specific weakness: "a thorn in the flesh … to harass me, to keep me from being too elated" (2 Corinthians 12.7). The reference is enigmatic and has been variously interpreted in terms of epilepsy or leprosy or even the stigmata (the wounds of Christ's crucifixion as experienced by some saints). Whatever the physical defect, the point of the reference is clearly the weakness and suffering experienced in contrast to Paul's other reasons for boasting.

Paul the Jew

One reason for Paul's boasting was his Jewishness. By religious background Paul was a Jew of the Diaspora (Dispersion). What made it possible for these Jews in exile to be Jews, though they were scattered through the Roman world, was the fact that all the Dispersion had Jerusalem as its focus and important links were maintained with this centre. For Paul to have been born (and brought up?) at Tarsus in Cilicia, Asia Minor (Acts 22.3), does not mean that he was different in any religious sense from a Jew brought up in Jerusalem. He was intensely proud of his Jewish ancestry and a strict observer of the Torah (the Jewish Law). Paul sums up his feelings about his Jewish background in his letter to the Philippians 3.5f: "Circumcised on the eighth day, of the people of Israel, of the tribe of Benjamin, a Hebrew born of Hebrews; as to the law a Pharisee, as to zeal a persecutor of the church, as to righteousness under the law blameless". For a Jew these were credentials of superlative orthodoxy, or more strictly orthopraxis – not only right belief, but the most scrupulous observance of the moral code.

In this context of Philippians 3, Paul is at his most outspoken and polemical, even vitriolic. But it is vital to realize that he is not attacking Judaism and renouncing his own heritage, even if any kind of boasting about it would be less compared with knowing Christ (3.8). Those he is attacking are the "enemies of the cross of Christ" (3.18), Jewish-Christian missionaries who boast of their present perfection and are self-consciously superior in the possession of spiritual qualities. They seem to attach little significance to the cross of Christ, and their centre of gravity is the present, where they are constrained rather than liberated. As Paul sees it, for Christians to *boast* of such Pharisaic attributes is ridiculous. If anybody could, Paul could. Although his Jewish upbringing had formed his character, it was no longer the driving force behind either his present actions or his future.

What happened to Paul at Damascus

This brings us to a further stage in the characterization of Paul, beyond his Jewishness. We normally speak of his conversion or apostolic commissioning, but the language used to describe the transition or turning-point must be chosen with care. The most neutral of historical descriptions is that "it was at Damascus during this period that Paul ceased persecuting the Christians and became their colleague".[3] But this side-steps the issue for our purposes by excluding any explanation or interpretation of events from Paul's point of view. In his letter to the Galatians (1.13–17) Paul describes the sequence as follows: "I persecuted the church of God violently and tried to destroy it …

The Damascus Gate of Jerusalem.

But when he who had set me apart before I was born, and had called me through his grace, was pleased to reveal his Son to me, in order that I might preach him among the Gentiles, I did not confer with flesh and blood, nor did I go up to Jerusalem to those who were apostles before me, but I went away into Arabia; and again I returned to Damascus."

The account in Galatians is clearly of a call to be an apostle, a commission to preach to the Gentiles. As far as Paul himself is concerned, there is an emphasis on the continuity of divine action. God's plan for Paul had begun before his birth; the same divine grace was active throughout his life, regardless of the contrasts in his activities. Serving the one and the same God, Paul receives a new and special calling in God's service. God's Messiah asks him, as a Jew, to bring God's message to the Gentiles. This sense of a call rather than a conversion is intensified when the language Paul uses is compared with that of the call of an Old Testament prophet. Look, for example, at Second Isaiah (Isaiah 49.1.6) and at Jeremiah ("Before I formed you in the womb I knew you, and before you were born I consecrated you; I appointed you as a prophet to the nations" – Jeremiah 1.5). The use of the word "conversion" is no more or less appropriate for Paul than for Jeremiah.

Paul in his letters and the Paul of Acts

Paul is quite secretive about the precise nature of the experience on the road to Damascus in Galatians 1.16. This is in accord with his other allusions to religious experiences, such as the rapture to "the third heaven" in 2 Corinthians 12.2ff. By contrast the three descriptions in the Acts of the Apostles

(9.1–19; 22.4–16; 26.9–19) are quite explicit and dramatized accounts of a series of events. They are broadly parallel but not exactly so; the variations repay careful study. Whether we think of Paul's temporary blindness and the visit of Ananias to restore his sight, or the sustained visionary experience and heavenly voice of Acts 26, it is clear that Paul is being commissioned as apostle to the Gentiles. It is the highly dramatic character of the event on the Damascus road, where Paul is stopped in his tracks, that suggests a conversion experience. It must be borne in mind, however, that these are Luke's narratives and his interpretation of the events.

There is no evidence anywhere in his own writings that Paul himself wanted to describe the experience as a conversion. This is an example of the kind of problem which recurs quite frequently, because there are considerable differences between the Paul depicted by Luke in Acts and Paul's own view in his letters. Whatever the historical value of Acts and whatever the credibility accorded to one individual's account of his own experiences, the fact remains that, in accordance with strict historical method, Acts is a secondary source for our knowledge of Paul and the primary source must always be his letters.

Paul's educational background

Paul's letters do provide documentary evidence of his Jewish education, referred to in Acts 22.3 ("at the feet of Gamaliel"). Some, but not all, of his own theological arguments operate according to the rules of rabbinic argument (for example the seven principles of interpretation enunciated by Rabbi Hillel). But this does not mean that Paul should be presented, on the grounds of his education, simply as a Christian "Rabbi" and one who has

Formal Jewish education: a class at a modern rabbinical school.

received a particular prophetic call. The results of other educational influences upon him can be seen in the writing of his letters, for example literary patterns such as the DIATRIBE (especially Romans). The diatribe consists of a series of objections, raised by a notional opponent, which were used as a technique of argument in the popular STOIC philosophy. Perhaps Paul had been influenced by Stoics in Tarsus and should be regarded as a Christian Stoic. The main question here is whether Paul emerged from such a background as essentially Hellenistic in his world-view and assumptions. There is also a theory which attributes Paul's knowledge of the mystery religions to his origins in Tarsus. Because of this, the transformation of the original Jewishness of Jesus into the new mystery cult of Christianity has often been attributed to him.

However, we should beware of splitting up the ancient Mediterranean world into separate cultural enclaves and insisting that Paul belongs in only one place. The world was much more cosmopolitan and someone in Paul's situation would have been exposed to a variety of influences. Just as Tarsus does not cut Paul off from Jerusalem, so Jerusalem does not cut him off from Tarsus. The traditional polarization of "Tarsus" versus "Jerusalem" is an artificial distinction. To have been brought up in Tarsus need not have committed Paul to a full rhetorical education, let alone a philosophical one (both of which were a matter of tertiary training involving much time and money), while being brought up in Jerusalem need not have excluded him from at least a general acquaintance with the Greek cultural tradition. Half of Gamaliel's pupils are said to have been trained in the wisdom of the Greeks.

Cultural influences

If Paul's writings show a knowledge of the mysteries or of Stoic thought, these are not arguments against his Jewishness, but merely demonstrate a breadth of cultural awareness not unusual in his day. In culture and language the frontier between Palestine and the rest of the world was in many ways not significant as far as Judaism was concerned. Paul's situation prior to conversion had much in common with that of his near-contemporary Philo of Alexandria, a prolific first-century philosopher who popularized Judaism in the wider world. Paul, like Philo, was fully aware of contemporary Pharisaic methods of expounding the Hebrew Bible, while at the same time making use of concepts from Hellenistic philosophy and spirituality within his theological teaching. Even if Paul's Pharisaism was more extreme and exclusive, with sectarian tendencies, the example of the Qumran community demonstrates that Jewish apocalyptic sectarianism did not exclude a wider interchange of ideas and language. In many ways this background would be an appropriate one for Paul's fuller statements of Christianity, which retain an emphasis on eschatology. But we do not know how easy it was in those days to cross the boundaries between the Pharisees and the sectarian Essenes who lived at Qumran, and what would be the prevailing reasons for doing so.

A Jewish rabbi teaching. Paul's teacher Gamaliel is sometimes depicted in this way.

In an area like this there is still a need for more adequate secondary information about the context. "Without such help we find it difficult to cope with the many-sidedness and directness of the way Paul has documented himself, and the severe demands this makes on our powers of analysis and judgement. It is akin to the difficulty we have in getting agreement about a controversial figure in our own day. We know him at too close quarters to be confident of our own reaction, until historical classification and interpretation can reduce the fullness of the evidence to a tidy order."[4]

The psychology of Paul

One of the most direct impressions communicated by Paul's letters is a sense of the temperament of the author. He is a torrential writer who sometimes does not finish his sentences, because he is carried away by the emotion of what he is saying. His great eloquence is not of the most polished literary kind, but is the eloquence born of an unshakeable conviction that problems can be solved because the gospel of Christ is the answer to them. His writings suggest a hot-blooded and tumultuous person. He could well have been experiencing a difficult time, spiritually, emotionally, and perhaps morally, even before he encountered Christ on the Damascus road. It is tempting to project a measure of psychoanalysis, but rash to do. We can interrogate the texts but we may read too much into them, because we cannot also interrogate the author.

Can Romans 7.7–25 give us some insight into Paul's psychology (e.g.: "I do not understand my own actions. For I do not do what I want, but I do the very thing I hate" [7.15])? There is an influential interpretation of this text by C. H. Dodd: "The reason why Paul found ... a story of how an individual fell into the power of sin and death was that he had had experience of it, and the old story fitted his experience ... Paul rarely, if ever, says 'I' unless he is really speaking of himself personally, even if he means to generalize from the particular instance ... It justifies us in accepting this immortal description as an authentic transcript of Paul's own experience during the period which culminated in his vision on the road to Damascus ... It is one of the most important teachings of modern psychology, and one most readily verifiable by analysis, that the attempt to repress an instinctive desire, directly, seldom succeeds in its object. If the desire is repressed, it is likely to form a 'complex' below the threshold of consciousness, and to break into the conscious life in fresh and perhaps even more deleterious forms."[5]

It is interesting to notice that Dodd wrote this at a time in the 1920s when he was himself exploring modern developments in the theory of psychology and when he was also undergoing therapy. Such thoughts were clearly in the mind of the reader of Paul; were they also in the mind of Paul himself? If it is pushed too far, this argument ends in absurdity by suggesting that Paul had anticipated prophetically the insights of modern psychology. Dodd was too much the scholar to go this far, but he used his own experiences to shed light on what Paul was saying, and suggested that Paul did the same for his readers. We must set out the options for interpretation when we consider an argument like this one from Romans, which is in essence a discussion of the Law of Judaism and its place in the story of God's dealings with mankind.

The alternative interpretations:

* Is Paul extrapolating from his own immediate and personal experiences as an enthusiastic Pharisee, providing a more widely applicable psychology from what he knew of his own reactions?

left A mass-produced Greek icon of St. Paul, showing his traditional facial features and the bundle of his letters.

The panel responsible for translating the New English Bible (published in 1961). The chairman is C. H. Dodd and J. A. T. Robinson is sitting on the far left.

* Or is he propounding theological statements on the basis of theological arguments (i.e. this is the nature of God's expectations of humanity, and the nature of humanity's response)?
* Are Paul's arguments conceived in abstraction (i.e. this is how things always are) or with regard to particular church situations?
* Are they presented with polemical or apologetic intentions (i.e. is he intending to attack others, or is he justifying himself)?

Options like these dramatically affect the meaning and application of what Paul is saying in a particular text. Does Paul start from his self-taught view of human nature, and work out his theology as an answer to it? Or does he begin from what he observes going on in the early church communities, and evolve his theology in response to the pastoral task? The further one goes in the direction of seeing Paul's argument as a kind of confrontational politics, the less one is compelled to see the Jewish Law as a menace and to adopt an anti-Semitic position for theological or humanitarian reasons. It may well be that what has been called the "introspective conscience of the West", demonstrated in the mind of Augustine or Luther, and building on the first option (the Pharisaical background), has been the root cause of Christian anti-Semitism. Paul's words may have been enlisted in support, but this was not Paul's intention.

A man of contrasts

So the deep insights of individual psycho-analysis are not applicable to the task of elucidating Paul's character. We have seen that he was a many-sided individual and a man of contrasts. The major contrast is that between the ferocity of his manner on some occasions and his periods of apparent self-denigration. However, it would be wrong to interpret this as a simple contrast between Paul the Jew and Paul the Christian, mainly because it presupposes a total conversion experience rather than a prophetic call. Rather, there is a real continuity in Paul's character from the period prior to his prophetic call to the period after it.

Paul the Pharisee was a man of fierce action ("I persecuted the church of God violently and tried to destroy it" – Galatians 1.13). We see him arresting offenders or perhaps more realistically organizing *ad hoc* lynching parties. Paul the Christian apostle seems not to have used physical force, but he was a man of fierce words. He urged the church at Rome to leave it to God to carry out the judgement ("Beloved, never avenge yourselves, but leave it to the wrath of God; for it is written, 'Vengeance is mine, I will repay, says the Lord.'" [Romans 12.19]). Despite this injunction, it is clear that Paul was implicated in – and urging on – the church decision in 1 Corinthians 5.1–5:

> *When you are assembled, and my spirit is present, with the power of our Lord Jesus, you are to deliver this man to Satan for the destruction of the flesh, in order to have his spirit saved in the day of the Lord Jesus.*

This sounds like the burning of heretics. It almost amounts to that, as a judgement of permanent excommunication or expulsion from the community, coupled with a curse. The purpose was to cleanse the community and ultimately to redeem the soul of the offender. As an anticipation of the Last Judgement such an action might well have had immediate and fatal consequences on the individual concerned (compare Acts 5.1–11). It is comparable with permanent exclusion from the Qumran community: banishment or being "rooted out of the pure thing of the Many" was the equivalent of a death sentence.[6]

If Paul did not himself use force, he was certainly a recipient of force, used against him by many people including his Christian opponents (e.g. "danger from false brethren" within the catalogue of sufferings in 2 Corinthians 11.26). His ideas about tolerance and turning the other cheek seem at odds with his personality. His acceptance that "My grace is sufficient for you, for my power is made perfect in weakness" (2 Corinthians 12.9) suggests that, if Paul was forced to make any transition, in response to the call to apostleship, it was the transition from power to powerlessness. Nevertheless, in Paul's dealings with his Christian communities, he still has authority as a Christian. He is the founding father of a church and so he has power over his converts. The theory of power defined in terms of powerlessness is an idea not always applied by Paul in practice; perhaps to apply it consistently in an institutional context is well-nigh impossible.

In Paul's defence one should also draw attention to the parental imagery, of both father and mother, which he uses of himself in relation to the enlarged family of his converts. "I became your father in Christ Jesus through the gospel" (1 Corinthians 4.15); "I fed you with milk, not solid food" (1 Corinthians 3.2); "My little children with whom I am again in travail until Christ be formed in you" (Galatians 4.19). The emotional implications are obvious. Perhaps this is the explanation of his fierce language and vehemence in protecting the integrity of the group, and the faith for which it stands, when his spiritual children are attacked. Paul obviously experienced a tension between the theory of power in weakness and the practical requirement to defend the gospel from enemies outside the church and within it.

Paul's social context

Loyalty to the state

What indications can the social context give us, to add to our character study of Paul? Here again there are conflicting pointers and Paul is hard to place with precision. It is often claimed that "Pauline Christianity as reflected in the epistles was not a movement of the disinherited classes. Paul himself was a master-craftsman and a Roman citizen, and explicitly repudiated resistance to the Roman Empire". It is true that Paul was not a revolutionary in the Marxist sense, but the text of Romans 13.1–7 has to carry more weight in asserting his loyalty to the Empire than is justifiable. "Let every person be subject to the governing authorities. For there is no authority except from God" (13.1). This text has been hopelessly overloaded by interpreters; it must be seen in the context of advice, which included advice to act loyally *in the present situation*. Paul is not propounding a theory of church–state relations for all time. His advice is put firmly in an eschatological perspective by 13.11–14: "the day of the Lord is at hand". In the same way, 1 Thessalonians 5.1–11 expresses Paul's sense of the very limited involvement by Christians in the concerns of this world, because the world to come was now their dominant concern.

It is an interesting possibility that what provoked the special localized comment on loyalty in Romans 13.1 was not some problem, like taxation, that the Roman Christians were having with the state authorities. If that were the case, Paul would have been intervening as the loyal politician. On the contrary, the problem could have been that the Roman Christians suspected Paul himself of having real difficulties over loyalty to the state. They would have good reason for this, because Paul had already been arrested several times by the civic authorities (e.g. in Philippi and Ephesus, on suspicion of disloyalty and trouble-making). The accusation in Thessalonica (Acts 17.7) was that "These men who have turned the world upside down have come here also, and Jason has received them; and they are all acting against the decree of Caesar, saying that there is another king, Jesus".

Paul saw his imprisonment as "for Christ" and "for the gospel" (Philippians 1.13; Philemon 9, 13), but it is unlikely that those were the official charges which put Paul's life at risk. In Romans 13.1–7, Paul is therefore an apologist for himself in the face of Roman suspicions, not for the first time in this letter. "It is rather different if someone who is suspect of disloyalty, who has tangibly felt this suspicion and yet continues acting in the way which makes him incur this suspicion, appeals to loyalty as though loyalty were ordained from above."[7]

Roman citizenship

The second aspect for which there are contrary indications is the matter of Paul's Roman citizenship. The evidence of Acts is that he was a citizen of Tarsus (21.39) and also a Roman citizen by birth (16.37f; 22.25–29; 23.27). Paul himself does not mention it in his letters. In fact some of the things he says have been taken as negative evidence, disproving his citizenship. If 1 Corinthians 15.32 means literally that Paul fought with wild beasts in the arena, then the fact that Roman citizens could not be treated in this way argues against his Roman citizenship. The idea would offend public decency, if not a particular law. If Paul had been a Roman citizen, he could have made his claim in 2 Corinthians 11.25 ("Three times I have been beaten with rods") sound even more telling by mentioning this fact, in the way the narrative of Acts does. But this is an argument from silence, and as such must be inconclusive.

More positively, Acts had very good reason for emphasizing Paul's status and Roman citizenship; it was important in this apologia for Christianity to stress its constitutional respectability. Luke thus attaches particular importance to these details. On the other hand, it would be reasonable to suggest that Paul himself did not attach much importance to the status of citizenship, especially because he is emphasizing his real humiliation, without wishing to gain credit for the extent of his sacrifice. He might well have been a citizen, but he boasts about his weakness, not about his status. There is, in addition, some evidence at this time of a general tendency to reduce the value of citizenship in itself. In the more remote Roman colonies of southern Anatolia, where Paul had worked, citizen status "might be a declining asset ... Roman citizenship may not have been so decisive a status factor in the Greek cities of the first century as has been supposed ... The social class ranking system that applied later was already beginning to cut across the distinction between citizens and aliens."[4] What was beginning to count for more was relative affluence and achievement, rather than pedigree.

There is some evidence that individual Jews acquired the citizenship of Greek cities in which they lived. That presupposes not only great prosperity but also a marked degree of Hellenization, or thoroughgoing adaptation to the Gentile environment. This raises a further objection in connection with Paul: by his own testimony, before he became a Christian he was a strict Pharisee; that should have precluded so total an adaptation to the Gentile environment. It leads to the inevitable conclusion that Paul would have attached little or no importance to citizen's status, whatever later apologists for his legitimate achievements might wish to claim.

This does not imply that social status was necessarily irrelevant to Paul and his society. His constant use of status terms and his emphasis on humiliations, as in the Corinthian letters, are the marks of a man caught up in serious conflicts of rank, and in the normal course of events entitled to considerable respect himself. However, it is clear that his primary aim was to integrate different classes of society, by recognizing their divisive nature and urging humility. He may have thought that it was good tactics to gain access to social groupings via the lower rather than the upper classes.

Paul as artisan

There are positive and negative aspects to Paul's sense of self-reliance as an apostle, derived from his status as an independent, self-supporting artisan. Even when Paul is in prison, his life's experience conditions his outlook: "Not that I complain of want; for I have learned, in whatever state I am, to be content" (Philippians 4.11). In Galatians 1.18–2.10, Paul argues for his essential independence from Jerusalem and for the economic self-sufficiency which allowed him to be so.

One thing can be stated very positively: the Pauline mission is one coherent movement within early Christianity, which contrasted sharply with the world of the Palestinian followers of Jesus. Paul's missionary arena is dominated by this economically self-sufficient figure whose primary role is that of community organizer. Paul's world is the world of cities, large urban centres, far removed from the villages of Palestine. In this world Paul is the sophisticated and rational urban man. He understands these large cultural centres among which he travels. He is capable of the planning and organization required by such a social setting, where one could not live from day to day on the generosity of alms or by gleaning a handful of wheat from a field. The distances involved required money, travel, and communication on a scale hardly compatible with the background of poor Galileans.[8]

While Paul's economic independence had positive advantages for the Christian mission, there were also some more negative aspects. He was a tentmaker by trade, who probably made tents out of leather. This is Luke's evidence in Acts 18.3, clarifying the more general reference by Paul in 1 Corinthians 4.12. It would be possible to see Paul's role of missionary-artisan as simply reflecting the rabbinic ideal of combining Torah and trade, but this ideal is probably later than Paul's time. He frequently had to defend his practice of supporting himself by trade, against both critics within the church and rival missionaries from outside it (1 Corinthians 9.1–19; 2 Corinthians 11.7–15; 12.13–16). This seems to have been a live issue among philosophers: should one charge fees, be a "philosopher in residence" in a wealthy household, follow a trade, or be reduced to begging like most CYNICS (street philosophers/preachers, despised as "dogs")?

"Paul's life was very much that of the workshop – of artisan friends like Aquila, Barnabas, and perhaps Jason; of leather, knives and awls; of wearying toil; of being bent over a workbench like a slave and of working side by side with slaves; of thereby being perceived by others and by himself as slavish and humiliated ... His trade may also have served directly in his missionary activities in the sense that workshop conversations with fellow workers, customers, or those who stopped by, might easily have turned into occasions for informal evangelization."[9]

What Paul himself says about his work, referring to it in terms of slavery and humiliation, suggests that he might well have begun his career with a higher social status. His education was hardly the most appropriate for a lifetime of working with his hands. Considerable loss is involved, even though he is not specific about what he has lost. Nevertheless, his work supplied relative independence, mobility, and a meeting-point with access to various classes of people.

In conclusion, four significant factors in Paul's background affected the nature of his Christian mission:

1 A difference in manner and style from that of the original preaching about Jesus by Palestinian Christians was one direct result of Paul's more sophisticated background. (This does not inevitably imply a change in content.)

2 Paul deliberately suffered some loss of status, which he interpreted as an appropriate experience of humiliation for the sake of the gospel.

3 As Paul conceived it, the Christian mission should be independent and self-supporting with a wide-ranging potential for expansion.

4 The working apostle's own background and present position gave him the maximum opportunity for access to all classes of society and a variety of contacts with different cultures.

The theology in Paul's letters

This section addresses the themes which are central to Paul's theology: those which occur most frequently and are given greatest emphasis; and their social as well as theological implications. The major themes include Paul's understanding of Christ (particularly his death); his characterization of Christian belief and its relation to Judaism; his wider panoramic perspective of the geographical setting of Christianity within the context of the Mediterranean world and the practical limits of the Roman Empire; and of its historical setting in the context of the whole history of salvation, from the beginnings with God's Israel right up to the last days in which Paul sees himself as living.

The death of Christ

Paul is preoccupied with the cross of Christ, in much the same way as the gospel of Mark (and not just his Passion narrative) is dominated by this theme. "Some explanation is required for Paul's preoccupation with the cross which, together with the themes of humility, weakness, suffering and death, constitute the negative side of Paul's gospel and the main focus of his attention – an interest which may be compared profitably with the dominant 'passion theology' of the Gospel of Mark."[10] When he writes to the Corinthians about the Lord's Supper, Paul says: "For as often as you eat this bread and drink the cup, you proclaim the Lord's death until he comes" (1 Corinthians 11.26). The eminent Protestant theologian Rudolf Bultmann maintained that the cross was so central for Paul that "Jesus' death-and-resurrection, then, is for Paul the decisive thing about the person of Jesus and his life experience, indeed in the last analysis it is the sole thing of importance to him."[11]

The idea of the cross has a twofold significance for Paul. Firstly it was a tradition received: "For I delivered to you as of first importance what I also received, that Christ died for our sins in accordance with the scriptures" (1 Corinthians 15.3). Secondly this was not a tradition derived solely from men, but it was a divine revelation: "For I would have you know, brethren, that the gospel which was preached by me is not man's gospel. For I did not receive it from man, nor was I taught it, but it came through a revelation of Jesus Christ" (Galatians 1.11f). Therefore Paul felt bound to preach this and nothing but this (Galatians 1.6–10).

Death and Resurrection

The expression "death-and-resurrection" brackets two ideas together. It is often assumed that for Christianity resurrection takes over from crucifixion, that the new life supersedes the death in importance. But for Paul this is not the case. In the tradition which Paul receives and communicates, death, resurrection, and the post-Resurrection appearances belong together in sequence (1 Corinthians 15.4–8).

The two events thus together constituted the main structure of Paul's message and must be regarded as complementary aspects of a single whole.

> *Jesus our Lord, who was put to death for our trespasses and raised for our justification.* (Romans 4.25)
> *All of us who have been baptized into Christ Jesus were baptized into his death. We were buried therefore with him by baptism into death, so that as Christ was raised from the dead by the glory of the Father, we too might walk in newness of life.* (Romans 6.3–4)
> *Christ Jesus, who died, yes who was raised from the dead.* (Romans 8.34)

Paul seems preoccupied with the cross, for a variety of theological and practical reasons. Although cross and resurrection belong together, are integrally connected, and essentially complementary as theological ideas, the priority of the cross is clear in his writings. And Paul takes up the cross and "makes it his own" in so far as weakness, suffering, and powerlessness are his principal boast (2 Corinthians 10–12).

Fighting with wild beasts in the arena (4th century mosaic from the Galleria Borghese in Rome).

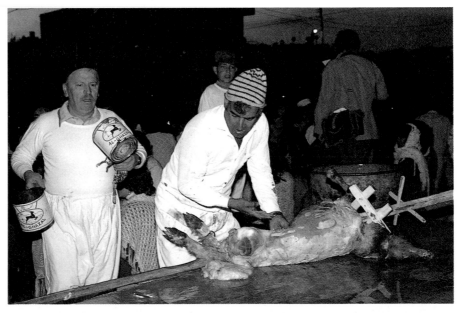

The sacrifice of the lamb for the Samaritan Passover at Mount Gerizim. The survivors of the Samaritan community in Nablus (Shechem) area preserve the old tradition.

The Christian believer's baptism by total immersion.

How Paul uses the theology of the cross

Where Paul is obviously arguing with and against others, his preference for this theology of the cross provides him with a powerful argument against his opponents. It enabled him to counter other ideas (alternative theologies) in places like Corinth and Galatia. For example, those Corinthians who were spiritual enthusiasts, who believed that they were already full members of the Kingdom of God, could base their argument on a one-sided doctrine of resurrection. They could conclude that if Christ was risen so also were his people. They had separated the resurrection of Christ from his death and spiritually left his death behind.

Such alternative theologies were associated with particular groups of people (opponents) in quite specific places and church situations. The arguments can therefore be considered in terms of Paul's relationships with the people in these communities. That is, there are cultural and social dimensions to these apparently theological questions.

Paul was a leader in a position of authority in relation to the church communities in places like Corinth and Galatia, but his authority was limited in two respects: it was limited by the authority of the Jerusalem church, and limited by Paul's own personal inadequacies (to which he refers in 2 Corinthians 10.10). The relation of Paul to the church of Jerusalem was unlikely to be the subordination which Luke depicts in his account of the Council of Jerusalem (Acts 15). However, when Paul himself asserts his independence (Galatians 2.6), he may well be protesting too much. "He is not subordinate, not an emissary of the Jerusalem church ... But he and his work are still dependent on the recognition of the church which is the source and centre, not only of the Palestinian Jewish Christian church but of *all* churches."[12] Paul's authority was not recognized by his opponents. In this situation what were the advantages of preaching the cross?

A mystery religion ceremony in the sanctuary of Isis (a wall painting from Herculaneum).

Preaching to the powerless

"For I delivered to you as of first importance what I also received, that Christ died for our sins in accordance with the scriptures" (1 Corinthians 15.3) associates Paul with the traditional authority of the Jerusalem church. We have also noted already, in respect of Paul himself, the appropriateness of the message of the cross for those who felt themselves lacking in power. This gospel for the powerless would have been welcomed by the majority of Paul's hearers, those who belonged to the lower levels of Greco-Roman society. "Not many of you were wise according to worldly standards, not many were powerful, not many were of noble birth" (1 Corinthians 1.26). "For such as these the symbol of the cross must have been very potent: it gave them access to an *alternative source of power* based upon an ideology which taught that the first would be last and the last first, that he who suffered most gained most, that the 'weak' had precedence over the 'strong'."[10]

The appeal of this message to the richer members of the church communities is less obvious, and this membership cannot simply be dismissed. The churches were not exclusively socially depressed groups. "If the Corinthians are at all typical, the Christians were dominated by a socially pretentious section of the population of the big cities. Beyond that, they seem to have drawn on a broad constituency, probably representing the household dependants of the leading members."[13] We cannot generalize solely from the Corinthian evidence, nor can we ignore it. It may be a special case contrasted with Asia Minor and northern Greece, but it is still our best-documented church situation.

Preaching to the rich

One of the attractions of the gospel message for the richer minority was that of patronage by the richer of the poorer, for which there is plenty of evidence in Greco-Roman society. The owners of the houses in which church groups met would automatically become leaders of those churches. The way Paul presented the message, with his wider perspectives on mission, gave an international character to the movement. The preaching had a philosophical appeal which was not too popularist and unsophisticated. As a social activity the work of the itinerant teacher or SOPHIST or the Cynic philosopher was much more marginalized. More specifically, the theme of a reversal of values would have a definite appeal to those who were in the middle ranks of the power structure and who felt their ambitions to rise being oppressed by those higher up.

Certain aspects of Paul's theology would also have been attractive to women, who might have been able to gain a prominence not usually permitted in Greco-Roman society. They could have mixed with men on equal terms, rather than be honoured at home like Jewish women, or be confined to single-sex societies or rash ventures into the dubious mystery cults. The Christian gospel, at least at the outset, offered women a new role apart from the approved sexual stereotypes. "For as many of you as were

left The competitor's entrance to the stadium at Olympia in southern Greece.

baptized into Christ have put on Christ . . . There is neither male nor female" (Galatians 3.27f).

The cross as the symbol of reversal

The cross as the symbol of reversal had dramatic propaganda value. When Paul writes to the Philippians he quotes from a traditional hymn that may well have been familiar to them. These words encapsulate what the symbol of the cross means, as they describe how God's agent is humiliated and punished as a slave would be: "but he emptied himself, taking the form of a slave, being born in the likeness of men. And being found in human form he humbled himself and became obedient unto death, even death on a cross" (Philippians 2.7–8). To celebrate Christ as the crucified one is to invert the conventional notions of honour and shame. For the Romans acceptable ideas of honour were based on the *cursus honorum*, the socially approved career structure. For the Jews acceptable ideas were concerned with gaining merit in a system of rewards and punishment. But the gospel's symbol is an inversion of such contemporary value systems, not an alienation from them. This meant that Christians remained in contact with those value systems and were able to relate to contemporary ethics and build upon them.

Paul the example

Paul can apply this symbol of reversal directly to his own person (although, as we have already noted, the theory of power in powerlessness is not always applied consistently in practice). Paul sees himself experiencing, and indeed embodying, reversal and negation:

> *For as we share abundantly in Christ's sufferings, so through Christ we share abundantly in comfort too.* (2 Corinthians 1.5)
> *We are afflicted in every way, but not crushed; perplexed, but not driven to despair; persecuted, but not forsaken; struck down, but not destroyed; always carrying in the body the death of Jesus, so that the life of Jesus may also be manifested in our bodies. For while we live we are always being given up to death for Jesus' sake, so that the life of Jesus may be manifested in our mortal flesh.* (2 Corinthians 4.8–11)

Paul himself (or a later writer in the spirit of Paul) even claims that he brought to completion the process of reversal, making up any apparent shortfall in what Christ had achieved:

> *Now I rejoice in my sufferings for your sake, and in my flesh I complete what is lacking in Christ's afflictions for the sake of his body, that is, the church.* (Colossians 1.24)

This might well be exaggeration for rhetorical effect, to focus attention on the extent of Paul's involvement in the experience of reversal. Taken literally, it seems at odds with the uniqueness and adequacy of Christ's sufferings, to which Paul attaches such importance. (See the more careful statement in Romans 5, especially vv. 3–6, 18f.)

Imitating Paul

Despite his emphasis on reversal and suffering, Paul *does* focus attention on himself as leader. This is the working out of the theory of power through powerlessness. In this way, he appears to urge the ethical principle of the imitation of Paul, as well as (and related to) the theological/ethical principle of the imitation of Christ:

> *You know what kind of men we proved to be among you for your sake. And you became imitators of us and of the Lord, for you received the word in much affliction.* (1 Thessalonians 1.6)

> *I have applied all this to myself and Apollos for your benefit, brethren, that you may learn by us to live according to scripture, that none of you may be puffed up in favour of one against another. For I became your father in Christ Jesus through the gospel. I urge you, then, be imitators of me.* (1 Corinthians 4.6, 15–16)

> *Be imitators of me, as I am of Christ.* (1 Corinthians 11.1)

> *Brethren, join in imitating me, and mark those who so live as you have an example in us ... What you have learned and received and heard and seen in me, do; and the God of peace will be with you.* (Philippians 3.17, 4.9)

Reversal in practice

In Paul's symbolic interpretation of experience his reversals become his triumphs, his punishments and hardships become the imitation of Christ, and the catalogues of his sufferings constitute (almost) the only boast which Paul is prepared to make as his apostolic claim to fame:

> *If I must boast, I will boast of the things that show my weakness.* (2 Corinthians 11.30)

> *For I think that God has exhibited us apostles as last of all, like men sentenced to death; because we have become a spectacle to the world, to angels and to men. We are fools for Christ's sake, but you are wise in Christ. We are weak, but you are strong. You are held in honour, but we in disrepute. To the present hour we hunger and thirst, we are ill-clad and buffeted and homeless, and we labour, working with our own hands. When reviled, we bless; when persecuted, we endure; when slandered, we try to conciliate; we have become, and are now, as the refuse of the world, the offscouring of all things.* (1 Corinthians 4.9–13; see also 2 Corinthians 4.7–12; 6.3–10; 11.21–33)

This is no mere rhetoric but a dramatic symbol embodied in Paul's life, as an example and a warning against complacency among his churches. The extent to which Paul lived out his symbol of reversal is indicated when he describes to the Corinthians how he decided to achieve recognition among

The crucified Christ,
12th century CE
German bronze.

them not by skilful argument but by a deliberate "self-emptying":

for I decided to know nothing among you except Jesus Christ and him crucified. And I was with you in much fear and trembling; and my speech and my message were not in plausible words of wisdom, but in demonstration of the Spirit and power, that your faith might not rest in the wisdom of men but in the power of God. (1 Corinthians 2.2–5)

"Christ crucified"

Paul's preoccupation with this symbol is summed up in the use of the slogan "Jesus Christ and him crucified" or, even more briefly, "Christ crucified". See 1 Corinthians 1.23f:

we preach Christ crucified, *a stumbling block to Jews and folly to Gentiles, but to those who are called, both Jews and Greeks, Christ the power of God and the wisdom of God.*

The modern world is largely inured to slogans and the power of advertising. But Paul clearly chose his summary phrase with great care. This is a slogan which would have a universal appeal, because it would be universally shocking.

The punishment of crucifixion was well known in the Roman world, and examples of it were familiar to those who lived around the Mediterranean. Particularly favoured as a punishment for slaves, it provided a repulsive public display of human agony (for which the theory of deterrence might have been cited as justification). For the Jew, this manner of death represented a divine curse on the individual so executed (Deuteronomy 21.22–23). This curse would be compounded if the victim was left unburied, as a further public example and deterrent.

At the least, then, there would have been widespread recognition of what the slogan meant: a named individual had suffered the form of capital punishment appropriate for the dregs of society. Even if the reaction was of repulsion and disgust, for Paul to have chosen such a focus would have attracted greater interest than the Jewish-Christian discussion of the extent of obligation to the Jewish Law (Torah). By comparison, propaganda about calculated adjustments of Torah would have had a limited relevance, and appeared restrictive and sectarian. In contrast, Paul's message gave the Christian missionary something to argue about with both Jewish and Gentile audiences.

The use of a simple slogan permits greater clarity in defining the boundaries of the faith and deciding who is on which side. Religious conversion usually entails a radical process of re-socialization, and the symbol of initiation by baptism likewise implies boundaries that are tightly drawn. But it has been widely recognized that Pauline Christianity was more ambivalent about boundaries, with "a more open, integrative response toward the macrosociety".[14] There are several reasons for this, including the missionary zeal of the community leaders, and the prominence, among the beliefs, of symbols which crossed boundaries.

Among the symbols which can cross the cultural divides is the slogan of "Christ crucified", especially emphasized as the focus of Paul's preaching. Thus the limits of the convert's acceptability were set purely by the acceptance of the crucified Christ, in apparently minimal terms such as Galatians 2.20:

> *I have been crucified with Christ; it is no longer I who live, but Christ who lives in me.*

This is not to disparage the depth of conviction or the intensity of identification which underlies this statement. The point is that, as a confession of faith, it is set in minimal terms, which therefore permit a high tolerance of diverse interpretations. It is a good example of a symbol that works on many levels and in many contexts.

There are clear exclusions: the outsiders are those (Jews and Gentiles) who reject the cross for whatever reason. But equally both Jews and Greeks can be included. Paul can thus be seen as contributing to cultural pluralism. In his language "both Jews and Greeks" is synonymous with "all"; he wishes to exclude nobody on racial or cultural grounds. As 1 Corinthians 9.19–23 demonstrates, Paul is prepared to work alongside anyone:

> *I have become all things to all men, that I might by all means save some.*

Paul is the "mediator of a new symbol system" which has its particular focus in the symbol of the cross. His symbols relate in many ways to existing and diverse patterns of meaning. He uses them to establish contact, but then transforms them with new meaning as a result of his understanding of the gospel.

The Jewish context of Paul's theology

Paul's approach to theology was initially from a Jewish perspective, using a range of Jewish symbols to talk about the death of Christ. Within this Jewish dimension of his theology, he explains the significance of the cross as a mechanism of salvation.

Ideally Judaism has a universal dimension. But in the Old Testament this tends to be expressed by the picture of a victorious Israel leading the conquered nations to worship Israel's God (see Isaiah 60, especially vv. 3, 14). To this end the expected Messiah might be a warlike leader of Israel; certainly the Messiah is God's agent for Israel exclusively. However, although his perspective is Jewish in origin, Paul's use of Jewish symbols in fact opens out this universal dimension in a quite unrestricted way. His thesis is that Jesus Christ is for everyone, that all humanity needs Christ, and that he brings all women and men equally to God. Christ is the final revelation and Christ is for all; God is thus the God of the Gentiles as well as of the Jews.

That is why Paul uses the Jewish symbol of Adam, as the representative human being from the creation story, to express his argument in Romans 5. This fits with what he has already said in Romans 4 about the symbol of the

Abraham receiving the promise: fresco from the synagogue at Dura Europos.

A basic guide to Paul's theology

Adam was the man who brought sin into human existence and Christ was the man who dealt with the problem.

Adam was tempted and sinned, thus bringing humanity out of the garden paradise into the wilderness.

Christ came into the wilderness, was tempted, and withstood the devil, thus opening the way back into paradise.

Adam is a symbolic figure, representing all humanity, so that Adam's sin was humanity's sin. (See Romans 5; 1 Corinthians 15.45–49.)

Similarly Christ is a symbolic figure, representing the whole of the new humanity, so that his righteousness is humanity's righteousness.

Humanity shares Adam's guilt, by virtue of its unity with him, and expresses this "original sin" by living sinfully. Similarly, by virtue of its unity with Christ in faith, humanity may be accounted as righteous as he is, and may express this righteousness by living like him.

Jewish nation, Abraham the "father of the Jews". The promise to Abraham (Genesis 12 and 17), which could be interpreted exclusively as to Israel, the covenant and circumcision, is opened out to emphasize that Abraham is "the father of many nations" and an example of the righteousness that comes through faith. Paul expresses this breadth of vision in a programmatic statement at the beginning of Romans (1.16–17):

> For I am not ashamed of the gospel: it is the power of God for salvation to every one who has faith, to the Jew first and also to the Greek. For in it the righteousness of God is revealed through faith for faith; as it is written, "He who through faith is righteous shall live/The righteous shall live by faith".

Characteristically, Paul's claim is supported by a PROOF TEXT, from the prophet Habakkuk 2.4. The point is that such a claim could be made by any Jewish idealist quoting his own scriptures (although he would prefer the second translation as giving the proper priorities: living by faith as a result of keeping the Law as a righteous Jew). Paul had enlarged the vision in a way consistent with the original scriptural insight (but perhaps sharpening the issue by reversing the emphasis of the quotation). A later view of the constitutional implications of this Pauline prophetic revolution can be seen in Ephesians 2.11–22.

The universality of Christ

It is Paul's ultimate conviction that Christ leads all to God, and that Christ is (potentially) for all. However, although the universal offer had been made, it had to be accepted. There are indications, particularly in Romans, that Paul had realistic rather than comprehensive and universalist expectations, bear-

Adam and Eve, conscious of their nakedness, being expelled from the Garden of Eden (13th century CE carving from the North Porch of Chartres cathedral).

ing in mind the short time left for the process of mission and salvation, as he projected it. Nevertheless, even if the numbers were practically limited, there would be no discrimination and exclusiveness: both Jew and Greek were included.

This enlarged vision had been brought about by what Christ had done – not by his teaching and example (rarely mentioned by Paul) – but by his death and Resurrection. Paul explains the mechanism by which one man's death achieved the possibility of life for all by using a large number of pictures and symbols to convey different aspects of his belief that at the cross of Christ something happened which changed the world. It changed the world because it changed the whole situation between God and humanity in respect of sin. Many of these ideas were part of a widespread system of thought in the Mediterranean world (Jewish and Greek and Roman) in which Paul and his readers lived. Let us concentrate on one particular explanation of how the cross worked. This functions within the Jewish understanding of suffering.

Salvation by sacrifice

The Jewish view of suffering

Many people from different cultures in the ancient Mediterranean world would have agreed that suffering was a fact of life. The Jews depicted this by the symbol of Adam expelled from the Garden of Eden and its paradisaical existence:

> *Cursed is the ground because of you;*
> *in toil you shall eat of it all the days of your life;*
> *in the sweat of your face you shall eat bread*
> *till you return to the ground.* (Genesis 3.17–19)

At the end of the Old Testament period, the belief was much strengthened among the Jews that the suffering would actually increase, and build up to a climax, before God brought about the end of the world.

> *For nation will rise up against nation and kingdom against kingdom;*
> *there will be earthquakes in various places, there will be famines; this is*
> *but* the beginning of the sufferings. (Mark 13.8)
>
> *O Lord of hosts, how long wilt thou have no mercy on Jerusalem and*
> *the cities of Judah?* (Zechariah 1.12)
>
> *O Sovereign Lord, holy and true, how long before thou wilt judge and*
> *avenge our blood on those who dwell upon the earth?* (Revelation 6.10)

Innocent suffering

In addition to this sense of climactic suffering – and the confidence which sometimes goes with it, based on the belief that it is darkest just before the dawn – there was also in Jewish thought a special importance attached to the idea of innocent suffering. This was significant, exceptionally honorific, and potentially beneficial to others. One who suffers innocently, like the Suffering Servant in Isaiah's prophecy, does God's will in suffering on behalf of others, suffering vicariously.

> *He was despised and rejected by men*
> *a man of sorrows and acquainted with grief;*
> *surely he has borne our grief*
> *and carried our sorrows.* (Isaiah 53.3–4)

At the time of the Maccabean revolt, in the middle of the second century BCE (reflected in the book of Daniel as well as in the apocryphal books of the Maccabees), the belief developed that such martyrs as suffered for the Jewish faith would, as "saints of the Most High . . . receive the kingdom, and possess the kingdom for ever, for ever and ever" (Daniel 7.18). The innocent who suffered martyrdom would suffer on behalf of others, and would themselves be vindicated in resurrection to God's kingdom. The circumstances of these times proved a major stimulus to the later idea of resurrection among the Jews.

Paul inherited these Jewish beliefs in the value of innocent suffering within the trials of THE LAST DAYS, but there is a serious complication, a major impediment to such belief, for him. There seemed to be no righteous people who could be involved innocently in this climactic experience of suffering and through it make a positive contribution on behalf of others. Paul sums up the situation of unrighteousness, of universal sinfulness, in words which he quotes from the beginning of Psalm 14:

> *as it is written,*
> *"None is righteous, no, not one".* (Romans 3.10)

This sounds only too conclusive, a final judgement after the catalogue of Gentile and Jewish sinfulness in the first two chapters of Romans. But it underlines for Paul the unique importance of Christ: the sole exception to this judgement, *the sole righteous man is Jesus Christ himself.* In the cross of Christ the whole climactic period of human suffering was located and concentrated. Here was the one righteous person suffering in such a way that others could enter into his suffering and be redeemed and vindicated by it.

Christ's death as sacrifice

While the Jerusalem temple was still standing, Judaism was primarily a religion of sacrificial acts; there were complex provisions for offerings and observances twice daily through the year and also on special occasions such as the annual festivals. It is not surprising that, when Paul explains the death of Christ as the vicarious suffering of the innocent victim, he should also use the symbolism of Jewish sacrifice, where suitable victims were selected with great care within the established conventions. The provision of particular sacrifices was prescribed for sin-offerings and guilt-offerings and for making ATONEMENT with God. In such contexts it would have been appropriate to speak of Christ's death in sacrificial, ethical, and penal terms. Because Paul is close to this Jewish background he does not need to explain the imagery. Other cultures in the Greco-Roman world shared an understanding of the principles of sacrifice, of propitiating the superior with whom one wished to be on good terms, and of expiating the sense of guilt from the offence. So Paul only needs to draw attention to where the death of Christ goes beyond what is expected of a sacrifice.

The Passover sacrifice

Paul recalls the circumstances of the Exodus from Egypt, and its annual commemoration at the Jewish feast of Passover, when he tells the Corinthians:

> *Christ, our paschal lamb, has been sacrificed. Let us, therefore, celebrate the festival, not with the old leaven, the leaven of malice and evil, but with the unleavened bread of sincerity and truth.* (1 Corinthians 5.7–8)

When God has acted to deliver his people anew, and acted with such tremendous sacrifice, it is only appropriate that Christians should respond by changing the quality of their lives.

There is an extension of this argument, from the actual sacrifice of Christ's death to the community's commemoration of that sacrifice in the Eucharist. While Paul has made only a brief reference to Passover, the relation between Passover and the Last Supper (apparently presumed everywhere in the New Testament apart from John's gospel) means that the Passover sacrifice is presupposed when the Pauline communities celebrate the Lord's Supper. The same sacrificial symbolism therefore underlies references, such as 1 Corinthians 10.14ff, to "participation" in the body and blood of Christ. By these sacramental means the Christians can identify with the sacrifice of Christ and its effects in unity and purity.

The sin offering

It is possible to find another specific reference to Christ's death as working within the Jewish sacrificial system, in Romans 8.3:

> For God has done what the Law, weakened by the flesh, could not do: sending his own Son in the likeness of sinful flesh and as a sin offering, he condemned sin in the flesh.

The emphasized phrase is a simple Greek expression ("concerning sin") which was used in the Septuagint on occasion to translate a Hebrew reference to making a sin offering. The work of Christ is in fulfilment of God's ultimate plan; it is a decisive act of expiation, in dealing with sin (and condemning sin, not sinners). The letter to the Colossians states in other words, but equally emphatically, the decisive nature of the action, but stresses the eschatological and penal aspects:

> The Father has delivered us from the dominion of darkness and transferred us to the kingdom of his beloved Son, in whom we have redemption, the forgiveness of sins. (1.13–14)

(See also Ephesians 1.7–8: "in him we have redemption through his blood, the forgiveness of our trespasses, according to the riches of his grace which he lavished upon us.")

The imagery here is of deliverance that works by transaction and purchase. The metaphor of ransoming and redeeming (as in Mark 10.45) sums up the general theme of Isaiah 53: it expresses the idea of vicarious and voluntary giving up of life, with the additional implication that the sacrifice was in some way mysteriously necessitated by sin. Christ has paid the penalty to ransom humanity.

Justification by God

The fullest explanation of how the death of Christ works in terms of the imagery of sacrifice is provided by Paul in Romans 3.21–26. It is a rather condensed and complicated explanation, beginning with the observation of universal sinfulness (Jews and Greeks) which we have already noted in Romans 3:

> *But now the righteousness of God has been manifested apart from Law*
> *– although the law and the prophets bear witness to it – the righteous-*
> *ness of God through faith in Jesus Christ, for all who believe. For there*
> *is no distinction; since all have sinned and fall short of the glory of*
> *God, they are justified by his grace as a gift.*

What has happened in the act of Christ's dying was prophesied in the Old Testament. The same point is made in the Passion narratives of the gospels, to emphasize that these events are the fulfilment of prophecy. The outcome of this death is a gracious gift from God, not something which has been earned by human obedience or stored up merit. It could not be otherwise, for all are sinners. But God has acted to acquit these sinners; by a creative act he has made them righteous. (It is much less likely that Paul's words mean that God uses a legal fiction and treats humankind as if they were righteous.) He has done this

> *through the redemption which is in Christ Jesus, whom God put*
> *forward publicly as an expiation by his blood, to be received by faith.*

This statement puts together several of the images of sacrifice we have been considering. It would be possible to understand these words as referring to a process of liberation which takes place in the public arena (like a revolutionary coup d'etat where blood is shed for the cause) but the added dimension of the sacrificial idea leads on to the question of whose blood is shed. It is not the blood of enemies of the revolution, nor even of innocent by-standers, but the blood of the liberator who sacrifices himself. The words can mean that God offers a sacrifice in the bloody sacrificial death of Jesus Christ. The sacrifice functions as an expiation: it wipes out the sins (the universal sin).

The Day of Atonement

It is likely that Paul is referring to a particular expiatory means of dealing with sin, the cover or lid of the Ark of the Covenant from Old Testament times. "This cover was sprinkled with blood by the High Priest on the Day of Atonement; it was here that the gracious God appeared, in thick darkness, once more reconciled with his people. There is much to be said for the traditional view that Paul represented Christ as the true 'mercy-seat'. What else to a Jew represented at once the place and the means of atonement?"[15] Just as Paul can describe Christ's death by the symbol of the Passover lamb, so he can represent it by the symbol of the mercy-seat, the means of reconciliation between humankind and God on the Day of Atonement. This demonstrates a creative use of a range of sacrificial images, microcosmic elements from the Old Testament that are prophetic of the macrocosmic achievement Paul is claiming for Christ. A similar claim by another author is supported by a similar range of symbols (the liturgy of the Day of Atonement, the covenant sacrifices, and the red heifer of Numbers 19) in chapters 9–10 of the letter to the Hebrews. But why does Paul think that God acted in the way described by these powerful images?

This was to show God's righteousness, because in his divine forbear-
ance he had passed over former sins; it was to prove at the present time
that he himself is righteous and that he justifies him who has faith in
Jesus.

The same Greek word is repeated here and translated "show" and "prove";
it has both meanings like the English word "demonstrate". The cross of
Christ is a demonstration of God's righteousness in action, a proof that God
is righteous (when the evidence might suggest God is being unduly compassionate), and a further demonstration of how easy it is for the believer to
be righteous in God's eyes.

In Paul's argument, the crucifixion has achieved two major purposes
within a single, highly symbolic, action. To do to death his own son in a
particular bloody way shows how much God hates sin; it shows that he is
prepared to throw the full weight of his anger against the fact of sin and pass
a punitive judgement upon it. In the past it might have seemed that God
disregarded sin; but God's justice is not thereby called into question. He had
delayed his hand out of mercy, wishing to give sinners every opportunity for
penitence. The other major purpose is concerned with the present rather
than the past. More accurately, it anticipates God's decisions at the Last
Judgement.

As God has taken upon himself (in Jesus) all the suffering traditionally
expected in the last days, he has vindicated himself and is able to vindicate,
now and at the Last Judgement, all who are believers and who appreciate
what God has done. In the first place the cross was the symbol of penalty, of
punitive judgement on sin. Now that the penalty has been fully exacted, the
cross can be seen as the symbol of God's love demonstrated in the ultimate
sacrifice. For those who see the cross, in the light of the Resurrection, as
God's act of redemption and reconciliation, the future is transformed.

Salvation by initiation

We have seen something of the range and depth of Paul's use of the symbols
of Jewish sacrifice to describe the death of Christ. These are not the only
symbols he uses, nor is Judaism the only cultural world which serves as a
source for his theology. As well as "salvation by sacrifice" there is "salvation
by initiation", which has as its model the practices of the mystery cults. We
see this most clearly in the argument of Romans 6.3–11, which begins:

Do you not know that all of us who have been baptized into Christ
Jesus were baptized into his death? We were buried therefore with him
by baptism into death, so that as Christ was raised from the dead by the
glory of the Father, we too might walk in newness of life. For if we have
been united with him in a death like his, we shall certainly be united
with him in a resurrection like his.

This idea starts from the earliest Christian use of baptism as a rite of
initiation, for the individual believer, modelled on the water baptism for

Head of Mithras, made of marble, from the temple of Mithras at Walbrook, London.

repentance of John the Baptist, and in particular the baptism of Jesus himself. Paul, however, interprets baptism using ideas associated with the mystery cults. This is not the same as saying that Paul turns Christianity into a mystery cult. Rather he uses the esoteric language of the cults as a source of imagery, to depict vividly the depth of the transformation of life which the convert undergoes. It is as if a modern writer, recognizing the popular appeal of the new cults, or the world of astrology and the occult, were to borrow such imagery to colour up and communicate what he wished to say.

Initiation in the mysteries

In a mystery cult the rite of initiation could be understood as in some mysterious way uniting the believer with the destiny of the deity. In the dramatized myth and ritual of the cult the mystic participated in these dramatic experiences and made them his/her own. The transforming life experience depended not on the ritual in itself, but on the divine exploit which the ritual symbolized. So a virile new life sprang up for the soldier-initiate of Mithras as a result of his identification with the deity's slaying of the bull. It was also thought that a permanent bond was established between the mystic (who received the initiation) and the mystagogue (who was directly responsible for preparing the initiate and imparting the secret knowledge). The implications of such a permanent bonding and allegiance were a cause of concern to Paul, if they were applied to Christians baptized and "worshipping" those who baptized them (see 1 Corinthians 1.12–16).

The following are two extracts which describe initiation in a mystery cult and clarify the nature of the comparison Paul is making. The first is by a Christian writer (which explains his critical remarks) and is a description of the consecration of a priest by the rite of *taurobolium*, a ritual which became a means of initiation in Mithraism. After this explicit narrative, the second is a more allusive account of what it meant to be an initiate of Isis. Examples of initiation rituals in the mystery religions:

> *The high priest who is to be consecrated is brought down under ground in a pit dug deep. Over this they make a wooden floor with an open mesh; they then repeatedly pierce the wood with a pointed tool that it may appear full of small holes.*
>
> *Hither a huge bull, fierce and shaggy in appearance, is led, bound with flowery garlands about its flanks, and with its horns sheathed. Here, as is ordained, the beast is to be slain, and they pierce its breast with a sacred spear; the gaping wound emits a wave of hot blood, and the smoking river flows into the woven structure beneath it and surges wide.*
>
> *Then by the many paths of the thousand openings in the lattice the falling shower rains down a foul dew, which the priest within catches, putting his shameful head under all the drops. Yea, he throws back his face, until he actually drinks the dark gore.*
>
> *Afterwards, the flamens draw the corpse off the lattice, and the priest, horrible in appearance, comes forth and shows his wet head and sodden*

*garments. This man, defiled with such contagions, and foul with the gore
of the recent sacrifice, all hail and worship at a distance, because profane
blood and a dead ox have washed him while concealed in a filthy cave.*
(Prudentius, *Peristephanon* x.1011–50)

*Soon after this she [Isis] gave me proof of her grace by a midnight vision
in which I was plainly told that the day for which I longed, the day on
which my greatest wish would be granted, had come at last.*

*The High Priest summoned me and took me to the nearest public
baths. There, when I had enjoyed my ordinary bathe, he himself washed
and sprinkled me with holy water, offering up prayers for divine mercy.
After this he brought me back to the temple and placed me at the very
feet of the Goddess.*

*As evening approached a crowd of priests came flocking to me, each
one giving me congratulatory gifts, as the ancient custom is. Then the
High Priest ordered all uninitiated persons to depart, invested me in a
new linen garment and led me by the hand into the inner recesses of the
sanctuary itself.*

*I have no doubt, curious reader, that you are eager to know what
happened when I entered. If I were allowed to tell you, and you were
allowed to be told, you would soon hear everything; but, as it is, my
tongue would suffer for its indiscretion and your ears for their
inquisitiveness.*

*However, not wishing to leave you, if you are religiously inclined, in a
state of tortured suspense, I will record as much as I may lawfully record
for the uninitiated, but only on condition that you believe it. I
approached the very gates of death and set one foot on Proserpine's
threshold, yet was permitted to return, rapt through all the elements. At
midnight I saw the sun shining as if it were noon; I entered the presence
of the gods of the under-world and the gods of the upper-world, stood
near and worshipped them.*

*That day was the happiest of my initiation, and I celebrated it as my
birthday with a cheerful banquet at which all my friends were present. I
went to the High Priest, now my spiritual father, clung around his neck
and kissed him again and again, begging him to forgive me.*
(Apuleius, *The Golden Ass* 11.22–26)

Initiation in Christian baptism

As we have already seen in Paul's argument in Romans, Christ is the second
Adam with whom all humankind could be united by faith. It is no secret
matter with a few initiates. The believer is baptized in the name of Christ,
and so baptized into Christ. Christians are united with Christ in his sufferings on the cross, and are united in (and vindicated by) his death. They are,
by their baptism, buried with Christ, and they will share in Christ's Resurrection. The basic affirmation, about what God has done in Christ, is
intimately related to the present and future state of the Christian believer. At
the cross the whole situation between God and humanity is changed. From
this is derived a new situation for each individual believer.

Traditional representation of Mithras slaying the bull. Mithras wears a Phrygian cap, and is accompanied by two torchbearers; the dog and the snake seek the bull's blood as it flows. The exploit happens in a cave while overhead the chariot of the sun crosses the heavens.

Romans 6.5 contains a contrast in time as well as parallelism of theme between the two parts of the verse. It could be translated: "If, through the representation [symbol] of his death, we have come to be joined with his death, then we shall certainly be joined with him through the representation [symbol] of his Resurrection." It is clear that the references to death and burial (and our involvement with them) are references to the past, while equally the references to the Resurrection experience are future. Salvation is through initiation. But, although Paul uses the language and ethos of the mysteries, he is not uncritical of the mystic's view of salvation (especially as this may have been adopted by Christians at Corinth).

While he speaks of baptism into Christ as incorporation into Christ's death and (potentially) into his Resurrection, he is obliged to combat the view that the individual Christian believer has already been raised to a new life that cannot be lost. Baptism does not bestow a material gift of salvation (a kind of foolproof insurance policy); but rather it subjects the individual Christians to the lordship of Christ, in order that one day they might be raised from the dead and finally united with Christ. For the mystic a vital divine power is imparted in the mystical experience, which is timeless (transcending historical time) and related to the cyclical order of nature. Through baptism the Christian is related to the historically unique event of the death of Christ, and to the offer of future life which the Resurrection of Christ embodies.

Baptism into death

At the heart of Paul's argument is a meditation on the fact of death, which shows how literally he takes the death of Christ to which the symbolic believer-baptism relates. It is widely recognized in many cultures that death pays all debts, that a dead woman or man has been freed of obligations by dying. The dead have thereby been freed from sin (6.7), just as in a Jewish rabbinic argument it is recognized that the dead are freed from the Law. This liberating effect is supremely true of the death of Christ, because he died sinless in a context of universal sin. Accordingly, to be incorporated into Christ's death by baptism is to share the prospect of that liberation from sin. The death and life of Christ are applicable to the death and life of Christians (6.11), but the ultimate application of the prospect of life and liberation depends upon the obedience of the believer to God, what Paul graphically describes as a "slavery" to God's righteousness (6.18).

Freedom with obligations

At the very point in his argument where Paul discusses "salvation by initiation", he also firmly rejects the notion that we should "continue in sin that grace may abound" (6.1), and exhorts the Romans: "Let not sin reign in your mortal bodies" (6.12). The prospect of liberation entails a new kind of freedom with obligations. The Christian initiate has begun with God's help on a long process of ascent to God, but he must conduct himself worthily and appropriately. Given the human limitations which would stay till the end, it would be a rash woman or man who abused the system of God's salvation and exploited Christian freedom from the Law. It is hardly surprising that later generations of theologians and church people were so concerned about post-baptismal sin. (Can Christians help being sinless after baptism? If they do sin, what should the church do about it?) When Paul speaks, as he often does, of the Christian life as "being in Christ", this is no mystical doctrine of perfectionism. It is a living relationship where the believer identifies with Christ and, with Christ's inspiration, strives to be obedient to his/her Lord.

Salvation by example

A third type of approach to salvation, after "salvation by sacrifice" and "salvation by initiation", may be characterized as "salvation by example", as it is concerned with the model or example set by Christ in his life and particularly in his death. It is a pattern of humility, of "service unto death", which is set for imitation. The context of thought is a secular philosophy and ethics, commonplace in the Greco-Roman world, and exemplified in particular philosophies such as PLATONISM and Stoicism.

To illustrate the powerful "saving" influence of such an "example", a very rough parallel could be drawn with the Buddhism widely popular in modern times: the *bodhisattva* figure of Mahayana Buddhism is one who, having attained enlightenment, is on the way to Buddahood but postpones the goal in order to keep a vow to help all life attain salvation. In popular devotion such figures are worshipped as symbols of compassion. These "examples" do not just act as teachers; in working indefinitely for the good of others, they gather others into their own being. In a broadly similar way, in Paul's theme, the salvation achieved by imitation is a kind of absorption, almost a "salvation by osmosis".

The foundation text which Paul uses is the quotation from a traditional hymn in Philippians 2.6–11 which begins: "though he was in the form of God, did not count equality with God a thing to be grasped" (seized for oneself or held on to). We have already noted (p. 106) how powerfully this hymn expresses the idea of the cross as a symbol of reversal, but it is also important to notice how Paul uses this quotation, in an ethical context in which he exhorts the Philippians: "Have this mind among yourselves, which you have in Christ Jesus". Jesus is the example for their imitation; they are to think as Jesus thought.

Imitation of Christ

Paul's line of argument through Philippians is concerned with the example of Christ to the church. Paul loved this community and urged it to stand firm in critical times and follow the example of Christ.

> So if there is any encouragement in Christ, any incentive of love, any participation in the Spirit, any affection and sympathy, complete my joy by being of the same mind, having the same love, being in full accord and of one mind. (2.1–2)

Paul is concerned about unity and unanimity in the church, with good reason (see 4.2). He is not just talking about being of one mind, but of having the mind and unifying love of Christ as example.

> Do nothing from selfishness or conceit, but in humility count others better than yourselves. (2.3)

The obedient mind and will of Christ, as demonstrated in the successive phases of humiliation which the quoted hymn records, is the clear pattern to follow when the church is involved in external as well as internal conflicts. Paul singles out the virtue of humility. (At first sight this is not the virtue most likely to be favoured in secular philosophies. Nevertheless, although the Greek philosophical tradition reserved a place for self-praise, it was more often critical of it, drawing the moral that pride goes before a fall.) Paul builds on this basis and relates all moral philosophy to the example provided by the cross. It is an inversion of the world's values, but it offers a working critique of them, rather than the total alienation of other-worldliness.

Therefore, my beloved, as you have always obeyed, so now, not only as in my presence but much more in my absence, work out your own salvation with fear and trembling; for God is at work in you, both to will and to work for his good pleasure. (2.12–13)

The example offered in the quoted hymn is the total obedience of Christ: "he humbled himself and became obedient unto death, even death on a cross" (2.8). The cross is the definition of utter humility and also the symbol of reversal which defines all subsequent existence. What Paul says (verses 12–13), at the triumphant close of his quoted exemplification of Christ, sounds rather like leaving the Philippians to work things out for themselves while he was in prison. But more literally, just as Paul's imprisonment is "for Christ" and "to advance the gospel" (1.12–13), so the Philippians' use of the pattern of Christ's obedience is the process of working out (effecting) their salvation, and God is indeed active within this process.

Paul's imitation of Christ

The pattern of "service unto death" is further demonstrated in Philippians 3 where Paul describes his own imitation of Christ. Paul writes in a context of polemic against a diametrically opposite point of view among his opponents. They preached a doctrine of spiritual perfection, already achieved by their fulfilment of the Jewish Law, and boasted about their exemplary achievements. Paul is driven by such circumstances to set himself up as an example (3.17), not in his own right but only as a model for those who are imitating Christ, who are involved in the suffering and death and turn away from self-glorification. The broad similarities between the picture of Paul and the picture of Christ are made theologically specific:

Whatever gain I had, I counted as loss for the sake of Christ.
[Christ "did not count equality a thing to be grasped"]
Indeed I count everything as loss because of the surpassing worth of knowing Christ Jesus my Lord. For his sake I have suffered the loss of all things, and count them as refuse, in order that I may gain Christ and be found in him.
[Christ "emptied himself . . . slave . . . humbled himself . . . obedient]
. . . that I may know him . . . and may share his sufferings, becoming like him in his death.
[Christ "obedient unto death, even death on a cross"]
. . . that if possible I may attain the resurrection from the dead."
["Therefore God has highly exalted" Christ] (Philippians 3.7–11 // 2.6–11)

Paul's imitation of Christ is a process of "gaining" Christ, without counting the cost, of "becoming like" Christ, particularly in his death, with the possibility of "attaining" the Resurrection. For this reason Paul can realistically expect to be put to death as the outcome of his imprisonment and trial (1.20; 2.17), much as he would hope to be freed and to visit Philippi (1.26;

2.24). "For to me to live is Christ, and to die is gain" (1.21). It is clear that, however much Paul wishes to know "the power of the resurrection", he does not see the process of "salvation by imitation" as already completed:

> *Not that I have already obtained this or am already perfect; but I press on to make it my own, because Christ Jesus has made me his own.* (3.12)

Paul emphasizes this point by using the secular metaphor of a competitor at the athletic games. Such an allusion would be understood universally in the Greek world, where such contests were an essential part of the culture (in Philippi just as much as in Corinth or Olympia). Many orators and writers used such metaphors in a similar way to Paul; the following example is from the letters of Seneca, a Stoic philosopher, a contemporary of Paul:

> *And when a man is in the grip of difficulties . . . he should put his whole heart into the fight against them. If he gives way before them he will lose the battle; if he exerts himself against them he will win . . . Stand your ground, willing yourself to resist, [and the overwhelming pressure] will be forced back. Look at the amount of punishment that boxers and wrestlers take to the face and the body generally! They will put up none the less with any suffering in their desire for fame, and will undergo it all not merely in the course of fighting but in preparing for their fights as well: their training in itself constitutes suffering. Let us too overcome all things, with our reward consisting not in any wreath [crown] or garland, not in trumpet-calls for silence for the ceremonial proclamation of our name, but in moral worth, in strength of spirit, in a peace that is won for ever, once in any contest fortune has been utterly defeated.*
> *(Letters from a Stoic, 78.16)*

The race is not yet over

As in the extract from Seneca, Paul has not yet finished the race.

Runner from a painting on a Greek vase.

> *But one thing I do, forgetting what lies behind and straining forward to what lies ahead, I press on toward the goal for the prize of the upward call of God in Christ Jesus.* (3.14)

Paul uses a similar metaphor from the athletic games in 1 Corinthians 9:

> *Do you not know that in a race all the runners compete, but only one receives the prize? So run that you may obtain it. Every athlete exercises self-control in all things. They do it to receive a perishable wreath [crown], but we an imperishable. Well, I do not run aimlessly, I do not box as one beating the air; but I pommel my body and subdue it, lest after preaching to others I myself should be disqualified.* (9.24–27)

This contest is one in which both Paul and his readers are still very much engaged.

The prizes

Paul's sporting metaphor raises the question of whether Christianity is like a race in which only one person wins a prize. Paul's argument emphasizes the role of the individual "athlete" only in relation to the rest of the social group, and the number of prizes is not necessarily limitless. We tend to assume that because Paul's mission has universal dimensions, he sees salvation as ultimately for everybody. While that might theoretically be the case, his ideal is limited by practical considerations because the strategy of mission has to be geared to the nearness of the world's end. Those who are ultimately saved may well be drawn from all kinds of people, but salvation is not total and comprehensive. When Paul writes in Romans 5.15 of the "one" and the "many", he seems to mean *many but not all*. This reservation increases rather than diminishes the importance of the present task in "running the race".

This metaphor of the race depicts (in familiar and accessible terms) the achieving of salvation for oneself and for others. The context of 1 Corinthians 9 shows that it involves preaching the gospel to others and is not just a personal quest for salvation. The same point should also be clear from the relationship (between Christ, Paul, and the community of Christians) which is represented in both versions of the metaphor. Christ is the example, Paul the imitator "becoming like" Christ in his death. Paul is thus eligible to enter the race. He describes the effort of his running and the goal at which he is still aiming. With such a prize ("the upward call of God") and an imperishable crown before them, Paul can only exhort his converts to join the race. They should follow the example of Christ, and only imitate Paul in so far as he is an imitator of Christ. "Therefore, my brethren, whom I love and long for, my joy and my crown, stand firm thus in the Lord, my beloved" (Philippians 4.1). Notice both how close Paul's moral advice ("stand firm") is to Seneca's, and also how the Philippian church ("my crown") has become identified with the goal to which Paul is aiming.

Service unto death

All of this theological statement, and ethical exhortation, this web of symbolism, makes creative use of secular parallels and metaphors. But its central theme is "salvation by imitation"; and at the heart of that is the death of Christ, which exemplifies the attitude of "service unto death". A philosophical explanation of how the fundamental experience of obedience and humiliation could lead to so extensive a process of salvation can be found in Aristotle's *Metaphysics*, which advanced the principle that "like seeks after like" and so "like is known by like". The knowledge of God and awareness of his plans for individuals depend therefore on a point of identification with him. This point is provided by human mortality in the experience of Jesus Christ. The counterpoint is found in the consequent progress toward God and growing experience of, and identification with, his nature.

It is the modern experience that daily living, like the sporting event, rewards the achiever not the failure. The media rejoice when the coveted prize is placed on the brow of the winning man or woman. Paul's creative use of this commonplace, of modern as well as ancient experience, alerts us to a striking fact. Central to his symbol of reversal is an achievement of salvation for the world, based on a rather special kind of failure. Can the believer afford not to follow this example?

Paul's use of symbolism: conclusions

We have now examined three of the symbols – imitation, initiation and sacrifice – which Paul uses in discussing the gospel of Christ's death and Resurrection. These are typical of the many kinds of symbols Paul uses. Each has its own context within a specific world of thought, of which Paul offers a careful criticism of by the way in which he uses each symbol. With his cosmopolitan experiences, Paul did not inhabit a single world of thought. His concern with the universal mission of Christianity leads him to use individual symbols as building blocks, combining two or more in a single letter, to create a new kind of construction, a distinctively new Christian theology and philosophy of life.

Whilst it is possible to identify themes and arguments in Paul's writings, and to examine his use of symbolism, the content transcends the style and the literary techniques. The whole is greater than the sum of the parts.

We have seen the range and depth in one small slogan of "Christ crucified" within the symbol-system. We have also noted that Paul's mission began with a minimal definition which enabled a high tolerance of diverse interpretations. When he is being tolerant, the only thing which makes him angry is the opposition and straight contradiction which comes from a narrow definition and tightly drawn boundary lines. This helps to explain why he is both extremely positive and also angrily negative about the Law: he is positive about the Jewish tradition, and incensed about the restrictive use made of it by Jewish Christians. We must ask whether there was a real danger in Paul's definition being too minimal and his outlook too inclusive? This sense of danger might be recognized in the immediate feelings of opposition and in the longer-term reactions which attempted to impose a structure on Paul.

Developments from the simple slogan

For many of Paul's converts his simple slogan and open exposition provoked an identity crisis. "It was too minimalist. Its effect was to relativize and transform every alternative identity symbol. Circumcision of the flesh became circumcision of the heart; the liturgy of synagogue and Temple became the liturgy of the whole life. That this proved too radical a transformation is seen in the search for additional identity symbols on the part of many members of Paul's churches."[10] The old symbols had been transformed, and alien symbols that might have been thought incompatible had been integrated in the faith. It was rather confusing and troubling; hardly surprisingly converts sought security in small group allegiances (as at Corinth – see 1 Corinthians 1.11ff) and personal commitment to the one who had initiated them into this "mystery".

There was scope in the Pauline communities for revisionists, who wished to re-establish the traditional patterns of observances in a more rigorous way (see Galatians 4.9–10). Others set great store by personal inspiration, using charismatic practices exclusively as a source for their own edification rather than of prophecy for the benefit of the church (see 1 Corinthians 14). In this way came also the claims to special knowledge (*gnosis*) and the esoteric movements of GNOSTICISM. Paul represents an early instance of wide-ranging, liberal "enthusiasm". The institutional kind of response (the imposition of a structured organization), which is often termed "early/primitive catholicism", was a natural reaction to Paul's freedom and personal leadership. We can measure the adequacy of Paul's transformation of existing structures by the extent to which his insights are preserved and by the strength of the alternatives proposed.

To read Ephesians, for example, is to enter a different world, that of the theological essay rather than the urgent communication to a community with problems. The original Pauline emphases can still be identified, however: the long sweep of salvation history within the purposes of God, the central role of Christ's death on the cross, the eschatological tension between present salvation and the battle which is still to be fought, and the close interconnection of ethics and theology. Even the structure of the church itself, which has become so much more a dimension of theology since the days of Paul, bears witness to the dialectic between theology and social structure which is so important in the writings of Paul.

Implications for the church

These aspects of continuity, between Paul and his successors, also provide some defence against the charge that Paul's approach is too inclusive and his definition of the Christian faith too minimalist. The future of Christianity (if this was in any sense Paul's problem) would only have been in danger, open and exposed, if Paul had merely used the simple symbol of the cross of Christ and left it unelaborated. But, as we have seen, Paul does investigate the implications of his symbolism within the constraints of local circumstances. He spells out these implications for the local community, the groups of converts who form the interim "church" of Christ. These localized hints and elaborations have provided in their different ways a number of bases for future institutional development. Paul is concerned with a foreshortened span of time, one that would last only until the strategy of mission is completed in Jerusalem and Rome, but various aspects have been extrapolated from his situation and found relevant for new contexts since his death.

The solidarity of the community

The cross of Christ serves as a potent symbol for community formation. It also lays the foundations for an "alternative" structure at odds with the world's social classifications. Paul's symbolism can interpret and justify the sufferings of Christians, as essentially related to the sufferings of Christ. Such shared experiences would reinforce a sense of solidarity within the church, as well as a collective relationship with Christ ("the body of Christ"; "in Christ") and a close bonding with the apostle ("engaged in the same conflict which you saw and now hear to be mine" – Philippians 1.30).

What progress can and should be made in the interrelationships of individuals, as distinct from the larger society around them, is seen especially in the Corinthian correspondence. With reference to 1 Corinthians 5 and 2 Thessalonians 3, it is plain that Paul "regarded the social relationships of individual members as a matter of concern for the whole Church. A man no longer lives for himself once he has entered the fellowship: he is responsible to God and his brothers in Christ... For the good name of Christ and the inner health of His body it is therefore essential that all should feel themselves equally obliged to maintain both."[16]

The threat of outsiders

Many of the shared experiences of suffering are also evidence of the hostility of those outside the Christian community. These outsiders were regarded as a threat, and special language is used to characterize them and to emphasize separation from them. The picture can be presented in the language of myth, highly coloured with dualist contrasts, and the expectation of the end of the world. See an example of this in 2 Thessalonians 1.4–10:

> We boast of you ... for your steadfastness and faith in all ... the afflictions which you are enduring. This is evidence of the righteous judgement of God, that you may be made worthy of the kingdom of God, for which you are suffering – since indeed God deems it just to repay with affliction those who afflict you, and to grant rest with us to you who are afflicted, when the Lord Jesus is revealed from heaven with his mighty angels in flaming fire, inflicting vengeance upon those who do not know God and upon those who do not obey the gospel of our Lord Jesus. They shall suffer the punishment of eternal destruction and exclusion from the presence of the Lord and from the glory of his might, when he comes on that day to be glorified in his saints.

This picture is a response to suffering, theologically interpreted. It represents the drawing of certain boundaries against the aggressor, but it does not exclude the outside world from missionary outreach. Eschatological language has a remarkable capacity for combining the threat of vengeance with the offer of salvation. Perspectives are foreshortened, to precipitate the end. In such a context the warning of exclusion may simply be a device to bring potential converts to their senses (at least to save their souls if not their

Suffering in the modern world: police and protester at Christian C.N.D. demonstration in London.

bodies), and the threat of divine vengeance can be a provocation to a change of heart. This kind of apocalyptic attitude has perhaps been taken to extremes in modern times: some "religious" politicians have threatened to use nuclear war as a way to bring about Armageddon, and thus save what is left of the world.

The strong and the weak

Jews distinguished themselves from pagan society by rules of purity, in the same way as the stricter sects of Judaism could differentiate themselves from the broader stream. Pauline Christians, on the other hand, had explicitly discarded the Jewish rules and rituals of purity. The rules of diet (affecting "meat offered to idols") and the rules of sex appear to have been extraordinarily ambivalent in the Pauline groups. This suggests that the "stronger" members of the community were still trying to live out the more open, integrative policy of the apostle, despite the scruples of the "weak". Paul's response to the problem this raises (as in 1 Corinthians 8) shows how he balances application of the original principle of openness with concern for the "weaker" members of the church. The theological doctrine of Christ's identification with the weak and vulnerable resolves the matter, and inevitably draws the boundary lines.

A new "alternative" community

The theological and practical pressures towards community formation ensure that eventually the individual and communal identities will be at odds with the social classifications of the day. They therefore lay the foundation for an "alternative" community. The term "Kingdom of God" is rare in

Paul's letters; when it does occur it denotes the future state in which promises are fulfilled and God's judgement has been executed (see 1 Corinthians 6.9–10). In the interim the church functions as the community of those who "are all one in Christ Jesus" (Galatians 3.28), "the body of Christ" as described in 1 Corinthians 12.12–27 and Romans 12.4–8. Different elements, with differing social backgrounds and functions, are conscious of their unification within the definition of relationship to Christ.

The text which makes the most radical statement, and seems to anticipate the future fulfilment of God's kingdom within the present situation, is 2 Corinthians 5.17:

> *Therefore, if anyone is in Christ, he is a new creation; the old has passed away, behold, the new has come.*

So great is Paul's reliance on what Christ has done through the cross that he can see the fulfilment of promises, even to the re-creation of the world, as accomplished by this event. More often, however, Paul sees himself as part of a process (inaugurated by the death of Christ) that still needs to be worked at, because it is in important respects still incomplete.

Nevertheless, the individual and communal relationship with Christ experienced within that process is of such an order as to lead to the redefinition of existence and a revolutionary change in self-understanding and self-designation. This applies as yet only to those who form the community of believers. But their experience anticipates the promised transformation of the world at the end time, even if the means to that end would strike outsiders as strange. "This Pauline phrase [new creation] is rooted in the social reality of Paul and of the communities of which he was a part. Paul had joined a new community. It brought him agony, beatings, hatred, jail."[17]

It must be stressed that these definitions of salvation were concrete claims, born of a political or social situation, and therefore part of a dynamic of power and conflict. Compare, for example, Paul's definition of Christian existence in 2 Corinthians 5.17 with that of a later writer, Ignatius of Antioch, early in the second century. Ignatius wrote, in his *Letter to the Smyrnaeans* 8.2:

> *Wheresoever the bishop appears, there let the people be, even as wheresoever Christ Jesus is, there is the catholic church.*

The difference appears to be the enormous gulf between an early prophetic "enthusiasm" and an institutionalized "catholicism". But "the Ignatian sentence goes farther only in degree, not in kind. Instead of the 'apostle', the 'bishop'; instead of an emerging primitive congregation, the 'catholic church' (whatever Ignatius may have meant by those words). Ignatius demanded obedience of the bishop in the same way that Paul demanded obedience. For both, it was ultimately obedience to Christ; yet for both, obedience to Christ meant obedience to their own person, in the church."[17]

The community's relation to Paul

Paul's position in relation to his Christian communities may be characterized by Ernst Troeltsch's model of "patriarchalism". In this the "basic idea of the willing acceptance of given inequalities, and of making them fruitful for the ethical values of personal relationships, is given. All action is the service of God and is a responsible office, authority as well as obedience. As stewards of God the great must care for the small, and as servants of God the little ones must submit to those who bear authority; and since in so doing both meet in the service of God, inner religious equality is affirmed and the ethical possession is enlarged by the exercise of the tender virtues of responsibility for, and of trustful surrender to, each other. It is undeniable that this ideal is perceived dimly by Paul, and only by means of this ideal does he desire to alter given conditions from within outwards, without touching their external aspect at all."[18]

It is not Paul's goal to reform the social order. Instead he has a vision of transcending that order, so that range and diversity are transposed on to a new plane. Paul's ethic has been described as "love-patriarchalism": "an integrative ethic which does not champion a particular social or economic status", while it "does not seek to challenge the forces which lead to economic or social stratification. Love-patriarchalism advocates transcending such distinctions within the framework of a religious community which generates mutual respect and love."[17]

Paul's ethic thus depends upon a patriarchal vision of the family, which is structured to acknowledge differences in roles and status. The dominant ethical motif of love serves the practical purpose of reducing friction where this is created within a differentiated structure. This social structure appears much more clearly authoritarian, within the framework of the status quo, in contrast to Mark's use of the family as a model for discipleship. Mark's picture is much more radical because it is adopted from the Palestinian context of the wandering charismatics in the Jesus movement. Paul's picture retains the traditional hierarchy of the Greco-Roman world.

The church of the household

The community was to see itself as a family with Paul as a patriarchal figure, the father of the growing family. It would not be surprising, therefore, if the community's practice, as well as its definition of itself, were found to have been modelled on the conventions of an extended family. This was a natural pattern for a basic community or house-church (although there are other models of societies available, such as the *collegia* of the Greco-Roman world). We can see the pattern firmly established at a later date, in Ephesians and Colossians particularly.

Here the metaphor of the "household" and its management has been extended, and transferred as a symbol for God's implementation of his plan of salvation (Ephesians 1.10; 3.9). The expression was also more literally applied to the church household and the conduct of its day-to-day affairs; the ethical rules of relationship within the family are therefore properly referred to by scholars as the "household codes" (Colossians 3.18–4.1; Ephesians 5.22–6.9; also 1 Peter 2.13–3.12). At the basis of this extended

Community meal – the Christian "Agape" or banquet (from the Capella Gracca in the Catacomb of Priscilla, Rome).

metaphor may well be Paul's own reference to his apostleship as "steward-ship", i.e. being in charge of the administration of the household. In 1 Corinthians 9.17 he says: "I am entrusted with a commission", which means literally "I am the manager of the household"/"I am the director of the company".

The community meal

The household finds its focus in the communal meals. At the heart of these is the celebration of the Lord's Supper, which proclaims the death of Christ ("as often as you eat this bread and drink the cup, you proclaim the Lord's death until he comes" – 1 Corinthians 11.26). This proclamation defines the community's identity and purpose for existing, in relation to the theological symbol of Christ's death as sacrifice; but by these same means the community begins to have boundaries drawn for it over against the outsider: "You cannot drink the cup of the Lord and the cup of demons. You cannot partake of the table of the Lord and the table of demons" (1 Corinthians 10.21). It has already been noted (p. 118f) how the rite of initiation into the community is defined in relation to the death of Christ (in the mystery language of Romans 6).

The ethics of the community

The way the community behaves, its ethical patterns, will be defined eventually in terms of "household codes". In the meantime, this ethical instruction (PARENESIS) is presented either in Old Testament terms of the two ways (a listing of good and evil deeds, with the accompanying promise of blessing or threat of destruction); or as a catalogue of vices and of virtues, supplemented by an exhortation to "strip off" the allegiance to evil and "put on" loyalty to the good. The last two metaphors probably derive from the ritual of baptismal initiation (by total immersion); these catalogues probably originated in CATECHETICAL instruction before baptism. There are parallels to these kinds of catalogue in, for example, Stoic philosophy, but there they are used to describe the ideal of the wise individual, while Paul uses the catalogue to emphasize the need for the communal holiness of the whole congregation. There are examples in Galatians 5.16–26; 1 Corinthians 5.9–11; 6.9–10; 2 Corinthians 6.14–7.1; Romans 1.19–32; 13.12–14. The way in which these ethical patterns are defined in terms of the cross of Christ

Early Christian figures in the posture of prayer (Orans): wall painting from the Roman villa at Lullingstone in Kent.

is particularly striking:

> *those who belong to Christ Jesus have crucified the flesh with its passions and desires.* (Galatians 5.24)

Conclusions

This survey of Paul's theology in its social setting has concentrated on the multiplex symbolism of the cross in order to show how central this was to Paul's theological explorations and his preaching. It has also highlighted the impact his preaching made on those who heard him, and how significant it became for the Pauline communities' definition of themselves. Given this whole sweep of evidence, as to Paul's theory and practice, it is remarkably difficult to decide whether he should be called a revolutionary or a conservative.

"Behind the glorious dynamic of Paul lay an uncertainty that lies behind all his writings, from Romans 7 to his very position as an apostle (2 Corinthians 10ff) and to his admission that he has not reached his goal, but that he was still running after the prize (Philippians 3.14)."[17] In the Philippian context, it becomes clear that he was torn two ways in his existential hopes: to be with Christ, or to remain alive for the sake of the church (Philippians 1.23f). He was eagerly awaiting the resurrection of the dead at the Parousia, or glorious Second Coming of Christ (1 Corinthians 15.20ff); but it seems that he also set great store by a transcendent mystical experience in the past, as far as his personal spiritual development was concerned (2 Corinthians 12.2ff).

To resolve these apparent contradictions into an harmonious picture is difficult and it is unlikely that we shall eliminate uncertainties concerning this supremely confident man. He can be measured alongside Abraham as the man of faith but perhaps some of his fellow Christians had grounds for their anxieties about him. It has been suggested that the "men from James" who figure in Galatians 2.12 were sent from Jerusalem to investigate what Paul was doing in Antioch, and to try to ensure a viable Christian community there. Paul's great resource, however, was his theological outlook and breadth of vision. At his most sensitive and vulnerable he was the epitome of his symbolic principle of reversal. In weakness and failure lay his greatest strength.

CHAPTER 3

Luke–Acts: the church and the world

The Evangelist Luke.

At first sight, Acts seems to be a direct historical account of the rise of Christianity in the Mediterranean world as a result of the personal activities of Peter and Paul. But Acts seen in continuity with the gospel of Luke (by the same author), and in contrast to the writings of Paul, offers an interpretation of events from a theological perspective, with the benefit of hindsight. The situation it describes is that of the evolved church of Luke's day; some of the early problems have already been replaced by later concerns.

When compared with the basic proclamation (the reconstructed "Preaching of the Cross") or with the gospel of Mark, Luke's gospel is very clearly the product of the third generation. Luke's is the gospel of ordered material for the considered response. We might almost say it is the gospel of "law and order". It was produced by a community which felt established, that they had crossed a frontier and were looking back to see their origins and to follow the route which they had taken. That at least is the claim they wished to make for themselves. It is an axiom of modern scholarship that the gospel of Luke and the Acts of the Apostles belong together, the work of a single author. We should therefore regard them as a single sequence of events, an integral theological interpretation. Acts then offers the evidence for the new situation of the community behind Luke's gospel. Acts is the confirmation of the gospel. It is the evidence for the community's definition of itself and its historical consciousness.

The problem: Delay of the Second Coming

The proclamation of the first Christians shared the sense of urgency and immediacy of fulfilment which was heard in the message of Jesus himself (see page 49). This sense of urgency accompanied the expectation of a decisive climax in world events, a transformation on a cosmic scale. But however significant the message of Jesus had been and still was, it became a puzzle that this "end" or climax had not actually happened. The sequence of major events, the material of history, proceeded. There were indeed local disruptions and catastrophes, but normal everyday life continued.

The author of Luke–Acts recognized the problem. It seems as if this particular evangelist deliberately set out to answer the kind of worries and difficulties of his generation and community, in regard to the gospel message and the continuing processes of history. If we assume, as modern scholarship does, that the man we call Luke was the originator of the idea of the two-volume work (Luke–Acts), then this in itself represents a major step forward in answering the problems faced by Luke and his church.

The addition of the Acts of the Apostles to the Christian documents meant that a great change had taken place. Luke was probably the first to represent the story of Jesus as the beginning of a continuing history of the church, with Acts following the gospel like the second book of a connected historical report. In this way the proclamation of Jesus, the story about him, is turned into past history and the report in Luke's gospel becomes in effect the first, the pioneering, "Life of Jesus". As a work it is of course centuries away from the lives of Jesus written in the nineteenth century CE, which featured in the celebrated "Quest for the Historical Jesus" but the intention (of producing a theological picture against a "realistic" historical background) was really quite similar; only the conventions of theology and historiography were different.

The solution: Importance of the church

Luke's enterprise indicates that a change in outlook had taken place among the early Christians, because it shows that the church in itself had become important. The church community had become explicitly interested in its own history and in defining itself. It is a truism that "one does not write the history of the church if one daily expects the end of the world". The addition of Acts therefore indicates that this writer did not expect the return of Jesus and the end of the world at any moment. Luke has changed the message of the world's end into an account of a meaningful historical development.

The text at the beginning of Mark's gospel, "The time is fulfilled, and the kingdom of God is at hand; repent and believe in the gospel" (Mark 1.15), has no parallel in Luke's gospel. In Mark 9.1 Jesus is reported as saying, "Truly I say to you, there are some standing here who will not taste death before they see the kingdom of God come with power". Luke 21.9 however reads, "the end will not be at once". In Acts 1.6f Jesus is asked, " 'Lord, will you at this time restore the kingdom to Israel?' and Jesus said to them, 'It is not for you to know times or seasons which the Father has fixed by his own authority' ".

In Mark 13 the general prophecy of the last days is presented in terms of the traditional images:

> *In those days, after that tribulation, the sun will be darkened, and the moon will not give its light, and the stars will be falling from heaven, and the powers in the heavens will be shaken. And then they will see the Son of Man coming in clouds with great power and glory.*

In Luke 21.20 a new element is introduced into this picture:

> *When you see Jerusalem surrounded by armies, then know that its desolation has come near.*

The general prophecy has been qualified by a specific reference to the historical fact of the fall of Jerusalem to the Romans in 70 CE. The prophetic hope concerned with the last days has not been extinguished. It has a living and strongly spiritualized relevance as part of the Christian message in Luke's day. There is still an eager and earnest expectation of the fulfilment of God's promises and the completion of the divine plan, but the urgency and imminence have been transformed by the establishment of an extended sequence of time in which particular events of world history can (and must) be included.

The Roman world and the history of salvation

As a development from the early Christian message of the last and critical moment for a decision to accept the gospel, Luke offers a schematized history of salvation, of the ways in which God has acted for his people, which (most significantly for Luke) interlocks at key events with the history of the Roman world. This is also evident in these "datelines" which Luke gives to his reports:

> *In those days a decree went out from Caesar Augustus that all the world should be enrolled. This was the first enrolment, when Quirinius was governor of Syria.* (Luke 2.1)

> *In the fifteenth year of the reign of Tiberius Caesar, Pontius Pilate being governor of Judea, and Herod being tetrarch of Galilee, and his brother Philip tetrarch of the region of Iturea and Trachonitis, and Lysanias tetrarch of Abilene, in the high-priesthood of Annas and Caiaphas, the word of God came to John the son of Zechariah.* (Luke 3.1f)

This is not simply a matter of chronology. There is a sense in which the entire context of the Roman world is seen as propitious for the events of Christ's life. "In 29 BC [BCE] Octavian put an end to the internecine wars that had ravaged the Mediterranean world. Upon his glorious return to Rome the senate proclaimed him 'Augustus' and moved to erect an altar to *pax Augusta* [the peace of Augustus] in the Campus Martius. Virgil could exult over the 'baby boy' who, having received 'the life of gods', reigned 'o'er a world at peace' ... Augustus had a part to play in God's plan for salvation. His edict set the plan in motion, Jesus the Messiah was born appropriately in Bethlehem, and the angels sang the doxology that the *pax Augusta* was completed [complemented] by the *pax Christi* [the peace of Christ]. 'Peace on earth' was God's good news brought to people of good will through the birth of a baby boy."[1]

Luke as a writer

Luke is a cultivated writer, familiar with classical and Hellenistic literature and at least as well-versed in the stories and theological ideas of the Old Testament. He seems to be strongly influenced by both classical and Hebraic traditions, and he makes a major contribution by his creative synthesis of these cultures in his writings. The prologue to the gospel is written in a well-balanced classical form:

> *Inasmuch as many have undertaken to compile a narrative of the things which have been accomplished among us, just as they were delivered to us by those who from the beginning were eyewitnesses and ministers of the word, it seemed good to me also, having followed all things closely for some time past, to write an orderly account for you, most excellent Theophilus, that you may know the truth concerning the things of which you have been informed.* (Luke 1.1–4)

We should probably take the author's own account of his purpose, as expressed in this prologue, more seriously than scholars have sometimes done. Luke very clearly locates himself in the third generation (1.3). He looks back systematically on the process of gospel tradition – eyewitnesses (1.2), compilers of narratives (1.1), and finally his own orderly composition. He wishes this to be his contribution, representing the tradition for his generation. He is the steward of that tradition, but his role is not simply that of a mechanical transmitter of information. He has a creative role, in reflecting on the nature of the tradition and defining his own standpoint within that chain of tradition.

Luke's recognition of his predecessors in the gospel tradition is clear, especially when we can compare his work with other gospels and their source materials. In the Acts, he is much more of an innovator, "inventing" the idea of church history and producing his own original pattern of material about the church. This difference between the circumstances of the two volumes of the single work (Luke–Acts) is demonstrated by the difference between the prologue of the gospel and the prologue of Acts. Again it is Theophilus who is addressed, but there is no reference in Acts to the author's attitude to any previous accounts. The preface serves to remind us of the literary connection between the gospel and Acts, and of its theological continuity but this is all Luke can say by way of formal introduction:

> *In the first book, O Theophilus, I have dealt with all that Jesus began to do and teach, until the day when he was taken up, after he had given commandment through the Holy Spirit to the apostles whom he had chosen.* (Acts 1.1–2)

Available source material

The prologue of each volume of this two-volume work shows that in one important respect Luke and Acts should be approached differently.

Marc Chagall *White Crucifixion* (1938). The bearded figure of the prophet Christ (in the tradition of Russian icons) is seen in the context of a Jewish disaster that was prophesied. This is a political work of art, painted in response to Hitler's persecution of Jews in Eastern Europe.

Although in both cases we are concerned with the writer's perspectives and the situation of his community, the means are different. In his gospel, Luke uses Mark, substantial material common to Matthew, and some sources of his own but there is no agreement about Luke's sources for Acts.

Some scholars see the speeches and sermons of Acts, which can be detached from the narrative, as valuable, independent source material. Others believe that ancient historians normally represented as speeches what people were likely, or ought, to have said. One section of the story of Paul sounds like eyewitness material because it uses the first person plural pronoun in the narrative. This could be from Luke's own travel diary, or be a fictional device to heighten the sense of immediacy. There may have been sources, but it is at present impossible to identify them because much is due to Luke's own creative treatment. One theory, now widely disregarded, suggested that the first part of Acts (until Paul becomes central to the narrative) was derived from two sources maintained in the church archives of Jerusalem and Antioch and that because these sources were combined,

Jerusalem as seen from across the Kidron valley. The Dome of the Rock marks the site of the Temple. The Golden Gate is towards the right, in the foreground.

below *The Destruction of the Temple by Titus* (70 CE): painting by David Roberts, 1848. The Jewish historian Josephus vividly described the destruction of Jerusalem in *Jewish War* books 5 and 6.

The modern city and landscape of Jerusalem.

some events were recounted more than once. It is, however, improbable that the churches would keep archives of this kind in the early years of their existence. What is important is that in Acts (as much as, or more than, in the gospel) the extent of Luke's contribution should be ascertained and the themes which are characteristic of him identified.

The design of the Acts of the Apostles

A programmatic statement of the contents and structure of Luke's second volume occurs in Acts 1.8:

> *You shall receive power when the Holy Spirit has come upon you; and you shall be my witnesses in Jerusalem and in all Judea and Samaria and to the end of the earth.*

This describes a kind of "ripple effect", whereby the movement travelled across the Mediterranean sea from Jerusalem and reached a farther shore at Rome. This is often taken as an historically accurate account of the outreach of the early church. Under modern critical scrutiny it seems less likely to be authentic, but Luke intended it to be both an historical and a theological account of the progress of the gospel. It describes a programme, regarded as established by Jesus himself, of mission to the whole world and not just for God's chosen people Israel. Acts 1.8 is in this sense a summary of the book.

Jerusalem ancient and modern: **left** the line of an ancient street, leading to the traditional site of Caiaphas' house; **right** a modern street scene.

The Jerusalem connection

The initial location of Acts in *Jerusalem* establishes a strong link with the gospel of Luke, reinforced by an overlap of narrative material. Jerusalem is the scene of the death of Jesus, of his Resurrection appearances to the disciples, and thirdly the setting of his Ascension. In the second and third respects we find a strong contrast with the gospels of Mark and Matthew which are not explicit about this kind of literal ascension, and which point to Galilee not Jerusalem as the scene of appearances of the risen Christ. For Acts it is in Jerusalem that the disciples wait and receive the promised gift of the Spirit. Jerusalem is therefore the setting for the first seven chapters of Acts. The early Christians are inspired to start their missionary activity in the place where Jesus' earthly ministry had ended.

Judea and Samaria

In Acts 8.1 we read:

> On that day a great persecution arose against the church in Jerusalem; and they were all scattered throughout the region of Judea and Samaria, except the apostles.

Roman coin marking the capture of Judaea and Jerusalem, issued by Titus in 71 CE.

This exception of the apostles is a curious aside. In all probability the twelve remained in the theologically important centre of Jerusalem, despite persecution, because of their obedience to Jesus' original commission. The reference to a general dispersion to *Judea and Samaria* is further substantiated by the particular statement in 8.5: "Philip went down to a city of Samaria and proclaimed to them the Christ". The regions of Judea and Samaria are thus the setting for chapters 8 and 9 of Acts.

And to the end of the earth

The third stage of the programme – "*and to the end of the earth*" – covers much of the Mediterranean world. Acts 10–28 describes the progress from Caesarea to Rome in the journeys of Peter and of Paul. Rome, as the centre of the Empire and the heart of the Mediterranean world, is a fitting goal for the Acts of the Apostles: "the victory of the word of God, Paul at Rome, the climax of the gospel, the end of the Acts"[2]. Acts 28.30f is not an anti-climax after all the trials and the shipwreck. It is true that the story of the shipwreck "amounted to a theological *tour de force* in the eyes of ancient readers. Paul was put to the test by forces and exigencies far more dreaded than the requirements of a human law court, and since [by winning through] he had been found guiltless, what need was there to recount the outcome of his appeal?"[3] But whatever the reason for Luke's not revealing the legal verdict on Paul, he nevertheless provides a triumphant conclusion, the true objective of this theological history, namely that the gospel should be preached unhindered in the city of Rome itself. Christianity has reached the capital city of the world:

Pentecost: the descent of the dove and the tongues of fire upon the apostles (Acts 2), as depicted in the Rabula Codex, completed at Zagba in 586 CE. Unlike the narrative of Acts, the mother of Jesus plays a central part.

And Paul lived there two whole years at his own expense, and welcomed all who came to him, preaching the kingdom of God and teaching about the Lord Jesus Christ quite openly and unhindered. (28.30–31)

Paul, in his own writing, regards Rome (however important to him) merely as a staging post. In Romans 15.28 he writes to the Roman Christians: "I shall go on by way of you to Spain". In terms of theological importance within the strategy of the Christian mission it was Paul's visit to Jerusalem with aid for the saints which for him provided the decisive (eschatological) moment. Luke sees things differently and presents Rome as Paul's final goal. Similarly we should note the contrast between *Acts* and Homer's great epic *Odyssey*, with which it is sometimes compared. Homer is concerned with the great travels and adventures of Odysseus on his return from the Trojan war. Luke tells the stories of Paul's epic missionary journeys. But in Homer's scheme the return of the wanderer to his home and to Penelope (though it raises other conflicts) is much less important than the journeying. While for Luke the arrival in Rome is all-important and the journeys are means to that end.

Ancient historians

Writing to a programme such as Acts 1.8 is certainly not expected in modern history, which sets standards of scientific precision and critical method but it is not necessarily incompatible with ancient standards and expectations of written history. A great German historian of the 1920s, Eduard Meyer, called Luke the one great historian between Polybius (the last of the classical Greek historians) and Eusebius (the first great ecclesiastical historian of Christianity). Examples from Greek and Latin, Jewish and Christian history illustrate the nature of historical writing in Luke's time.

Classical historians

The Greek writer Lucian in the second century CE produced a tract *On Writing History*:

The one aim and goal of history is to be useful; and this can result only from its truth. The one task of the historian is to describe things exactly as they happened.

Lucian learned his lesson, his passion for truth, from Thucydides, who aimed to write history not for passing entertainment but for permanent usefulness. The historian must aim at accuracy and usefulness in order that, when circumstances recur, men have the lesson of the past to teach them how to act in the modern crisis. This is a lofty ideal, but Lucian does not imply that all historians worked in this way. Rather he attacks his own contemporaries who emphasize the agreeable at the expense of the useful: "such are the

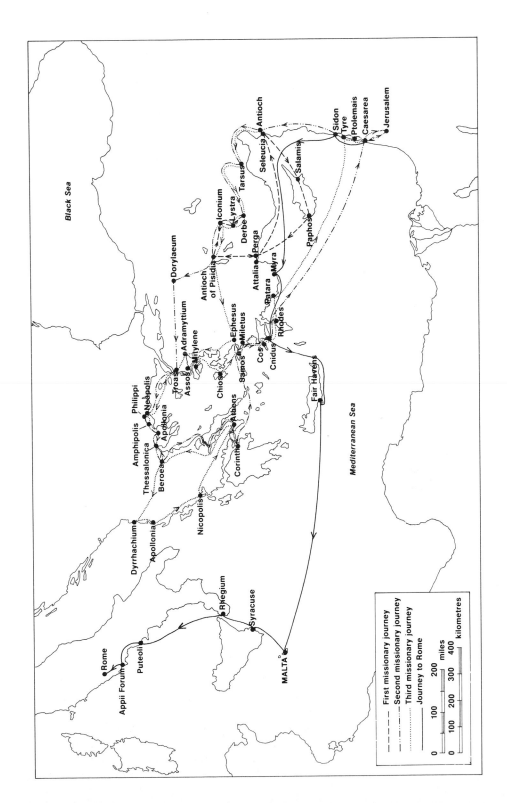

MAP 3 Paul's missionary journeys.

majority of historians who serve the present moment, their own interest, and the profit they hope to get from history".

It is not just a matter of a simple distinction between historians who write to please, and historians who write for the sake of truth. Few historians are uninfluenced by some doctrine or philosophy of history: Lucian and Thucydides both imply a cyclic view of history, so that their readers are ready to cope with these events when they recur. It is also possible to write history in the interests of a cause for which one is campaigning; one can distort the narrative of events in such a way as to illustrate more effectively the moral which one wishes to draw. So the Roman historian Livy can commend the national cause:

> *Whatever may come of my work, I shall at least have the joy of having played my part in perpetuating the memory of the finest people in the world; and if in the midst of so great a multitude of writers my fame remains in obscurity, I shall console myself with the glory and the greatness of those who shall eclipse my repute.*

Livy also advocates a moral purpose in writing history:

> *This is the most wholesome and fruitful effect of the study of history: you have in front of you real examples of every kind of behaviour, real examples embodied in most conspicuous form: from these you can take, both for yourself and for the state, ideals at which to aim; you can learn also what to avoid because it is infamous either in its conception or in its issue.*

Because Livy's primary concern is to promote these two causes, he does not distinguish too precisely between history and edifying legend.

Another Roman historian, Tacitus, is of particular interest to those who study early Christianity. Tacitus wrote *Annals* of the early Roman emperors, and described how Nero reacted to the fire of Rome. The historian suggests that he made unpopular Christians into scapegoats, to divert suspicion from himself. Tacitus appears more of a rationalist and less of a moralist than Livy. He did not hesitate to rewrite the record of an emperor's speech, to say what he himself thought appropriate. In his characteristically succinct narratives, while he appears to be giving the facts straightforwardly, he allows his political prejudice to present facts with some distortion, or suggest an alternative construction by means of innuendo.

Jewish historians

Luke also very clearly recalls the Jewish tradition of writing history, and looking at the course of events from a religious standpoint. The historical tradition in Israel goes back at least as far as the court history of king David, with its narrative of the reign of David and the accession of Solomon (2 Samuel 7–20; 1 Kings 1–2). This Jewish tradition persists through and beyond the Old Testament and can be seen in the Greek form of the later Books of the Maccabees. Again, within this tradition, Josephus was a Jewish

Bust of the emperor Nero (Capitoline Museum, Rome).

historian in the first century CE who wrote history to a classical Greek (Thucydidean) pattern. His account of the Jewish War in which he participated contains much eyewitness material. His work is specially informative because of his own involvement, but it is also distorted because of his own personal perspectives. In his introduction he promises to be impartial, but it is clear that his work is written from an apologetic standpoint.

Josephus is a Jew trying to gain the sympathy of his Roman readers; he minimizes or omits all that might offend Roman susceptibilities. Here is an example of his interpretation of the fall of Jerusalem, in which theological and apologetic instincts are combined.

> *In these events we may signally discern at one and the same time both the power of God over unholy men* [the Jewish leaders of the revolt whom he called "tyrants"] *and also the fortune of the Romans. For the tyrants stripped themselves of their security and descended of their own accord from those towers, in which they could never have been overcome by force; while the Romans, after all the toil expended over weaker walls, mastered by the gift of fortune those that were impregnable to their artillery.*

When Josephus speaks about the "fortune" of the Romans he does not just mean good luck; in Roman religious terms this is their "destiny" or divine guidance, the spirit of Rome. The interpretation makes sense in terms both of Jewish theology and of Roman imperial philosophy. Josephus has taken the bold step of introducing, into conventional "secular" history, the Jewish notion that God has a direct role within the historical process.

Josephus' other works, notably the *Antiquities of the Jews*, also have clear apologetic motives. He demonstrates the antiquity of the Jewish faith, and tries to prove the unique validity of Jewish conceptions of history, in terms intelligible to a secular readership. Josephus also wrote an "autobiographical" and polemical appendix to the *Antiquities* usually entitled *Life*. "His career embodies in a distinct way the principal themes and conflicts of the Roman Middle East during this period: the tension between local patriotism and the claims of the imperial order, between native culture and the allure of Greco–Roman civilisation, between Semitic languages and Greek, between pragmatic flexibility and committed sectarianism, between class loyalty and group loyalty."[4] In many respects there are close resemblances between Josephus and Luke, their situations, the ways in which they embraced and related to two cultures, and their uses of historical writing for these ends.

Christian historians

To look extensively at Christian (as opposed to classical or Jewish) traditions of writing history would demand an examination of writers in later centuries, perhaps as far as St Augustine of Hippo. It has been said that Luke's work made the second century CE portrayals of church history seem old-fashioned even before they appeared. This was because such works did not present history for its own sake but only as a case for Christianity. By

MAP 4 Palestine in the Jewish War.

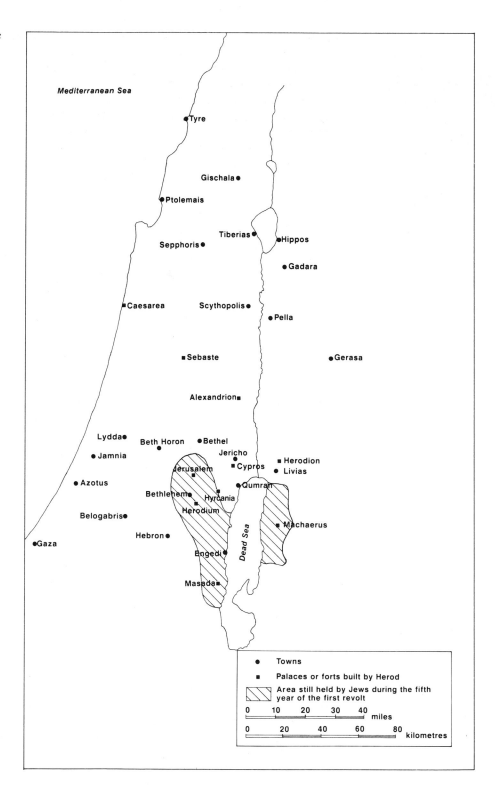

Mediterranean Sea

Tyre

Gischala

Ptolemais

Tiberias Hippos

Sepphoris Gadara

Caesarea Scythopolis

Pella

Sebaste

Gerasa

Alexandrion

Lydda Beth Horon Bethel

Jamnia Jericho

Herodion

Jerusalem Cypros

Livias

Azotus Qumran

Bethlehem Hyrcania

Belogabris Herodium

Machaerus

Hebron

Gaza

Engedi

Dead Sea

Masada

● Towns

■ Palaces or forts built by Herod

Area still held by Jews during the fifth year of the first revolt

0 10 20 30 40 miles

0 20 40 60 80 kilometres

contrast, the author of Acts appears to have been intellectually closer to Eusebius in the fourth century. For a very long time Christian history and classical (Greek and Roman) history had little in common, and classical history remained a pagan preserve.

Christians did concern themselves with a particular group of historical events associated with Jesus of Nazareth, but new converts from paganism did not really know where the history of Jesus fitted in with their own history (although they might have been helped to some extent by comparative frameworks of dates). Quite a different order of historical activity was the tradition of ecclesiastical history developed by Eusebius; clearly this was a more esoteric tradition of church-based studies bred within the church. Finally it was Augustine who became conscious of the need for a new kind of Christian historical apologetic, where Christians and pagans could meet on common ground and the same time-scale, so he commissioned from Orosius a work called the *Seven books of histories against the pagans*, but this happened as late as the fifth century CE.

The nature of Luke's theology of history

These comparisons between historical writings in different traditions attempt to define what kind of history Luke's work is. The question of what kind of theology, or theological history, it is can be answered on the basis of what was said earlier about the significance of Luke's two volumes in relation to the established "one-volume" gospel. Luke–Acts is a major development from the early Christian message of eschatological crisis. The writer offers a schematized history of salvation, a religious history (not exclusively a church history) which interlocks with key events in the history of the Roman world. Like its Old Testament predecessors this is often referred to by the German theological term *Heilsgeschichte*, which simply means "salvation history". Luke's particular pattern was first described in detail by a German scholar (Hans Conzelmann) in 1954; the title of his book would translate literally into English as "The Middle of Time". For the significance of this title we need to look at the scheme. There are three stages in Luke's history, which can be set out as follows:

1 The time of Israel, of the Old Testament, the Law and the prophets. See Luke 16.16: "The law and the prophets were until John [the Baptist]; since then the good news of the kingdom of God is preached."

2 The middle of time, the time of Jesus' ministry, which anticipates in a real but preliminary way the coming salvation. The nature of this is described in such texts as Luke 4.16ff, Acts 10.38: "how God anointed Jesus of Nazareth with the Holy Spirit and with power; how he went about doing good and healing all that were oppressed by the devil, for God was with him".

3 The time between Jesus' ministry and his Second Coming (Parousia), the time of the church and of the Spirit. This third age is the last age, but Luke does not say that it will be short. It is possible, by virtue of looking back to

the time of Jesus (the time of anticipation), also to look forward to the Parousia. The Parousia itself represents not a stage within the course of salvation history but the completion of it. It corresponds to the opposite pole, the very beginning of things, creation itself.

This provides a very useful overall guide to the structure of Luke–Acts. But it should be used critically and not regarded as the last word on the theological perspectives of Luke. It clearly attaches great significance to the time of the church, giving it great scope and not simply thinking of it as a moment of crisis. For Luke, those who find salvation in Christ (Acts 4.12) are members of a community which lives between the Ascension and the Parousia and which is directed by the Spirit. Thus Luke defines salvation as membership of the church in which the Spirit reigns.

This also provides a new perspective on the time of Jesus, regarded as a life in the past, but offering promises for the church and for the future. The traditions of the Old Testament period are seen as more important than one would expect in a writer for the Greco–Roman world. John the Baptist is a significant figure on the boundary between the Old Testament and Jesus. He stands clearly on the Old Testament side, as a prophet and preacher of repentance. He does not appear as Elijah, the expected forerunner of the new age which the Messiah will usher in, although Luke's sources regarded John in this way. Instead, Jesus himself seems to have some of the characteristics of Elijah as prophetic forerunner in Luke's picture.

The importance of prophecy (interpreting history)

The strong element of continuity, through these three stages represented in Luke's work, is the succession of prophecy. The "prophets" are categorized in three generations: the Old Testament prophets and John the Baptist; Jesus himself; the apostles and prophets of the church. "Just as it did not diminish reverence for Jesus to identify him as . . . prophet, so it did no damage to the authority of the apostles to describe their work in prophetic categories: 'I will send them prophets and apostles, some of whom they will kill and persecute' (Luke 11.49). Luke's organization of the traditions in both volumes is fully consistent with that prophecy. This may not seem to apply to the long circumstantial accounts of Paul's trip to Rome, although even the bizarre details of that trip verified, albeit in naive ways, Paul's gifts of charismatic discernment of hearts and his power to foretell the future (Acts 27.9, 22–6, 31, 34–6; 28.5, 8). However that may be, Paul's vocation as a prophet comes clearly to the fore in the closing paragraphs of Acts (28.23–28). Here Paul disclosed how Christ had fulfilled the hope of Israel, and he supported this disclosure with a reinterpretation of Scripture that provoked a dissension with Jews, which he explained in terms of the Holy Spirit's voice in Isaiah (parallel to Jesus' sermon at Nazareth). It was against this background that Paul defended the Gentile mission and witnessed to the presence of the kingdom as 'the salvation of God'. Luke saw alike in Paul's chains, in the blindness of Israel, and in the response of the Gentiles a fulfilment of Jesus' prophecy."[5]

right The Ascension of Christ, to which Luke refers explicitly in the gospel and Acts. This primitive representation comes from a Coptic tombstone from Egypt (5th century CE).

below Rome: the forum at dawn, showing the sacred way, the temple of Vesta, the arch of Titus (page 15), the temple of Castor and Pollux, and the Colosseum.

The Journeys of Paul: the Roman road, the Egnatian Way, near Philippi in northern Greece (Macedonia).

The Acropolis of Athens: this view of the Propylaea (the processional entrance) is seen from the hill of the Areopagus where Paul preached (Acts 17.19ff).

Thessalonica: in the modern town centre the Egnatian Way passes the Roman Arch of Galerius, built in 303 CE.

The location of Luke's church

To seek the location of the community for which Luke writes may appear to risk constricting such large matters in a localized setting, denying Luke's breadth of vision. Few people are likely to relate quite so positively to more than one culture as both Luke and Josephus did. It is not surprising that no one has been able to reduce Luke to one sociological setting. Most likely, Luke, who writes from a Pauline community, is an author who has had considerable experience in Christian communities. He addresses himself to the Christian world at large.

Indications of the kind of members of the community from which Luke is writing may lie in the special preaching material, unique to Luke in the gospels, which is found in the words of John the Baptist in Luke 3.10–14. John is represented as addressing ethical messages to three particular groups: the Jewish "crowd" or proletariat, the "tax-collectors" or local agents loyal to the Roman Empire, and the "soldiers" or army officials who are the guardians of imperial order. This is in addition to the sermon beginning "You brood of vipers" (3.7–9) which Luke shares with Matthew (3.7–10). In Matthew that is addressed, more convincingly, to the Jewish leaders, Pharisees and SADDUCEES.

Luke applied this sermon and the following message generally to the Jewish proletariat, among whom both John and Jesus historically made their initial appeal. For Luke's community, which still saw the mission in prophetic terms such as John the Baptist had used, the question of relations with the ordinary Jewish people was still important. But equally Luke takes a positive view of those who help to administer and defend the Roman Empire. This indicates well the twin perspectives of Israel and Rome which Luke strives to keep in balance for his Christian and potentially Christian readers.

The church and the world

To some extent Luke distinguished between the world outside and the people of God, that is the church. Circumstances forced him to do this and to frame some social and political directives for the people of God which took little account of the ways of the world, but his convictions about the universal relevance of the gospel and about God as the God of all history would have inhibited the drawing of any rigid and final distinctions between church and world. Potentially everyone was intended to do God's will. As Peter says in Acts 10.34f: "Truly I perceive that God shows no partiality, but in every nation any one who fears him and does what is right is acceptable to him". A symbolic example is the parable of the Good Samaritan (Luke 10.30–7), which follows this argument to its limits. The answer to the question "Who is my neighbour?" was intended to be an open one.

Since the church was apparently going to continue its earthly existence within the political context of the Roman Empire, there were two possible ways of reacting to the situation – total withdrawal damning society to an

The elaborately decorated Altar of the Augustan Peace (13–9 BCE), set up in Rome by the emperor Augustus to symbolize his restoration of peace to the Roman empire.

apocalyptic hell or some accommodation to the political, cultural, and social context for the sake of further church expansion.[6] Luke's choice of the second option, in an attitude of "positive thinking" and "creative theological accommodation", is evident throughout his work. For example, Luke (unlike Josephus) takes a positive view of the Augustan census associated with the time of Christ's birth. "Organized government had at last come to Judaea... The beginning of a new order for the holy land under Caesar Augustus also marks the beginning of a new order for the holy people under Jesus Christ. Luke had no intention of positing an affinity between the rise of the Zealots and the birth of Jesus, nor of challenging the ideal of *pax Augusta*. Rather, the 'world-wide' decree which Luke records united the world under a universal politic of peace, and it provided a fitting birth announcement for him who would found a universal religion of peace."[7]

Even politicians obey God

"God stands behind all human institutions as the power who delegates all authority."[8] This is the lesson which is amply demonstrated in Israel's "history of salvation", the foundation on which Luke bases his Christian historical perspective. Not only is Israel in the palm of God's hand, he is all too aware of the good and bad actions which fit his plan, but even Israel's adversaries, the Pharaohs of Egypt, the armies of Assyria, the Babylonian conquerors, and Cyrus, king of Persia, are all in their time the agents of Israel's God, implementing his purposes. Thus, from Luke's point of view, all political situations serve God's purpose, and no political force (even the might of the Roman Empire) can overcome God's plan. A typical expression of this view can be found in the apostles' speech of Acts 4.27–8:

> *For truly in this city* [Jerusalem] *there were gathered together against thy holy servant Jesus, whom thou* [God] *didst anoint, both Herod and Pontius Pilate, with the Gentiles and the peoples of Israel, to do whatever thy* [God's] *hand and thy plan had predestined to take place.*

The Passion and death of Jesus are explicitly stated to be necessary (because they are God's will), to be carried out by the world's representatives as God's agents, and to be seen as the precise fulfilment of prophecy (here interpreted in the words of Psalm 2.1–2 and not just the prophetic books of the Old Testament).

There are enormous problems for modern readers in this "history of salvation" perspective, when it is carried to such lengths of determinism and predestination. In one sense it is seeing events with the benefit of a particular religious hindsight, and therefore being able to identify those prophecies which are fulfilled in the events. There soon also develops a doctrinal and ethical corollary for future behaviour: activity and initiatives are unnecessary, since the outcome has already been determined by God, whose agents have no choice but to act. One can see these kinds of problems more sharply, if one focusses on modern events and their consequences (e.g. the Holocaust in Nazi Germany, or the foundation of the modern state of Israel) seen from the religious point of view of one group of participants.

Luke's two-volume work has pushed this "salvation history" perspective to its limits. He emphasizes the necessity of the fulfilment of prophecy and the implementation of God's plan by the world powers. When viewed more critically, Luke's theological claim for God's power may lack rational authority. It is like the conclusion to which Job is forced, to see great events as the responsibility of an inscrutable God whose ways are not our ways and whose thoughts are not our thoughts.

Because Luke does seem to go to the lengths of acknowledging that those who act as God's agents are not ultimately responsible for their own actions, he is then able to suggest that those who put Christ to death are thereby exonerated. In Luke's account the Romans are not actually responsible for Jesus' death, but rather acknowledge his innocence; and the Jews, who are responsible, are ultimately forgiven. (See Luke 23.34; Acts 7.60; 3.17; 13.27.) What God wills, and what fulfils the prophecy, also appears to the outside observer tò be an accident (in human terms) for which nobody is in the least account responsible. God alone brought about the death of Jesus (all others being but unwitting tools – with some help from Satan [Luke 22.3]), for the sake of his age-long, deep-laid purposes of salvation.

Luke's community in relation to Judaism

At its most extreme, the position of Luke–Acts could be characterized as anti-Semitic and pro-Roman. To substantiate the charge of anti-Semitism one would have to say that the enemies of Jesus were not merely individuals or groups who ignorantly or selfishly opposed Jesus and engineered his death, but that they were so prejudiced, because they were Jews, that they put to death the one who came in the name of the God they claimed to serve. The story of the church was the story of the realization of Christianity as the faith for the Gentiles and the obliteration of the traces of the Jewish context in which the faith originated.

Inscription recording the name of Pontius Pilate (in the second line) found on the shore at Caesarea, now in the Israel Museum in Jerusalem.

A small boy and other Jews being arrested by German soldiers in the Warsaw ghetto 1943. This classic photograph from World War Two, symbolic of anti-semitism, was used as evidence in the trials at Nuremberg.

Such an attitude of anti-Semitism might well have arisen at the end of the first century CE in Christian circles responding to the intense pressures of Jewish propaganda. Judaism was reconstituted and accepted, while potential Christians might feel especially vulnerable in what was a persecuted and marginalised situation. "The onset of persecution, or even of sustained psychological pressure from the Jews through dispute over the meaning of the scriptures and the credibility of a crucified Messiah, will have shaken many people's confidence in their faith. How could non-Jews hope to find any value in something which has its roots in Judaism, yet seems to be repudiated by the leaders of the Jews? This problem is not unique to Luke . . . In an earlier form, it also lies behind Paul's Epistle to the Romans . . . The chief difference between Paul's situation and Luke's is that the breach with Judaism is now wider and deeper: for Luke there is apparently no longer any reason to hope that the Jews as a whole will accept the gospel."[9]

Hostility to the Jewish leaders

The Jewish religious leaders in Luke–Acts are enemies of Jesus and the church. In several ways the Lucan account exceptionally heightens this impression. The Jewish authorities themselves make the arrest of Jesus (Luke 22.52). The "chief priests and scribes" are consistently those who bring the accusations (22.66; 23.10). The charges made before Pilate (23.2) are a uniquely political indictment: disturbing the peace, forbidding payment of tribute to Caesar, and proclaiming himself as king. It sounds as if the charge of blasphemy, discussed at the Jewish trial, has been suppressed; in place of it new charges have been produced, which are to Luke's readers patently false, and seem designed to be the kind of charges on which the Roman procurator might convict. In fact their very absurdity supports Pilate's judgement of Jesus' innocence. But the voices of the Jewish leaders prevail (23.23) against the threefold declaration of innocence; by emphasizing the authority's attempts to release Jesus, Luke also strengthens the role of the Jews in bringing about his death. And finally Luke gives the impression that the Jews actually carried out the crucifixion (23.25–26).

Luke treats the Jewish officials negatively in the Passion narrative. This is particularly true of the chief priests, members of the Sadducee party (the religious conservatives within Judaism), who are in the centre of the stage. On the other hand the more radical Pharisees are treated more positively. There is no explicit indication of their involvement in the Passion narrative, and particularly in the narratives of Acts they are sometimes more favourably regarded. (See Gamaliel in Acts 5.34–39; Paul's perhaps opportunist reference to Pharisaism in Acts 23.6–10; and Paul's defence before Agrippa in Acts 26.4–8 – "on trial for the hope of Israel"; cf. 28.20.)

It is doubtless significant that in Luke's situation, after the fall of Jerusalem in 70 CE, it was the Pharisees who were the relevant party to represent and reconstitute Judaism. They were the ones with whom Christianity would have to deal. And just as some Jews were the accusers of Jesus, and went on accusing the Christians, there were also some Jews who intervened positively, or at least showed signs of pity and support, for Jesus and for the Christians. Among the ordinary people there were women of Jerusalem who wept for Jesus (Luke 23.27); and the crowd's response to the crucifixion was to return home "beating their breasts" (23.48). Such an act of repentance by those on the sidelines would indicate the possibility of forgiveness rather than a blanket (or a general) condemnation for those implicated.

The wider concern for Israel

A case has not been made for a total judgement against Judaism, characteristic of anti-Semitism. Rather the judgement has been selective, concerned with particular actions and attitudes, but a judgement expressed with all the power and trenchancy of the Old Testament prophets (who spoke from within the system). In that sense it seems more a critique of Israel as the people of God, rather than an outright denial of her birthright. This fits better with Luke's positive and extensive use of the traditions of Israel's salvation history, his sense of God's all-embracing purpose, and his indication that God will exonerate those involved as hapless accessories in the furtherance of his plan. Luke is not denying the idea of Israel as God's people, rather drastically redefining her terms of reference, and her membership (so as to include the Gentiles as of right). He reminds his readers of the proven dangers in working with a much narrower definition and resisting new and prophetic insights. In this respect alone, Israel of old, and the more militant Judaism of Luke's day, stands condemned.

The rejection of the gospel by Israel posed a major problem for Theophilus and the circle of readers he represents. Luke–Acts argues that this rejection was not a catastrophe but a fulfilment of God's plan and purpose. The death of Christ, the sufferings of the Old Testament prophets and the experiences of Christian apostles are instances of the rejection of God's spokesmen by those who are supposed to be God's people. (Luke addresses the parable in Luke 20.9–18 to "the people" instead of the chief priests and scribes with whom Jesus is engaged in controversy. They still react to the implications of the parable – 20.19 – but Luke's aim is to help the wider audience of the Jewish people understand.) There is a struggle taking place *within* the people of God. This is the spur and the justification for the missionary activity of the gospel, seen within God's total plan for his people.

Luke's larger context, his concern for the wider Jewish audience as the continuity of the people of God, can also be seen in the way he tells the story of the experience of the Holy Spirit at Pentecost in Acts 2.5ff:

> *Now there were dwelling in Jerusalem* Jews, *devout men from every nation under heaven. And at this sound* [the wind and the speaking in tongues] *the multitude came together, and they were bewildered, because each one heard them speaking in his own language.*

Luke proceeds to list the range of languages. But this is not a universal Gentile audience: Luke calls them "Jews and proselytes [Jewish converts]" (2.10), and the word he uses for "multitude" in 2.6 denotes the full assembly of Israel in the last days. (In the same terms the Jewish sect at Qumran saw themselves as standing for the whole Israel.) In Acts this variety of tongues makes an address of ultimate significance to the Diaspora (Israel as scattered through the Roman world). The audience at Pentecost is nothing other than Greater Israel:

> *Let all the house of Israel therefore know assuredly that God has made him both Lord and Christ, this Jesus whom you crucified.* (2.36)

This verse brings together both aspects of the struggle for and within Israel, both the accusation and the evangelistic communication.

The real, as well as the symbolic, importance of Israel, and its history of salvation, is evident for Luke. Before the event of Pentecost, the account is at pains to restore the full total of twelve apostles (representing the twelve tribes of Israel), which was diminished by Judas' betrayal. (See Acts 1.13–26 in relation to Luke 6.14–16; in both texts the representative community is established before the definitive sermon.) Even though, in terms of the mission, Luke thinks of more than twelve missioners, witnesses or apostles, the pattern is established by the gospel precedents (Luke 9.1 and 10.1). Beyond the twelve, the seventy (or the seventy-two) represent Greater Israel (the Diaspora). The number is the traditional total of the translators involved in the Bible of the Dispersion, the Greek translation of the Old Testament (the Septuagint). It is the total of the elders chosen to assist Moses in the late tradition of Numbers 11.16, and the symbolic number of the nations of the earth in the genealogy from Noah in Genesis 10. Luke, who saw the story of Pentecost as a reversal of the effect of the tower of Babel (Genesis 11.9), builds his picture of the Christian mission upon the way that Israel had testified to her faith throughout the known world.

Luke in relation to the Roman Empire

While Luke treats selected Jews (the Jewish leaders) very negatively within his narrative, he does not condemn all Jews. He also treats named Romans very favourably and positively. The most famous of these is Pontius Pilate, who attests Jesus' innocence and makes efforts to free him. The first recorded Gentile convert to Christianity is the Roman centurion, Cornelius (Acts 10.1–11.18). There is another very favourable picture of a centurion in Luke 7.1–10. Here Luke notes the imperial virtues of friendship, respect for authority, and piety ("not even in Israel have I found such faith"–7.9). And Sergius Paulus, the proconsul at Paphos on Cyprus, becomes a believer as a result of witnessing Paul's cursing of Elymas the magician (Acts 13.6–12).

In Luke's narrative Roman citizenship is highly regarded and provokes anxiety among those who infringe its rights (Acts 16.35–40; 22.22–29). There is great concern for Roman law and order (see Acts 19.40). Gallio, the proconsul of Achaia (the Roman province of Greece), rests his refusal to adjudicate on the Jewish attacks against Paul upon the basis of Roman law: "If it were a matter of wrongdoing or vicious crime, I should have reason to bear with you, O Jews; but since it is a matter of questions about words and names and your own law, see to it yourselves" (Acts 18.14–15). The Roman tribune, Claudius Lysias, is responsible for rescuing Paul from the Jewish mob on more than one occasion (Acts 21.27–36; 23.27; 23.9–10, 12–22). The procurator Felix is well informed, if somewhat corrupt, and seems to recognize Paul's innocence (Acts 24.22–27). Roman law again protects Paul against the Jews when he appeals to Caesar through Porcius Festus (Acts 25.11–12).

On the way to Rome the Roman centurion Julius of the Augustan cohort treats Paul kindly and fairly (Acts 27.1–3, 42–43). This is an impressive list, to which we should probably add the freedom which Paul enjoyed to preach and teach in Rome itself.

With examples such as these, Luke seems to have been saying that "the activity of Christians and the tenets of their religion create no difficulty for a sensible, reasonable system of government. Only an irrational government or people, led by religious prejudice and/or hatred, could find fault with Christianity. In any nation ruled by reason, Christians make good citizens."[10] But how far can we press this picture of Luke, like Josephus, making a good case for his imperial patrons? While Josephus says that the majority in Judaism are not really rebellious, Luke is saying that the Roman administrators need have no fear that Christianity is a subversive influence.

The dilemma of Luke's apologetic

Part of Luke's problem would be that he has to present two faces at once within his narrative. He needs to demonstrate the essential continuity of Christianity with Israel as heir to the promises of salvation history. He is not condemning Greater Israel, but rather indicating the exoneration of the

Roman coin (sestertius) issued under emperor Nero in 64–66 CE to commemorate the rebuilding of the port of Ostia on the Tiber. The reverse shows ships in the harbour surrounded by colonnaded warehouses. The figure of Neptune is at the bottom.

> The themes in Luke's apology (Luke–Acts) according to Hans
> Conzelmann
>
> Two themes side by side (especially in the Passion narrative):
> A: Dogmatic theme that suffering is "necessary" in the divine plan
> B: "Historical" reconstruction which makes the Romans innocent (B.1)
> the Jews guilty (B.2)
> The consequences are: B.1: The Romans appreciate the non-political
> character of the gospel
> and therefore: B.2: Jewish terms are interpreted by Luke in a non-
> political sense (e.g. Messiah = Son of God) contrary to the Jewish
> understanding
>
> As a result Luke produces (especially in the Passion narrative):
> A threefold demonstration of the "new" facts of the case:
> 1 The Jews must be telling lies
> 2 The Romans objectively define the legal position
> 3 The client ruler (e.g. Herod) owing allegiance to Rome agrees with the
> findings of the Roman representative.
>
> (Hans Conzelmann, *The Theology of Saint Luke* 1960, pp. 140f)

Jewish leaders, as God's agents in the death of Christ. At the same time Luke needs to distance Christianity from Israel for the benefit of his politically sensitive readers. Unlike the Judaism which brought about the costly Jewish War (despite the fact that the faith was permitted and its peculiarities tolerated in the Empire), Christianity was neither rebellious nor legalistic, and was widely recognized as normal and supportive of good government. The Christians did not set themselves up as critics of Rome's political supremacy.

In these matters both Jesus and Paul were acknowledged by Roman administrators to be totally innocent. In the death of Jesus, and in subsequent disturbances in the Empire, the fault lay with Jewish troublemakers who had incited protest and discontent. Christians blamed the Jewish agitators, and not the Romans, for the crucifixion of Christ. It was not simply that Christians took an exalted view of the divine necessity for Christ's death, which would exonerate the executioners, but that it actually was the Jews and not the Romans who carried out the critical stages of the process to eliminate Jesus.

The writer of Acts is concerned to present Paul's case – which to him is the case for Christianity itself – as completely innocuous from the viewpoint of Imperial Rome. In Acts 28.17–19 Paul is made to say that the Romans – after having investigated the charges preferred against him – wished to set him free, but were hindered from so doing by Jewish opposition. One might argue whether Paul's defence has points of reference unique to him, or whether he is being tried as the representative Christian. If Paul had already been executed in Rome and the author of Acts came from a Pauline community which was under attack because of this event and Paul's teaching, a defence of Paul himself would not be out of place. It is clear, however, that Paul's defence is only the last section of a sustained apologetic, running through the whole of Luke–Acts, and that what happens to Paul is in fact predicted for all Christians. (See Luke 21.12–19 in relation to Acts 26.)

The lessons of Thessalonica

One text which illustrates the possibilities of the Lucan apologetic best of all is the account of the incident in Thessalonica, where an uproar is instigated by Jews from the synagogue at which Paul had been teaching (Acts 17.1–9). If this were the true nature and extent of Paul's mission here, it would certainly call into question what we see of the church in Paul's own Thessalonian correspondence. It is unlikely that such a church could be founded on the basis of three weeks' teaching in the synagogue, so perhaps the account is contrived to present the Jews as troublemakers and the Christians as victims. Luke invites the reader to consider the representation of the Christian gospel as subversive. ("These men who have turned the world upside down have come here also" – 17.6). It is obvious from this particular incident, as well as from the whole tenor of the Acts narrative, that the accusation is transparently false, and that it has been deliberately framed by the Jews to cause trouble for Paul and Silas. There is no evidence that the Christians "are all acting against the decrees of Caesar, saying that there is another king, Jesus" (17.7), any more than there was evidence in Luke's gospel to substantiate the political charges against Jesus in Luke 23.2. The account of the Thessalonica episode is so effective because it will outrage the reader at the injustice of it all; the audience can draw its own conclusions.

Luke's work as an apology

However important this theme of the innocence of Christians, like the innocence of Christ, is for Luke, it is unlikely that such an apology and defence is the sole reason for Luke's work. It is not very plausible that the main audience of Luke–Acts was the officialdom of the Roman Empire, whoever Theophilus was and whatever his job in the imperial administration might have been.

This argument has been even more strongly expressed. Acts "was not addressed to the Emperor, with the intention of proving the political harmlessness of Christianity in general and Paul in particular; a few passages might be construed to serve this purpose, but to suggest that the book as a whole should be taken in this way is absurd. No Roman official would ever have filtered out so much of what to him would be theological and ecclesiastical rubbish in order to reach so tiny a grain of relevant apology."[11] So, even if the moral of Acts 17.1–9 is self-evident, it is unlikely that an administrator would have read as far as this.

Luke's attitude to existing government

It is also possible that some passages in Luke–Acts would have raised genuine, rather than fabricated, suspicions about Christianity. Jesus' teachings and actions might be said to have revolutionary consequences by advocating a new social order, and Jesus certainly did not defer to existing (Jewish) authorities. On the other hand, just because Christianity was *ultimately* a revolutionary faith and could subject existing social patterns to fundamental critical scrutiny, this did not mean that all Christians intended to be politically subversive. And just because Luke's social concerns, and his bias to the poor and disadvantaged, are now being quoted as key texts for Liberation Theology, this does not mean that Luke himself had the intention of writing a "Marxist" political manifesto.

A distinction must be made between long-term consequences and results (such as the perception that ultimately Christianity entails a new social order), and the immediate intentions of the writer and his community. The latter, rather importantly, includes the apologetic concern about living co-operatively and at peace with the Roman administration (as we have recognized this in Luke's work). Even a conservative political programme can have radical implications for future generations.

The evidence for the identification of opponents in Luke–Acts, the question of anti-Semitism, and the generally favourable attitude to the Romans in the narratives suggest that two issues are particularly important for Luke. One is the continuity of the traditions of Israel in the history of salvation; this must be retained but with a prophetic critique and a wider frame of reference. The other issue, which needs to be balanced with it, is a positive attitude to social structures and to good government as represented by the Roman Empire. What Luke is saying is consistent with writing an apology for the virtues of the Roman Empire to the Christian churches. In this way the positive political and religious issues can be woven together, and the arguments make sense. Luke does not wish to argue one-sidedly either for radical religion or for radical politics. From what he has seen, his defended position will be essentially conservative and harmonizing.

Luke's representation of Christ

We must now look at Luke's perspectives on the person of Christ. Luke places the gospel of Christ in a social context. He provides an orderly account of Jesus' life and a record of the church's preaching about Christ.

There is a striking contrast between his account and Paul's teaching about the death of Christ. Luke depicts Jesus as a prophetic figure, the prototype of the prophetic ministry undertaken by the apostles and the wider church; and the death of Jesus is shown as a martyrdom, akin to the death of a prophet. "Most striking is the entire absence of a Pauline interpretation of the Cross . . . There is indeed no *theologia crucis* [theology of the cross] beyond the affirmation that the Christ must suffer, since so the prophetic scriptures had foretold."[12] For this theme of the fulfilment of prophecy in Luke, see especially Luke 24.25–27.

Christ's death as a Christian prophet

A significant parallel is drawn between the deaths of Jesus and of Stephen, both presented as martyrdoms. (The details of the parallelism can be seen in the table below.) What this means, in respect of the death of Jesus, is that an unjust murder is at the heart of God's plan, an innocent man is done to death by the established earthly powers, and the actual human responsibility rests with the Jewish leaders. The pattern then repeats itself as the first Christian martyr, Stephen, follows in the steps of his Lord (according to Acts 7). Before Stephen dies, the reader is offered, in a defence speech which aggressively attacks the Jews, an interpretation of the meaning of Christ's death:

> *Which of the prophets did not your fathers persecute? And they killed those who announced beforehand the coming of the Righteous One, whom you have now betrayed and murdered, you who received the law as delivered by angels and did not keep it. (7.52–3)*

Today the word "martyr" is used of one who suffers fatally for the cause; the original Greek word meant "witness" and came to mean witnessing through dying as a result of the persecution of the first Christians. Stephen is here a prophetic witness to Christ, and in his testimony Christ's death is put in the context of the prophets who suffered in Israel.

Death of Christ // Death of Stephen		
Signs and wonders provoke popular awe		Acts 6.8
Prophetic activity provokes rejection	Luke 24.19–20 (20.1–7, 13–16)	Acts 7.57–58
Trial before Jewish "council"	Luke 22.66f	Acts 6.12f
False witnesses: accusations of blasphemy and of wish to destroy the temple	[Mark 14.55–59, 63–64] ?transferred in Luke →	Acts 6.11–14
Vision of heaven: glory of God and Son of Man (unique)	Luke 22.69 (21.27)	Acts 7.56
Prayer for forgiveness of persecutors	*Luke 23.34	Acts 7.60
Martyr's death ("receive/commit spirit")	*Luke 23.46	Acts 7.59
Influence of death (spread of gospel)	*Luke 23.39–43, 47–48	Acts 8.1–4; 11.19
Death of Stephen fulfils Jesus' prophecy	Luke 21.12–19 (esp. 16) cp. Luke 12.1–12	
Ultimate Jewish responsibility for execution	Luke 23.25–26	Acts 7.57–58; 8.1
(*Note:* * = distinctive Lucan material.)		

Jesus as prophet

That Christ's death is seen as the death of a prophet is confirmed by the way that Luke (and Luke alone) records Jesus' prediction of his death in these terms:

> *Nevertheless I must go on my way today and tomorrow and the day*

following; for it cannot be that a prophet should perish away from Jerusalem. (Luke 13.33)

Repeatedly Jesus is spoken of as the prophet (see Luke 7.16; 24.19, 21), and he behaves like one (as in Luke 4.16–30 at the Nazareth synagogue). Again and again Luke emphasizes that Jesus suffers innocently for his prophetic activity, in a way that had itself been prophesied.

The term "righteous one" which was used in Stephen's speech (about Jesus' death) is found in Luke 23.47, when the centurion at the cross described the dying Jesus as "innocent". Perhaps Luke prefers this word for its limited, and appropriately non-theological, sense in the mouth of a Roman centurion. It corresponds to the secular Hellenistic use ("he is a really good man/a saint") while claiming Jesus' innocence. But Luke uses the same term elsewhere in more Jewish and theological ways (see Luke 2.25 [Simeon] and Acts 10.22 [Cornelius – a nice combination of the secular and Jewish possibilities]).

The term is also a potential title, for such a person as the expected messianic prophet, like Moses (Deuteronomy 18.15, 18). "I will raise up for them a prophet like you from among their brethren; and I will put my words in his mouth, and he shall speak to them all that I command him." In Stephen's speech in Acts 7.52 the word "Righteous" has strong echoes of an Old Testament designation for the Messiah (see Jeremiah 23.5f; 33.15; Zechariah 9.9; Wisdom 2.18). In Luke's hands this is a good example of the creative use of parallelism. The effect of putting the two senses of secular innocence and Jewish righteousness together in a parallel structure (referring to the death of Jesus) is to create resonances, to allow the meaning in one context to spill over into the other. Luke again shows his capacity to work creatively in both worlds.

Jesus is not being diminished by being categorized as a messianic prophet. In Luke's day prophecy was a powerful and world-wide phenomenon. (It never had been exclusively Jewish.) Luke could use such terminology to unite the world of the Old Testament with contemporary prophetic activity in the Christian church, and to make it intelligible to Greece and Rome. To identify Jesus as the central figure in the divine plan of redemption, the expected prophet who would be God's agent, was an ultimate theological statement that became thus widely accessible.

While Luke views Christ's death as divinely ordained martyrdom, he makes no reference to that death as a sacrifice (in the technical sense such as Paul derived from the Old Testament). The death is not connected explicitly with the church sacraments of baptism and Lord's Supper. It is not described as an atoning death, to be effective for many; where Mark records (10.45): "The Son of man also came not to be served but to serve, and to give his life as a ransom for many", Luke has only: "I am among you as one who serves" (22.27). Isaiah 53 is quoted both in Luke 22.37 and in Acts 8.32–3, but in neither case referring to the servant's sacrifice.

No connection is made between Jesus' death and the forgiveness of sins (contrast 1 Corinthians 15.3; Matthew 26.28). Instead Luke 22.19–20 and

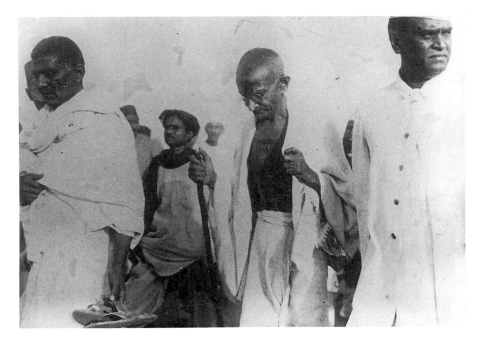

Mahatma Gandhi leading the Salt March in 1930. A large crowd accompanied him for 100 miles from Ahmedabad to make salt freely at the seaside. This was a non-violent protest against the British tax on salt, widely perceived as unjust.

Acts 20.28 both speak of the death of Jesus as the blood which seals the new covenant. Peter and Paul in Acts preach the forgiveness of sins (e.g. Acts 2.38; 13.38), as commanded by the risen Christ in Luke 24.47; but the forgiveness of sins is not combined with the death of Jesus on the cross. With evidence like this, at the very least one should avoid reading Luke with the presuppositions of Paul or Matthew. It is best to concentrate on what is accredited to Luke himself.

Prophets are rightly conceived to be forceful communicators, fired with the power of the message they have to convey. They have a transcendent experience of the divine (as in the vision in the temple in Isaiah 6), a sense of the other world but a variety of attitudes to this world. There is a well-received suggestion that Luke's picture of Jesus as a prophet closely resembles Mahatma Gandhi, both in his inspirational character and in his advocacy and practice of non-violent resistance. This comparison is attractive, but, because of the different contexts and the gap of many centuries, the resemblance must be examined critically.

Violence and non-violence

Jesus teaches and acts assertively and aggressively. He shows no deference towards political rulers, as when he calls Herod a fox (which may be cunning, but is more likely to have been conceived as destructive, or even worthless vermin) in Luke 13.32. This could be non-violent resistance, but more likely an indifference to political rulers, comparable to that displayed by the Pharisees. Within Luke's perspective is a Jesus who believes that all power and authority ultimately belong to God, and the course of history follows the divine plan. Thus human rulers were actually of little consequence at the last account, even though the reality of their present authority was recognized (Luke 22.25). Jesus was silent in their presence (e.g. Luke 23.9) because he had nothing in common with them. Such a Jesus is unlikely to advocate violence, like the Jewish fanatics the ZEALOTS, or offer Christians a model of political activism.

While Jesus does offer resistance towards Jewish structures, which verges on the violent, on balance the example offered to Christians is one of non-violent resistance and civil disobedience, in the Jewish rather than the Roman context (see Acts 4.19–20 and 5.29). The episode which comes closest to an example of violence is the traditional story of the cleansing of the temple, after Jesus' entry into Jerusalem. But notice what Luke 19.45–48 does with the story from Mark 11.15–18. Luke has reshaped the story to suppress most of the cleansing activity, so that it becomes an account of Jesus' entry to the place of his subsequent teaching; and Luke, by introducing 19.47, makes the plot of the chief priests, scribes, and other leaders into a response to the teaching rather than a reaction to the cleansing.

The question of violence is raised again in Luke 22.35–38, with the new instruction to the apostles to buy a sword. This is a small basis on which to build a whole theory of Jesus' advocating armed Zealot-style resistance. On the contrary, the sword may symbolize the "cutting-edge" of the Christian mission (compare Luke 2.34–35), and the fate of Jesus warns that it is no light matter. However, it may be more important to notice how this passage actually urges restraint on armed resistance.

> *And they said, "Look, Lord, here are two swords." And he said to them, "It is enough."* ["That is enough of that" is an equally possible translation] (22.38)

Even if we take the translation which allows for two swords, this is hardly adequate for an armed insurrection. The more negative reading is further corroborated by the later incident at 22.47–51. Jesus says, "No more of this [idea of striking with the sword]" (22.51). His own activity is directed in the opposite way, towards healing and restoring rather than maiming and killing. Even if the text allows for limited violence, i.e. towards the Jews but not the Romans, that limit is being clearly set. "You can go thus far, but no farther." The patterns of law and order are being clearly set within Christian political organization.

The sermon at Nazareth

The role of Jesus as prophet is particularly enhanced by Luke in his special account of the sermon at the Nazareth synagogue, early in Jesus' ministry. Luke 4.16–30 sets the programme for Jesus' teaching in Luke's gospel in the same way as the much briefer Mark 1.14–15 does in Mark. It is a matter of debate whether Luke derives this episode from Mark 6.1–6, or from a conjectured early Palestinian tradition which Matthew knew but did not use (Matthew 13.53–58 follows Mark closely). It is likely that Luke has given the account its distinctive shape and theological emphasis. Jesus stands (in respect for the word of God) to read in the synagogue the prophecy from Isaiah 61.1–2:

> *The Spirit of the Lord is upon me,*
> *because he has anointed me to preach good news to the poor.*
> *He has sent me to proclaim release to the captives*
> *and recovering of sight to the blind,*
> *to set at liberty those who are oppressed,*
> *to proclaim the acceptable year of the Lord.*

Jesus then sits down (according to the convention of rabbinic teachers and some Greek philosophers) in order to deliver a sermon, or explanation of the text. But instead of conventional teaching, Jesus speaks authoritatively as a prophet: "Today this scripture has been fulfilled in your hearing" (4.21).

Jesus is seen both as an interpreter of scripture and as a prophet, because the fulfilment of the text goes beyond the normal processes of exposition. The eventual reaction to his words (along with initial compliments) is incomprehension and rejection of what he stands for, the response of the lynch mob. This one episode can thus be seen as programmatic of the whole ministry. The episode is also prophetic, as it prefigures the similar experiences of Jesus' apostles. (The consistency of the refrain in Luke about the necessity of prophetic suffering for the Christian, as for Jesus himself, can be seen in the table overleaf.)

Luke seems to have added the details of the setting of a synagogue service, the references in 4.25–27 to the traditions about the prophets Elijah and Elisha, and the violent ending (4.29). The context of material taken over from Mark 6.1–6 has been changed, to create this statement of the programme of the ministry and the prefiguration of church history. All these changes accentuate the theme of Jesus' teaching as prophecy; this prophet (like his predecessors and successors) challenges the assumptions of the privileged group. "No prophet is acceptable in his own country" (4.24) takes on a much deeper meaning in Luke's context.

Understanding of Old Testament prophecy

This episode in the synagogue contains one of the clearest allusions to the traditional Jewish idea of the jubilee year. The basis of this year (the Sabbath of Sabbaths) is explained in Leviticus 25:

> *Six years you shall sow your field, and six years you shall prune your vineyard, and gather in its fruits; but in the seventh year there shall be a sabbath of solemn rest for the land, a sabbath to the Lord ... And you shall count seven times seven years ... And you shall hallow the fiftieth year ... It shall be a jubilee for you, when each of you shall return to his property.* (verses 3–4, 8, 10)

In this jubilee year all debts would be wiped out and the land would lie fallow. As a recipe for agriculture or for the economics of banking, the idea was both radical and potentially disastrous. Various devices were developed

Prophecies of Christ's suffering and the prophetic suffering of the Christian

1 Predictions and omens of the passion of Jesus:

Luke	6.11, 16	Judas as traitor
	9.22	Son of Man
	9.44	Son of Man (*9.45)
	12.49–50	Fire and baptism
	13.33–34	Jerusalem and lament
	17.25	Son of Man
	18.31–33	Son of Man (*18.34)
	22.22	Son of Man
	22.37	(Isaiah 53.12)
	24.6–7	At the tomb
	24.25–27	Interpreting prophets
	24.44–46	Understanding scripture
Acts	13.27–29	Paul explains

(* indicates accompanying theme of incomprehension)

2 The necessity of prophetic suffering:

Luke	6.22	Blessed are those who suffer on account of the Son of Man
	11.47–51	The blood of the prophets
	13.33–35	Jerusalem killing the prophets
	22.14–22, 28–34	Passover, Kingdom, shared trials
Acts	26.23	Christ must suffer, the first to rise from the dead

3 Christ's predictions of Christian self-denial:

Luke	9.23–26, 57–62	Take up cross daily
	12.4–12	Acknowledgement before men
	13.24	The narrow door
	14.25–33	Total renunciation
	21.12–19	Testimony and endurance

to ensure that the people were fed and the moneylenders remained in business during this fiftieth year. But the idea of jubilee could be championed by the prophet to defend the poor against the privileged. It became part of the eschatological perspective of future hope. The year of remission, to which the poor looked forward, rapidly became a metaphor of that larger future hope. It features, for example, in the Isaiah 61 references to "release" and "acceptable year", mentioned in the passage which Jesus read.

The presence of such ideas within Luke's picture makes clear that this evangelist has not eliminated all traces of future eschatological expectation as a result of his preoccupation with the past (the life of Jesus and the record of church history). These traditional prophetic perspectives of time remain important for him within the scheme of salvation history, but they are metaphors of time, not literal dates. His emphasis is on the fact of fulfilment: "Today this scripture has been fulfilled in your hearing" (4.21). These prophetic words are for Luke a reference to the past, to an event which happened in the life of Jesus many years before. He is dealing with an

The vision of the prophet Ezekiel, from a 9th century CE miniature in the Homilies of St. Gregory Nazianzus.

historical process of salvation which continues to encompass the experience of the church.

The difference can be seen by comparing Luke's reference to historical prophecy with Paul's interpretation of another Isaiah quotation in 2 Corinthians 6.2 ("Now is the day of salvation"). For Paul this is grasping in the present for a reality long awaited in hope, while for Luke this is a projection

above Aerial view of the coastline at Caesarea, showing the extent of the city and now-submerged harbour constructed by Herod the Great.

right The synagogue at Chorazin (Luke 10.13), in the hills above Capernaum. It was built in black basalt, full of decorative carving; its doors (at the far end) face Jerusalem.

from the past. The further consequence in Luke is that, although some of the implications of the jubilee year for social revolution still remain intact, essentially its emphasis is in the area of ethical practice by the new and relatively privileged society which is the Gentile church. There is a prophetic reminder of the appropriate "bias" to the poor, but it does not amount, for Luke, to any future programme of liberation.

Jesus' teaching in parables

The Good Samaritan is one of the most familiar parables Jesus told. It is also found only in Luke, at 10.29–37. (See the accompanying table of parables and miracles found only in Luke.) So it is appropriate to ask what this story reveals of the distinctive interests of Luke and his community, and what it might add to Luke's picture of Jesus the prophetic teacher.

Miracles and parables found only in Luke		
Miracles:		
Luke	7.11–17	Widow's son at Nain
	13.11–14	Woman bent double (Sabbath healing)
	14.2–4	Man with dropsy
	17.12–19	Ten lepers
	22.50–51	High Priest's slave
Parables:		
Luke	5.38–39	Old and new wine compared
	10.30–37	Good Samaritan
	11.5–8	Importunate friend at midnight
	12.16–21	Rich fool
	13.6–9	Barren fig tree
	13.25–28	Locked out of the Kingdom
	14.7–11	Place of honour at the feast
	14.12–14	Invite the poor to your feast
	14.28–30	Builder of a tower
	14.31–32	King going to war
	15.8–9	Lost coin
	15.11–32	Prodigal son (the "lost" son)
	16.1–9	Unjust steward
	16.19–31	The rich man and Lazarus
	17.7–10	Expectations of servants
	18.1–7	Importunate widow and unjust judge
	18.9–14	Pharisee and publican

The parables of Jesus, like the narrative of the Old Testament, are concerned primarily with the world of nature (seed sowing and harvest, vineyards and fig trees). Unlike the Old Testament, Jesus' stories concentrate attention on teaching about the Kingdom of God and its nature. To this end they employ all kinds of shock tactics, dramatic contrasts with the natural world, and literary devices including jokes and puns. The prophetic challenge, the controversial elements, and the fundamental criticism of the Jewish religious leadership should not be underestimated. So much is true generally of Jesus' parables, but it is also important to distinguish between the stories which he told (which provoked the hostility of the Jewish leaders) and the process of retelling and reapplication of these stories within the first Christian communities. Subsequently the gospel writers record a selection of these and similar stories, providing interpretations; thus each individual evangelist characterizes the teaching of Jesus in accordance with his gospel's theological emphasis. A further stage came when the fathers of the Greek and Latin churches recorded their own interpretations, often highly elaborate, of the "simple" story Jesus told.

The real contrast may not be between simplicity and complexity, for Jesus' stories often have the subtlety of precise prophetic criticism. Rather there are contrasts in the way the stories are applied. Whereas Jesus' stories are challenging statements about the coming of the Kingdom, the early churches and the evangelists often turned them into models and examples of how Christian groups or individuals should behave. Jesus was above all the example of good behaviour, and the parables (as illustrations of good behaviour given by him) were welcomed in the zeal to imitate Christ. The Good Samaritan could obviously be an instance of such a model, for it concludes: "Jesus said to him, 'Go and do likewise'" (10.37).

In the parable of the sower (Luke 8.4–15 / Mark 4.2–20) the basic story is of seed broadcast in different soil conditions, which is an illustration from nature fully in conformity with Palestinian agricultural practice. The emphasis here, as in the parable of the mustard seed (Luke 13.18–19 / Mark 4.30–32), is on the sheer size of the harvest from wholly unpromising beginnings. Herein lies what is called "the secret of the Kingdom of God" – the full significance embedded in the small-scale beginning to the ministry of Jesus. But by the time the sower parable came to be interpreted (and the interpretation derived from the experience of the early church), the issues were rather the problems of Christian preaching, the extent of resistance, rejection, and persecution experienced by the church. The wonder is that in such circumstances there is any harvest at all!

Just as the emphases of the early Christians can be compared with the emphases of Jesus, so the way the individual evangelists use the parables can be distinguished. Mark tends to preserve the context of the natural world in which Jesus set his illustrations. Luke often leaves the countryside behind and his preferred parables have, implicit or explicit, town settings and urban orientation (debtors, builders, travellers, visitors at midnight, dinner guests). While Matthew enlarges and exaggerates the stories, increasing the scale and multiplying the numbers for effect, Luke is more modest and down-to-earth in the situations described; the stories are homely, even if some characters are rich.

The Good Samaritan

The Good Samaritan is the story of a wayside robbery, set on a specified road between Jerusalem and Jericho, involving a pack-animal, oil and wine, and a couple of denarii. It sounds like an exemplary story, used for ethical purposes in the church, as several of Luke's special parables could be. If the unjust judge behaves like this, how much more (by contrast) will God? How much more should Christians follow the patterns of behaviour exemplified by the unjust steward, the friend at midnight, or the despised Samaritan? Luke is often credited with developing (if not creating) this ethical use of parables. It is sometimes said that Luke created the whole story of the Samaritan, as a teaching aid, on the basis of a piece of Old Testament tradition from 2 Chronicles 28.15 (the Samaritans who clothed the naked captives from Jerusalem and "provided them with food and drink and anointed them; and carrying all the feeble among them on asses, they brought them to their kinsfolk at Jericho, the city of palm trees").

One problem with the idea that the story is a Lucan creation for ethical purposes is its inconsistency, which is like the inconsistency between the parable of the sower and its interpretation. The typical question, introducing a parable in Luke ("And who is my neighbour?" – 10.29), is at odds with the answer expressed in 10.37 ("Go and do likewise"). This answer actually belongs with a different initial question, such as "How am I to be a true neighbour?", but would match the church's ethical emphasis on the behaviour model. In contrast, the answer which corresponds with the original question would be: "The Samaritan is the neighbour, the one who showed mercy". Such evidence of inconsistency might well justify an attempt to reconstruct the original parable and the subsequent history of its development.

The Good Samaritan: the parable represented on an 18th century CE ledger from Rochester cathedral. The Latin moral (from Luke 10.37) reads "Go and do likewise".

If Jesus tells the story to illustrate how the Jewish religious leaders, priest and Levite, are inadequate in helping a man in a desperate situation, the man at the wayside, beaten and abandoned, then tended and having his wounds dressed with oil and wine, could represent God's pilgrim people, Israel. This Israel is described in such terms in Isaiah 1.6:

> From the sole of the foot even to the head, there is no soundness in it [the whole rebellious nation], but bruises and sores and bleeding wounds; They are not pressed out, or bound up, or softened with oil.

The image of the parable might have appealed to Luke, and confirmed his negative view of the Jewish leaders in relation to the people of Israel.

The Samaritan as Christ

Is Christ then depicted as the Samaritan? Did Jesus tell the story with himself in that role? Such shock tactics in a prophetic statement as deliberately using the pejorative term for the hated and despised race would not have been impossible. Another gospel tradition exploits the idea in John 8.48 ("Are we not right to say that you are a Samaritan and have a devil?"). It is also true that Luke's story states that the Samaritan "had compassion" on the wounded man, a verb which the New Testament only uses of God and Christ. There is also the possibility that the term "Samaritan" is itself an elaborate pun (quite acceptable in parables), using the fact that the Hebrew word also means "watchman" and a kind of "shepherd" (see 1 Samuel 17.20; Hosea 12.12). So to call the hero of the story a Samaritan is therefore to pick up a term which his enemies used of Jesus, and also to allude to the Davidic shepherd/Messiah of Israel. There is a further pun on the words for "Samaritan" and "neighbour", which have two similar Semitic roots that were occasionally confused (e.g. in some rabbinic commentaries on Proverbs 27.10).[13] Beneath the drama and the word-play, then, the parable would have been told originally to answer the question, "Who is the true shepherd?" And Christ thereby makes a claim for himself, that he (rather than the priest and the Levite) fulfils the prophecy of Ezekiel 34.11–12, 16:

> Behold I, myself will search for my sheep, and will seek them out. As a shepherd seeks out his flock when some of his sheep have been scattered abroad, so will I seek out my sheep; and I will rescue them from all places where they have been scattered on a day of clouds and thick darkness . . . I will seek the lost, and I will bring back the strayed, and I will bind up the crippled, and I will strengthen the weak.

The imagery of shepherd and flock is familiar enough in Luke (as in the other gospels) applied to Christ and Israel; see especially Luke 12.32; 15.3–7; Acts 20.28.

This parable about the person of Christ, contrasted with the Jewish leaders, then undergoes a transformation within the early Christian communities. It comes to represent a moral challenge for good neighbourly relations. In the first instance such a challenge derived its force from the identification of Christ as the Samaritan, but gradually the action of the Samaritan became more important than his person. Both the original context, of Christology and Jewish polemic, and the ethical corollary may have appealed to Luke. It could well be that Luke reshaped the parable (unless of course he created it) and emphasized the return of the Samaritan in 10.35. This could make the parable of Christ into a vehicle for Luke's view of the history of salvation. It may well represent the history of the people of God (identified as the wayfarer) from the Fall, through the Redemption, to the Last Day of Christ's return. Christ is the central figure of redemption, but the church is charged to carry on this prophetic and compassionate ministry until the end. This reconstruction is conjectural but within the limits of the evidence; such examples of "salvation history" interpretation appear in the church fathers (e.g. in Origen and Augustine and especially Severus of Antioch's sermon on the parable of the Good Samaritan).

The Christ figure in the baptism and temptation stories

The understanding of the purpose of Jesus' historical ministry might also be illuminated by considering the narrative of his baptism and temptations. Both Matthew and Luke develop considerably the brief but dramatic account of Mark 1.9–13. Differences in the emphases of Luke and Matthew can indicate Luke's interest in, and theological understanding of, these episodes. Luke 3.21–22 and 4.1–13 describe the commissioning of Jesus and his prophetic inspiration, followed by a process of testing. As his life's work begins, so his credentials are presented, in the form of a genealogy (3.23–28) which traces his ancestry through David and Abraham back to Adam as the first man. This is certainly a good beginning for a universal mission which will use Jewish channels and relate positively to the traditions of the Old Testament.

According to Luke, the experience immediately after the baptism by John comes as Jesus is praying (3.21). Luke often mentions prayer as being important within the life of Jesus and, by virtue of his example, within the life of the church. In this state Jesus is particularly receptive to divine communication, and receives the inspiration of the Holy Spirit for his prophetic ministry. (See Luke's references to the Holy Spirit in 1.15 and 2.25–27 and compare Acts 2.4.) In Luke's narrative, distinctively, the visual experience of the dove is public, while the aural experience of the heavenly voice is personal, confined to Jesus himself. The divine communication (interpreted as a combination of Psalm 2.7 and Isaiah 42.1) is regarded, like the temptations, as relevant only to Jesus himself and to the definition of his ministry. On the other hand, it is stressed that the dove is "in bodily form". This Old Testament symbol for Israel is now seen as a public declaration; in the Christian community (as the new Greater Israel) there is emphasis on the

A synoptic comparison of the three gospels:

Matthew 3.13–17	Mark 1.9–11	Luke 3.21–22
Then Jesus came from Galilee to the Jordan to John, to be baptized by him. John would have prevented him, saying, "I need to be baptized by you, and do you come to me?" But Jesus answered him, "Let it be so now; for thus it is fitting for us to fulfil all righteousness." Then he consented.	In those days Jesus came from Nazareth of Galilee	Now when all the people were baptized
And when Jesus was baptized, he went up immediately from the water, and behold, the heavens were opened and he saw the Spirit of God descending like a dove and alighting on him; and lo, a voice from heaven, saying, "This is my beloved Son, with whom I am well pleased."	and was baptized by John in the Jordan. And when he came up out of the water, immediately he saw the heavens opened and the Spirit descending upon him like a dove; and a voice came from heaven, "Thou are my beloved Son: with thee I am well pleased."	and when Jesus also had been baptized and was praying, the heaven was opened, and the Holy Spirit descended upon him in bodily form, as a dove and a voice came from heaven, "Thou art my beloved Son: with thee I am well pleased."

reality of the Spirit within the community orientated around Jesus.

The scriptural quotations uttered by the heavenly voice show a merging of the themes, firstly of the enthronement of a king (from the royal Psalm), and secondly of the prophetic servant figure who suffers (from Second Isaiah). These two texts represent the tension between alternative possibilities, resolved in Jesus uniquely as the one who must suffer, the Christ who is servant, king, and "prophet mighty in deed and word" (Luke 13.33; 22.27; 23.3; 24.19). The symbolic trials which he undergoes (4.1–13) are the testing of this vocation by standards which would be appreciated in the Roman Empire, using the models of economics, politics, and of permitted religions. These options for power are considered in turn, and rejected with reasons. He is not an economic manipulator, using bread and circuses as an enticement. He is not a threat to the political dominance of Rome in the Mediterranean world. Although he will heal the sick, he is not a conjuror who relies on magical spells or the mysterious powers passed on through initiation rites. These options are closed for this prophetic teacher as he goes to preach his programmatic sermon at Nazareth (4.14ff). His symbolic Old Testament adversary retires from the fray, but, like Satan in the book of Job, he is allowed to intervene again in the story, in furtherance of God's ultimate purpose (see 22.3, 53 and compare 10.18 – in the context of the church's mission).

The birth stories as theology

A final area where the Lucan view of Christ emerges clearly is the birth narratives in Luke 1–2. These two chapters comprise materials found only in Luke, although it fulfils a similar function to the special birth material in Matthew 1–2, with which it should be carefully compared.[14] Despite their obvious differences from the rest of the gospel, such texts, like the infancy stories of the Buddha, have much to contribute to a religious understanding. In Luke 1–2 the evangelist has outlined a theological context with which to preface the gospel. There is no such material in Mark, which begins abruptly with a title and John the Baptist. Matthew and Luke each in his own way use the birth stories to comment upon the meaning of the gospel and the incarnation. Thus the chapters fulfil the same purpose as the generally recognized prologue to the fourth gospel.

In these chapters Luke's Old Testament style of story-telling is most obvious in the ethos and the language. In fact, this section provides a bridge between the gospel and the Old Testament, in much the same way as the beginning of Acts provides a bridge between Jesus and the church. It seems that Luke has created these narratives to express the theological purpose of his work. Previously unknown characters (e.g. Zechariah and Simeon) appear as Old Testament figures, while known characters (such as Mary) come from within the gospel traditions. These chapters express a theology which is entirely consistent with, and sometimes more explicit than, the main part of the gospel.

Luke based his story of Jesus' birth on the Old Testament precedents of the birth of Samson in Judges 13 and of Samuel in 1 Samuel 1–2. Luke and Matthew both know a tradition of an angel announcing the birth of Jesus (to Mary or to Joseph). Luke develops this material using the charcterization of Mary from the gospel, and statements about the person of Christ derived from Christian preaching. He also shapes a parallel narrative about the birth of John the Baptist, whose role is that of the Old Testament prophetic forerunner. Appropriately, then, the story of his birth also prepares the way for Jesus, intensifies the effect by the parallels drawn between John and Jesus, and enlarges the scope for prophetic interpretation of the significance of these events.

Authentication by the Holy Spirit, prophecy, and titles

There are three particular theological emphases to notice in relation to the birth of Christ. Firstly, the action of the Holy Spirit is repeatedly emphasized. The reference is to the prophetic and creative spirit of God, the word of God as seen in creation and in the call of the Old Testament prophet. The Holy Spirit prophetic inspiration is particularly mentioned in the case of Simeon (2.25–27). Further, Zechariah is told that John the Baptist:

will be filled with the Holy Spirit, even from his mother's womb. And

> *he will turn many of the sons of Israel to the Lord their God, And he*
> *will go before him* [be a forerunner] *in the spirit and power of Elijah.*
> (1.15–17)

In fulfilment of this prophecy "the word of God came to John the son of Zechariah in the wilderness" at 3.2. John is identified with Elijah (according to the higher theology of this prologue), in that he is the Old Testament prototype for the true prophet (that is Jesus himself).

The role of the Spirit is again vital at Luke 1.35, when the angel tells Mary:

> *The Holy Spirit will come upon you, and the power of the Most High*
> *will overshadow you.*

This is a new creative undertaking (compare Genesis 1.2). The importance of the birth is the action, the personal intervention, of God. Luke's poetry in the Old Testament style emphasizes this by drawing a parallel (synonymous parallelism) between the activity of the creative Spirit and the localized overshadowing of divine power (as in the pillars of fire and cloud at the time of the Exodus). The birth of Jesus stands not merely as one among many in the long series of millions of births; it took place not merely through the creative will or drive of a man, but through God's own will as creator.

A second theological emphasis concerns history and eschatology. Luke's perspective of a divine plan in history is reflected in the birth of Christ. What was prophesied in the past is now fulfilled, and with Christ there is a new beginning, the dawn of a new age which is identified as the time of the church. While Matthew expresses the fulfilment of prophecy by means of extended quotations (e.g. Matthew 1.22–23) which serve as the interpretative climax of stages in his story, Luke makes a similar point more comprehensively in the Old Testament-style hymns and songs. Like the hymns of Revelation, or the choruses of Greek theatre, these provide a commentary on the action. The most striking thing about the songs of Mary (1.46–55), Zechariah (1.68–79), and Simeon (2.29–32) is how the future tenses of prophecy have now become the past tenses of fulfilment, because of the announced birth of Christ, e.g.

> *Blessed be the Lord God of Israel,*
> *for he* has visited and redeemed *his people*
> *and* has raised up *a horn of salvation for us*
> *in the house of his servant David.* (1.68–69)

The third emphasis concerns Christ most directly, for it is the way he is named and designated. "Behold, you will conceive ... and bear a son, and you shall call his name Christ" (1.31). This presupposes knowledge of Isaiah 7.14 (which is actually quoted by Matthew in 1.22–23 as his proof-text) but, unlike Matthew 1.21, Luke seems to take the name "Jesus" for granted, and does not seek to explain the Hebrew name by its popular etymology (= "God [Yahweh] is salvation"). If Luke does not expect his readers to know Hebrew, he still takes pains to underline the same theological equivalent (Jesus = salvation) by repeating the words "saviour" and "salvation" (see 1.69; 2.11; 2.30).

Exorcism: Christ casts out a devil, as depicted in the upper circle of the initial letter **B** from Psalm 1 in the Winchester Bible (12th century CE) from the Cathedral library. The lower circle depicts the harrowing of hell (see page 331).

The Evangelist Luke from the Lindisfarne Gospels, made *c*.698 CE on the
Northumbrian island.

The baptism of Christ, from the 14th century mural in the Church of "The Lady of Our Pastures" at Asinon in Cyprus.

Luke 2.11 also collects together in a few words several important statements about Jesus. As well as Saviour he is Messiah and Lord. The fact that the birth takes place in Bethlehem underlines this, because Bethlehem is associated with David (the prototype of the messianic king). There are several ways to translate this text:

* Messiah (and) Lord
* Christ (proper name) the Lord
* anointed Lord.

A comparison of 2.11 with 2.26 might suggest (instead of "anointed Lord") "the Anointed of the Lord" or "God's Messiah". Luke seems to be making good use of the earliest Christian titles with their inherent ambiguities. "Christ" might be a proper name or a function. The Greek word *Kyrios* may be translated as "God" (as in the Greek version of the Old Testament) or "Sir" (that is, eminent person or master, as in secular Greek). Luke has assembled these titles in a solemn-sounding formula, rather like an imperial

Christ in the House of Simon the Pharisee by an imitator of Dirk Bouts (1415–75) from the Flemish School in the first half of the 16th century. According to Luke 7.36–50, while Jesus is at table, a woman anoints his feet.

proclamation. Once again we see Luke living in two worlds simultaneously, the world of the Old Testament and the world of the Roman Empire. Paul uses the term "saviour" in Philippians 3.20 of the awaited return of Christ. He is the once and future saviour. But Luke proclaims the salvation differently, as an historical process, achieved in these gospel events and carried forward by the church.

Wherever one looks in Luke–Acts, at the birth or the death of Christ, at the sermons or speeches of the first apostles, at the parables, teaching, and life experiences of Jesus himself, there is a clear and consistent thread of theological statement. Christ is the centre of an historical process which spans the Old Testament and the life of the church in the Roman Empire. The plan is God's and his is the ultimate power, but Christ is the true prophet who has proclaimed God's ultimate will, and sealed the new creation and new covenant by an exemplary martyrdom which was foreordained.

The nature of Luke's church

In conclusion we must now try to sharpen the focus on the nature of the church or society for which Luke writes. Inevitably the church was at some remove from Jesus himself, because these people looked back to his lifetime as to a sequence of past history. These events, however, were interpreted as possessing a *definitive* religious meaning for the church. They represented a new beginning, a new creation, a redemption which brought about salvation. They also belonged to and had continuity with the previous salvation process of the Old Testament. The Jewish legacy of the Greater Israel could be appreciated by this community which had points of contact with the Jewish Dispersion. Like Josephus, however, they renounced the tyranny of the old Jewish leadership and placed their trust in the political structures of the Roman Empire. They were prepared to defend what Rome stood for, and to encourage a more positive attitude to the Empire on the part of Christians. Their emphasis on Paul's activity for the majority of Acts suggests a Pauline church, founded by or closely attached to him, although this does not mean that they necessarily understood Paul very well.[15]

The church of the Ascension

Luke's was a church which interpreted and applied the theme of the new beginning, prophesied and historically achieved by Christ, as a "new start" in the Christian life, within the context of the church. The Ascension, which Luke records explicitly as an actual event, and emphasizes by recording it twice (Luke 24.51; Acts 1.9–11), represents a clear dividing line at the close of the middle section of salvation history. No other New Testament writer is as explicit as Luke, or treats the Ascension in quite this way. Christ is removed from the most direct physical involvement in the arena of history. The church of the apostles is then inaugurated as the beginning of the next (the current and final) stage of the history of salvation, with the gift of the prophetic spirit at Pentecost. The church carries out its ministry, inspired by Christ and working in accordance with his example, healing and prophesying, suffering and dying. Paul in particular is seen as the representative Christian, and his activity corresponds with Christ's and obviously imitates the example of Christ. So Paul's missionary journeys in Acts thus match the Lucan theme of Jesus' journey to Jerusalem (the travel narrative section which begins at Luke 9.51). Paul's trial in Acts 25 and 26 corresponds closely in Luke's account with the trial of Jesus in Luke 23 (see table on p. 182).

The imitation of Christ

Just as Paul is a supremely representative Christian, there is also a visible correspondence between the gospel and Acts, as the activities of the other apostles match the activities of Christ (see table on p. 183).

In the same way, the death of Stephen is recorded as though modelled upon, and imitating, the death of Christ. In all these respects what is seen is the interpretation by Luke and his community of these seminal events in the life of the church. These examples of the imitation of Christ are to be pondered and put into practice daily within the church: this is the ideal. Special emphases are found in Luke's unique additions of the words "daily" and "all," to the well-known saying of Jesus:

> *And he said to* all, *"If any man would come after me, let him deny himself and take up his cross* daily *and follow me."* (Luke 9.23)

The imitation of Christ should be a matter of daily practice within the world-wide church.

Parallels between Jesus and Paul in the final scenes

	Luke	Acts
Good reception: praise of God for works seen/things done	19.37	21.17–20
Entry into temple (basically positive and friendly attitude toward it)	19.45–48	21.26
Sadducees do not believe in Resurrection; in contrast scribes supportive	20.27–39	23.6–9
Meal at which bread is taken, thanks given, bread broken	22.19	27.35
Mob arrest	22.54	21.30
Struck by priest's assistants/at High Priest's command	22.63–64	23.2
[Scheme of four trials (Jesus before Sanhedrin, Pilate, Herod, Pilate) (Paul before Sanhedrin, Felix, Festus, Herod Agrippa) Parallelism of roles of four main characters: Roman, Herodian, Jewish accusers, and defendant]		
1 Introduction to Roman trial	23.1	25.1
2 Hearing before Roman procurator with Jewish accusers (High Priest and leaders of Jewish people, demanding death penalty, on charge of activity against Jews and Caesar)	23.2–5	25.2–12
3 Coincidence of presence of Herodian who wishes to see the prisoner*	23.6–7	25.13–27
4 Hearing before Herodian prince*	23.8–11	26.1–23
5 Dialogue	23.13–23	26.24–29
6 Threefold declaration of innocence (motif of Suffering Servant?)	23.4, 14, 22	23.9; 25.25; 26.31
7 Intention/possibility of release of prisoner (could and should be freed)	23.16, 22	26.32
8 Jews cry "Away with him"	23.18	21.36
9 Conclusion – "innocent except . . ."	23.24–25	26.30–32
10 Centurion has favourable opinion	23.47	27.3

* Herodian episode could be omitted from narrative sequence. Description in Luke's own terms, rather than in his source? Real audience intended is not Herod, but Luke's own readers.

Parallels between the activities of Christ and the activities of the apostles		
	Luke	Acts
Baptism (fire and spirit from heaven)	3.16, 21–22	2.1–4; 11.16
Preaching commenced (prophetic preaching interpreting scripture)	4.16–27	2.14–40 see 28.23–28
Storm at sea	8.22–25	27.13–26
Journey motif (Christian community to go on a Christ-like journey)	9.51–19.44	13–21
Going up to Jerusalem	9.31, 51; 13.33	19.21; 21.15f
Authority in heavenly vision	9.28–36; 24.44–49	7.55f; 9.4ff
Working of miracles (example) (word of command)	8.40–42, 49–56; 8.54, 9.40	9.36–42
The Roman centurion	7.1–10	10
Forgiveness of sins	23.34	2.38
Hostile reactions – sufferings and persecution	22.2, 63; 23.2	5.33, 40; 12.2; 16.37; 22.19; 26.10
Jesus and Paul on trial	23.1–25	25–26
Verdict of innocence	23.47	23.29; 26.31–32; 28.18
Witnesses of resurrection	24.48–49	1.22; 10.39–42

The social gospel

A particular feature of Luke's narrative which can shed light on the nature of the community and society for whom he writes is the concern for the weak and downtrodden, the sinners, and the despised. This can be seen in Jesus' ministry of healing and in the symbol of the Good Samaritan. Even if in this parable Christ is considered to be rescuing Greater Israel from the Jewish leaders, there are clear ethical implications in the wounded and abandoned figure by the wayside. And it is these categories of "the poor and maimed and blind and lame" who Luke specifies should be rescued not only from the streets of the city, but also from the highways and hedges, in his version of the parable of the great banquet (Luke 14.16–24, compare Matthew 22.1–10). "Until Pentecost the community of the poor had been seen as recipients of the gospel; after Pentecost they become channels of the power of the Spirit."[5]

This is the most critical point of all in the identification and description of Luke's community. It would be easy to conclude from this emphasis on the social gospel that here was a mission station in the third world or the inner city, a group identifying with the poverty of those they wished to help. But it must not be forgotten how Luke's gospel and Acts begin: they are addressed in literary terms to what appears to be a socially privileged community. And the positive attitude to Rome and its representatives would support that impression. If Luke 22.25 is compared with Mark 10.42, it can be seen that the authority of government is acknowledged as both real and beneficial in Luke's view, whereas for Mark there is a note of irony about its *apparent* power contrasted with true greatness in the Christian community.

> *The kings of the Gentiles exercise lordship over them, and those in authority over them are called benefactors.* (Luke 22.25)

Luke's perception is no longer the view from below, of the oppressed. Just as the Empire is viewed positively, so the Christians are not to be regarded as political agitators and rebels.

The symbolic poor

For Luke, in part, the historical situation has changed from that of the earliest days of the church. He tries to record faithfully the historical ministry of Jesus, as a wandering prophet among the poor and disadvantaged of Israel. But the age of the church represents a major transition to a new world of dialogue with Pharisaic Judaism and the Roman imperial administration. The continuity and parallels between the ministries of the church and of Jesus are stressed so much because the differences were so apparent to Luke. Symbolically the Gentile proselyte (like Cornelius) is part of the mission of Greater Israel, but he is not poor. Rather it was Israel who was poor, but is now made rich by God's redemption. Much of this concern for the poor is therefore a symbolic concern. The prophecy used by Jesus in the Nazareth synagogue (Luke 4.18f) is converted to apply to the church, which has been so "released" and "liberated". This then constitutes the church of Israel as a privileged community, separate from those outside, but there are still ethical and missionary implications in the message of Jesus, which maintain in the community a concern for those still to be reached.

So the Lucan themes of poverty and disadvantage are distanced somewhat, just as the historical Jesus is distanced. The effect is rather like that of a theologian from the affluent Western world, on the advantageous side of the North/South divide, who writes about Liberation Theology, showing that he cares for those to be set free, and that he respects the Biblical basis of this tradition, but, because he does not write from within the situation of hardship, he is not respected; indeed he is condemned as a theoretician not a practitioner (much as Jurgen Moltmann's *Theology of Hope* has been criticized by the Liberation Theologians).

The church and social construction and accommodation

Luke's concerns are with social construction, with seeing the church functioning, like the leaven of the Bible parable, within society. The church organization can help society to grow to full maturity. A specific example is Luke's interest in the role of women within the church. Women are frequently mentioned in his narratives and play a significant part in Luke–Acts. Elizabeth, Anna, Joanna, Susanna, Mary Magdalene, Lydia, and Priscilla are among those named who make an important contribution. Mary the mother of Jesus can be regarded as the ideal of discipleship (Luke 1.38; 8.19–21; Acts 1–14). "Women are a continuing theme and example used by Luke as he tries to teach the qualities of a true disciple – one who is loyal and faithful to Christ through trials and joy; and who witnesses to the person and work of Christ; one who serves the Lord and the brethren freely from their [*sic*, her?] own means."[16] Luke's attitude to women's gifts is certainly a socially progressive one by New Testament if not by modern standards.

All this is evidence of how Luke has tried to come to terms with the political, cultural, and social context. He makes a positive assessment of the

	LUKE'S GOSPEL	
	1.1–4	Formal Preface
1.5–4.13 The Coming of the Messiah who was prophesied	1.5–38	Parallel announcements of the birth of John the Baptist and the birth of Jesus
	39–45	Mary visits Elizabeth
	46–56	Mary's song of praise
	57–80	Birth of John the Baptist and Zechariah's prophecy
	2.1–20	Birth of Jesus
	21–40	Jesus' circumcision; presentation in the Temple; Simeon's response
	41–52	Jesus in the Temple at the age of twelve
	3.1–22	Preaching of John the Baptist and Jesus' Baptism
	23–38	Jesus' ancestors
	4.1–13	Temptations of Jesus
4.14–9.50 Jesus' ministry in Galilee	4.14–30	Jesus begins his ministry and is rejected at Nazareth
	31–44	Exorcism and healings; Jesus at prayer
	5.1–11	First disciples
	12–26	Healings of the untouchable and paralysed
	27–39	Call of Levi; question of fasting
	6.1–11	Actions on the Sabbath
	12–16	Choice of the Twelve
	17–49	Sermon on the Plain
	7.1–17	Healing the officer's servant and raising the widow's son
	18–35	Questions from John the Baptist
	36–50	Jesus anointed at Simon's house
	8.1–3	Women with Jesus
	4–18	Parables (including the Sower)
	19–21	True relations of Jesus
	22–56	Four miracles (the storm; the demoniac; a resurrection; a healing)
	9.1–17	Mission of the Twelve; feeding of five thousand
	18–27	Peter's confession; prediction of the Passion
	28–36	The Transfiguration
	37–43	Healing of epileptic boy
	43–50	Teaching to disciples, on greatness and exorcism
9.51–19.44 The Journey to Jerusalem and the Way Beyond this world	9.51–56	Rejection by a Samaritan village
	9.57–10.24	Discipleship and the mission of the Seventy
	10.25–37	Parable of Good Samaritan
	38–42	Mary and Martha
	11.1–13	Teaching on prayer
	11.14–12.3	Controversies and criticism of the Pharisees
	12.4–53	Exhortations to the disciples on the critical time
	12.54–13.5	Exhortations to the people on the crisis
	13.6–30	Parables of the Kingdom and a controversial Sabbath healing
	31–35	Focus on Jerusalem
	14.1–24	Dinner-table discourses
	25–35	Cost of discipleship
	15.1–32	Parables of the lost (sheep, coin and prodigal son)
	16.1–31	Parables of the dishonest steward and the rich man
	17.1–19	Instructions and example for the disciples
	20–37	Shorter eschatological discourse
	18.1–14	Parables of the judge and the widow, the Pharisee and the publican
	15–43	Teaching on children, eternal life; healing of blind man
	19.1–10	Zacchaeus meets Jesus
	11–27	Parable of the pounds
	28–44	Approach to Jerusalem
19.45–24.53 Suffering and Vindication	19.45–48	Jesus enters the temple
	20.1–21.4	Controversies and the widow's mite
	21.5–38	The fall of Jerusalem and the last things
	22.1–6	Judas' betrayal
	7–38	Last Supper and Farewell Discourse
	39–53	Mount of Olives and Arrest
	54–62	Peter's denial
	63–71	Mockery; Jesus before the Sanhedrin
	23.1–25	Jesus before Pilate (including 6–16 Jesus before Herod Antipas)
	26–49	Crucifixion
	50–56	Burial
	24.1–12	Resurrection
	13–35	Walk to Emmaus
	36–49	Jesus appears to the disciples in Jerusalem
	50–53	Ascension

The angel of the agony (Luke 22.43) and the crown of thorns from the chapel of Christ in Gethsemane, Coventry cathedral. The angel holds the cup of suffering which must be drained; in the dark panel to the right are the apostles sleeping in the garden of Gethsemane.

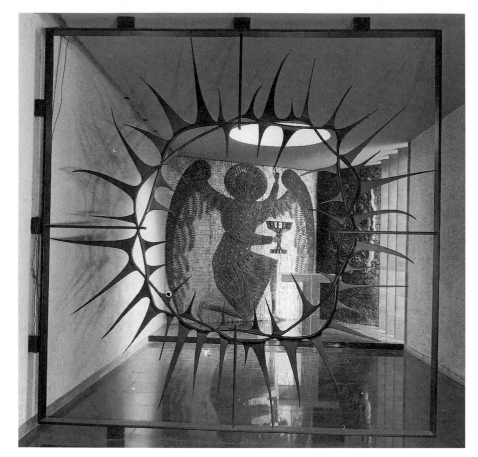

situation and its advantages for the church. It is an attitude of "positive accommodation". What is wrong seems, to Luke, due to abuses of the system (as documented by past evidence such as the trouble caused by Jewish leaders), rather than to any flaws in the system itself. The Roman concepts of slavery (as in the example of Christ's service) and of the respected woman (the Roman *matrona* or lady and patroness) can be seen as positive features of society. They are not attacked as symbols of inequity, subordination, and privilege. At its best, with enlightened masters and rulers, the Roman system worked well and to the advantage of the church. In other writings at the end of the first century the situation is regarded rather differently. In the gospel of John, the Roman cohort of soldiers sent to arrest Jesus fall back in awe before him at Gethsemane (John 18.3–6) but, according to the Revelation of John, the Roman Empire is setting tests for the Christian churches and probably persecuting them. In the religious dimension at least, the writer sees the state as setting up a major challenge for the churches in Asia Minor. This can be contrasted with Luke's positive accommodation and Paul's seeming ambivalence on such matters.

CHAPTER 4

The Matthean Church and Judaism

There are striking comparisons to be drawn between Paul and Matthew, particularly in their relationship with Judaism. The gospel of Matthew supplied the most anti-semitic of texts ("his blood be on us and on our children"), but thought in the most Jewish way about an ethic of righteousness, and labelled non-Christians as "Gentiles". The Sermon on the Mount may have been misread, and the familiar parable of the sheep and the goats misunderstood.

The order of precedence among the gospels

Within the order of books of the New Testament, the official arrangement known as the New Testament canon, Matthew stands first in the sequence of four gospels. Until the rise of modern Biblical criticism in the eighteenth century, Matthew's gospel was reckoned to be first also in the order of writing, the gospel on which the others depended. Not all modern theories of the relationship among the four gospels have removed Matthew from that primary position, although a majority view among modern scholars holds that Matthew and Luke are both dependent upon Mark as the first full gospel to be written. If these scholars are right, and it is historically true that Matthew was written after Mark, there should be an explanation of why Matthew was then placed first in the New Testament. It is likely to be a matter of church politics. Matthew's gospel was supported by an influential centre of early Christianity. Antioch is strongly favoured as a possible candidate. As a result, this gospel was used much more widely than the other gospels in the churches. In the church lectionaries (the lists of Bible passages set for public reading in the church meetings Sunday by Sunday) Matthew was dominant and provided the gospel framework. Other gospels only filled in the gaps where Matthew was felt to be incomplete.

The nature of this gospel

Matthew's has been described as "an authoritative gospel, a gospel for popes, prelates and priests."[1] Thus the historical outcome of early church politics is reflected within the text itself by an impression that here is a thoroughly ecclesiastical production, indicative of church authority. The irony is that this gospel, with its universal range and catholic authority,

St. Matthew the Evangelist in a miniature from the Lindisfarne Gospels made *c.*698 CE on the Northumbrian island. The scribe and illuminator of this Latin text of the four gospels was a monk named Eadfrith, who later became Bishop of Lindisfarne.

seems to have had its beginnings in the very narrow and limited circumstances of a Jewish-Christian sect. Only the subsequent sponsorship of this gospel by an influential church could have made the transition possible. But perhaps one can note similar instincts in the authoritarian discipline of a world-wide church and in the protective security of a sect which feels threatened. The scale is vastly different, but, given a certain temperament, the methods may well be similar.

"For seventeen centuries Matthew's gospel was regarded as the first gospel, both in order of composition and in importance. Matthew's gospel possesses certain characteristics which ensure that, if it is taken as the first gospel, it will overshadow Mark almost completely. Firstly, it is clearly *gospel*. Matthew gives a clear and structured account of the Lord Jesus Christ as the Messiah and Lord of the Church. Matthew has Jesus founding the Church. Jesus authorises the Church's ministry, its discipline, its mission and its theology. Matthew has the disciples sent out as missionaries to spread the faith by preaching and baptism. Matthew also recognises that the new kingdom, like the Old Israel, requires scribes and judges. Matthew's is a spectacular gospel of miracles and unambiguous signs. It lays the foundation for a certain kind of triumphalism which can always be assured of a popular response and is mirrored in the contemporary style of the papacy. Matthew's gospel is also judgmental. Matthew knew that the Lord forgave, but, try as he might (and he does try), he finds it very difficult to understand forgiveness. So he hedges it about and limits it in certain important ways. Matthew believes in clerical punishment. He thus lays the foundations for a Church-sanctioned morality which has been enormously influential, creative and damaging."[2]

These characteristic features of Matthew will be examined in more detail later but here they serve to give an initial impression. It is important to insist on the work's character as "gospel". To think of it as an ecclesiastical

Remains of a Roman aqueduct near Antakya, ancient Antioch on the Orontes (Syria). Antioch was an influential church centre authorizing Matthew's gospel.

The Deposition (or taking down of Christ from the cross) an oil painting by Graham Sutherland (1903–1980). Joseph of Arimathea's tomb may be seen bottom right.

product, perhaps designed as a handbook for teaching, administration and discipline within the church/sect, suggests similarities with the *Manual of Discipline* (1QS) at Qumran, or an early Christian writing outside the New Testament such as the *Didache* (or *Teaching of the Twelve Apostles*). But while such church needs may have coloured the presentation of key passages, and influenced the overall structure to some extent, the work's primary purpose is as gospel. It proclaims and interprets the story of Christ for the needs of Matthew's community and for that community's mission.

The distinctiveness of Matthew

The interests of Matthew and his community can be identified by a careful comparison of his gospel with those of Mark and Luke. The existence of parallel texts in the synoptic gospels offers a controlled comparison, where quite small changes can be significant. Matthew's distinctive theology can emerge from the way he handles a source (Mark, or the other material shared by Matthew and Luke which is referred to as Q), or develops a proof from an Old Testament quotation, used as prophecy by Matthew and other early Christian writers. Here are three examples, quite different in scale:

1 Matthew 27.57–61 shows one of his special emphases. Matthew does not present Joseph of Arimathea as an honoured member of the Jewish council, the Sanhedrin, and yet positively inclined towards Jesus, in the way that Mark, Luke and John do. Matthew depicts him as a disciple rich enough to own a tomb in the vicinity; Matthew may intend a deliberate allusion to Isaiah 53.9 (the suffering servant who is associated "with a rich man in his death"); with this rich man, Joseph, Matthew sees the Old Testament prophecy being fulfilled in Jesus' death. Thus Matthew makes opportunities to reinforce the idea of prophecies being fulfilled in the story of Jesus.

2 Matthew 18.10–14 shows how he applies source material differently. In Luke 15.4–7 the parable of the lost sheep exemplifies Jesus' attitude towards sinners, in contrast to the criticism voiced by the Pharisees. In Matthew the parable is applied in a context of church discipline; it deals with the brother who has lapsed from the community or is in danger of doing so. Here the "little ones" are the ordinary "rank and file" believers (a similar term is used at Qumran). Thus Matthew shows concern primarily for the discipline of the Christian community, rather than the wider field of mission to outsiders.

3 A major structural change in Matthew is his arrangement of the teaching of Jesus into discourses, like the Sermon on the Mount. There are five discourses, interspersed with narrative sections, and these give the entire gospel its shape. Because the plan has five parts, it is sometimes argued that Matthew is consciously imitating in the New Testament the structure of the five books of the Law (The Pentateuch: Genesis–Deuteronomy) in the Old Testament.[3] The argument is not conclusive although, if the gospel presents Jesus as the teacher and giver of a new authoritative law, it would support the case. This makes him look like a new law-giver greater than Moses.

Another way of identifying Matthew's special concerns is to see the gospel in a mirror as a reflection of a situation, or a reaction against a particular set of circumstances. This recognizes that the gospel does not chronicle the life of Matthew's community but that it does, though less directly, reflect that community. It seeks to strengthen particular aspects of the church, offering an answer to community problems by measuring them against the traditions of the gospel. One major area with which Matthew is concerned is the relationship of the church to Judaism, or perhaps more accurately the definition of Christianity over against Judaism.

Plan of the five discourses in Matthew

Chapters 1–2 The birth of Jesus
Section 1
(a) Narratives: the announcement of the Kingdom; glimpses from the ministry in Galilee (chs. 3–4)
(b) Discourse: Sermon on the Mount; Ethics for the Kingdom; higher righteousness as a requirement for entry to the Kingdom (chs. 5–7)
     Editorial conclusion: 7.28f
Section 2
(a) Narratives: Ministry as one in which disciples are to share (chs. 8–9)
(b) Discourse: Mission and martyrdom of disciples; preaching the Kingdom entails persecution (ch. 10)
     Editorial conclusion: 11.1
Section 3
(a) Narratives and debates: indicating the difficulties for outsiders to understand that the Kingdom is at work in Jesus (chs. 11–12)
(b) Discourse: understanding the nature of the Kingdom (the parables in ch. 13)
     Editorial conclusion: 13.53
Section 4
(a) Narratives and debates with disciples rather than with outsiders (chs. 14–17)
(b) Discourse on fraternal relations among disciples and on church discipline; the necessity of humility and forgiveness (ch. 18)
     Editorial conclusion: 19.1f
Section 5
(a) Narratives and debates in Jerusalem, sharpening issues with Pharisees and authorities (chs. 19–22)
(b) Discourse on the danger of hypocrisy – which leads to expulsion from the Kingdom – and on the nature of the last things and the Parousia (Christ's Second Coming); the proper way to wait for this coming (chs. 23–25)
     Editorial conclusion: 26.1f
Chapters 26–28 Passion and Resurrection
             The charge to the disciples

Relations with Judaism

Where Matthew's community stood in relation to Judaism is a much disputed issue among scholars. Almost all positions have been maintained – from the Gentile church hostile to (or ignorant of) Judaism, to the Jewish-Christian community which had not separated itself from Judaism. Such a range of possibilities is astonishing, and only exists because the gospel provides a range of evidence which appears inconsistent if not self-contradictory. It is a question of discovering a situation where this apparent paradox will fit.

Ignorance of Jewish conventions

At one extreme is the theory that Matthew's was a Gentile community for whom Jewish issues were irrelevant. This could be combined with a charge of profound ignorance of Judaism. It is one thing to note Matthew's concern for a world-wide mission to the Gentiles (on the basis of 24.14 and 28.19), although even this is debatable. It is much more difficult to sustain the case for Matthew's ignorance of Jewish customs, manners, and teaching. In fact the modern academic knowledge of first-century Judaism is far from complete. One suggestion is that, although Matthew used the Old Testament and Jewish-Christian traditions as his source material, he did not really understand Hebrew poetry. This is not based on stressed syllables and rhyme but on PARALLELISM, where words and ideas balance one another in each part of the verse.

So, it is said, when Matthew quotes Zechariah 9.9 at chapter 21.5:

> *Behold your king is coming to you,*
> *humble and mounted on an ass,*
> *and on a colt, the foal of an ass,*

he does not understand the parallelism between the last pair of lines and so he tells the story of the triumphal entry of Jesus to Jerusalem using two animals rather than one (21.7). It is clear that the Old Testament prophecy has deeply influenced Matthew's telling of the story. Jesus' activity is demonstrably the fulfilment of prophecy, and Matthew sometimes tries to intensify the impression by doubling numbers, but it is not so clear how precisely Matthew understood this prophecy. Certainly any confusion is not the result of Matthew's failure to understand Jewish parallelism. Repeatedly he uses this poetic technique himself, to intensify in his own words what has already been said in his source material. See, for example, in this same chapter, 21.41 and 43 (verse 43 is a special Matthean composition).

Judaism rejected?

If the idea of ignorance of Jewish methods and teaching is rejected, then another suggestion is that Matthew's Gentile community had decisively and permanently rejected Israel and the Jewish option for Christianity. The most striking evidence from the gospel for this view is at 27.25: Jesus' trial before Pilate. The procurator protests that he is innocent of Jesus' blood and ceremonially washes his hands. By the addition of this symbolic action Matthew further shifts the responsibility for Jesus' death from the Romans to the Jews; and, in confirmation of this, he makes the Jewish people say: "His blood be on us and on our children!"

Another section of the gospel often quoted in support of the permanent rejection of Israel is chapter 23. This is a powerful sequence of woes uttered against the scribes and Pharisees, which might sound like a denunciation of all that Judaism stands for. In fact it is quite specific in naming in the attack not all Jews, but only a certain group of the Jewish leaders: "Woe to you, scribes and Pharisees, hypocrites!" (The Pharisees were the more innovative teachers of the Jewish Law, on whom the future of Judaism depended after the Temple was destroyed.) It is also quite a restricted criticism, attacking not their teaching but their practice. The focus is then a condemnation of hypocrisy.

It is important to notice the way Matthew introduces this chapter. Jesus is speaking "to the crowds and to his disciples" and he says very positively:

> *The scribes and the Pharisees sit on Moses' seat; so practise and observe whatever they tell you, but not what they do; for they preach, but do not practise.* (23.2–3)

This sounds like an affirmation of the credentials of these Jewish leaders, by virtue of their maintenance of the law of Moses. What is at fault is not their teaching but their hypocritical practice. However polemical the ensuing statements, the positive attitude to the written Law and to Jewish teaching is entirely consistent with the principles expressed earlier in Matthew 5.17–20 ("Think not that I have come to abolish the law and the prophets").

It is significant that the whole discourse of Matthew 23 is addressed to the people at large, and not staged as a doctrinal controversy with the Pharisees. It is also addressed to the disciples, who stand for the Christian church in Matthew. This opens the possibility that the discourse is really intended to warn the leaders of the church against the dangers of hypocrisy. Christ's treatment of the hypocrisy of the scribes is then an educational warning to Christians, and the Pharisees are counter-examples to the positive models of Christian disciples in this gospel. It is certainly not clear from such evidence that Matthew intends to disown Judaism; such arguments against hypocrisy might be more powerfully effective if Matthew's audience rather had a strong sense of affinity with Jewish traditions.

Judaism accepted?

At the opposite end of the spectrum of Matthew's possible relationships with Judaism is the suggestion that Matthew's community still belongs within Judaism, even if the gospel was written in the last quarter of the first century. By this time, it is usually thought, Christianity had separated decisively from Judaism. One episode which particularly supports this idea is Matthew 17.24–27, a discussion unique to Matthew about the payment of the Jewish temple tax. The point of this story about Peter's penny is probably that Peter is shown to be an obedient disciple by his willingness to pay the tax. There is no reason then for Jews to reject the Christian gospel, because Jewish Christians do not behave in a radically different way, nor disown the central tenet that the Jewish dispersion is orientated on the Jerusalem Temple and positively supports its upkeep.

Even if Matthew's gospel shows some signs of friction with Judaism, nevertheless it is argued that the eventual break-away of Christianity had not yet happened in Matthew's locality. Other churches, perhaps encouraged by Paul's example, had become thoroughly Gentile and separated long ago. But

The Synagogue over against the Church: two symbolic figures from the 13th century south portal of Strasbourg cathedral. The Synagogue is represented as blindfolded in its ignorance of the truth represented by the Church. Matthew's church, literally or symbolically, is just across the street from the synagogue.

for Matthew's community any struggle with the concept of Israel was internal and not against the Jews as outsiders. After the fall of Jerusalem to the Romans in 70 CE, at the end of the Jewish War, many of the traditional aspects of Judaism were disrupted, just as the temple was devastated. A major reconstitution of Judaism took place in a council at Jamnia under the influence of the Pharisees, in particular Rabbi Johanan ben Zakkai. Many of the traditions of the temple were spiritualized within a pattern of worship (without sacrifice) and of ethical practice based on the synagogue communities. It could be argued that Matthew's gospel, and in particular the discourse of chapters 5–7, represents a Christian answer to the Pharisaic statements of Jamnia. The gospel offers a critique not so much of the theory as of the practice, but a critique from within the range of Jewish options. Accordingly the historical tradition of the Jerusalem temple is symbolically cherished.

This raises an important question about the boundaries of Jewish tolerance towards the end of the first century. The prayers called the Eighteen Benedictions were among the oldest parts of the Jewish synagogue service. Probably by the end of the first century CE an additional prayer was included which cursed certain heretics; this was clearly a test formula which Jewish Christians would not be able to utter:

> *For the renegades let there be no hope, and may the arrogant kingdom soon be rooted out in our days, and the Nazarenes and the* minim *perish as in a moment and be blotted out from the book of life, and with the righteous may they not be inscribed.*[4]

This is obviously an act setting limits to Jewish tolerance and drawing boundaries to exclude.

It has become normal practice to speak of Matthew's church as the one "across the street from the Jewish synagogue". This could be physically true, because archaeologists have provided actual examples of house-churches adjacent to house-synagogues but in Matthew's case what is often meant is a similarity of outlook as well as a physical proximity. There had been a smooth transition from the basis of Judaism to the development of Christianity, with none of the Pauline trauma that can be seen in a reading of the letter to the Galatians. If there is an argument in Matthew, it is a local one between the Pharisaic leaders of the Jewish community ("their synagogue") and Matthew's community ("our synagogue"). But if Matthew's church could see itself as still part of a federation of Jewish synagogues, this did not mean that the Jews were equally happy to see it that way.

Matthew 10.17 refers to judicial punishments of flogging administered to Christian disciples within the Jewish synagogue (in contrast to Mark 13.9 – a more general reference to mob violence):

> *They will deliver you up to councils, and flog you in their synagogues.*

"In all probability the charge for which Christians received this punishment was breach of the peace. This charge could only be made while Jewish Christians were still clearly identified with the synagogue community and

The Jerusalem temple as built by king Herod the Great (a reconstruction that is part of the Holy Land model in Jerusalem). The temple tax (Matthew 17.24–27) was paid by Jews throughout the Dispersion to maintain the temple.

propagating their faith in that community. When Christians, ostracized from the synagogue, withdrew into the Gentile community for both fellow-ship and missionary activity, they were no longer liable to the disciplinary action of the synagogue, nor could any legal charge be raised against them except before the civil courts."[5] Jews who moved out of the Jewish quarter of a town, and then became identified with a Gentile community, effectively removed themselves from the jurisdiction of the synagogue, even in the Dispersion. However, if Christians still lived in the Jewish quarter, the Jewish and the civil authorities would have to regard them as Jews, and the Jewish synagogue would have to punish them if they caused trouble.

Jewish-Christian community in transition

The interior of the synagogue at Dura Europos (north-west corner). The synagogue is important for its elaborate wall-paintings (see page 110); and the whole site is interesting because of the proximity of an early Christian house-church to the synagogue. There is also a pagan temple to the gods of Palmyra, and a Mithraeum.

If Matthew's community is accurately described as "a church in transition, a transition which has by no means ended",[6] it is reasonable to ask whether any visible split between Jew and Christian had already taken place. In terms of Matthew 10.17, is the prophecy by Jesus (of Christians being flogged in the Jewish synagogues) regarded by Matthew as fulfilled in the present circumstances, or in the past experiences of his community? Had Matthew's church already left the Jewish quarter? Several scholars, who are totally convinced about the Jewishness of Matthew's community, nevertheless believe that a final separation had by then taken place between Jew and Christian. The Christians had been forced out by Jewish pressure, and the boundaries of Judaism had been redrawn more tightly. The Christian "synagogue" no longer qualified and this would have had a devastating effect on its group identity.

According to this view, Matthew's community was located between the two extremes of complete Jewishness on the one hand, and of a Gentile situation where Judaism was unknown and irrelevant on the other. This Jewish-Christian community had only recently been forced across the frontier and away from strictly orthodox Judaism, after protracted hostilities. Matthew is puzzled – indeed pained – by the Jews' continued rejection of Jesus, and of Christian messengers, who have proclaimed Jesus as the fulfilment of Israel's hopes. He is only beginning to come to terms with separation from Judaism and the threat of persecution and unceasing hostility.

The evidence for this dramatic and recent change, beyond the general sense of an appropriate context for Matthew's paradox (the tension between his positive and negative attitudes to Judaism), lies in a single verse. This verse, already noted (on p. 193) as occurring only in Matthew, at 21.43, is particularly appropriate as a prophecy of exactly this situation of transition. The prophecy is placed in the words of Jesus following, and interpreting, the parable of the wicked tenants of the vineyard (= Israel):

> *Therefore I tell you, the kingdom of God will be taken away from you and given to a nation producing the fruits of it.*

This prophecy relates to a time when historical Israel (as continued by Judaism) will forfeit all the rights of the covenant. At that point a new nation (represented by Matthew's community) will inherit these rights, by virtue of its appropriate beliefs and practices. The phrase "producing the fruits" is similarly used of living the Christian life at 3.8, 10; 7.17–19; 12.33. Matthew combines the prophecy of 21.43 with the quotation from Psalm 118.22f also found at the end of this parable in Mark:

> *The very stone which the builders rejected has become the head of the corner; this was the Lord's doing, and it is marvellous in our eyes.* (21.42)

To read verses 42 and 43 together suggests that Matthew sees the new nation (his community) as the stone which the Jewish leaders rejected. The Psalm quotation, which is usually applied (by Mark 12.6–11 and elsewhere in the New Testament) to Jesus, is here applied by Matthew to his church: although rejected by the Jews, this community is acceptable to God.

This theological justification – a divine blessing on the change – suggests that the transition has already taken place, and only recently, so that it still needs explanation and justification. Another text which makes clear the distancing between Matthew and traditional Judaism is at 28.15: the soldiers who were bribed to spread the story that Jesus' body had been stolen by the disciples "took the money and did as they were directed; and this story has been spread *among the Jews* to this day". Matthew here uses the expression "the Jews" in the same way as it is used in John's gospel (e.g. 8.48), indicating separation, distance, and hostility. "Whereas the Gentile Luke speaks of the synagogue with the detachment natural to one for whom it is a foreign institution, Matthew speaks as one for whom it has only recently become an alien institution."[7]

Matthew's community in an eschatological atmosphere

Matthew's community has to be located in such a way as to explain *both* the intense Jewishness of the tradition to which he belongs *and* the sense of distance and hostility to the Jews or their Pharisaic leaders. The gospel shows evidence of a strengthening both of the polemic against the Jews (represented by their role in the trial of Jesus before Pilate), and also of the themes of apocalyptic (which are rightly regarded as characteristically Jewish ever since the book of Daniel). There is one situation which can explain satisfactorily both the addition of such eschatological language and the increase in anti-Jewish polemic. Matthew's community identified strongly with Judaism, but a recent redrawing of the Jewish boundaries in a narrower way had forced them outside. This decisive and traumatic break would explain the current sense of alienation and the polemical reaction against the Pharisees in particular. With this alienation from the outside world (where they really felt they belonged), Matthew encourages in the members of his community a sense of group solidarity. For this purpose, the language of eschatology was appropriately used to reinforce solidarity. Just as in the pattern of later millenarian sects, the minority group which feels excluded by cataclysmic events from the wider society uses the imagery of apocalyptic to re-define both the cataclysm and the purpose of its own future existence.

Matthew is responsible for adding numerous features to the gospel which make the narrative more spectacular and the events more stupendous. Among these are the images of heightened eschatology, for example, in the closing sequences: the "angel of the Lord" who takes the place of the young man at the tomb (28.2–4); the earthquakes, one which accompanies the appearance of the angel and enables him to roll away the stone (28.2), and the other associated with the tearing of the temple curtain (27.51); and the general resurrection of "the saints" at 27.52–53. Certainly this eschatological view of resurrection is cross-referenced by Matthew to Jesus' own Resurrection from the new tomb provided by Joseph. It is even possible that Matthew, by placing the resurrection of the saints just after Jesus has died, is deliberately including an allusion to an early tradition that Jesus rose and ascended to heaven straight from the cross. By the phrase "after his Resurrection" at 27.53, Matthew tries to accommodate this tradition along with the later and much more widely accepted belief in Resurrection on the third day.

Comparison with Mark

Further support for this view of the alienated community can be derived from observing how Matthew handles the main block of eschatological material in the discourse of chapters 23–25. When Matthew is most dependent on Marcan material as his source, his practice is to tidy up and clarify meaning, often within a considerable expansion, and so he does here, on the basis of the "Little Apocalypse" from Mark 13. A section of the Marcan source (13.9–13) contains instructions as to how Jesus' followers are to behave if they are arrested and put on trial. Matthew moves this section out of the eschatological sequence of chapter 24 and locates it within a set of instructions for Christian missionaries at 10.17–21. There is obvious appropriateness in considering how missionaries should behave when they are arrested by the authorities. This "tidying up" makes Matthew 24 more consistently supernatural in its subject-matter, and it acknowledges the realities of daily life for missionaries, as Matthew's community is now experiencing them. It does not mean that 10.17–21 is any less "apocalyptic" than Mark 13.9–13. This "sign of the end" is still a sign of the end, even when it has become a daily fact of life for Matthew's eschatological sect.

Matthew 24 provides a consistently supernatural package of eschatological symbols and portents. As prophecied by Jesus, their fulfilment is not necessarily far into the future (in Matthew's perspective). Matthew has considerably extended the scope of the discourse into chapter 25, by adding much material either of his own or from the source he shares with Luke. A block of this material consists of sayings and parables (24.37–25.46). The most celebrated of the parables is the vision of last judgement at 25.31–46. This is not so much a parable as a revelation discourse or apocalyptic warning. However, Mark 13.33–37 shows that the imagery of parables or educational stories has an important warning role in the eschatological context. Mark's brief story may well have been the inspiration for Matthew's extended sequence of parables.

Another significant addition from Matthew's own material is at 24.9–12:

> *You will be hated by all nations for my name's sake. And then many will fall away, and betray one another, and hate one another. And many false prophets will arise and lead many astray. And because wickedness is multiplied, most men's love will grow cold.*

It would be hard to find a more graphic account of Matthew's own situation than this. His community had experienced oppression from outside, and tensions and potential schisms within, as they faced up to their official disinheritance from Judaism. This prophecy was to be a solemn warning and explanation of why this had happened. This eschatological context sustains a call to be vigilant and to strengthen their corporate identity as a sect. Matthew associates this call firstly with the responsibility of the sect to proclaim and live out the "gospel of the Kingdom" with which they have been entrusted (24.14), and secondly with the promise (which he shares with Mark and Luke) that "he who endures to the end will be saved" (24.13).

Comparison with Qumran

A comparison of the Jewish sectarian community which lived at Qumran and produced the Dead Sea Scrolls with Matthew's community demonstrates how eschatology (language and ideas) can strengthen group solidarity. It offered an explanation, in terms of God's will and predestined

The Temple Scroll from cave 11 at Qumran (11Q TS), this text was copied in the 1st century BCE, and the original may have been composed early or late in the 2nd century BCE.

The Temple Scroll: one of the manuscripts before it was unwound. The state of the material (as discovered) shows what a delicate task it was to unravel.

purpose, of why that group was an isolated sect. It generated a "symbolic universe" (a world of ideas) opposed to that of the dominant society. This "universe" gave them security and purpose. More importantly still, they were able to perceive that theirs was the legacy of God's historic promises to Israel, and theirs was the kingdom which Israel had forfeited by its inadequacies and impure practices. One of the most recently published texts from Qumran is the *Temple Scroll* (11Q TS), perhaps more accurately described as the Torah (Law) Scroll. It is a recasting of legal traditions from Exodus to Deuteronomy, in the form of a direct and authoritative speech of God to Moses. This Jewish law-book, while essentially based on the Old Testament text, makes direct and authoritative claims for the law of the last days, as revealed here. It can be argued that it was a special revelation to this sect, although not all scholars agree with this interpretation.

The claims are at least for equality with, and probably for superiority over, the Torah of the scroll (the law of Moses) possessed by the official teachers of Judaism. The author of the Qumran scroll asserts that the temple-sanctuary, prescribed by the fundamental legal texts of the Pentateuch, is not to be identified with the tabernacle used by the Israelites in the wilderness; nor is it identifiable with the temple built by Solomon (much less the temple of king Herod). The satisfactory implementation of these legal commandments has never been completed in the past; but it is to be fulfilled in the conditions of the last days. This is the final Law, the Torah for the end of time (the *eschaton*), and it is only within the confines of the Qumran sect that the proper conditions of purity, holiness, and covenant renewal can lead to the fulfilment of God's promised redemption, according to the beliefs of the founder and members of that community.

This eschatological sect had effectively appropriated the traditional legal texts which formed the scriptural basis of Israel's faith and Israel itself (at least as represented by current orthodoxy) was being subjected to searching criticism by the sect. The theological problem addressed was why Israel had fallen short. In view of the long history of God's promises to Israel (recorded in the Old Testament), why was God's chosen people in such a plight and facing such a crisis? From the perspective of the Qumran sect, it appeared as if God was removing himself from the traditional establishment of Israel and coming to dwell with the sect, as the last refuge of God-given purity and holiness. (See the imagery in Ezekiel chapters 10, 11 and 43.)

In the *Temple Scroll* the royal covenant with David and the Mosaic Torah are seen in the same perspective. In column 59 of this text the former king of Israel is castigated for the past and present sufferings of God's people. Israel has been inadequate and backsliding but God has foreseen this impiety and therefore prescribed a law of the last days, to redeem his chosen from just such a situation. In the belief of the sect, Moses had been entrusted with another law book, a hidden one, which could now be revealed within the Qumran community. The sect's activity enshrined the last (desperate) hope that the remainder of the nation would learn from experience and from the example of the sect and ultimately repent. If not, there was still confidence that the remnant (the sect itself) would be saved.

Qumran's use of the Old Testament

The eschatological sect at Qumran used a distinctive method of interpreting the texts which it valued from the Old Testament. This method is often referred to technically as *Pesher* or *Midrash-pesher* (which simply means "interpretation" or "interpretative commentary"). It was a free, creative, imaginative, and quite audacious method of explaining the meaning, a

The ruins at Qumran. In the foreground is the traditional site of the Scriptorium (the place where the scrolls would have been copied on analogy with a monastery). The ink bottle found on site is inconclusive evidence, because ink would also be needed for commercial operations. The Dead Sea scrolls were used and hidden at Qumran, but may not have been produced there.

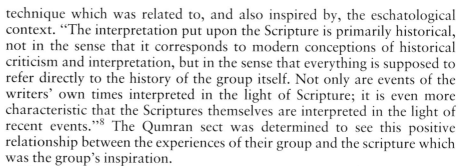

above The Habakkuk commentary found in cave 1 at Qumran (1Qp Hab). This was copied at the end of the 1st century BCE.

below A scroll jar from Qumran. Just as the Dead Sea scrolls were discovered in jars such as this, so now they are housed in the Shrine of the Book (at the Israel Museum in Jerusalem) the roof of which is designed like the lid of this jar.

technique which was related to, and also inspired by, the eschatological context. "The interpretation put upon the Scripture is primarily historical, not in the sense that it corresponds to modern conceptions of historical criticism and interpretation, but in the sense that everything is supposed to refer directly to the history of the group itself. Not only are events of the writers' own times interpreted in the light of Scripture; it is even more characteristic that the Scriptures themselves are interpreted in the light of recent events."[8] The Qumran sect was determined to see this positive relationship between the experiences of their group and the scripture which was the group's inspiration.

There are three main assumptions of this *Pesher* method:

1 Scripture has a veiled meaning which belongs to the last days and the eschatological crisis. These secrets of scripture are only open to a "teacher" properly trained to read the text. Those outside have no access to the secrets, even though they possess the sacred texts themselves.

2 This concealed meaning may be discovered by all manner of devices which might seem to take liberties with a sacred text: e.g. putting two or more texts together; choosing to interpret a variant reading of the text; changing the text by transposing letters; extracting a spiritual or allegorical meaning rather than the literal meaning of the text.

3 The meaning so revealed can be applied directly to the events or circumstances of the present day, as a proof of fulfilment.

Qumran, using such interpretative techniques, was able to take an authoritative reading of the Jewish Law, as applying uniquely to the sect (as in 11Q TS, the *Temple Scroll* or Torah scroll). In the same way the words of Old Testament prophets were applied to the situation of the sectarian community, as in the *Commentary on Habakkuk* (1Qp Hab):

> *God told Habakkuk to write down the things that were to come upon the latter age* [the last generation], *but He did not inform him when that moment would come to fulfilment. As to the phrase, "so he may run who reads it"* [Habakkuk 2.2], *this refers to the teacher who expounds the Law aright, for God has made him aware of all the deeper implications* [the secrets] *of the words of His servants the prophets.* (1Qp Hab 7.1–5)

The parable of the sower (Matthew 13.3–9), as depicted in Les Tres Riches Heures du Duc de Berry. The realistic Palestinian setting of the original parable is here transformed into 15th century French realism.

above Painting by David Roberts showing the view from Nazareth towards Sepphoris. After the Roman conquest of Palestine, Sepphoris was selected as the administrative centre of Galilee.

right Sketch by David Roberts of the Shrine of the Nativity in Bethlehem (1839). The niche on the left contains a representation of the glory that guided the Magi – shown worshipping above the niche.

Matthew's use of the Old Testament

It has been strongly and convincingly argued that a very similar kind of scriptural scholarship to that of Qumran (and quite distinct from the methods of the orthodox rabbis) existed with Matthew and his community. The similarity is confirmed not only by the practice but also by the reasons for the practice. Matthew's community shows all the signs of a beleaguered minority group, cut off from its Jewish roots (through no wish of its own), a sect which expresses its sense of alienation through the medium of eschatological ideas. Within this eschatological context the community defines itself as the last sanctuary for the preservation of those fundamentals of Israel's faith. It tries desperately to live up to its high calling, as represented in these responsibilities to preserve true holiness. But it is also inclined to be bitter and vengeful; this typical, and entirely understandable, desire for vengeance (upon the Pharisees in particular) is expressed in the notion of eternal punishment and the principle of just requital (21.41; 13.41–42; 16.27).

Matthew can be described in his own words (unique to Matthew) as a "scribe trained for the kingdom":

> *Therefore every scribe who has been trained for the kingdom of heaven is like a householder who brings out of his treasure what is new and what is old.* (13.52)

The scholar who applied this description to Matthew himself explains: "The author of the gospel of Matthew ... was a Jewish-Christian author thoroughly familiar with the Old Testament and with Jewish traditions of its interpretation. He employed this knowledge as a key to the organisation of a number of the parts of his gospel ... He especially showed his understanding of the relationship between his Christian faith and the Old Testament, and the relationship of both to the problems of Christians of his own day. He was, therefore, 'a scribe' ... I do not mean that it can be shown that Matthew was actually a Jewish scribe, or that he had been trained as one, *although both might be true* [my italics]. I do think that Matthew would not have objected to this description of himself."[9]

Matthew the scribe

It is important that the term "scribe" should be defined with care. As a scribe, Matthew is an interpreter and exegete of scripture, commenting on its ultimate meaning in relation to the role of Christ in the Christian community. His church stands within Jewish Christianity and is permeated by those Jewish traditions which are the context of Christ's teaching. For the same reasons as the Qumran community, Matthew feels estranged from Pharisaic orthodoxy, and in sharp conflict with them, and he preserves the essence of true Israel in sectarian ways. Only so will the purist ideals survive in the bitterness of the current crisis. Matthew's special concerns are featured in the exact knowledge about questions of defilement (chapter 8), and in the precise answers given in the debate on cleanness/uncleanness (15.1–20). He is a scribe with the original Jewish traditions in his heart, but trained (or obliged by events) to pursue sectarian rather than mainstream disciplines. He sees the true Israel as centred on Christ the teacher, in much the same way that Qumran was formed by, and focussed upon, the Teacher of Righteousness.

It has long been emphasized that Matthew is, by training and theological temperament, a commentator upon and interpreter of scripture. He differs from Luke, for example, in this respect. Luke is a theologian of salvation history who sees the impact of large theological issues on the public stage. Matthew is a pastoral theologian within a relatively small community, working at an internal education programme, using teaching from scripture to shape the attitudes of the group. He has been variously characterized: as a Jewish rabbi converted to Christianity, a provincial schoolmaster, or a church educator or catechist. His gospel is related to a programme of catechetical training for his church, or is seen as an extended homily or midrashic exposition, which reinterprets Old Testament themes and earlier gospel traditions in a new synthesis. Matthew seems concerned to present a faith that has been *proved*; what is required within the community, to

---

Old Testament quotations in Matthew

Emphasis on fulfilment of scriptural prophecy

Matthew 1.22–23	(Isaiah 7.14)	Simple fulfilment text
2.15	(Hosea 11.1)	Clue to link with Moses
2.17–18	(Jeremiah 31.15)	Simple fulfilment text
2.23	(?Isaiah 11.1/?Judges 13.5)	Source disputed but key text for Nazareth move
4.14–16	(Isaiah 9.1–2)	Validates start of ministry
8.17	(Isaiah 53.4)	Inclusively applies to healings
12.17–21	(Isaiah 42.1–4)	Jesus as the servant, structural importance for ch. 12
13.14–15	(Isaiah 6.9–10)	Structural importance for theory and interpretation of parables
13.35	(Psalm 78.2)	Jesus as the revealer of secrets through parables
21.4–5	(Zechariah 9.9 + Isaiah 62.11)	Text is source of *two* animals in the story
27.9–10	(Zechariah 11.13 is quoted; ?influence of Jeremiah 19.1–13; compare 32.6–9; 18.1–2)	Interpretation of Judas' fate, interweaving of texts

This group is distinctive because of the precise introductory formula used ("in fulfilment of that which was spoken"). Another distinctive feature may be the unusually mixed nature of the Old Testament text used.

Compare:

Matthew 3.3	(Isaiah 40.3)	
11.10	(Malachi 3.1)	
15.7–9	(Isaiah 29.13)	
21.42	(Psalm 118.22–23)	
also 2.5–6	(Micah 5.2)	Integral to the story – cited by the scribes and priests

These examples have less rigid introductory formulae; the idea of fulfilment is still essential to their use in the gospel, but that precise term is not used. There are at least sixty direct citations of the Old Testament in this gospel, apart from those which are introduced by the fulfilment formula.

The parable of the wise and foolish virgins (Matthew 25.1–13) below. Above sits Christ in judgement flanked by Peter, with the keys, and Paul. From the 12th century CE north door of Basel Minster, Switzerland.

strengthen its identity and self-confidence, is an objective and irresistible basis for belief. This, however, is for internal consumption, to reassure the faithful as they look out on a scene of disobedience and unbelief. It cannot be an explanation for the outsider, or a missionary work to attract new converts.

To arrive at a fair description of Matthew's role his particular methods of using quotations from the Old Testament have been studied intensively. Special attention has been focussed on those citations which emphasize in the way they are introduced that these prophecies have been fulfilled in the events of the gospel. These proof texts were for the Christian community around Matthew what the *Pesher* method of interpretation was for Qumran. It can be seen how closely his methods of eliciting the desired meaning from scripture correspond to Qumran's practice (including the creative use of a variety of text-readings, interpreting one text in the light of another, and allowing the secret meaning to dominate the plain meaning of the text). As has been noted (p. 204), they arise from the same causes in a similarly alienated and self-justifying community.

In some of these examples it is not simply the fulfilment of prophecy that is expressed by the Old Testament citation. The selected text has a structural importance for the particular sequence of argument in that section of the gospel. The section is formed around the text which links quite disparate materials together. It gives the passage its organizational principle, as Matthew works forward to the quotation at the heart of the section, and then moves outward again to the end of the passage. This procedure can best be seen in a working example, Matthew's presentation of the parable of the sower:

Matthew's parable of the sower

Matthew 13
1–9   Jesus' parable
9   Concluding exegetical formula
       "He who has ears, let him hear!"
10   Question – why speak in parables?
11–12 Answer initially in terms of apocalyptic "secrets"
13–17 Parables are secrets – a further explanation in terms of the
       prophecy of Isaiah 6.9–10
       It is natural that the people as a whole will not understand, while
       you (the disciples = the church), who have the secrets explained,
       will understand
18   Responds to 13.9, offering exegesis
18–23 Interpretation of the parable for the disciples by the teacher
       The meaning of the interpretation is itself derived from the
       prophecy of Isaiah 6.9–10
       The interpretation is therefore *doubly* in accord with the
       "theory" of parables in verses 11–17
       Matthew's distinction is really between two kinds of people
       (instead of four) because the four examples are grouped into two
       categories:
       those who hear and understand (verse 23)
       and those who hear but do not understand (19, 20, 22)
       Interpretation based on key words:
                                   kingdom (11)
                                   hear (13, 16, 17)
                                   understand (15)

Matthew's use of parables

It can be observed that Matthew's theory of parables is the opposite side of the coin to Mark's. For Mark the parables challenge people to see Jesus who is himself the "secret" of the Kingdom (Mark 4.11). Those who do not respond to the challenge (which is open) are left with puzzling riddles. But for Matthew the disciples (= the church) have the parables/the secrets, which are unlocked for them by Jesus' teaching. Other people outside the sect do not have access to this meaning. There is substantial (threefold) evidence that Matthew has revised the reading of the parable material in his sources, in accordance with a secrecy theory appropriate for an eschatological sect:

1 Matthew replaces the singular "secret" in Mark 4.11 by the plural "secrets" at 13.11. (So does Luke at 8.10 but for a different reason.)

2 Matthew omits "in parables [riddles]" at 13.11. He is not making Mark's contrast between the insight of those within and the riddles/parables for those without, because for Matthew the parables (rightly handled within the community) are the means of insight.

3 Matthew makes it clear by "this is why" and "because" in 13.13 that he is providing a causal explanation, based on Isaiah 6.9–10, of his use of parables. He is not interested in Mark's or Luke's sense of the missionary challenge of faith, which recognizes, as a possible corollary, that it may be God's will that some do not respond. Mark expresses this hard truth by the "purpose" expressions ("so that" and "lest") in 4.12.

Matthew's community: the church which held the secrets

Several passages, such as Matthew 10; 22.8–9; 28.18–20, suggest a positive view of mission by Matthew's community. But these passages, especially the last, should not have their significance exaggerated beyond the bounds set by this gospel. Matthew cannot be made to advocate a universal Gentile mission, or to agree with Paul.

Mission to Israel

Firstly Matthew makes it clear that the historical mission of Jesus himself was confined to Israel. The meeting of Jesus with the Canaanite woman from the area of Tyre and Sidon is the context for the most explicit statement:

> *I was sent only to the lost sheep of the house of Israel.* (15.24)

If Matthew 15.21–31 is compared with Mark 7.24–37 (there is no parallel in Luke), it is obvious that Matthew has added this narrow definition of Jesus' mission. For him there can be no question of two stages in the process, first a Jewish then a Gentile mission; he rules this out by omitting the significant first clause of Mark 7.27: "*Let the children first be fed*, for it is not right to take the children's bread and throw it to the dogs". The clever repartee of the woman's reply remains:

> "*Yes, Lord, yet even the dogs eat the crumbs that fall from their master's table*" (15.27)

but the focus has altered. The bread clearly belongs to the children in perpetuity; there is only the possibility of some scraps which might fall for a few of those outside the family. This woman is promised just such an isolated opportunity, on the grounds of her "faith". Matthew also omits Mark's reference at 7.31 to the region of the Decapolis (outside Israel to the east of Galilee). This confirms the general impression which Matthew gives of Jesus' ministry within the bounds of Israel. (See Matthew's summary at 9.35.) In the same way the mission of the disciples is also confined to Israel, closely following the pattern of Jesus' ministry. The charge to the twelve is:

> Go nowhere among the Gentiles, and enter no town of the Samaritans, but go rather to the lost sheep of the house of Israel. (10.5–6)

The general impression is of activity within Israel (10.17 refers to "synagogues" and 10.23 concludes: "you will not have gone through all the towns of Israel, before the Son of Man comes"). These twelve representative disciples are chosen and commissioned, with a mission that typifies the church's mission. Curiously Matthew does not say that the disciples went out, or came back, on this occasion (contrasted with Mark 6.7, 12 and Luke 9.2, 6). In fact, the editorial conclusion at 11.1 shows that the mission charge has turned into a discourse containing instructions on discipleship. From this one can conclude that Jesus' instructions are to be fulfilled *after the Resurrection*; these are guidelines on mission for the church which are to be valid for all time but the eschatological note struck by 10.23 stays as a reminder that the time is short.

Mission to the Gentiles

In addition to the mission to Israel, there are some indications of a mission to the Gentiles in Matthew. One slightly discordant note is found in the mission instructions of chapter 10:

> and you will be dragged before governors and kings for my sake, to bear testimony before them and the Gentiles.

If, as was suggested earlier, this reflects the stage when Matthew's community finds itself outside the Jewish boundaries, excluded by the synagogue and therefore on trial before civic authorities, then giving evidence in a court of law can amount to witnessing to the faith before the Gentiles (non-Jews). But this is more like a sign of defiance to the world than a mission strategy, embarked upon voluntarily.

"On the one hand Matthew rejects the Gentiles most decisively, yet on the other hand he criticises the Jews very severely and it seems often that according to his opinion ultimate salvation will be given to the Gentiles."[10] To say this is to take a significant further step, and suggest that eventually for Matthew Jewish mission becomes Gentile mission under force of circumstances. This is not necessarily the way he looked at it. The parable of the vineyard tenants (wicked husbandmen – 21.33–41) and the parable of the invitations to the marriage feast (22.2–10) are both concerned with the rejection of Jesus by Israel – his rejection as Messiah and the rejection of his invitation to the Kingdom. The historical rejection does not exclude the idea of a mission to Israel for Matthew's church as identified with the disciples; rather the original reaction to Jesus and the subsequent failure of the church's mission serve to confirm Israel's guilt and the justice of God's judgement. This is a situation that can be interpreted theologically, and involves the principle of just requital and retribution which is so important to Matthew's eschatological experience. Thus Matthew 23.34–36, in the context of the fiercest criticism of the Pharisees:

> *Therefore I send you prophets and wise men and scribes, some of whom you will kill and crucify, and some you will scourge in your synagogues and persecute from town to town, that upon you may come all the righteous blood shed on earth, from the blood of innocent Abel to the blood of Zechariah the son of Barachiah, whom you murdered between the sanctuary and the altar. Truly, I say to you, all this will come upon this generation.*

Matthew's parable of the marriage feast (22.2–10) can be compared with Luke's parable of the great banquet (14.16–24). In Matthew the invitations are delivered by two sets of servants; it is natural to think of the first set as the prophets who were sent to the Jews (22.3), and the second set as the Christian prophets and missionaries of Matthew's church operating within Israel (22.4–6). As a result of this equally negative response to the second set of servants, the prophecy of an earlier parable (21.43) will come into effect. "The Kingdom of God will be taken away" from historical Israel and given to the "rejected" nation (Matthew's community now seen as the "new" Israel). As the consequence of this new state of affairs, it could be said that a mission to the Gentiles will take the place of the mission to the Jews. But when would this radical transition take place? The conclusion of Matthew 28, verses 18–20, might suggest that the Gentile mission is a consequence of Jesus' death and Resurrection. But this cannot be, since Matthew's church (the disciples) have a mission, of which the terms of reference match Jesus' own, that is, a mission exclusively to Israel.

The point of transition might therefore have been well after Jesus' death, at the time of Jerusalem's fall in 70 CE. Again the symbolism of the parable of the marriage feast could point to this conclusion. The king responds to the treatment of the Christian missionaries by the Jews:

> *the king was angry, and he sent his troops and destroyed those murderers and burned their city.* (22.7)

This brief allusion could be compared with Luke 21.20 and the detail of Josephus' description in *Jewish War*. After the events of Matthew 22.7, the new era of the Gentile mission begins (22.8–9). It is possible that the symbolic happening – the curtain of the temple being torn from top to bottom – which is described in eschatological terms in 27.51 is a further "prophecy" of this cataclysm which befell Israel in 70 CE. A Jewish thinker could see the destruction of the temple as the judgement of God, executed by the Romans as agents. In the Old Testament the earlier destruction by the Babylonians had been interpreted in this way. But it is one thing to interpret

Roman action as a divine agency of judgement; it is quite another to identify the Roman emperor as the king who is angry (as the parable would require), because the king who sent the invitations at the start of the parable is God himself. We must conclude that this timing of the beginning of the Gentile mission does not exactly work for a reverent Jewish mind which would not confuse God with a man.

Mission restricted to the true Israel

Matthew is different from Paul, who went out of his way to welcome Gentiles, in order to make Jews jealous enough to be saved (Romans 11.13–14). Matthew would not leave the Jewish tradition, even if he had been excommunicated from the synagogue. It was quite improbable that a man who was very proud of standing in the Jewish tradition would have been convinced that his present period was the time of the Gentile rather than the Jewish mission, for any reason whatsoever. For Matthew the whole idea of a distinct Gentile church is inconceivable. The added conclusion (found only in Matthew 22.11–14) to the parable of the marriage feast makes this uncomfortably clear. As a result of the servants' activity, the wedding hall has been filled with guests, both bad and good (22.10). Already there is a hint of an internal judgement, to correspond with the king's judgement on historical Israel at 22.7. And so it proves to be, for there is at least one man at the party without a wedding garment.

The nature of the wedding feast has not changed, even though the servants have brought people out of the streets. (Unlike Luke 14.23, people are not brought from outside the town.) The parameters are those of true Israel, which should have been the historical people of God, but is now constituted by the new nation (Matthew's church), which produces the proper fruits. If there is any Gentile mission in Matthew, it is only the missionary activity to introduce Gentiles into the true Israel.

At the end of the day it is appropriate that this "mixed" community of Christian Israel should be judged, to make sure that it lives up to the identity and moral standards set for Israel. This way of understanding the wedding garment is supported by another text in an apocalyptic context, Revelation 19.8, where the garment of "fine linen, bright and pure ... is the righteous deeds of the saints". In Matthew's story the lesson of this last judgement (22.13) is clearly expressed: "many are called, but few are chosen" (22.14).

Gentiles are non-Christians

Because Matthew's church was so closely identified with Israel, the term "Gentiles" (the plural word at 10.18; 25.32; 28.19) meant those who were not Christians (of Christian Israel), just as a Jewish speaker would designate non-Jews. It is foreign to the context of Matthew's gospel to translate this word more neutrally as "nations", and thereby open the way to a more universalist scope of mission. Matthew's disciple stands up before civic authorities to witness to his faith. His community functions after the model

Life in ancient Antioch on the Orontes: a man and a sundial in the suburbs at Daphne (from the Hatay Museum, Antioch).

of Old Testament Israel, obeying the noble calling of being a sign, a symbol, a light to those who are Gentiles, outsiders, non-Jews. The sense of being a beacon-light in a darkened world must have been intensified for Matthew's eschatological sect, estranged from corrupt and condemned Jewry. Theirs was the great responsibility, as inheritors of all the Old Testament promises, to live up to this standard and to conduct themselves worthily in holiness and purity. They were a small remnant, an eschatological community; they could not expect hordes of converts to their rigid lifestyle. Any who came were more than likely to vanish away.

Locating Matthew's community

With a community so sharply defined and rigorously principled as Matthew's church, it should be possible to locate it with some geographical precision. It has been observed (p. 187) that for a gospel produced by a narrow sect to become the mainstay of the catholic church's lectionary required some political influence from a major church centre such as Antioch. In fact Antioch in Syria is the place traditionally held to be where Matthew's gospel was written. There are several indications from internal and external evidence to support this origin and there is much less to say on behalf of other candidates, such as Alexandria (the other main centre of eastern Christianity which debated with Antioch) and Pella (the rather insignificant place of refuge for some Christians at the time of Jerusalem's fall in 70 CE).

The location at Pella would make Matthew's gospel into a symbolic statement of reconstituted Jewish Christianity, a manifesto for the continued existence of the Jerusalem church, and clearly in opposition to the Pharisaic pronouncements from Jamnia (see p. 196). This is an attractive idea but it lacks hard evidence. The story of the Christian flight to Pella, used by the third-century CE church father Eusebius in his history of the church, was derived from Aristo of Pella in the mid-second century. It is at least possible that Aristo contrived the story to give an apostolic ancestry to the community at Pella. Such legends were important ammunition in rivalries between churches.

The case for Antioch in Syria

To accept the identification of Antioch would have the interesting consequence of associating the central position and authority of Peter in this gospel (16.17–19) with the primary influence of Peter at Syrian Antioch. This would have been Peter's area, compared with the power of James (the Great) in Jerusalem. The New Testament evidence comes from an obviously one-sided account by Paul (in Galatians 2.11–15) of a major confrontation with Peter at Antioch. The issue is table-fellowship, and whether Jewish Christians should keep themselves apart like Jews or eat with Gentile Christians. Paul, as apostle to the Gentiles, holds one view, while James presumably holds rigidly to the opposite and separatist position. The trouble with Peter is that he does not act consistently (perhaps influenced by his experiences at Caesarea – Acts 10). The exact situation probably cannot be reconstructed, because only Paul's version is available. But it seems likely that the Antioch incident confirmed Paul in his mission to the Gentiles (and made him very angry). He probably lost the argument with Peter, who reverted to a more disciplined practice of purity for the sake of Jewish Christianity. Peter's apostolic authority over the Jewish-Christian communities at Antioch is thereby confirmed.

"In Antioch the disciples were for the first time called Christians", at least according to Acts 11.26. The circumstances which produced this extent of Christian self-definition over against Judaism would be useful to know, and possibly very relevant to the crisis which Matthew's community faced. Sadly Acts does not explain, beyond saying that Jewish Christians from Palestine started the church in Antioch and Gentile evangelism developed there (11.19–21). For the rest, scholars simply speculate. It is reasonable to suggest that to take the formal name of "Christ-people" was a way of claiming adherence to Jesus; to set up a "Jesus-school" of disciples was to maintain continuity with him as teacher, perhaps as a check against wider freedoms or spirit-enthusiasm in a more Hellenistic environment.

There is strong evidence for growing and thriving Jewish communities in Antioch, ever since its foundation in 300 BCE by Seleucus Nicator. The city attracted Jewish settlers because of its proximity to Palestine and its importance as an administrative and commercial centre (ranked third or fourth in the Roman Empire). It was also a vital stepping-stone between Palestine and Asia Minor, on both overland and sea routes. In many ways it seemed a bridge city to the outside world and a place of compromises. Where there are easy compromises, so eventually reactions set in and sharper distinctions are made.

A substantial Jewish population would have had numerous synagogues; the main one (the Kerateion) was in the southern Jewish quarter, but there were others out in the suburbs at Daphne, and for Jewish tenant-farmers in the surrounding countryside. Among the Jews also there was a wide range of social class, from the most affluent to the poor and the slaves. It was from this mixture that Christianity emerged and eventually became strong. In the aftermath of the Jewish War, some Christians might have wished to separate from Judaism because of anti-Semitic feelings in the population at large. But although there is evidence of Gentile–Christian pressures, it is clear that there was no clear and final break. For many, including the "first Christians", the Jewish Christians under Peter's influence, and Matthew's community, the strong influences of Judaism persisted. These groups would probably have been happy to remain one special synagogue among many in Antioch, but it was not to be.

Other small clues to this location in Antioch are found in the gospel. Matthew 4.24 mentions "Syria" in place of Mark's "Tyre and Sidon" (Mark 3.8; Luke 6.17); this suggests an interest in some other place in Syria than Tyre or Sidon, otherwise there is no reason for the substitution. Where Tyre

A Syrian coin (stater) of the 1st century CE, mentioned in Matthew 17.27 in the story, unique to Matthew, of the coin in the fish's mouth.

and Sidon are mentioned, in 15.21, Matthew carefully makes the geography fit *his* understanding of the story (contrasted with Mark's at 7.24–30). Jesus is still in the coastal area (of Jewish influence) when he encounters a woman, clearly labelled as a Canaanite, and therefore non-Jewish, who "came out from beyond those boundaries" to meet him (15.22). The geography sets the scene for the point of the story, the restriction in principle of Jesus' mission to Israel.

There is one further clue in the story, unique to Matthew, of the temple tax (17.24–27). The coin in the fish's mouth is a "*stater*" (17.27), which, only in Syria (particularly Antioch and Damascus), was the exact equivalent of two double-drachmas ("*didrachma*" – 17.24). That Peter supported the payment of the temple tax does not mean that the Temple was still standing when Matthew wrote. Nor, if Matthew wrote after 70 CE, as seems likely, does this mean that he made Peter support the transfer of this tax to the upkeep of the temple of Jupiter Capitolinus in Rome. Peter was not so pro-Roman! Most naturally in Matthew's community, the temple tax was a symbol from the past of positive support for the traditions at the heart of Judaism.

The survival of Matthean tradition in Syria

Later external evidence of the use of Matthew's gospel provides further indications of a Syrian origin, associated with Antioch. Ignatius, the bishop of Antioch at the beginning of the second century, quotes Matthew 3.15 (in a form which depends particularly on Matthew's redaction) in his letter to the church at Smyrna 1.1:

> baptized by John, in order that all righteousness should be fulfilled by him.

This seems clear evidence of a strikingly early use of the gospel at Antioch.

There is much evidence of a more sustained use of Matthew within the tradition represented by a puzzling early Christian writing called *The Didache*. This work appears primitive in its picture of church organization and practice, with emphasis on a prophetic ministry that was still itinerant for some of the time. It can perhaps be dated to the end of the first century, or as an old-fashioned survival in the second century; it seems to reflect a more detached and isolated community, perhaps in a rural backwater (the countryside adjacent to Antioch?). From later quotations of *The Didache*, and allusions to its beliefs and practices, it has usually been located within a particular Christian tradition in Syria. The most relevant feature is the extent to which it uses Matthew's gospel, and indeed many of the characteristics typical of Matthew's church recur. It therefore establishes evidence for a real continuity of tradition in a community in this part of Syria. It is possible to see how the original Jewish-Christian and eschatological community might have survived, once the immediate crisis was past.

The Apocalypse of Peter, a document from the Gnostic library (found at Nag Hammadi in Upper Egypt) and probably to be dated in the third century

Quotations from Matthew's gospel in *The Didache*:

Didache	Matthew	
1.2	Matthew 22.37ff; 7.12	The two commandments and the golden rule (negative/positive)
1.3	5.44ff	Pray for your enemies
1.4	5.39ff	Turning the other cheek
1.5	5.26	The last farthing
2.1f	19.18f	Commandments
2.3	5.33	Commandment on oaths
3.7	5.5	The meek shall inherit the earth
5.1	15.19	List of vices
6.1	24.4	See no one leads you astray
7.1, 3	28.19	Baptismal formula
8.1	6.16	Fasting (contrast hypocrites)
8.2	6.5	Prayer (contrast hypocrites)
8.2	6.9–13	Lord's Prayer
9.5	7.6	Do not give what is holy to the dogs
10.5	24.31	Elect from the four winds
10.6	21.9, 15	Hosanna
11.3	10.40f, 10	Ordinance of the gospel on apostles/prophets
11.7	12.31	Unforgivable sin
11.8	7.15f	Awareness of false prophets
12.1	21.9	He who comes in the name of the Lord
13.1	10.10	Worthy of his food
14.2	5.23f	Be reconciled
15.3	5.22ff; 18.15ff	Reproof as in the gospel
15.4	6.1–4, 5–15	Prayers, alms etc. as in the gospel
16.1	24.42ff; 25.1–13	Lessons of parables
16.4	24.10	Hatred and betrayal
16.4	24.24	Deception by signs and wonders
16.5	24.10	Many shall be offended
16.5	10.22; 24.13	Enduring to the end
16.6	24.30f	True signs of the end
16.8	24.30; 26.64	Coming on the clouds of heaven

CE, gives a description of this kind of group (an isolated survival of an eschatological community) which appeals to key ideas from Matthew's gospel.[11] They called themselves "these little ones who are seen [by God]" (Matthew 18.6, 10) and they were highly critical of those who "let themselves be called bishop and also deacons, as if they had received authority from God, who recline at table after the law of the places of honour" (Matthew 23.6–12). They maintained the ideals of poverty and chastity, and attacked "people who love possessions" and "serve their desires, loving the created things of matter". The visionary forms of this apocalypse show that prophetic inspiration and interpretation were still highly valued.

"We thus see in Syria an independent Christianity of poor itinerants who live in passionate expectation of the Coming One and therefore often renounce marriage, wine and meat. Like Matthew they reckon seriously with evil, including evil in the community, and ... they understand [Christian] teaching as guidance for pilgrimage along this 'way'. It is interpreted totally as cutting loose from the world in imitation of the unmarried, poor and itinerant Jesus."[11] This appears to have been a route by which the insights of the prophetic movement were translated into the structures of monasticism.

Christ and the church in Matthew

Terracotta figurine of a priest preaching (3rd century CE Smyrna).

It is sometimes debated which is more important to Matthew's gospel, the person of Christ or the pattern of the church. Such a debate suggests an unrealistic polarization, for both are vital and they are intertwined within the gospel. At the beginning and end of the gospel are representative passages (1.21–23 and 28.18–20) which demonstrate the interrelationship. The salvation brought by Jesus applies to the people of God with whom he dwells. And the authority of Jesus is communicated to his church of disciples, who have a baptizing and a teaching role until the end of time. However, for practical purposes it is appropriate first to make some observations about Matthew's picture of the person of Jesus, before returning to the theory of the Christian life and the structures of the church.

Matthew's picture of Christ is set in the frame of discipleship and the church. As has been observed, his view of the church is inescapably linked with the expectation of the last days, precisely because of the crisis which defined the shape of Matthew's community. To say the same thing in theological jargon: Christology is set in the context of ecclesiology, and ecclesiology is linked with eschatology. The particular idea which links the church and the End is the Law (in Matthew's special term, "the new righteousness"). The way this is to be understood sets the disciples of Jesus apart from the scribes and the Pharisees. This distinguishing feature is itself the standard according to which the members of the church are to be assessed at the last judgement by the one who judges all. Because of this it is hardly surprising that the principal function of Jesus in Matthew's gospel is to interpret the Law. As Messiah, Jesus is the great teacher who gives the Law and interprets it.

Matthew's pictures of Jesus: teaching and glory

Matthew maintains a significant balance between two definitive aspects of his picture of Jesus: there is Jesus as the great earthly teacher who makes searching ethical demands by the way he interprets the Law; but there is equally Jesus as the exalted heavenly figure who conducts the final judgement, possesses the power and authority which lasts for ever, and who meanwhile shares that power with his church. Among Matthew's special material, the parable of the sheep and the goats (25.31–46) establishes in story-form the essential relationship between earthly experiences and the last authoritative judgement, but the key text which exemplifies this significant balance and sums up the entire message of Matthew's gospel is the conclusion in 28.18–20:

> *And Jesus came and said to them, "All authority in heaven and on earth has been given to me. Go therefore and make disciples of all nations,*

> *baptizing them in the name of the Father and of the Son and of the Holy Spirit, teaching them to observe all that I have commanded you; and lo, I am with you always, to the close of the age".*

This final episode of the gospel, more than comparable in power and influence with John 20.19–23 as a final commissioning, has the effect of establishing Jesus' relationship with the world in terms of authority for ever (28.18), while his relationship with his followers is one of closest intimacy (28.20). The eschatological context of this definitive episode is established by Matthew's reshaping of Daniel 7.13–14 (where the Son of Man comes with the clouds of heaven and is given an everlasting dominion). The central element for Matthew is the teaching of Jesus, mediated by his followers; the world is to be confronted both with this teaching and with the authority of the exalted master. Perhaps this can be seen as a strategy of power, designed to dispose of the doubt which still remained for some after the experiences of Easter (28.17). The confidence of Matthew's church is that the gospel message, presented authoritatively in eschatological times through a purified community, will prove to be irresistible.

It is notable that the story does not end, like the Ascension narratives in Luke–Acts, with the disappearance of Jesus, but rather with the emphasis on his abiding presence (28.20). In this experience of the church, the transcendent exalted being of God is also particularly immediate and imminent. The opposite poles of religious experience, as traditionally described – God being distant and almighty, and God being close in a mystical way – are here combined in one church-centred claim. As the gospel ends, so also it began. For the stories of Jesus' birth which Matthew uses claim that Jesus is the fulfilment of the prophecy of "Emmanuel (which means, God with us)" (1.23). So Jesus is here on earth and Jesus is God. Matthew's birth narratives scarcely overlap in content with those of Luke, but both of them are using such stories to make claims about Jesus and to interpret the significance of his earthly life and ministry. The beginning and the end of the whole story are good points at which to sum up its meaning.

Jesus as God with us

Matthew chapters 1 and 2 can be analysed as answering a series of questions about Jesus:

Who? The genealogy (1.1–17) establishes *who* he is;
How? The announcement to Joseph (1.18–25) shows *how* the birth would happen;
Where? The account of the birth at Bethlehem (2.1–12) answers *where*;
Whence? The hostility of Herod and the Jewish authorities (2.13–23) emphasized *whence* (from where, and against which) the destiny of Jesus (and his followers) would be set in motion.[12]

This provides an outline of the structure, but close attention to the content is also needed. The initial heading (1.1) makes a deliberate statement about Jesus:

> *The book of the genealogy of Jesus Christ, the son of David, the son of Abraham.*

According to the intention expressed in 1.17, if not completely borne out by the actual lists in the present state of the text, Matthew has three sets of fourteen generations. Fourteen is double the highly symbolic religious number seven (used frequently in apocalyptic texts). Number symbolism was much more prevalent in the ancient world than it is today, and its possibilities should not be neglected. For Matthew it could mean that, after six groups of seven generations (42 in total), the Messiah is awaited who by his birth will inaugurate the significant seventh group of sevens.

The genealogy as the plan of history

Jesus is presented as the goal of divinely ordained history. Abraham and David are specially named as turning-points in this history (in the genealogy and at 1.17). Abraham was the father of the Jews and David the chosen king; both were selected by God, responded positively, and became partners in legal covenants with God which were handed down to their successors; and both were recipients of promises now seen as fulfilled in Jesus. The pedigree is not simply historical and chronological, but also embodies theological themes, truths about Jesus. That Jesus was born at Bethlehem (2.5f – one of the few facts on which Matthew and Luke agree) underlines his identification as the Son of David. There are many echoes in these first chapters and throughout the gospel of a royal Davidic theology which was for Matthew an important context for understanding Jesus. This is because David was the symbol of Israel's historical success and the prototype for the future Messiah (the pledge of the destined survival and salvation of Israel). The Hebrew letters of David's name, according to a counting system used in the number symbolism which Matthew seems to favour, add up to the total of fourteen. The structural importance of the number fourteen (twice seven) in Matthew's genealogy has already been noted.

Important though David is for Matthew's theology, he is not the only figure in Matthew's tapestry of Old Testament images fulfilled in Christ. Joseph (in the Old Testament tradition the premier dreamer and interpreter of dreams) may well be recalled by Matthew's reference to the significance of dreams, repeated five times in these first two chapters. Highly significant, because of Matthew's concern for the Law, is Moses, the recipient of God's Law on Sinai. Jesus' birth stories echo some details of Moses' early life: his birth and naming, the early persecution, from which he escapes and then significantly returns. The text from Hosea 11.1, cited as a "proof" from prophecy at Matthew 2.15 – "Out of Egypt have I called my son" – sums up this identification. Herod is probably cast here in the role of Pharaoh, and the astrologers feature in the story of Moses just as they do at the birth of Jesus. Finally the vision of the star, which the astrologers/magi see, recalls

Balaam and the
prophecy of a star
(Numbers 24.15–17)
together with Mother
and Child, from the
catacomb of Priscilla,
Rome (early 3rd
century CE).

Balaam's vision of the star which "shall come forth out of Jacob" (in
Numbers 24.15–17). The early Christian artists in the catacombs of Rome
recognized, as Matthew did, the importance of this "messianic" prophecy
from the Old Testament as a type (prototype) of Christ.

El Greco *Repentant Peter*. El Greco painted several versions of this picture, all reflecting the moment when Peter realizes that he has fulfilled Jesus' prophecy by denying him (Matthew 26.74). The apostle implores forgiveness. Peter as the first Pope provides an example of repentance; his tears symbolise the sacrament of confession.

The truth of Israel before the world

The magi are sometimes seen as the symbol and prototype for some universal mission to the Gentiles in Matthew but their significance should not be distorted like this. They worship at the birth of Christ, and leave gifts symbolic of majesty and grief (actually elements used in their rituals and alchemy), but they do not stay to become disciples. Their role is that of foreign celebrities who come to pay homage to, and are more than overawed by, Israel's light to the nations. It is like the prophecy of Isaiah 60.1–3

The ride of the Magi, as depicted in the stained glass of the north choir aisle, Canterbury cathedral.

Christ in glory – the all-powerful Pantocrator figure from the apse of Cefalu cathedral in Sicily.

(comparable with Isaiah 9.1–2 which Matthew actually quoted at 4.15–16):

> *Arise, shine; for your light has come,*
> *and the glory of the Lord has risen upon you.*
> *For behold, darkness shall cover the earth,*
> *and thick darkness the peoples;*
> *but the Lord will arise upon you,*
> *and his glory will be seen upon you.*
> *And nations shall come to your light,*
> *and kings to the brightness of your rising.* (Isaiah 60.1–3)

As the Hebrew poetic parallelism shows, these kings and celebrities represent "the nations" before whom Israel's gospel is proclaimed (see 28.19). Matthew's emphasis is on the true Israel, rather than the mission to the Gentiles.

The magi are a good illustration of Matthew's repeated emphasis on the worship and reverence paid to Jesus. Notice especially 2.2, 11; 8.2; 9.18; 14.33; 15.25; 20.20; 28.9, 17. Jesus deserves worship because he is

"Emmanuel" (God among us). While there is debate over the inclusion of the words "Son of God" in the title of Mark's gospel (1.1), and also debate about whether these words make an ultimately theological claim or are a Greek term of respect for a hero, there can be no disagreement whatsoever that Matthew makes increasing use of this title in its most theological sense. For him the acclamation "Son of God" is defined in terms of the Isaiah prophecy (7.14) of "God with us".

Thus in Matthew, Simon Peter confesses to Jesus: "You are the Christ, the Son of the living God" (16.16). Jesus then acknowledges that Peter knows this by divine revelation (16.17); in accordance with the Q saying at Matthew 11.25–27, the knowledge that Jesus is the Son can only have come from God. Matthew's distinctive use of the epithet "living" for God is a conscious adoption of an Old Testament term. This is seen for example in Hosea 1.10 ("Sons of the living God"); if Matthew uses this term "sons" in the plural for those who are members of the new Israel (e.g. 5.9 – "the peacemakers . . . shall be called sons of God"), he clearly sees the distinction. The disciples are "sons" of God by virtue of Christ's being "Son" of God. The unique theological title was applied to Jesus repeatedly at key points:

14.33 "Truly you are Son of God" (14.27 has already made a statement about Christ – he walks on the water and identifies himself with the divine title "I am" [Exodus 3.14]).

16.16 "You are the Christ, the Son of the living God"

18.20 "Where two or three are gathered in my name, there am I in the midst of them" ("Emmanuel")

26.63 "I adjure you by the living God, tell us if you are the Christ, the Son of God" (even in the mouths of opponents the affirmation was made for Matthew's readers)

27.40, 43, 54 "If you are/for he said, I am/truly this was/Son of God"

One can see how rapidly the birth stories convey the reader to the heart and the conclusion of the gospel. As T. S. Eliot's magi speculate:

> *"were we led all that way for*
> *Birth or Death? There was a Birth, certainly,*
> *We had evidence and no doubt. I had seen birth and death,*
> *But had thought they were different; this Birth was*
> *Hard and bitter agony for us, like Death, our death.*
> *We returned to our places, these Kingdoms,*
> *But no longer at ease here, in the old dispensation,*
> *With an alien people clutching their gods.*
> *I should be glad of another death."* [13]

Theologically there is hardly any distance from the birth stories to the passion narrative.

Adoration of Kings
(*c*.1500 CE) attributed
to Hieronymous
Bosch, painting from
Petworth House, West
Sussex. In another
cultural context, exotic
visitors greet Christ's
birth in squalid
surroundings.

Christ in the Passion narrative

Matthew's use of Mark's Passion narrative is characterized by relatively small but highly significant modifications. The main points can be summarized, because most have been touched on already. There is a heightening of the Christology by means of titles which emphasize the majesty and the divinity of Jesus. Increasingly stress is placed on the responsibility of the Jews for the death of Jesus. This is summed up in 27.24–26, where Pilate symbolically washes his hands in a valid renunciation of responsibility for this death; his attitude is authenticated by another significant dream (27.19) which Pilate's wife had experienced; and even more clearly the Jews take responsibility (27.25). It is not appropriate to regard this apportioning of the blame simply as anti-Semitism. There may have been particular cause in Matthew's community for antagonism against the Pharisees, but often Matthew's interest is not engaged by the hostility of the Jewish leaders as such. Instead it serves as an effective foil to the majesty and dignity of Jesus. Matthew's portrayal of the responsibility of the Jews, while it is evidently a characteristic of his presentation, is ultimately subordinated to his fascination with the majesty of Jesus.

The characters in Matthew's Passion narrative also have moral significance as exemplars of types of behaviour. The Pharisees and other Jewish leaders are then providing educational counter-examples to the positive leadership of Jesus. Matthew had already enunciated (in an addition to Mark) his principle of requital, of rewards and punishments in the tradition of Deuteronomy:

> For the Son of man is to come with his angels in the glory of his Father, and then he will repay every man for what he has done. (16.27)

The narrative specific to Matthew about the fate of Judas (27.3–10) is an illustration of this requital principle in action. Matthew has intensified the nature of his betrayal (26.15, 25) and shows Judas no mercy. In the same way it is recognized that the Jewish leaders, who took upon themselves the full responsibility for Jesus' death, will suffer for it, or have already done so in the fall of Jerusalem (24.15). The immediate cause may be the desire for vengeance of a wronged eschatological community. But one has to conclude that in the tension between mercy and justice, Matthew cannot see God's love as ultimately having free rein.

Jesus as the giver of the Law

These moral issues of reward and punishment raised by the Passion narrative are very relevant to Matthew's picture of Christ. As Jesus is the great law-giver, who also enunciates the principle of love (e.g. 5.44; 22.39), this tension between mercy and justice is at the heart of the gospel message, as Matthew conveys it. For Matthew the priority is ascribed to the traditional Jewish view of Law, albeit a radical re-evaluation of any existing laws. Jesus insists on a higher righteousness which is significantly more demanding than the inherited Law; but Matthew tends to be legalistic in his interpretation of Law (as in his modification of the teaching on marriage: compare Mark 10.2–12 with Matthew 5.32 and 19.9). He therefore gives the impression that, however rigorous the ultimate standards are, human beings cannot always sustain the finest and most far-reaching moral principles. Therefore the commands need to be hedged about with legalistic safeguards, to ensure the fulfilment of the Law. Paul, in his practical concern for the weaker sister or brother, and also Luke, in his humanitarian theology, might have been disappointed in Matthew but in fairness their situations are different.

Matthew claims the abiding validity of the Law, over against those groups of Christians who taught that the Law had been in force only until John the Baptist, and that Jesus had abolished it. On the contrary in Matthew's discourses, Jesus gives and interprets the Law. Matthew is linked with the orthodox Jewish rabbis in holding fast to the whole law; he parts from them in the way he interprets the Law. It is not merely a matter of the interpretation of particular questions: the contrast between them is fundamental and leads to a quite different understanding of the Law. For Matthew the law of Moses is the law of God for the church as well as for the synagogue. Essentially Jesus' interpretation of the Law does not conflict with the Mosaic law; this is proved by passages in which Jesus' commands are corroborated by the Old Testament (e.g. 12.1–7; 15.1–20; 19.1–9). Matthew is less concerned to set Jesus' teaching against the law of Sinai, than to set it in opposition to certain rabbinic interpretations of that law.

A convincing proof text for this point of view is found at Matthew 5.17–20, where the binding nature of the law was emphasized:

> *Think not that I have come to abolish the law and the prophets; I have come not to abolish them but to fulfil them. For truly, I say to you, till heaven and earth pass away, not an iota, not a dot,* [not the smallest letter or part of a letter] *will pass from the law until all is accomplished. Whoever then relaxes one of the least of these commandments and teaches men so, shall be called least in the kingdom of heaven; but he who does them and teaches them shall be called great in the kingdom of heaven. For I tell you, unless your righteousness exceeds that of the scribes and Pharisees, you will never enter the kingdom of heaven.*

The Law at the end of time

At its heart Matthew 5.17–20 is a traditional and conservative statement about the Law, with the addition, significant for an eschatological community, of the words "until all is accomplished" (5.18). The binding force of the Law is related to the final events of the end of time. Some would say that "the last days" are inaugurated with the death and Resurrection of Christ, and so the Law is now superseded. However, Matthew (in whose view Jesus speaks directly to the church when he speaks to his disciples) does not suggest this; rather the last things are the future resolution for which his community is

Coins from the first Jewish revolt (66–70 CE) from the Israeli Museum, Jerusalem.

working. The Law is sacrosanct and its revealed text is not to be altered, even by the removal of one small letter. But the scribal exposition and interpretation has the necessary flexibility, because it is this which makes the Law relevant to daily life. Hence there is emphasis on the importance of "teaching" for Matthew the scribe and on criticism of the false teaching of the Pharisees. There is a recognition of the variety in attitude of the Christian groups, or more likely of the "mixed" nature of Matthew's own community. The Matthean parable of the weeds (13.24–30, 36–43) makes a similar point about the difficulty of separating good from bad within the growth of the community, notwithstanding the zeal for purging and purifying within the community. The moral is that all will be resolved at the judgement/harvest at the end of the age.

While false interpretations are criticized, the correct interpretation of the Law can be summed up in the commandment to love (5.44; 22.36–40) and in the terms of the golden rule (7.12):

> So whatever you wish that men would do to you, do so to them; for this is the law and the prophets (see 22.40).

The positive form of the golden rule demands positive acts of love towards others, and not merely avoiding hurting other people. If Matthew's use of this traditional motif is compared with Luke 6.31, it can be seen that Matthew is referring particularly to God's giving of gifts; this is a pattern for Christian disciples to follow. In Matthew's interpretation of the Law, however, there can be no single all-encompassing summary, to which all human responsibilities can be "reduced". Unlike John's gospel, the whole teaching is not orientated around the single commandment to love. At the conclusion, in 28.20, it is clear that there is a range of commands which must be taught ("teaching them to observe all that I have commanded you").

Law and righteousness

The Christian's objective is "righteousness", according to Matthew 5.20. The Greek word *dikaiosune* is the one Paul uses, but Matthew's meaning could not be more different. For Paul righteousness is the very nature of God, and it is also projected as an active, saving power from God which makes men righteous, or "justifies" them, entitling them to be called righteous. For Matthew righteousness is that which is realized by human effort, in the same way as a Jew can earn merit by keeping the commandments of the Law. The term relates to the demand which God makes, and the expectations God has of what humankind should be; it is their task to respond and to live up to these expectations. This sense of "righteous" and "righteousness" directly reflects the understanding of the sectarian literature of Qumran. Matthew is most different from Paul in distinguishing ideas of righteousness from ideas of salvation, while Paul unites them. Matthew does speak about salvation as a gift from God (e.g. 1.21; 26.28), but essentially it is the continuing and authoritative presence of Jesus as Lord within the community, and not in the same context as "righteousness".

One text, unique to Matthew, which defines righteousness in relation to Jesus himself, is at 3.15. It was a cause of embarrassment for the early church to think of the Messiah (by definition "pure from sins" – Psalms of Solomon 17.41) undergoing a baptism "of repentance for the forgiveness of sins" as Mark 1.4 defines the baptism by John. Matthew 3.14–15 is a direct response to this problem. John the Baptist hesitates at the idea (3.14) and thus acknowledges Jesus' superiority. The response, "Let it be so now; for thus it is fitting for us to fulfil all righteousness" (3.15), explains what is being done, in terms appropriate to Matthew's understanding. In this way the baptism of Jesus can be the model and motivation for baptism in Matthew's community. In respect of the nature of Christ, while any such action is unnecessary because of his divinity, it nonetheless represents a thoroughly realistic identification by Jesus with every aspect of human life and the demands and expectations which God has of humankind. It completes the sense of God's nearness, while at the same time emphasizing the divine superiority and capacity to save.

Christ and the miracle stories

The Sermon on the Mount (Matthew 5–7) presents the readers with a picture of Jesus as law-giver and teacher, the Messiah who brings the authoritative Word of God. In the same way the following section of the gospel (Matthew 8–9) is also concerned to tell the readers about Jesus; but this time, in narratives rather than discourse, it is the complementary picture of Jesus as the Messiah of deeds and action, shown in miracles (healings and exorcisms and dramatic reassurance). These complementary pictures of the Christ in word and action are not simply historical information "at one remove". (He gave this teaching then; these stories are told about what he did.) Rather, this law and these narratives are treasured because of their direct relevance to Matthew's community in particular. Discourse and narrative alike are for the instruction of the church. Matthew interprets them for his community, to concentrate attention on the essential points, concerned with faith and discipleship. Thus the pictures of Christ as teacher (expounding the Law) and as healer (explaining what he is doing) are important as evidence for the historical Jesus but they are equally important for what they reveal of the interests of this eschatological sect and the models for Christian discipleship which it chose. The concerns are with academic discussion of issues of law, and with the training of the community (as remnant/true Israel) to fulfil its share of the ministry of Jesus in those critical days.

Again it has proved impossible to separate the issues of Christology and ecclesiology. This gospel is structured so that these themes intertwine and even merge together. The miracle stories in the earliest tradition may have been simply advertisements, to attract attention to Jesus. In Matthew's gospel they are retold in a refined and sophisticated way. The actual narrative of the event has been abridged (compared with Mark), but the interpretative comment (in the mouth of Jesus as well as in the evangelist's summaries) has been much expanded. This is a conscious technique of interpretation, after the manner of the scribe, so that the conversation, what Jesus says and the discussion which follows, becomes the most significant feature of the story. When the healing miracles are stylized as conversations, they look very like controversy material (a separate formal classification in the tradition, e.g. much of Mark 12). They resemble the scholastic dialogues of the time.

There are four aspects of the person of Christ which Matthew wishes to emphasize in his retelling of the miracle stories:

1 Christ's activities (particularly in healing) are fulfilments of Old Testament prophecy: e.g. 8.17 (Isaiah 53.4)

                        11.5 (Isaiah 35.5–6; 61.1)

                        12.18–21 (Isaiah 42.1–4 – this quotation was of structural importance for Matthew 12).

The use of the title "Son of David" in the miracle stories is a reminder that the mission of Jesus is designated as being for Israel (9.27; 12.23; 15.22; 20.30f).

2 While Matthew 12 speaks of the activity of the Servant of God, it is clear that it is victorious activity, displaying features of the exalted and triumphant Lord. There is a heightening of the dramatic and miraculous in Matthew's use of the tradition, with doubling and repetition. These are events which should compel belief, because they are stupendous and irresistible.

3 Jesus as Lord is seen directly as the helper of his church. These past events are clearly prophetic of the contemporary situation. The circumstances of the church have an influence on the telling of the miracle stories. See especially the stillings of the storms (8.23–27 and 14.23–31), which reflect the immediate anxieties of the sect and are designed to offer reassurance. From later Christian tradition interpreting this passage, there is a good example in Tertullian: "That little ship presented a figure of the Church, in that she is disquieted in the sea, that is, in the world, by the waves, that is, by persecutions and temptations, the Lord patiently sleeping, as it were, until roused at last by the prayers of the saints, he checks the world and restores tranquillity to his own" (*On Baptism* 12).

4 Jesus is seen as the one who gives his disciples a share in his authority. With understanding and faith, anything becomes possible (as 17.20 indicates: "If you have faith as a grain of mustard seed, you will say to this mountain, 'Move hence to yonder place,' and it will move; and nothing will be impossible to you"). As a means to this sharing in faith, the feeding miracles become in Matthew much more explicitly related to the Eucharist than they were in Mark. See 14.15–21 and 15.32–38. But the feedings are not completely eucharistic, for in both cases the use of the fish recalls the lakeside setting of the original historical tradition.

Christ in the parables

Similarly it is to be expected that the traditional parables of Jesus would be interpreted by Matthew in special ways related to the theological beliefs and eschatological expectations of his community. This has already been demonstrated in particular examples (the tenants in the vineyard, the invitations to the marriage feast, the Last Judgement warning about the sheep and the goats), which are applied directly to the community's understanding of itself. Again the teaching of Christ bears directly upon the realities of Matthew's church, and helps them to understand and to survive the crisis.

A few general observations about Matthew's parables support this conclusion. By means of his introductions, Matthew uniquely applies the parables to what he calls "the Kingdom of Heaven". Other evangelists, but less regularly and explicitly than Matthew, use the term "Kingdom of God". It is reasonable to suggest that these terms are virtual synonyms, but that Matthew uses a more orthodox Jewish formulation which preserves the sense of reverence by avoiding direct use of the name of God. The four sacred Hebrew letters of God's name in the Old Testament text are not normally read aloud, but the vowels are replaced by those of another Hebrew word meaning "my Lord". But Matthew is not just being reverential and ultra-Jewish; he is also emphasizing the coming of the Kingdom by the way he has linked the parables to this expectation. He is insisting that the Kingdom relates to the sectarian community, the church of the last days, to which he belongs. It is true that the phrase "Kingdom of Heaven" introduces a cosmic dimension – this Kingdom is as wide as the heavens and as full of majesty. It could stress the universality of the dominion exercised by Jesus and his Father. This means that when the last day breaks, the lordship of Christ will be universally recognized, and Matthew's eschatological community, now so beleaguered, will finally be vindicated as the true people of God.

The prominence of the theme of vengeance and appropriate punishment within this gospel has already been observed. The principle of requital was demonstrated in the fate of Judas after his betrayal of Christ. This theme is also underlined in several parables, where Matthew seems to have added a characteristically fierce conclusion:

13.40–43 the parable of	the weeds (tares)
18.34–35	the two debtors
22.11–14	the wedding garment
25.10–13	the foolish maidens at the wedding
25.28–30	the talents
25.41–46	the (sheep and the) goats

The doctrine of eternal punishment ("there men will weep and gnash their teeth") is most explicit in Matthew, using settings like these parables of Jesus. With the single exception of Luke 13.28, only in Matthew was this prophecy attributed to Jesus.

A Roman oil lamp from Sepphoris in Galilee.

The Kingdom of Heaven

Matthew's presentation of the Kingdom of Heaven sets the theme of justice in the context of God's law. It does matter what people do and how they respond to the gospel proclamation. While for Mark and Luke the emphasis is on the Kingdom as the initiative of God (God begins the secret process of growth from seed-sowing to harvest, or God is the determinative power in control of the whole process), for Matthew the stress is different and the Kingdom essentially is something which challenges response from human beings. There is no denying that in the Last Judgement the ultimate power belongs to God. In Matthew's eschatological scenario this truth is reaffirmed. But in the meantime the progress of the Kingdom, like the progress of the church, has much to do with the human process of response and development. It is on their contribution to this process that individuals will be judged ultimately. The preoccupation with eternal punishment and appropriate requital suggests that for Matthew's community (as heirs to the Kingdom) there was some desire for vengeance on their enemies. Those who had expelled and rejected the true Israel would surely receive their deserts.

The different emphasis on the Kingdom in Matthew can be observed by comparing Matthew 19.14 with Mark 10.14–15 and Luke 18.16–17. Matthew simply records: "Jesus said, 'Let the children come to me, and do not hinder them; for to such belongs the kingdom of heaven.'" Mark and Luke continue by relating the meaning of that saying to the child's attitude of receptivity ("whoever does not receive"). The Kingdom is seen as a gift of God, a direct intervention in the realm of human life. It is therefore something to be received, not earned by merit. But Matthew does not include this saying about "receiving" the Kingdom. And in a related piece of teaching at 18.3–4 (not found in Mark or Luke) he records Jesus as saying, "unless you turn and become like children you will never enter the Kingdom of Heaven. Whoever humbles himself like this child, he is the greatest in the Kingdom of Heaven". In the overall comparison one simple verb "receive" (in Mark and Luke) has become three verbs "turn", "become", and "humble" (in Matthew). So the emphasis has shifted from receiving to doing in relation to the Kingdom. And as Matthew's church proclaimed the Kingdom in the last days, what those who heard actually did in response, and how they treated the missionaries/envoys of the Kingdom, would determine the eternal destiny of the hearers (Matthew 25.40, 45).[14]

Jesus, the kingdom, and the church

At the centre of Matthew's gospel is a church or sectarian consciousness which explains why a particular theology and picture of Jesus is emphasized, and relates that gospel to community structures and the practice of discipleship. Like the sectarians at Qumran the members of Matthew's community refer to themselves, the brethren, as the "least" (25.40, 45) and the "little ones" (10.42):

> *And whoever gives to one of these little ones even a cup of cold water because he is a disciple, truly, I say to you, he shall not lose his reward.*

Here is a community which has learnt, from the bitter experience of rejection by the world around them, to value the most basic hospitality and positive response when it is offered. Such acceptance appears to be a rarity, but when it happens it indicates that discipleship has some success in the world. The Buddhist monks who regularly depend on the villagers near their monastery for their basic provisions are likely to fare better than Matthew's disciple-group did, because the Buddhists' neighbours respect their ideals.

> *He who receives you receives me, and he who receives me receives him who sent me. He who receives a prophet because he is a prophet shall receive a prophet's reward, and he who receives a righteous man because he is a righteous man shall receive a righteous man's reward.* (10.40–41)

Ministry and discipleship

Matthew's church had experience of an itinerant prophetic ministry, a practice which was still recognized in the pages of *The Didache* within the Matthean tradition. They were aware of the warnings against false prophets (7.15ff) which would offend their hearers, but critical circumstances left them no alternative but to speak as prophets.

> *You serpents, you brood of vipers, how are you to escape being sentenced to hell. Therefore I send you prophets and wise men and scribes, some of whom you will kill and crucify, and some you will scourge in your synagogues and persecute from town to town, that upon you may come all the righteous blood shed on earth.* (23.33–35)

The note of just vengeance is strong because of the way the Christian prophets had been treated (like the Old Testament prophets before them).

The prophets were associated with the wise and righteous members of the community; it is not clear whether these were alternative descriptions of the same people, or different roles which were equally despised in the eyes of the world. The righteous were traditionally those obedient to the Law (redefined in Matthew's terms as higher righteousness), and the wise were those responsible for interpreting the laws and applying them to the business of living. The wise were closely associated or identified with the scribes; their role is best described in the verse (13.52), previously noted as a possible designation of Matthew himself:

> *Therefore every scribe who has been trained in discipleship for the kingdom of heaven is like a householder who brings out of his treasure what is new and what is old.*

"Trained in discipleship" is a fuller translation of a word that only Matthew uses (see also 27.57 and 28.19); it emphasizes the integral relationship between discipleship and scribal interpretation and teaching, as Matthew sees it. This is his task and that of his community. Notice also how close the connection is between discipleship and the Kingdom. This helps to explain the use (already noted) of the parables of the Kingdom as guidelines for discipleship, warning the disciples of what to expect as the Kingdom is recognized/realized in their teaching.

Again there can be no doubt that the situation of Jesus' teaching of his disciples relates directly to the circumstances of Matthew's community. The gospel narratives and discourse are thus instructive for the next generation of readers. Effectively the original disciples are the medium of communication, so that through them Matthew addresses his own community and the active Christian membership of his day. The discourses destined for this new audience are both legal/prescriptive (e.g. chapters 5–7), offering a community rule, and also advisory (e.g. chapter 18), giving practical teaching towards a higher righteousness.

There is one point at which Matthew consistently improves on the image of the disciples as seen in Mark's gospel. Mark records the failure of the disciples to understand what Jesus says or does, in relation to the gospel's overriding theme of secrecy (see Mark 4.13, 40f; 6.50ff; 7.18; 8.16ff; 9.5f). But in Matthew the disciples do come to an understanding of Jesus' teaching (Matthew 13.16, 51; 16.12; 17.13), for Jesus is a good teacher. It is the disciples (not the crowds) who actually hear the Sermon on the Mount (5.1). They may well be men "of little faith" (8.26; 14.31; 16.8; 17.20; 21.21; 28.17) but they do have an understanding of Jesus' teaching. Matters of trust (in which they may be deficient) are separated from matters of intellectual understanding. It is of course vital that the disciples grasp what Jesus has taught them, if they in their turn are to be commissioned for the task of teaching, indeed of proclaiming the gospel to the world (28.20). The commissioning in Galilee for this teaching ministry of the disciples has a deliberate continuity with Jesus' own teaching, predominantly in Galilee. Matthew wants to emphasize this continuity of teaching and understanding, thus binding the vital post-Easter preaching of his own community by indissoluble links of trained and reliable discipleship to the preaching of the earthly Jesus. If Luke's apostles are primarily the eyewitnesses of Jesus' Resurrection (Acts 1.22; 10.39), Matthew's disciples are those who *heard* and understood Jesus' teaching.

The later besetting problems of leadership and institutional structure and arrangements did not bulk large for Matthew's community. Matthew 23.8–12 represents an isolated (and straightforward) treatment of such issues: "But you are not to be called Rabbi, for you have one teacher, and you are all brethren" (23.8). This view of discipleship sees the ministry particularly in terms of teaching and the practice of informed scribal interpretation. But there is a clear sense that the primary authority in all teaching and interpretation is Christ's, just as in historical Israel the ultimate authority was God's (although mediated through the Law given to Moses, or through the kingship of the Davidic dynasty). Thus Matthew's community depends on Christ alone (although Christ's authority may in some circumstances be shared with those whom he has chosen).

Matthew's understanding of "the church"

Central to Matthew's gospel is the church which Jesus has founded, of which Matthew's community is the true succession. This centrality lies both in the importance of the theme, and literally in its location at the heart of the gospel in two passages (16.17–19 and 18.15–18) which contain the only uses of the word "church" (*ekklesia*) in the canonical gospels:

1 Matthew 18.17–18: "If he refuses to listen, tell it to the church; and if he refuses to listen even to the church, let him be to you as a Gentile and a tax collector. Truly I say to you, whatever you bind on earth shall be bound in heaven, and whatever you loose on earth shall be loosed in heaven." The authority of Christ, which is delegated here through the church, is a disciplinary authority which enables individual cases (such as the sin of a brother or member of the community) to be adjudicated. If this authority vested in the church is spurned, the offender will be excommunicate like the non-Jew or the proved collaborator. Although forgiveness is mentioned explicitly at 18.21–22 in the case of the brother who is sinned against, it seems a scarce commodity when the brother who sins comes up against the discipline of this embittered church. It could be argued that the expulsion of the sinner was to save his soul if not his body (compare 1 Corinthians 5.4f and the practice at Qumran).

2 Matthew 16.18–19: "And I tell you, you are Peter [*Petros*], and on this rock [*petra*] I will build my church, and the powers of death shall not prevail against it. I will give you the keys of the kingdom of heaven, and whatever you bind on earth shall be bound in heaven, and whatever you loose on earth shall be loosed in heaven." The same charge is here given in a delegation of fundamental authority to Peter alone. Since Matthew often repeats a statement after an interval, to emphasize and intensify it, this is *not* necessarily a matter of a different authority (a prince-bishop in place of a council of elders). And Peter could be regarded as the model or type of the Christian among other Christians, whose authority is Christ's vested in his church.

However, this text is often seen as evidence of Peter's primacy and the foundation of a succession of bishops or a papal authority. Such a monarchical view seems contradicted by 23.8–12 (the isolated text on the problems of leadership), nor is there any evidence in Matthew of a special revelation to Peter (as Mark 16.7; 1 Corinthians 15.5).

What should be noted is the context: while Matthew 18 is concerned with church offences and discipline, Matthew 16 focusses on the confession of Jesus as "the Christ, the Son of the living God" – the centre of Matthew's picture of Christ. Peter is the first disciple to be called by Jesus (4.18) and it is his perception and understanding of Jesus that leads to this confession.

In Matthew's terms Peter is a disciple, that is, an interpreter of the kingdom and a teacher about Christ its king. He is the supreme disciple/teacher from the point of view of Matthew's community, not least because of his influence at Antioch, in the ministry to the Jews. He is the guarantor of the gospel tradition and the Law, by virtue of the authority delegated to him by Christ. Unlike the Pharisees and scribes who "shut the Kingdom of Heaven against men" (23.13), Peter is the disciple/teacher who has "the keys" to unlock "the Kingdom of Heaven" (16.19). He remains the authoritative guide for this embattled community. They were fearful that excommunication by the Jews might have cost them the Kingdom; now reassured, they wait eagerly for the gates of the Kingdom to open before them.

CHAPTER 5

John and the Community Apart

The fourth gospel is clearly a very different book from those assumed to have been written by Matthew, Mark, or Luke. John is capable of being read at many levels. It uses fewer stories about Jesus, and these are interwoven with the teaching to express the author's theological views about him as the Son of God and his significance for humankind. This teaching occurs in the form of discourses and not in the parables and short sayings familiar from the other three gospels (the synoptics). In an exploration of deeper levels of the gospel, its success as an evangel (bearer of good news) must not be forgotten.
John is a gospel which can be read at a far greater depth than this, and unexpected levels are reached when the complex thought-patterns and symbolism (which John derived from the cosmopolitan world in which he lived) are unravelled.

The background to John's gospel

It has been held that John's gospel was only intelligible in its day to "insiders", members of his own church, who already understood its vocabulary and symbolism.[1] The key to that code, which may have been given in former times by training in his special community, is no longer available. Fortunately, John's source material, from which he built up this highly individual piece of writing, still exists at least in part in the Old Testament scriptures, the Qumran texts, and reconstructions from rabbinic writings show us some of the diversity of thought in the Judaism of John's day. Many writings from the Mediterranean world contain the kind of philosophical ideas which formed the framework of an educated man's thought and show the diversity of religious experience in the cults of the day. While the New Testament offers other versions of the Christian tradition in which John's thought was steeped, we must also acknowledge the originality of his mind. He took raw materials but the end-product is more than the sum of its ingredients. The mind behind the fourth gospel was that of a creator.

Authorship

The authorship of this gospel is a vexed issue. From the time of Irenaeus in the late second century CE until a hundred or so years ago, Christian scholars

This Rylands Papyrus is a 2nd century CE fragment showing John 18.31–33, with .37–38 on the reverse.

Plan of John's gospel

I: The Beginning

1.1–18　　　The Prologue – a theological assessment of the origin and nature of Jesus: God's word incarnate bringing grace and truth.

II: The Ministry

1.19–51　　Witness to Jesus is given by various individuals and by various titles.

2.1–11　　　The first Sign: Jesus transforms the water of Judaism into the wine of Christianity at the wedding of Cana.

2.13–25　　Passover number one: Jesus claims to replace the Temple of Judaism.

3.1–21　　　In conversation with Nicodemus – Jesus shows he brings judgement as well as light, salvation, and spiritual rebirth.

3.22–36　　Jesus' status over against John the Baptist is considered.

4.1–42　　　Jesus' offer of the water of salvation, and of himself as the approach to God, is accepted by Samaritans, who claim him as Saviour of the world.

4.46–54　　The second Sign: Jesus heals an official's son at Capernaum

5.1–47　　　The third Sign: Jesus' cure of a cripple at the Pool brings about a major theological dispute on his right and authority to work on the Sabbath and his status as Son.

6.1–71　　　Passover number two, and the fourth Sign: Jesus feeds the five thousand. The crowd take this action as messianic. Jesus attempts to explain that he is a new and greater Moses offering food for spiritual survival.
The fifth Sign may be included: Jesus walks on water, showing God's control of the natural elements.
He scandalizes some disciples and brings out the faith of others.

7.1–8.59　　Controversy with the Jews further erupts over the Sabbath breaking of chapter 5, and widens out into greater issues. Jesus takes the opportunity of Tabernacles to offer the water of salvation. Jesus narrowly escapes with his life.

9.1–41　　　The sixth Sign: Jesus as light of the world gives a blind man sight; the exasperated authorities' reaction shows them to be the blind ones.

10.1–21　　Jesus' claim to leadership, through his life's work and sacrifice.

10.22–39　At the feast of Dedication (Hanukkah) is Jesus Son of God or a blasphemer?

11.1–57　　The seventh Sign: the raising of Lazarus. Jesus is seen as the Resurrection and Life, but brings about his own death.

12.1–19　　In preparation for his "Hour", Jesus is anointed, and hailed as he enters Jerusalem.

12.20–50　The arrival of the "Hour" is heralded by the appearance of Greek visitors. Jesus reviews the ministry as it closes.

III: The Hour

　　　　　　The climax of Jesus' ministry – his Passion, death, glorification – is now reached, and is explained before events unfold.

13.1–38　　Passover number three. Jesus washes the disciples' feet, to show the cleansing service of his death for them.

14.1–16.33　Farewell Discourses. Jesus explains the love, joy, and peace that will flow to the fellowship of disciples (in communion with him) after his departure from a hostile world.

17.1–25　　Final prayer. Jesus commits the disciples to the Father's care in the Hour of glorification.

18.1–19.16　Jesus' arrest, trials, and condemnation.

19.17–42　Crucifixion and burial. Jesus dies as king and as Passover lamb.

IV: The Resurrection

20.1–18　　The empty tomb, and the appearance to Mary Magdalene.

20.19–29　Appearances to the disciples and Thomas in the upper room (Easter and Pentecost combined).

20.30–31　Conclusion to the gospel.

V: Appendix or Epilogue

21.1–24　　Editorial addition of an appearance at the lakeside breakfast, establishing the respective roles of John and Peter.

The King's Game was played by Roman soldiers and the marks were scratched on this Jerusalem pavement. Strategic moves with special pieces were made as in chess today; one move was the "king's move" and a crown and a **B** for Basileus = king, may be seen. Jesus may have been dressed up as part of this game.

were satisfied that a readily identifiable individual was the author – John son of Zebedee.

Westcott summed up the internal evidence for apostolic authorship in his classic statement of concentric circles. By careful and detailed analysis of supporting evidence he deduced that the author was a Jew, of Palestine, an eyewitness, an apostle, the Beloved Disciple, and therefore the apostle John. Having eminent authorities like Irenaeus, Clement of Alexandria, and the Muratorian Canon (a list of approved books) from the late second century in support made the position seem secure and unassailable.

In the years after Westcott, many assaults were made on this secure fortress, and little by little its defences crumbled. When the evidence was investigated detail by detail rather than taken *en bloc*, it began to look different. The external evidence for apostolic authorship began to seem very late indeed for a book supposedly published over a century earlier. Investigations among Gnostic writings (see Chapter 7) revealed the curious phenomenon that the unorthodox had used this gospel long before the orthodox. It was already known that an argumentative Roman theologian of the third century CE called Hippolytus found it difficult to convince a rigorist party, nicknamed the *Alogoi* (minus the Logos = Word) that John was orthodox and acceptable for Christians in Rome *c*.200 CE. Surely this was odd for a gospel apparently bearing the signature of a senior apostle?[2]

On the internal evidence, few would dispute nowadays that the author was a Jew; that he was a Jew of Palestine is arguable on the assessment of how well he knew places there before their destruction in the Jewish War 70 CE. This itself is subject to recent archaeological dating of various sites, e.g. the Gabbatha (19.13) – the Pavement, complete with etched King's Game, is still displayed to tourists in Jerusalem as the site of Jesus' final appearance before Pilate, while current expert opinion dates this great stone pavement later, to the second-century Roman city Aelia Capitolina. That he was an eyewitness is usually dismissed, despite the gospel's claims (1.14, 19.35, 21.24) – partly because of his alleged reliance on sources (Mark and ?Luke), partly because of the amount of reflection and impression of distance conveyed in his telling of stories. Details which Westcott found compelling and accurate reminiscences of the apostle have been disregarded by a later generation as the accretions of legendary detail. A peasant fisherman, however apostolic, is also thought incapable of the degree of sophistication and culture that this gospel displays.

Thus the majority of modern scholarship has moved well away from the earlier position; only a few still maintain apostolic authorship. With the movement away from apostolic authorship of John there has been considerable fluidity in the date assigned to the gospel – no longer is it placed within the normal working lifespan of a contemporary of Jesus himself. Views on the date have even accepted *c*.150 CE as a norm. Mid-second-century dates had to be abandoned, however, when papyrus evidence proved that the gospel had not only been published by then, but also copied several times and circulated to fairly remote corners of the Roman Empire. The date has gradually receded until *c*.90 CE seems to be achieving some degree of consensus, although John Robinson's radical challenge to current scholarship involved a date of publication in the sixties.[3] Whereas for convenience we shall continue to refer to the evangelist as John, apostolic authorship is not thereby denoted in anything which follows. We take as a working hypothesis that this gospel was published *c*.90 CE, even if it had gone through several preliminary stages of composition and editing prior to this.

Even if John was not the apostle John, the evangelist seems to have had a particular relationship with a disciple close to Jesus, whom he describes with some awe as "the Beloved Disciple". It is possible that the Beloved Disciple, who was as intimate with Jesus ("in the bosom of " [John 13.23]) as Jesus was with the Father (1.18), was himself John the Apostle. This would certainly explain the confusion in the minds of the early church between the apostle and the author of the gospel which contained his teaching. The

Beloved Disciple may well have gathered around himself a group of Christians who listened to his distinctive set of teachings of and about Jesus, and their writings may be all that we have left.

Whether the community whose mind found expression through this gospel can be called a school is arguable. A number of interesting points have emerged from recent research, demonstrating the likeness in several characteristics between the Johannine (John's) "school" and those "schools" of Pythagoras, the Teacher of Righteousness at Qumran and other ancient teachers.[4] Certainly a "school" would provide an intelligible context in which to set such closely related yet disparate works as the gospel of John, the epistles and the Apocalypse. At least three pupils of the founder figure Beloved Disciple applied his teaching, which by long usage they had made theirs, to the varying situations in which they found themselves. If it is felt that "school" is too artificial a category, then the more flexible one of "community" will serve.

The evangelist was one representative of that community, his gospel preserves the traditions of that community; various other members may have assisted in the editing process and final publication. Others from the group were responsible for the epistles and Revelation. The somewhat unsatisfactory conclusion to the question of the gospel's authorship is thus an anonymous evangelist, who wrote down the reminiscences of a revered teacher, preserved and developed by himself and the community for whom he wrote. The Beloved Disciple may have been close to Jesus, but have died before the final and complete publication of the gospel (21.23). John was not totally dependent on the Beloved Disciple's verification of events and teachings, as he was also conscious of Spirit-leadership (the PARACLETE – see p. 271f). John's book was also probably the result of years of teaching in which materials in continuous use were honed down, shaped, and moulded to fit the purpose, and then various attempts were made to write it down.

This process may not have been entirely complete and so the gospel went out to the public in a rather rough-hewn state. The "Farewell Discourses" (Jesus' final teaching at the Last Supper: John 14.1–16.33) might well have been shorter than its present form, as the draft might have been included with the final copy; various discrepancies should have been edited out. The fact that these things were not done despite John's impressive craftsmanship as a writer may mean either that such details were unimportant to the author, or for his premature demise. If the latter were the case, then whoever was responsible in the community for the final issue of the gospel might also have been the author of chapter 21 and its resurrection stories. (Chapter 21 seems a later appendage for all that it is not missing in any reasonable manuscript of the gospel.)

Christians remembered, adapted, preserved, and shaped reminiscences of Jesus in response to their contemporary church conditions and problems. This gospel reflects the same process but, with its distinctive brand of Christianity, indicates a very unusual church community. The gospel has various distinctive features which we will look at in turn:

1 A strong evaluation of the person and purpose of Jesus – what is technically known as a "high Christology" – where the divine side of Jesus has a high profile.

2 An argumentative approach to the Jews.

3 A positive re-evaluation of previously held ideas about the end of the world – what is technically known as "realized eschatology".

4 A strong emphasis on the person and work of that power of God known as the Holy Spirit.

5 A surprising lack of what might be termed church-indicators – namely sacraments – Jesus does not apparently institute these; ministers – no kind of church organizational structure is in view for the succession to Jesus; apostles as such are not mentioned, and the "Twelve" get scant attention. John lacks a clear ecclesiology or church organizational structure.

6 An absence of positive ethical advice such as abounds for instance in the Sermon on the Mount.

As we investigate these features we shall be able to build up a portrait of a first-century church tackling its problems in such a way that its own growth and structure were formed in the manner of points 1 to 6 above.

The person of Jesus

1 Pre-existence

In the gospel claims are made for Jesus by the evangelist, the Baptist, and by Christ himself:

> *In the beginning was the Logos (Word), and the Logos was with God*
> *… he was in the beginning with God; all things were made by him*
> (1.1–3).
> *After me comes a man who ranks before me, for he was before me*
> (1.30).
> *Before Abraham was I am* (8.58).
> *Father, glorify thou me in thy own presence with the glory which I had*
> *with thee before the world was made* (17.5).

Such statements about Jesus – that he was associated with God (as God) in the creation of the universe – contrast with the presentation of him in other gospels:

* Mark – Jesus appears as Son of God at his baptism;
* Luke and Matthew – Jesus' Sonship dates from his conception by the Holy Spirit.

It is uncertain whether even Paul in his use of the image of God goes as far as John. The pre-existence of Christ is unique to this gospel. It is clear that the evangelist meant this idea to be the key to the meaning of the events he then goes on to describe, by the way in which, at the very outset in the Prologue, he uses the title Logos (or Word) for the pre-incarnate Jesus.

The ultimate source for the title *Logos* is probably the Greek philosophical school of Zeno *c.*300 BCE called the Stoics. Logos was for them that divine reason which organizes and controls the universe and intelligent human beings alike. Thus the laws of nature and the controls we exert over our own passionate natures are subject to this rational power. There is nothing said by John about the Logos in the Prologue right down to the Incarnation (but not including it) which would have seemed unacceptable to a Stoic. Jesus could thus be defined as the intellect of God. This was not alien to a Jewish way of thought either: not only did the thing said of the Logos frequently bear a resemblance to those said of the Jewish Law or Torah by the rabbis, and of Wisdom by her devotees, but a cosmopolitan Jew called Philo had adopted "Logos" some years before the fourth gospel was written. He used Logos many times to explain the workings of God, in relation to the world and to humankind, in a more modern fashion that the traditional scriptures would allow. In the Greek-orientated world it was a relevant word and concept to employ. It need not be assumed that John copied Philo in his usage, just that he, as another Jew in a Greek world, saw it as a suitable and available idea.

Logos may even have had a special attraction for John, in that it is the code-word for "gospel" in the Marcan parable about preaching the kingdom ("The sower sows the logos [or word]" [Mark 4.14]). Thus Christ would not only be seen as the creative mind of God, but as the proclamation of the gospel himself. Even more appropriate to a Jewish mind would be the use of Logos in the Old Testament. In creation in Genesis 1, God speaks and things happen or come into existence; clearly his word is creative and all-powerful (compare Psalm 33.6). Later, in the time of the prophets, God's word is not only seen as creative but as communicative – "The Word of the Lord came to me saying, 'Go . . .'" (Jeremiah 2.1). Logos was the preferred translation of the original Hebrew word (*dabar*) in Greek versions of the Old Testament, like the Septuagint (LXX).

Logos was therefore a term with powerful associations and it placed Jesus' origin beyond his earthly existence and defined his divinity. After John, others went on to use Logos, as in the Hermetic Literature and the Gnostic writings (see Chapter 7). In these cases John is the source and not vice versa.

Christ's pre-existence as God, with God, would pose a direct challenge to Jewish readers reared on the daily prayer called the Shema:

> *Hear O Israel the Lord our God is ONE God.*

Further, unlike the figure of Wisdom or Philo's Logos, this pre-existent being had committed the scandal of becoming incarnate, carrying over the divine attributes of glory, grace, and truth. Because knowledge of his origin is hidden from all but the faithful in John, it does seem like blasphemy to his audience when Jesus utters the taboo divine name *I am* (see below), in proving his priority to Abraham in 8.58 (quoted above). His followers had stressed his pre-existence to those who saw him as only a rabbi or prophet.

Divinity

In addition to the passages using the title "Son of God", also used in the other gospels, discussed below, and in addition to the passages concerned with Jesus' pre-existence set out above, there are a number of other passages to be examined. In some discourses and dialogues with the Jews, Jesus is portrayed as belligerently setting out his claims to divinity. The synoptics (Matthew, Mark, Luke) are remarkably reticent about this topic during Jesus' ministry, but the gospel writers' underlying assumption every time Jesus is involved in a controversy is that his authority is divine, even if John is the only evangelist to make this explicit. Thus in John 5 Jesus' defence develops into an assertion of his privileges as Son, the one sent by God and dependent on Him for glory.

Jesus' rights were: to override the Sabbath by working
to raise the dead and give life
to execute judgement.

These were all clearly functions of God, and exclusively of God. The debate continued in the extended controversy in chapters 7, 8 and 10 (chapter 9 is a related, yet separate episode). Some key sayings are the statements made by Jesus:

> *"For I proceeded and came forth from God; I came not of my own accord, but he sent me"* (8.42), which comments on his origin.
> The sacred name *I AM* (cited in 8.58 above).
> *"I and the Father are one"* (10.30).
> *"I am the Son of God"* (10.36) – note context here.
> *"The Father is in me and I am in the Father"* (10.38).

All of these are very exalted claims indeed, but are consistent with those made in the non-controversial setting of the Farewell Discourses and the "prayer" of chapter 17.

Titles

Each New Testament writer's understanding of Jesus is indicated by the titles that he applied to him. John contains some titles which are fresh (e.g. Logos above), and some which sound Biblical or Jewish enough, but on closer inspection prove to be new creations (e.g. Lamb of God – see below). Yet a third category appears familiar from other New Testament usage, but John is very selective in how he employs these titles: in chapter 1 he appears to heap titles upon Jesus, but does not do this again, after setting the scene for the rest of the gospel. A short list of Christological titles in the fourth gospel includes:

1 Lamb of God
2 Son of God
3 Messiah/Christ
4 King of Israel
5 Son of Man
6 Saviour of the World
7 Lord
8 The "I am" sayings

They will be discussed in order.

1 Lamb of God At first sight it seems most natural that John should derive the image of the "Lamb of God" from the Passover lamb, particularly as he portrays Christ's death in this role, by the careful editing of some details: e.g. the inclusion of the herb, hyssop, from the Passover ritual into the story of the crucifixion – John 19.19 = Exodus 12.22, see further below. The

Pharaoh Rameses as king is also seen as divine, here embraced by Amon and Mut (Museum of Antiquities, Turin).

left Hercules – the strongest man who ever lived – had his superhuman powers attributed to his divine father Zeus.

right Isis was traditionally wife of Osiris and Queen of Egypt. By the 1st century CE, however, she had joined other deities as a fertility figure and patron of mystery cults.

The goddess Ishtar is here portrayed as riding on a lion. Relief from the 8th century BCE in the Louvre.

problem lies in the further description "who takes away the sin of the world" – no one had ever thought that this lamb had this function. Another possibility is that Jesus' role is being seen in the light of the description of the Suffering Servant of Second Isaiah 53.7: "Like a lamb that is led to the slaughter"; but whereas early Christians might well have understood Christ's work in terms of suffering and dying, it is most unlikely that John the Baptist would have done. Because his ideas were shaped by apocalyptic traditions, a background has been sought in the wrathful conquering lamb of some inter-testamental literature (compare Revelation 17.14, but be aware that a different Greek word is here being rendered "lamb"). Yet John gives no support to this apocalyptic idea. Elements from all these sources may be included, but this is an original Johannine title.

2 Jesus as the "Son of God" Acclamation at the baptism and Transfiguration (and by Peter at Caesarea Philippi in Matthew 16.16 only), with the implied accusation at the trial, are the only synoptic uses of this very significant title. John was prepared to go much further. In the ancient Orient most reigning monarchs like the Pharaohs claimed divine parentage; eventually such ideas were to infect the Emperor cult in Rome. Greek mythology had also paved the way for a realization of superhuman and divine elements in human heroes calling them sons of God.

Judaism, on the other hand, did not blur the distinction between human and divine; kings might be acclaimed as sons of God in the Psalms, e.g. 2.7, but this was recognized as just the high-flown language of the coronation. Between the Jewish and the oriental and Greek thought worlds John had plenty of choice; he was not using symbols but describing a divine relationship: "No one has ever seen God; the only Son, who is in the bosom of the Father, he has made him known" (1.18). This relationship is the presupposition of the rest of the gospel, and becomes the touchstone of Christian belief: "These are written that you may believe that Jesus is the Christ, the Son of God" (20.31). It is of course entirely possible that, within his total understanding of the term Son of God, John did intend to include a level of meaning which embraced, as synonyms to it, Messiah/Christ and King of Israel – these would be in line with the Son of God title's Jewish origins.

3 The title of "Messiah/Christ" Here was such an entirely Hebrew category that John was forced to give his Greek readers a translation (1.41 and 4.25). Jesus' nation had long hoped that God would revert to Old Testament precedent and send them a Messiah, a special eschatological deliverer anointed like the kings and priests of old, to rescue them from their political enslavement to the Romans. Christ (= Anointed One) was a very special title entailing instant expectations. The synoptics show Jesus resisting open proclamation as Messiah because of the unfortunate nationalistic hopes of a leader to conquer the Romans which were tied to it. John does not share quite the same preoccupation. He requires faith that Jesus was the Messiah (see 20.31 quoted above). More importantly, from our present point of view, the Messiahship is discussed during the ministry, in 4.29, 7.26, 12.34.

opposite Doubting Thomas (John 20.24–29) from the Benedictional of St. Ethelwold, Winchester c.980 CE. In contrast to this picture, John does not record that Thomas actually touched Jesus, but the invitation to do so is certainly anti-docetic.

Fishing at sunrise is still a way of life on Galilee.

4 King of Israel This is, of course, interlinked with those of Son of God and Messiah. The Davidic monarchy was blessed by a peculiar closeness to God in its covenant:

I will be his father and he shall be my son. (2 Samuel 7.14)

That Nathanael's proclamation in John 1.49 is to be understood in a religious rather than a political way is very likely, particularly as Jesus hails him as a true Israelite (contrasted with the unbelieving Jews?). Jesus in fact goes out of his way to escape the political implications of kingship, hiding from the restless crowd after the Great Feeding (6.15), and explaining to Pilate the spiritual nature of his authority: "My kingdom is not of this world" (18.36). Not as King of Israel, but as King of the Jews he is executed on a trumped-up political charge which he had tried so hard to evade as misleading.

5 Son of Man When the prophet Ezekiel was greeted as "Son of Man", it was as the representative of humanity, but it would be a mistake to regard this title as merely denoting the humanity of Jesus, for by New Testament times it carried other meanings from apocalyptic literature. It was the symbol of God's victorious people Israel in the book of Daniel (7.13), and a pre-existent saviour in 1 Enoch (46.2–3). So Son of Man was a mysterious eschatological figure which Jesus could interpret as he chose. With the exception of Stephen at his martyrdom, it does not seem to have been a title others applied to Jesus either in his lifetime or retrospectively. Jesus seems to have chosen it as an alternative to the constraints of messianism, open acceptance of which would have confined him in a straitjacket of nationalistic expectations. In the synoptics, the classes of saying involving this title are three:

* Reports on Jesus' earthly condition
* Predictions of his Passion, death, and Resurrection
* Predictions of his triumphant return in glory

In his gospel, John has dropped the first category altogether, but he found in the other two groups enough material to reshape for his unique contribution to the Son of Man sayings. He fused together the second and third classes by means of the key word "raised up", which refers to both the raising up in execution and the raising in enthronement and exaltation. It is interesting that the glory of Jesus in Johannine theology does not require a second coming to express it; it is already there in the means of death. Thus John achieved his supreme portrayal of the death of Christ not as ignominious failure, but as the moment of glorification. This class of sayings is also the vehicle for his distinctive portrait of Jesus as the descending and ascending redeemer in whom heaven and earth are joined (1.51).

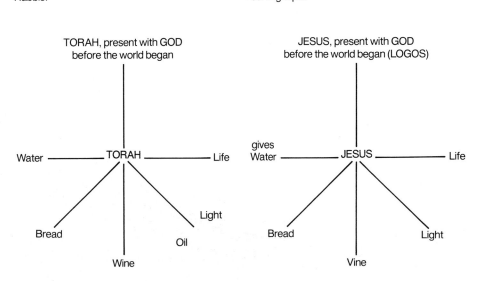

Symbolism and the signs in John

6 Saviour of the World This pagan-sounding title is applied to Jesus when he was off Jewish soil visiting Samaria (4.42). It was usually used to describe gods of healing and Roman emperors, but it is not inconsistent with Johannine theology when read in conjunction with "For God so loved the world that he gave his only Son, that whoever believes in him should not perish but have eternal life" (3.16).

7 Lord The meaning of the word "Lord" covers a broad spectrum ranging from the courteous "Sir" to the full acclamation of Godhead – the latter from both its use in Diaspora Judaism for the holy name of God, and its use in paganism, e.g. "Our Lord and God" applied to the Emperor Domitian. It is possible that Jesus' followers moved from the one use to the other through their acquaintance with him – from politeness to faith. Broadly speaking, in the first half of John "Lord" is used in only a few and significant contexts, which may show the effects of a post-Resurrection faith:

> *Lord, to whom shall we go? You have the words of eternal life.* (6.68)

> *"Lord, I believe;" and he worshipped him.* (9.38)

Christ the Good Shepherd caring for his flock, as portrayed at Galla Placida, Ravenna (5th century CE).

Otherwise "Jesus" is in common use, and he is usually addressed as "Rabbi", i.e. Teacher.

Whereas in the "Book of the Passion", or "of Glory", as the closing chapters centred on the Last Supper are sometimes called, although "Jesus"

One of many artistic representations of the Great Feeding miracle, this mosaic from Tabhge in Galilee shows how important the story was to early Christians. They saw links with the Last Supper, the Resurrection meal of John 21, and their own celebrations of the Eucharist.

is still in common use, he is normally spoken to as "Lord" (13.9; 14.8 etc.). Jesus comments on this (13.13):

You call me Teacher and Lord; and you are right, for so I am.

On Easter Day Mary Magdalene reported that the "Lord's body" had been stolen (20.2, 13) and that she had seen "the Lord". When Jesus joined the apostles that evening he identified himself by the wounds, "then were the disciples glad when they saw the Lord"(20.20). Finally we have the ultimate acclamation by the convinced Thomas: "My Lord and my God"(20.28). The Resurrection had put the seal on their belief. Jesus was certainly Lord.

8 The "I am" sayings   These provided John with a new opportunity to give Christological teaching in a symbolic way, using different "titles". *I am*, in Greek *EGO EIMI*, is a special formula in this gospel. Pagan readers would be familiar with it as the revelatory introduction of a god, e.g. "I am Isis" or "I am Ishtar" at a THEOPHANY, or the showing of the deity to the worshipper. This usage is comparable with Wisdom's self-description in Proverbs 8 and Yahweh's acclamation of himself in Isaiah 41.4: "I, the Lord, the first, and with the last; I am he". It was especially significant when it was used without a predicate ("I am" rather than "I am the Good Shepherd" etc.), because it was then a claim to divinity. This echoed the sacred name of God Yhwh, normally studiously avoided, but muttered once a year in the ritual, and then only by the high priest. Traditionally the name Yhwh was thought to be derived from the similar Hebrew expression revealed to Moses (Exodus 3.14):

God said to Moses, "Say this to the people of Israel, 'I am has sent me to you'".

It is very likely that we are to see in this formula the self-expression of the incarnate Logos – God's Word is doing his job: communicating.

We shall now look at the various uses of the *I am* titles.

a I am the bread of life (6.35, but also expounded in 6.22–71). (See below under the heading of Sacraments.) That this passage has eucharistic links is very likely, but there is more in this saying than communion imagery, just as there is more here than the claim that Jesus is/offers the spiritual nutrition for humanity's survival. The whole miracle of the feeding has its background both in the messianic feast at the End-Time, and in the miraculous feeding of the refugee Israelites with manna and quails in the wilderness. In the miracle Jesus has functioned as the new Moses, but in the later synagogue sermon the focus has switched to the manna. Jesus is the new manna descended from heaven according to what was expected in the last days. More than this, the Jews had used the symbol of the manna for the Torah (Jewish Law), which they also received in the wilderness wanderings and treasured very much. It is noticeable that John employs each main image which the rabbis used for the Torah, and applies it to Jesus. What the Jews thought they had in the Law, Christians have in the Logos (see diagram).

b I am the light of the world (8.12 and 9.5 in context). John sets this saying during the feast of Tabernacles, one of the great pilgrim feasts of Judaism. Held during the autumn, it celebrates both the harvest and the complete reading through of the Law. According to eyewitnesses, in Jesus' time the Court of Women in the Temple was so brilliantly lit at night-time, that all of Jerusalem shared the glow for the festival week. It was then an appropriate setting for Jesus to claim that he is the one who shines out, enlightens, and brings life for mankind. John uses the saying twice, the second time in the context of the curing of the man born blind; here it is caught up in the themes of light and darkness, and of the necessity of judgement being worked out.

In the Sermon on the Mount it is said that Christians are to be the light of the world (Matthew 5.14), and it may be that John has recast this traditional saying to apply to Jesus in his gospel. Its background is particularly interesting. Light was the first of all created things in Genesis 1.3, and John was careful not to confuse Jesus, the creative Word with it; the fourth gospel's use is purely symbolic as in:

> *Thy word is a lamp to my feet and a light to my path* (Psalm 119.105).
> *The Lord is my light and my salvation* (Psalm 27.1).

Light might accompany God and his appearances, but was distinct from him in Judaism, unlike the god=light equations in contemporary pagan and oriental religions; the distinction remained for the evangelist despite his immersion in the light/dark language of dualism he shared with the Qumran sect. It is interesting that the author of 1 John was not so sensitive to the distinction (see 1 John 1.5).

c I am the door of the sheep/good shepherd. Granted the Old Testament background and the rural landscape of much of Palestine at the time, the

The Palestinian shepherd is completely identified with the welfare of the flock he tends and protects from danger. He has no dogs, yet the sheep follow him as their natural leader. John 10.1–18.

imagery of sheep and shepherds was natural for Jesus to choose, especially given the association of leadership with the role of the shepherd. Ancient kings, two great leaders of the Old Testament, Moses and David, and, significantly, God himself were perceived as shepherds of their people thus:

> *The Lord is my shepherd* (Psalm 23.1).

The corollary was that God's people were the flock (compare Psalm 100.3 and especially Ezekiel 34, as this provides thorough background to this whole passage, including the dismissal of those unfit to be shepherds). This image seems to have been used by Jesus:

> *He had compassion on them, because they were like sheep without a shepherd* (Mark 6.34).
> *Fear not little flock* ... (Luke 12.32).

The parable of the lost sheep (Luke 15.4–7) appears to identify Jesus with the searching, caring shepherd.

John developed the image to show Jesus as the archetypal shepherd who

Lazarus' death provided Jesus with the opportunity to give an acted parable on his own power to conquer death, John 11.1–53.

leads and protects his flock from danger, even at the risk of his own life. Unlike ordinary shepherds (who slept across the opening of the pen at night) this "door" led to salvation, and there was much emphasis on the gift of life. The good shepherd has ultimately only one flock (John 10.16). This powerful image of leadership and unity will be discussed again below.

d I am the resurrection and the life – John 11.25. This title is set in the story of the raising of Lazarus, which both enshrines and illustrates it. As a saying, it embraces all that Pharisaic Judaism taught of the after-life, all that Jesus has already claimed for himself as Son of God (5.21, 24, 25–29), and all that was implied by the Easter story. Not all Jews accepted the concept of resurrection, but the Pharisees, Jesus, Paul, and the early Christians did; as God was the agent of resurrection, for Jesus to say this was tantamount to saying that he was divine. With the added provocation of the revival of Lazarus, it secured Jesus' death sentence (11.50).

e I am the way, the truth and the life (John 14.6). The origin of the "Way" (i.e. to salvation) is probably not to be found in Gnosticism but in Judaism; "Halakah", from a Hebrew word meaning literally "to walk", was the Jewish development of rules applying the Torah to everyday conditions; i.e. correct ethical behaviour was the way to God. Thus for John, Jesus, not the keeping of the Torah, is the way to approach to God. The "Way" was also the name given to early Christians (Acts 9.2). John may have adopted the Way and made it a Christological image, in the same manner as he did for the light of the world.

That Truth was an important idea for John is shown by the number of times he uses it. Here it is probably synonymous with that reality which is God.

Life, like light, was a basic concept introduced in the Prologue and developed subsequently. John shares the Biblical belief that God is the source of essential energy, both in creation (Genesis 1) and in restoration (Ezekiel 37). Much of the attention to life in the fourth gospel is directed to that eternal life which it was Jesus' special mission to bring to those who believed in him (3.16).

f I am the vine (John 15.1). As in the Bread of Life it is quite common to find a eucharistic reference here, related to the cup of wine at the Last Supper. Examination of the context shows that this is a symbol primarily concerned with the close relationship between Jesus and the disciples. The unity of Christ and believer is conditional on keeping the commandments, and the believer is expected to bring forth good fruits (15.2, 4, 5) or risk expulsion. This then is no relationship wholly mediated by sacraments, and is best seen as John's equivalent of the Pauline body, the relationship of the community in Christ. (On ethics in the community, see below.) In the Old Testament the vine or vineyard was a frequent symbol for Israel, the people of God, e.g. Isaiah 5.1–7. In this respect it matches the image of the shepherd and his flock.

Reverence

The only person in this gospel whose stature approaches that of Jesus is John the Baptist. Yet to the reader familiar with the synoptic characterization (of the wild-eyed ascetic, preaching fire and judgement), the Johannine picture comes as something of a surprise (1.1–36):

* John the Baptist is sent from God; he has authority.
* John the Baptist is a witness to Christ's pre-eminence and pre-existence, and he is to reveal him.
* His special witness is that Christ is Lamb of God;
  the one on whom the Spirit descended and remained; the one who baptized with the Holy Spirit; the son of God.
* John the Baptist is not to be confused, however, with the Messiah himself; the prophet like Moses; Elijah.

The last one, Elijah, is surprising – the synoptics certainly thought of the Baptist in that connection (e.g. Matthew 17.12) and so, by implication, did his contemporaries.

Now the fact that John the Baptist should so carefully be distinguished from other figures suggests an argumentative approach on John's part, countering the mistake of overrating the Baptist's relative importance in the story of salvation history. In chapter 1 the Baptist is reduced to the function of a voice/witness from the rank of prophetic forerunner, and still protesting that he is not worthy. Other passages reinforce this picture:

* The Baptist is only the best man   Jesus is the bridegroom
* The Baptist must decrease   Jesus must increase
* The Baptist is a lamp   Jesus is the Light of the world

N.B. a lamp is irrelevant in the full glare of the sun.

So, the Baptist was demoted and put in his place – as a witness:

> *John did no sign, but everything John said about THIS MAN* [Jesus] *is true* (10.41).

The Vine was a powerful image of unity and fellowship for the disciples to perceive their relationship to one another and to Christ. It also placed them under judgement – as expulsion from the vine and destruction followed unfruitfulness, John 15.1–8.

If Jesus was promoted at the Baptist's expense, the most obvious reason for this is that the Johannine community was in dispute with those who had elevated the Baptist beyond what was reasonable. According to Acts 19, Paul discovered a group of Baptist disciples at Ephesus, long after their Master's execution; they were baptized by Paul and received the Holy Spirit, but others might not have been converted. Some scholars see a continuing story of Baptist sectarians in the scriptures of the Mandaean movement (see the chapter on the Gnostic writings); if this is so, it means that, despite John's polemic, some were unconvinced (even if the two disciples of 1.37 stand for others who *did* come across, because they were sure of Jesus' superiority).

Reality

Despite the references to Jesus' pre-existence, divinity, and possession of impressive titles, some given by no less a figure than the Baptist himself, John's picture of Jesus was not only that of a celestial hero-figure. In fact, John underlines the flesh and blood reality in certain key verses about the Incarnation:

> *And the Word became flesh and dwelt among us.* (1.14)
>
> *The bread which I shall give for the life of the world is my flesh.* (6.51)
>
> *One of the soldiers pierced his side with a spear, and at once there came out blood and water.* (19.34)

Moreover in John Jesus admits to tiredness, thirst, and grief at the loss of a close friend. No one else carries the cross for him; there was no risk of Simon of Cyrene suffering crucifixion as a substitute in John's telling of the tale. All this was not accidental. John's church must have found itself in contact with the Gnostics (see below), who undervalued the human element in Jesus, and who thought that the divine hero was not to be identified with this world. To them, he only *seemed* (the Greek word *dokeo* = I seem gave us the name Docetists for the group of people following this line of thought), he only seemed to be a man, only seemed to die – in fact by evading his own destruction on the cross. John's underscoring of the tangibility of Jesus has then a corrective purpose. It does, incidentally, also serve to humanize the picture John has himself built up of a Christ who is an uncomfortably omniscient and divine companion at times, one for whom Gethsemane's agony was condensed to the passing comment:

> *Now is my soul troubled. And what shall I say? "Father save me from this hour?" No, for this purpose I have come to this hour.* (12.27)

The purpose of Jesus

It has been recognized for some time that John's distinctive presentation of the manner and purpose of Jesus' appearance among humankind is what sets him apart from so many other New Testament writers. The manner of Jesus' coming and going can be described in terms of downward and upward movements.

Christian theology has traditionally understood the moment of *descent* as at the birth in Bethlehem. Thus John 1.1–18 provides "the gospel" at many Christmas church services, accompanied by hymns and carols with a full complement of stables, shepherds, stars and kings (harmonizing the various gospel accounts). While there is no need seriously to question this interpretation, it should be remembered that it is not one which John himself makes explicit. Indeed Jesus' earthly appearance is recorded at the moment of approach to John the Baptist, and only later are dismissive and ironic references made to the Bethlehem story, 7.27, 41–42, and the virgin birth, 8.41.

On the *ascent*, however, John is in fact much clearer, marshalling a series of events into a unique collection of Passion, Death, Ascension and Glorification – all of which take place in the great eschatological moment of the "hour", anticipated throughout the gospel (e.g. 2.4 "My hour has not yet come"). The Hour's events are also covered by John's phrase "the lifting up of the Son of Man" (see p. 251). This curious phrase of "gallows humour"[5] covers both the hoisting of the condemned man on his beam into the upright position for the cruel work of execution to begin, and the exaltation of Christ on his throne. Thus John intends us to understand the Hour as containing the events of several hours – the suffering and death of Jesus, and his enthronement on the cross, which involves his return to the Father and Glory. Thus the whole movement is ascension.

Not for the first time the evangelist has compressed into one unit events that other writers have treated separately.[6] Return to the Father as an expression for his death was not, of course, confined to the Son of Man category of sayings. Jesus introduced the idea in a controversial dialogue with the Jews (7.33); but he developed it more fully in the Farewell Discourses (14.12 and 28), where it is the necessary preliminary to the coming of the Paraclete (that is, the Holy Spirit in a role unique to John) in 16.7.

The purpose of the coming of Jesus into the world is both salvation, the granting of eternal life, and judgement, the Greek word *Crisis*. John saw Jesus' presence in the world as extremely divisive. He offered men a choice of coming to him, but they were also free to turn away; in that offer and their rejection of him was their judgement. Symbolically expressed, Jesus was Light, and humankind could be attracted or repelled by that light. If they were repelled by that light they retreated even deeper into the darkness (3. 16–21). Light and dark here are more than poetic symbols; they are part of a dualistic system in which light is associated with good, knowledge, truth, and love, whereas darkness represents evil, ignorance, the lie, and hate. Thus in 3.2 Nicodemus comes in the night to approach Jesus, and in 13.30 Judas Iscariot departs into the night at the Last Supper. Similar dualism is to be found in other contemporary writings, e.g. those of the Dead Sea Scroll community at Qumran, and among the Gnostics.

Now if Jesus came for reasons of salvation, how was it to be achieved? Firstly through his teaching ministry, which sought to attract humankind to

an understanding of him and a belief in him, and a relationship with him. This he maintained was all that the Father required of them, provided that it was characterized by the mutual love which was at base the relationship between the Son and his Father. To this end he drew about him a close-knit group of companions who would be the pattern and exemplar of this faith and relationship. This then was the choice: for him, or against him; but when human society (the *cosmos* = the world) made its choice and its leaders decided that Jesus was an uncomfortable threat to political stability, then we see the other side of the coin – judgement. Ironically they sought to judge Jesus and condemn him; in so doing they brought about the second phase of salvation which comprised Jesus' death and their own condemnation.

John, like all the evangelists, naturally saw events in the ministry from the perspective of the cross – it had happened; it was the culmination of the three years' work. Thus Jesus and the evangelist were able to warn the disciples and the readers, and prepare them for the event with an interpretation or, more correctly, several interpretations of the crucifixion.

Christ's death as ascent

This view holds the crucifixion as the supreme moment of the Incarnation, and, far from being a reverse in Jesus' personal history, the achievement of the following purposes:

* the bringing of eternal life to believers (3.15)
* the establishing of Jesus' authority as "I am he" (8.28)
* the drawing of all humankind to himself (12.32).

In the main body of the gospel this has been given as "Son of Man" teaching, and in the narrative of the crucifixion Jesus, apparently still wearing his thorny crown, is lifted up on a cross surmounted by a trilingual proclamation of imperial type proclaiming his status. With his dying breath Jesus is able to claim that the purpose is achieved.

Christ's death for others

That Jesus died for others (i.e. vicariously) is most clearly expressed in the symbol of the good shepherd prepared to die for his sheep (10.11), and the man who would lay down his life for his friends (15.13).

Christ's death as cleansing

This is suggested by one possible understanding of the footwashing episode, especially when we bear in mind John's careful use of vocabulary, such that the same key verbs describe Jesus' activity with his robes and his life. Thus he lays aside robes and life, performs the cleansing activity, and takes up his robes and life (i.e. in the Resurrection). The death of Jesus will enable the believer to be washed from sin and share in Jesus (13.8).

Hyssop is too insubstantial a plant to bear a sponge of wine to Jesus on the cross. The possibilities of textual error (hyssos = spear), and incorrectly identified plant, must be weighed against the fact that hyssop played a significant role in Passover ritual – the festival which informed John's understanding of Jesus' death. Historical accuracy was not a high priority.

A modern charismatic church lays claim to Spirit-filled worship. Would John have recognized this kind of religious experience?

Christ's death as an example

Yet another layer of interpretation of the footwashing sees Christ's death as an example. Some have traced it to the Lucan comment, "But I am among you as one who serves" (Luke 22.27). Jesus held up his self-effacing role in performing even a menial chore for his disciples as a pattern for emulation. They were to express their love for one another in service, even if the cost was high; for it may well be that 13.14 should be read in the light of 13.34.

Christ's death as a sacrifice for sin

The title "Lamb of God, which takes away the sin of the world" is a new creation – probably from material supplied by the Suffering Servant passages and ancient Passover ritual. John's closeness to Passover ritual is shown in his changes to the traditional story of Christ's death to enhance the Passover symbolism.

* Christ died at the hour of slaughter for Passover lambs in the temple (i.e. 24 hours earlier than synoptic time)
* Christ was offered a drink on some hyssop (a herb unsuited to this type of assignment, but used to sprinkle blood at Passover time – Exodus 12.22)
* Christ was spared the crurifragium = the smashing of the legs to hasten death (John saw this as direct fulfilment of the text regarding the Passover lamb – "you shall not break a bone of it" Exodus 12.46).

It is curious that John never brings out the "sin" aspect again after 1.29, not even repeating the whole formula at 1.36, and of course no one ever

The Marriage Feast at Cana, painting by Juan de Flandes.

associated the Paschal Lamb with sin at all. Other creatures and other rituals were involved in sin-bearing ceremonies.

It would then appear that John's main interpretation of Christ's death is in terms of his ascent and return to the Father; the benefits wrought by this ascent do not explicitly include the traditional ones associated with sin etc. In fact none of the other interpretations plays a major role in John at all; so much is this the case that the evangelist has been accused of portraying Jesus as a Gnostic redeemer! Thus Forestell says, "the Cross of Christ in John is evaluated precisely in terms of revelation in harmony with the theology of the entire gospel, rather than in terms of vicarious and expiatory sacrifice for sin".[7]

Conflicts with the Jews

Every gospel provides some rationale for the final conflict with the Jewish authorities which led to the crucifixion – this was no sudden, unpremeditated attack on a "harmless" religious teacher. The synoptics pile up controversy stories during the ministry, which show Jesus outraging Jewish susceptibilities by healing people chronically, rather than acutely, ill on the Sabbath, and claiming his authority to rule the Sabbath and to forgive sins. Although indications of the same tendencies are at work in John – thus the cured cripple from Bethesda carries his bed on the Sabbath and attracts unwelcome attention, and the healing of the blind man is similarly offensive – far greater forces are also at work, and the whole theological question of the status of Jesus over against Judaism is explored more profoundly than the synoptics could or did do.

The wedding at Cana

What actually happened at this wedding (2.1–11), when Jesus performed his first sign, of turning water into wine, does not concern us here, but the significance of it does. A wedding setting may suggest a messianic background; the six water jars for purification rites do suggest the Jewish Law or Torah as an incomplete or imperfect number (1 less than 7). This water has to be totally transformed before it can be offered to the guests; the wine which is poured out is vastly superior to what might have been expected (2.10). Thus Jesus offers something new and radically superior to the Torah – "grace and truth" (1.17).

The cleansing of the temple

This event (2.13–25) is frequently regarded by commentators as being anachronistically placed at the start of Jesus' ministry – for they point out that Jesus would scarcely have been allowed on the premises again after this, and they prefer the synoptic dating of the story. This sparked the antagonism which concluded in Jesus' death during Holy Week, i.e. at the close of his ministry. Theologically, however, the episode does have a place at the start of Jesus' ministry. Here Jesus is attacking the principal cultic institution of Judaism. When he was challenged to produce a legitimizing sign of his authority to do this, he offered to replace the Temple with his body. The Temple is on the way to becoming redundant. As the meeting place between God and humankind the Temple, like the desert "tent of meeting" before it, has served its purpose. Now that God's presence has "dwelt among us", literally "has pitched a tent", in Jesus the incarnate Logos (1.14), and not in the Holy of Holies, Jesus and not a building is the proper meeting place between humankind and God. As Jesus later told the Samaritan woman:

> Neither on this mountain nor in Jerusalem will you worship the Father
> . . . true worshippers will worship the Father in spirit and in truth.
> (4.21, 23)

This 2nd century CE synagogue was undoubtedly built on top of the one in Capernaum where Jesus preached the Bread of Life sermon in John 6.

Both of these sayings are conditional on the arrival of his Hour and Jesus' death.

The Jewish festivals

The wedding at Cana and the cleansing of the temple set the pattern for what is to follow, because Jesus is to replace the best that Judaism can offer in teaching and worship. This is borne out in John's treatment of Jewish festivals —Jesus surpasses all that was previously available.

Passover
– year 1 – Jesus offers his body 2.21
– year 2 – Jesus offers the bread of life 6.48
– year 3 – Jesus dies as Paschal Lamb 19.30

Tabernacles
Jesus offers water 7.37–38
Jesus is the Light of the world 8.12
Jesus gives the mysterious name of God 8.28

Dedication (Hanukkah)
Jesus consecrates himself 10.36

This is in fact a very Jewish gospel, steeped in a knowledge and love of the Old Testament.[8] Apart from direct quotation, every section of the gospel is redolent of its symbolism. The author was also conversant with his contemporaries' interpretations of the Torah – even if he remains independent of it. He was well able to enter into rabbinic style argument and debate – the argument in chapter 7, based on circumcision as the legitimizing Sabbath-breaking precedent for a healing, was appropriate for 2,000 years ago, if not readily acceptable today. The evangelist even makes the stupendous claim that salvation is "of the Jews", in the context of controversy with the Samaritan woman. Thus John plainly sees Jesus as replacing or fulfilling all that was most significant in Judaism, but his gospel shows that this was not universally appreciated.

"The Jews"

As John employs it, the term "the Jews" is usually synonymous with "opposition", and an increasingly hostile opposition at that. Some of the Jews believe, some are ashamed or afraid to admit their belief, most are antagonistic and disbelieving. Thus "the Jews" has virtually the same meaning at times as the dualistic term "*cosmos*" or "the world". The cosmos represents human society organizing itself apart from God. This does not mean that God stops loving his obstinate wayward cosmos, but it does mean that the cosmos has deliberately cut itself off from communion with God and the benefits which he has to offer. Moreover the hatred that the cosmos has for God and his forces of good and light infects its attitude to Jesus, and subsequently to the disciples. Thus the opposition of the Jews to Jesus is theologically perceived as the work of the powers of darkness.

Misunderstanding of the heavenly aspect

John employs a literary technique frequently called "Johannine misunderstanding". According to this, Jesus responds to questioners, who then fail to comprehend Jesus' answer in the correct spiritual manner; in their pedestrian reply Jesus is provided with the opportunity to develop his theme further. Here are three examples:

1 Nicodemus is gently(?) mocked by Jesus (3.10) after his failure to understand the language of rebirth "from above" and spiritual things.

2 At Capernaum after the feeding of the five thousand the synagogue congregation's preoccupation with the earthly makes them think:

* Jesus can deliver daily bread (6.34);
* Jesus is intelligible in terms of his known human ancestry (6.42);
* Jesus is making a cannibalistic offer (6.52).[9]

It is noteworthy that some of Jesus' erstwhile disciples are so offended by the last misunderstanding that they desert Jesus. In each case Jesus has given a valid statement when seen in terms of the heavenly perspective (e.g. 6.63, where Jesus is the *spiritual* nutrition basic to humankind's survival, but this is only possible because his origin is divine, and the feeding will only become available after his death).

3 In the Temple at Tabernacles the crowd labours under similar misconceptions:

* Jesus lacks messianic qualifications because they know where he comes from 7.27 cp 7.41–2;
* Jesus must be going to the Diaspora because he is going away 7.35;
* Jesus must be going to commit suicide because he is going away 8.22.

These are sufficient instances to show that Jewish misunderstanding is motivated by a lack of perception of the spiritual dimension in Jesus and what he had to offer.

The status of the Son

Jesus' defence of the cure of the cripple in John 5 is based not on an appeal to humanitarian principles (compare Luke 13.15), but on an elevated theological discourse on the status of the Son. In terms inimical to those Jews raised on daily repetitions of the prayer called the "Shema" –

Hear O Israel the Lord our God is ONE Lord

– Jesus explains that he works seven days per week as his Father does. He claims that he works precisely as he saw his Father work, and will be given specific functions of God to carry out in judging, raising the dead, and giving life. These functions would demonstrate Jesus' authority and glory. Testimony to the status of Jesus as the Son is borne by:

* John the Baptist
* the works Jesus does
* the Father himself
* the scriptures
* Moses – "But if you do not believe his writing, how will you believe my words?" (5.47)

These themes from John 5 are renewed in chapter 7, to be developed in the acrimony of chapter 8, in which Jesus' parentage is attributed by his hearers to fornication, and his odd religious views to Samaritan heresy and demon-possession (compare 10.20). Meanwhile the Jews' claims to be free-born children of Abraham are rebutted by Jesus, who counter-claims that their father is the devil (see above, p. 265 under *cosmos*: this is a theological description of their opposition to Jesus).

This heated atmosphere naturally means that when Jesus reveals his essential unity with the Father in 10.30, the Jews' reaction is that he has committed the ultimate sin of blasphemy (10.33). Jesus then points to the mute evidence of "the works" he has done (e.g. healings) to prove his status as Son (10.38).

The automatic response to blasphemy was to stone the blasphemer. A list of all the references in John 7–10 to intent to arrest or kill Jesus is surprisingly long. In chapter 9 the persecution is widened to include excommunication from the synagogue of those who confess him too (see below, p. 268). Not surprisingly, Jesus retreated from the public domain after this harassment, emerging to raise Lazarus, despite the disciples' comment in 11.8. Thomas' brave resolution, "Let us also go that we may die with him" (11.16), shows how seriously the disciples took the threat to Jesus' life. As a result of the attention the raising received, Lazarus was similarly under threat (12.10–11).

Attitudes and responsibilities in the hour

> *The hour has come for the Son of Man to be glorified. Truly, truly, I say to you, unless a grain of wheat falls into the earth and dies, it remains alone; but if it dies, it bears much fruit.* (12. 23–24)

The "Hour", comprising the Passion, Death, Ascension, and Glorification, was presented as part of the divine purpose and brought about Jesus' departure to the Father. On another level, the execution of the operation was the responsibility of the devil, who inspired Judas Iscariot to betrayal (13.2), who was threatening even at the Last Supper (14.30), and was unconsciously bringing about his own judgement (16.11); but what of the human agencies involved? It appears that John wrote with a desire to clear the Romans from as much blame as possible (a shrewd political move for the world in which he lived). Jewish responsibility is correspondingly stated and underlined in statements of great dramatic irony:

> *It is expedient for you that one man should die for the people, and that the whole nation should not perish.* (Caiaphas: 11.50)

> *They themselves did not enter the praetorium, so that they might not be defiled, but might eat the Passover.* (18.28)

> *We have no king but Caesar.* (Chief priests: 19.15)

The overwhelming desire to be rid of Jesus permitted them to use political expediency, to defile themselves by murder, and to abrogate the sovereignty of God.

Conclusion

The traditional titles of Jesus, the pervading use of the Old Testament language and imagery as well as quotations, show that the Johannine church was originally made up of Christians reared in Judaism. The relationship with Judaism had not, however, remained friendly. Jewish Johannine Christians came to feel that Jesus had surpassed Judaism in its teaching, worship, festivals, and traditions; he had fulfilled to overflowing the traditional categories and titles of Messiahship. Such Christians had therefore to leave the synagogue. Possibly their departure from the ranks of Judaism was not entirely voluntary; Jews who did not accept their view expelled them from the synagogues (compare 9.22, 16.2). Some of them may also have been hounded to death (16.2), just as other early Christians had been tracked down by the unconverted Saul in his zeal and piety (see Acts 9.1). Dialogue of a kind may have continued, with the Johannine Christians determined to encourage the departure from the synagogue of reticent Christian believers (e.g. 11.42) and to convert and convince others. Doubtless the church/synagogue debate had in this way considerable influence on the shaping of the more contentious debates between Jesus and the Jews in John's gospel. The real point at issue for the evangelist's community was not the keeping of the Law, as it had been for Paul – that seems to have been no longer a live issue – but the place of Jesus in Christian belief.

As the discussion above on the status of the Son has shown, high Christology emerged and was sharpened in conflict with those who denied any superior status at all to the wandering preacher from Galilee. In fact the most outstanding statements of the whole New Testament in regard to the Sonship and divinity of Jesus are made in this gospel, and in opposition to the Jews.

Thus consideration of John' emphasis on Christology and controversial relationship with Judaism has furnished us with a background against which to place the Johannine community, on the borders of the Judaism from which it had emerged. Some distance in time from Jesus' ministry is probable. Firmer dating would be possible if the excommunication from the synagogues which occurred in John could be placed as the one officially ratified by the Synod of Jamnia in 85–90 CE. At this time, the Birkath ha-Minim, or so-called Test Benediction,[10] was introduced, a formula inserted in the morning prayers which no true Christian could speak. This would have effectively excommunicated all Christians from Jewish synagogues. If this was a reality for John, then this controversy could be placed at the end of the first century. It is not, however, entirely clear whether this, rather than the everyday disciplinary power of some local synagogue, as seen at work in Acts and the letters of Paul, was the case here.

Christians and the end of the world

Study of the synoptic gospels gives us the impression that at the close of his life Jesus warned of disasters that would befall believers and humankind alike in the future. Believers were to have confidence in God throughout that trying time and were to await Jesus' triumphant return, and the outcome of the Last Judgement. Jesus, the evangelists and Paul used language and ideas which had been fashionable in some Jewish circles since the demise of prophecy –collectively they were known as "apocalyptic". Whole books had been written in this vein between the Old and New Testament periods

The Last Judgement from St. Mark's Venice shows *conventional futurist eschatology*. Christ sits in judgement at the end of time, sorting out the good for life in heaven, and the evil for destruction.

(the time known as intertestamental Judaism). Such looking forward to a future dénouement of history at the End-Time is called "futurist" or "conventional" eschatology. There are only a few traces of it in John (e.g. 5.25–29), and even these may be from a later editor.

The fourth gospel's main preoccupation is with a reworked eschatological framework which redirects Christians' vision from the distant horizon to their present situation. The decisive End-Time event has in fact happened for them already – it was caused by the departure of Jesus to the Father. John's

The realization of conventional eschatology in the fourth gospel

Conventional (futurist) eschatology: Signs of the End	Targets fulfilled in Johannine realized eschatology
1 The preaching of the gospel to all nations	1 12.32??
2 Troubles for Christians – family break-up – expulsion from the synagogue – appearances before civil authorities – false prophets – men's love growing cold	2 The hatred of the cosmos for Jesus, spills over on to the disciples 15.18–19 persecution 15.20 expulsion from the synagogues 9.22, 16.2 } Present Christians killed in God's service 16.2 } reality?
3 Disturbances – natural: earthquakes, famines, plagues, etc. – cosmic: signs in the heavens – international: wars, uprisings, etc.	
4 The culminating sign is the siege of Jerusalem and attendant disasters (Lk), the abomination of desolation (Mk)	
5 The Son of Man comes – the Parousia, with power and clouds and glory – to gather his elect from the corners of the earth	5 Jesus has come again in the person of the Paraclete who is his working and teaching presence with the disciples 14.26, etc. Jesus' glory was present throughout the ministry, visible in the mini-transfigurations of the signs; his pre-existent glory was regained at his death in H-Hour 17.1.
6 The resurrection of the believing dead (1 Th)	6 Judgement occurs in the crisis of men's reaction to Jesus Resurrection is available here and now in the faith in the one who is the Resurrection and the Life 11.25–26.
7 The life of the world to come – happiness and plenty – messianic banquet	7 Joy, peace, fellowship, and unity with Christ are all present possessions of the believer 15.11, 14.27, 15.5, 16.20–24 Eternal life is on offer now 17.3, etc.
(Sources: Mk 13, Lk 21, Mt 24, Lk 17.22–end, 1 Th 4.14–17.)	

"realized eschatology" maintains that Christians already possess all that they might reasonably have expected to receive in the future:

* they have passed through the judgement;
* they have eternal life;
* Jesus has in a very real sense returned. (This will be discussed further in the next main section on the Holy Spirit.)

As a consequence the joy and peace Christians had been hoping for in some distant age of bliss were already the hallmarks of Christian existence. (The accompanying chart should be studied for more detail.) John had radically altered expectations to concentrate Christians' attention on the present, rather than the future. It must be recognized that all that still had to happen had been pre-determined by the crucial events which the gospel claimed as history. Why John might have arrived at this radically altered perspective will now be discussed, in relation to the Holy Spirit.

The role of the Holy Spirit

The Holy Spirit plays a much more significant role in John than in the other three gospels, and this can be seen in the later chapters. Despite John the Baptist's statement that the Holy Spirit descended on Jesus at his baptism, and that Jesus would baptize with the Holy Spirit (1. 32–34), the Holy Spirit is not much in evidence during the Ministry. It is the Spirit's function as a future gift which is important; the giving of the gift was apparently consequent on Jesus' death:

> *the Spirit had not yet been given, because Jesus was not yet glorified.*
> (7.39)

This promised gift arrived on Easter Day, when John combined in twelve or so hours what Luke and the church calendar spread over fifty days. He telescopes Resurrection, Ascension, and Pentecost into one day. Thus that evening the risen ascended Jesus breathes on the assembled disciples saying, "Receive the Holy Spirit" (20.22). The Holy Spirit was clearly God's gift to the church for the new age (thus Peter cites the prophet Joel to show that the coming of the Holy Spirit is an event of the End-Time – Acts 2.17). As such the Holy Spirit brought authority to his recipients to forgive sins (John 20.23).

The presence of the Holy Spirit was most distinctive when released to function in the church, by the return of Jesus to the Father, in the form of the Paraclete, announced and described in the Farewell Discourses (i.e. discussions led by Jesus in chapters 14–16 at the Last Supper).

The Paraclete

The term Paraclete is used of the Holy Spirit in John and in no other gospel. Indeed, this word is so distinctive within the New Testament, that it appears to be a creation of the Johannine community. John may have had in mind one or all of the possible meanings derived from the family of related words:

* a defence counsel, one called alongside to help;
* a mediator or go-between;
* a person bringing comfort and consolation;
* someone who encourages.

No one of these definitions fits exactly the role of the Holy Spirit with the disciples – in John the Spirit is a prosecutor, who does not act for the defence. The Spirit does not act as a mediator between God and the disciples; only in 1 John 1.2 does this intercessory role come to the fore – and then it is filled by Jesus, not by the Holy Spirit. Similarly there is no evidence that the last two possibilities of comfort and encouragement are John's priorities. A composite of these features is probably more acceptable than an isolated definition, but this composite and the ways in which the role is developed are all unique to John. The Paraclete is closely related to and modelled on Jesus; both come from the Father (15.26), the Father sends them (14.26), the Father gives them (14.16). The Paraclete is clearly seen as the successor to Jesus, taking over where Jesus has left the close relationship with the disciples, guiding and teaching them (14.26), so that they are not abandoned, but have his abiding presence reminding them of what Jesus said and did.

Other parts the Paraclete has to play are to testify to Jesus and to glorify him (14.26, 16.14). Consequently he finds himself ranged against the cosmos in a judgemental role (16.8–11). In this way too it replaces Jesus. The Paraclete, whom Brown so aptly describes as the "personal presence of Jesus in the Christian while Jesus is with the Father",[11] is clearly identified with the Holy Spirit, and also as the Spirit of Truth (a title familiar in Qumran literature). It would seem that, in his role as Jesus-substitute, the Holy Spirit was able to satisfy the desperate longing felt by some early Christians for the arrival of the apocalyptic Son of Man.

Particularly in the Farewell Discourses the Johannine community is portrayed as one which is very conscious of being Spirit-led, even if not charismatic in the Pauline (or the modern) sense. Certainly it was aware of Spirit-guidance both in relation to internal matters of teaching, and also in relation to the hostile world beyond the community's walls. This Paraclete-centredness is its charter and manifesto for church life.

A review of John's distinctive eschatology and his Spirit-led church will lead us to further conclusions about John's community and its situation. It is usually suggested that John's unusual emphasis on the fulfilment of the End-Time (at least in part) would be explained if the whole idea of the Second Coming of Jesus at the end of the world had become a problem, and John was offering a radically different solution to it. Evidence shows that many first-century Christians thought that the End was imminent; Paul himself seems to have gone through such a phase, though without the extreme reaction of some of his Thessalonian converts, who found daily employment an irrelevance in such circumstances!

Certainly the End was expected during the lifetime of many first-generation Christians, and when they began to die – a natural process hastened by persecution in places like Rome in the sixties – disquiet grew. The prospect of a future without any eyewitness contacts with the Lord himself may have been one impetus towards the writing down of the gospel tradition, in order to preserve it. A sharper anxiety was to overcome this, though. In some quarters the Second Coming of Jesus was closely tied to the anticipated fall of Jerusalem and destruction of its Temple in 70 CE. The Jewish War came and went, the Romans razed the Temple to ruins. The Parousia did not come. This calamity occasioned a severe crisis of faith – some must have doubted the whole gospel as a consequence of the non-appearance of a verifiable event (2 Peter 3.4). There was much "falling away".

John's answer is that Jesus had in fact come again – the Paraclete was his Parousia. There was no need for eyewitnesses with the Holy Spirit inspiring the teachers. Even eyewitnesses were dependent on the Holy Spirit to interpret events correctly after Jesus' death (compare 2.22, 12.16). "What need do you have to sigh after future happiness – when joy and peace are yours now?" At a critical stage in the development of the Johannine community it had been troubled by precisely the same problems that troubled other Christians – the delay of the Parousia, and the death of the first-generation Christians – but here it was especially acute in the loss of the Beloved Disciple (21.23). John or John's church had solved these problems by the doctrine of the Paraclete as the living presence of Jesus in the church, and the reassessment of eschatology in order to see the benefits of the end of the world accruing now from the immediate end of the world. The fourth gospel was a major influence in helping the church to adjust to the problem of living in history. (A parallel but independent and different solution to these problems was of course offered by Luke–Acts.)

Signs of the Church

Jesus and the sacraments

It is well known that in the fourth gospel Jesus nowhere issues a command like "Go therefore and make disciples of all nations, baptizing them in the name of the Father, and of the Son and of the Holy Ghost" (Matthew 28.19), which would clearly have instituted the sacrament of baptism. More strangely, John's Last Supper includes no activity with bread and wine, with the unmistakable command "Do this in remembrance of me" (1 Corinthians 11.24). The substituted story is of the washing of the disciples' feet. Why this should be so is quite an intriguing problem, especially when there are indications that the sacraments were known to John, and probably played quite a part in his community's life.

Baptism

John shares with the synoptics a recollection of Christian origins related to the baptizing group of John the Baptist; John goes further than them in stating that Jesus and his early group of disciples also engaged in baptizing activity, even though for some reason he saw fit to distance Jesus personally from this (3.22, 4.1–2). That the Johannine disciples should continue this practice after Jesus' death is a reasonable assumption, particularly as it is very likely that the discussion with Nicodemus focusses on the saying:

> Truly, truly, I say to you, unless one is born of water and of the Spirit, he cannot enter the Kingdom of God (3.5)

to make a distinct allusion to baptismal ideas. In John's community baptismal ideas were thus linked to spiritual birth and entrance into the spiritual realm of God (contrast the Pauline ideas of death and resurrection connected with immersion in Romans 6.3–4).

Further ideas appropriate to baptism, such as a coming to faith and enlightenment, are to be found in the sign/story of the man born blind in chapter 9. These are in addition to a clear importance assigned to washing, when the blind man visits the Pool of Siloam; anointing and possibly the laying on of hands are also to be seen as integral to the ceremony. Certainly since ancient times the man, cured on both the physical and spiritual levels, has been seen as the type of the convert; the story was read to converts at their own baptism service. Appropriately the convert advances to such faith that he worships Jesus: Lord, I believe. (9.38)

Other themes in the story include the working out of judgement (the other side of salvation, which is certainly not unconnected with baptism.

The story of the footwashing adds yet more information. Baptism is a cleansing whose efficacy is rooted in the death of Jesus (this story is an acted parable of that idea). Baptism is not automatic in its effect – afterwards Judas was able to go out and betray Jesus. However, the washing enables the faithful believer "to have a part in Jesus" (13.8).

Baptismal allusions are not automatically intended every time John mentions water, because water which is drunk is also a symbol of eternal life. The wedding at Cana, and the interview with the Samaritan woman, for example, are not baptismal in allusion. It is hard to see how the cure of the cripple in chapter 5 can be considered baptismal, when the man never dips in the pool.

Where one might have thought to have something akin to the Matthew 28.19 command to baptize quoted above, at the Pentecostal giving of the Holy Spirit on Easter Day, Jesus commissions the disciples to forgive sins. This could possibly have a baptismal significance; but an acceptable alternative interpretation would be to find here a reference to the powers of absolution enjoyed by the community in the regular process of discipline. Thus while an explicitly organized church initiation rite is not mentioned, John does seem to provide indications that baptism not only happened, but had received a fair degree of theological evaluation.

Communion

The Last Supper in chapter 13 is where one might have expected Jesus, in line with synoptic and Pauline traditions, to explain the coming trauma of Good Friday, with the symbols of bread and wine. Instead John uses another highly symbolic story, that of the footwashing, to explain the significance of the death to follow. In addition to the baptismal layer of this parable, we are surely meant to see a parallelism of the vocabulary in the laying aside of the clothes and life, and the taking up again of the clothes and life. This mirrors the death, and the resurrection which follows, when the cleansing is achieved. Death is viewed as an act of humble service, the supreme expression of love, and as such can be held up as an example to the disciples. This is a good sacramental background, but hardly teaching which is explicitly eucharistic in thrust, despite the fact that this is the "night in which he was betrayed" (1 Corinthians 11.23).

Explicitly eucharistic teaching was placed in an earlier episode in the gospel – the Great Feeding of chapter 6, and its related synagogue discourse centred on "I am the bread of life". That there was a clear link between *all* special meals recorded in the gospels (the 5,000, the 4,000, the Last Supper and the Resurrection meals) and the commemorative meals kept in the church was early recognized. The *Didache* (the so-called "Teaching of the Twelve Apostles", an early work of disputed date) recalls elements of the Great Feeding in the eucharistic prayer, while refugee Christians painted the bread and fish of the feeding miracles in clearly eucharistic contexts, in their wall paintings in the catacombs. The plainest indication of the link is in the use of the same vocabulary:

Jesus **took** *the bread,* **blessed/gave thanks** (= eucharistein), *and* **gave** *it out.*

These words are common to the synoptic and Johannine feeding miracles, and the synoptic and Pauline Last Suppers. (John does not share with them the commonly reported act of Jesus, that he broke the bread. Perhaps his account of the 5,000 was overshadowed by the recollection of 19.36, "Not a bone of him shall be broken". This omission is the more interesting as Luke makes it clear that this breaking of the bread was a very recognizable characteristic of Jesus: Luke 24.30–31, 35.)

Exegesis of John 6 reflects two traditions of Christian thought. The one which places a high value on the Eucharist identifies Christ as bread of life in the sacrament. At the other end of the scale, "I am the bread of life" is interpreted in line with the other "I am" sayings (see above, p. 254). It means that Jesus offers in his teaching, like the figure of Wisdom in the Old Testament, the spiritual nutrition, revealed understanding, vital to human-kind's survival, not sacramental feeding. The passage 6.51–58 is the obstacle in the way of this latter interpretation, as its crude realism has shocked not only the Jews in the audience of the time, but also others more recently. Some have felt so strongly that the verses are alien to John's general ethos, that one option taken has been to dismiss 6.51–8 as non-Johannine (the work of a later editor who had to bring the gospel into line with church sacramental expectations, prior to publication). It is probably unnecessary to take up such an extreme position as this, but rather to see 6.51–8 in context with the rest of the dialogue, which is explained by Jesus in these words:

It is the spirit that gives life, the flesh is of no avail; the words which I have spoken to you are spirit and life. (6.63)

The crude realism is then a misapprehension; nor must we forget that these words were represented as spoken ahead of their realization in the death of Jesus.

Further eucharistic interpretation is possible in the wedding at Cana and the "I am the true vine" saying. Cana can probably be dismissed fairly summarily; here the emphasis is on the new wine of Christianity (Mark 2.22), rather than on the blood of Christ. "I am the vine" is much more promising, particularly as it was said in the significant context of the Last Supper, during the Farewell Discourse. It is more likely, however, that the primary meaning was connected with the unity of the disciples with Jesus in the church fellowship he initiated (which replaces the old Israel, formerly known by the vine symbol – see above, p. 256). Eucharistic teaching here can only draw upon associated ideas of love, fellowship, mutual abiding, and keeping the commandments, which Jesus rated as very important.

Baptism and communion have been dealt with at some length because they are important ideas, and receive developed teaching, despite the lack of an explicit account of their institution. Various theories have been proposed as to why John is like this:

1 The discipline of secrecy, which dictated high security to preserve the sacraments from scornful pagans.

2 The existence of Christians who over-valued the sacraments. Ignatius' view of the Eucharist as the "medicine of immortality" can be instanced here. John feared that Christianity would become a mystery religion like many others, acting out the night that the god died, to gain benefits for initiates. Thus he gives corrective teaching and broadens the base of ideas connected with the sacraments.

3 The problems with DOCETISTS, who had a totally mistaken view of the sacraments because they misunderstood the significance of Jesus' death, claiming that he only "seemed" to die. Some of John's teaching can be seen as specifically anti-docetic – it may not be coincidence that blood and water flow from the crucified Lord on the cross (19.34). This is where baptism and Eucharist begin for the church.

Ministry

The synoptics give some prominence to the call and commissioning of the twelve apostles, who have the authority of Jesus to act on his behalf, like ambassadors and plenipotentiaries:

> *And he appointed twelve, to be with him, and to be sent out to preach and have authority to cast out demons.* (Mark 3.14–15)

In view of the importance in rank and status that the apostles achieved in the early church (see Galatians, Ephesians, and Revelation), it is probably not unimportant that John prefers the less official, intimate teacher/pupil image of "disciple". He gives those disciples in their call no authority, and sees their status as consisting of "following" Jesus (compare 1.43). These "called" men are five in number:

* an unnamed disciple (=Beloved Disciple?)
* Andrew
* Peter (fetched by Andrew)
* Philip (called by Jesus)
* Nathanael (fetched by Philip)

The first two originally came from John the Baptist.

Thereafter, however large the group grew, it was usually known as "his disciples" (e.g. 4.2). The "twelve" as such are mentioned only at the close of the "Bread of Life" discourse, when their spokesman Peter affirms faith in Jesus (6.68–69), and the evangelist explains that Jesus always knew of

Judas' potential treachery (6.70–71). As the time of the Passion approaches, other disciples are identified by name – brave, loyal Thomas in 11.16 becomes obtuse Thomas in 14.5, doubting in 20.25, and believing in 20.28. There is also another Judas who is puzzled in 14.22. Beyond this circle are others who were plainly disciples, even if not called such – Lazarus, Mary and Martha of Bethany, Mary Magdalene, and secret disciples like Joseph of Arimathea, who risked much at a politically sensitive time in marking his allegiance when he attended to Jesus' burial (20.38).

The most significant figure is, however, that of the Beloved Disciple, probably correctly identified with the other disciple (compare 20.2) who was close to Jesus (13.23), helped Peter gain entrance to the high priest's palace (18.16), understood what was happening and was the first to believe in the Resurrection (20.8). This disciple receives further prominence in chapter 21, where Peter was given the pastoral status, but it was the Beloved Disciple who followed Jesus without being told what to do. (A fuller discussion of chapter 21 will be given below.)

John's reinterpretation of apostleship as discipleship without prestige or power cannot be accidental or coincidental, any more than is his re-assessment of sacraments. From these two indicators it is possible to deduce that the Johannine community did not share the preoccupations of the Great Church with such institutions, and had its own criteria to assess what was valuable and important in the life of the church: fellowship, unity, loving, and, above all, following Jesus.

Ethics in the community

The Farewell Discourses have as twin ethical themes the necessity for Christians to love one another as Christ loved them (13.34), and the Lord's insistence to keep the commandments. Although no precise information is given on how to work this out in everyday life, it is apparent that the Johannine community recognized these twin poles as providing the rules for community and individual life. The first command is more narrowly defined in scope than the Lucan "love your neighbour" (anyone regardless of race or creed) or the Q "Love your enemies" (compare Romans 12). The restriction to "one another" within the circle of faithful disciples left at the Last Supper may well indicate a closed sectarian mentality in the Johannine community. It is often inferred that friction with outside agencies – pagans, Jews, and Christians of varying doctrinal complexion – had so scarred the Johannine group that it had turned inwards upon itself, and the intensity of relationship which burned within the community was remarkable to outsiders (13.35).

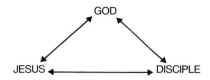

Theologically the love which John urges Christians to show each other is grounded in the reciprocal love which flows in the Godhead between Father and Son, which is the love made manifest to the world in the mission and incarnation of the Son (3.16). This love for Christ is conditioned by obedience to his commandments – which are never made explicit. Nevertheless, Johannine Christians were expected to abide in Christ and "bear much fruit" (John 15.5 – language which elsewhere bears an ethical connotation, e.g. Galatians 5.22). So are we to assume good ethical conduct on the lines of the Ten Commandments, or on a more general basis for good behaviour as taught by the Stoic philosophers? This much is certain, that love is the theological ground. Love clearly involves humble service of others, as Jesus showed in washing the disciples' feet (13.14), and the extreme to which this might have to be carried was illustrated in his death:

> *Greater love has no man than this, that a man lay down his life for his friends* (15.13).

But even here the risk taken is for a well-defined group; there is no indication of the church involvement in wider issues. There is no indication that they were committed to service outside their walls.

Conclusion

Thus in a survey of the indications of the church and ethical teaching in John, it would appear that John had no time for the formal structures of church organization and discipline so apparent in Matthew:

> *You are Peter, and on this rock I will build my church, and the powers of death shall not prevail against it. I will give you the keys of the kingdom of heaven, and whatever you bind on earth shall be bound in heaven, and whatever you loose on earth shall be loosed in heaven.* (Matthew 16.18–19)

> *If your brother sins against you . . . tell it to the church; and if he refuses to listen even to the church, let him be to you as a Gentile and a tax collector.* (Matthew 18.15–18)

John's church may have been slow to develop organically; development was patchy in the early church, as far as is known, but it is more likely that such growth was alien to the whole nature of the Johannine community, who were unhappy too at the way the sacraments were generally handled. His community then owned no hierarchy and trusted its members to comport themselves in accordance with the love ethic, rather than laying down a list of ethical requirements, let alone providing disciplinary measures should these requirements not be met.

St. John's Basilica at Ephesus, which is the traditional home of St. John the Evangelist and his work (and still a likely one despite the alternative suggestions of Antioch and Alexandria).

Only John records a successful mission into the enemy territory of Samaria during Jesus' ministry – in 4.1–42 cf Luke 9.51–56. Jesus offered the woman the water of eternal life, and the resultant crowd acclaimed him as saviour of the world.

Just as Salvador Dali saw another dimension to the Last Supper, so did John. He substituted the acted parable of the footwashing for that of the bread and the wine, and thus interpreted Jesus' death in terms of loving service and cleansing.

Summary of the gospel evidence

From the fourth gospel we gain a picture of a church which had originated from Judaism and had carried on a lively and acrimonious dialogue with it. While remaining deeply conscious of its great scriptural debt to Judaism, the church has been separated from its parent body, possibly at the time of the promulgation of the Birkath ha-Minim in 85–90 CE (see p. 268 and note 10). A correspondingly distinctive feature of this church's faith was therefore a highly developed Christology, or understanding of the person and significance of Christ. Another formative early influence in moulding the Christology was the theological dispute with the followers of John the Baptist, and a later one was the conflict with "heretics" who mistakenly took the period of the Incarnation to be only a shadow of apparent reality. The community had passed through various crises of its own, the passage of time had led to a falling away in disillusionment that the Parousia had not materialized and yet founder members of Christian society had died. John had to teach it how to come to terms with existence in history. It appears to have been a community only on the fringes of the kind of activities in church management which are evident in other gospels and epistles in the New Testament, and a community which offered a radically diverse approach to Christian discipleship and behaviour; it also understood its initiation and worship differently.

John's community viewed from the epistles

For a fuller discussion of the relation of the epistles to the gospel in matters of date and authorship, the reader will need to refer to the commentaries but it is superficially clear to the reader that the Johannine epistles reflect the same thought world as the gospel of John; Johannine vocabulary (like images of light and darkness, truth and love) is common to both. On closer inspection there are considerable differences, too, and there has been much debate as to whether or not the differences are sufficient to indicate that there were different authors for John and the epistles (the present author's position). If that question can be resolved, then how does it affect relative dating? Are the indications of a more primitive position held in 1 John sufficient to argue that it is therefore necessarily the earlier work, or do they represent a reversion to an earlier position (for whatever reason), after the publication of the fourth gospel? The view taken here is that the epistles are later than John, although not by a very great margin, and were not written by the evangelist himself.

The epistles, mostly 1 John, by reason of its length, will be examined for the same distinctive features as occur in the gospel, and any differences will be noted.

The person and purpose of Jesus in the epistles

Jesus' divine status as Son of God is secure in 1 John 1.3, 2.23–24, 3.8, 4.15 etc.; but it does not receive much in the way of special emphasis, or elaboration by titles. The mission of the Son in 5.9 has its Johannine purpose, which was eternal life (1 John 5.11–12). This itself was the great act of divine love. The titles employed are:

* Saviour of the World (4.14), which is in no way commented on;
* Christ (5.1), which does seem to have become an article of faith, though it is unclear whether this was in Jewish messianic vein or not.

There is nothing to suggest that a Jewish-oriented debate on his divinity had been causing problems, as in John, or that Baptist sectarians had been relegating Jesus to a status lower than their master. What does seem to have been under dispute is the reality of Jesus' Incarnation and the achievement of his death, as these do receive repeated emphasis, e.g.

> *Every spirit which confesses that Jesus Christ has come in the flesh is of God, and every spirit which does not confess Jesus is not of God. This is the spirit of Antichrist, of which you heard that it was coming, and now it is in the world already. Little children, you are of God, and have overcome them* (1 John 4.2–4).

The reality of Jesus

Jesus Christ has come in the flesh (1 John 4.2).

This is said in the context of the testing of the spirits for authenticity, by the correctness of the doctrines which they quote (see below).

This is he who came by water and blood, Jesus Christ, not with water only but with the water and the blood (1 John 5.6).

These two texts taken together appear to correct the misapprehensions that Jesus was not fully human from the start, and that the divine Christ was not involved in the suffering on the cross. This is known to have been the view of some second-century heretics; and it is possible to read 1 John as suggesting that humanity and divinity came together at the baptism by John (although this was probably not the author's intention). 1 John was concerned lest any thought Jesus was not really man, and probably the reference to blood is to be seen as two-edged: a real man could really die. 2 John 7 describes deceivers "who will not acknowledge the coming of Jesus Christ in the flesh". This is the one piece of doctrinal information in this epistle, and is therefore important. The reality of the incarnate Lord is plainly an article of faith for the Johannine community.

Salvation by the cross

1 John claims that the most remarkable privilege that Jesus brought and offered to humankind – the eternal life which he shared with the Father – was not automatic; it was bought at a cost. In the fourth gospel we noticed traces of the idea that Jesus died to cleanse humankind from their sins, and that his death was a vicarious offering. There the main thrust of the teaching about his death was concerned with ascent to the Father and glorification. In 1 John, by contrast, it is these very traces which offer the main theme, that of sin-bearing and sacrificial offering by the One who is supremely righteous (2.1, 2.29):

The blood of Jesus his son cleanses us from all sin (1.7).

He will forgive our sins and cleanse us from all unrighteousness (1.9).

[Jesus] *is the expiation for our sins, and not for ours only but also for the sins of the whole world* (2.2).

The Son of God appeared . . . to destroy the works of the devil (3.8).

[God] *sent his Son to be the expiation for our sins* (4.10).

With scant attention to ethics and no concept of repentance, the fourth gospel had in fact little place for sin (John 5.14). By contrast 1 John has, for its length, a considerable, convoluted discussion of the place of sin (which will be discussed later in the section on ethics). Thus Jesus' fundamental work was bound to be seen as providing the cleansing of the believer, the covering of the sin, and reconciliation between God and humankind.[12]

Jesus' relationship with the church

Although 1 John has no reference to the departure of Jesus to the Father, or to his glorification, such beliefs do seem to underlie his thinking and to be assumed. Thus the Son is plainly with the Father in 1.3, 2.24 etc., and he acts as an intercessor – Paraclete (2.1) – on the disciples' behalf. Such a use of Paraclete is very unexpected, being neither the role of the Spirit in the Farewell Discourses, nor a role applied to Jesus in the fourth gospel (except perhaps by implication in 14.16). This switch in function from the Holy Spirit to Jesus in 1 John is mirrored in a corresponding change in roles for the disciples. Instead of relating to the Spirit as in the fourth gospel, they must now relate to Jesus – i.e. to have fellowship with him (1 John 1.3), abide in him (2.24), and live through him (4.10, compare 5.12). They are also challenged to believe in him (5.10), or in his name (4.10).

Opponents in 1 and 2 John

The author of 1 and 2 John has enemies clearly in mind, but they are no longer the adherents of the Jewish synagogue to whom the fourth gospel was hostile. The new enemies are treacherous renegades, former members of the Johannine community, who have withdrawn and are being castigated for their breaking of the common fellowship (1 John 2.19). They are described variously as "deceivers" (2 John 7), and "false prophets" (1 John 4.1), whose spirit-inspired utterances were causing problems. They were branded in very strong language as "anti-Christs" (2.18, 4.3), for they plainly did not share the author's interpretation of Christianity. In fact, the author revives the old scheme of eschatology, whose futurist traits had lain largely dormant in the fourth gospel, to show how even their activities fit into the predicted pattern of the End-Time (2.18). That they would ever have read his comments seems highly unlikely; instead the author's tactic in 1 John was to make faithful members of his church more secure, and reinforce them against attack by these people and their specious arguments. That the closer was the former relationship, the more bitter would be any later rift, seems a law of human nature which applied here even in the loving community of John. So he comes to call them "children of the devil" (3.10), "liars" (2.22), and "murderers" (3.15). (Compare the debate of Jesus with the Jews employing the same range of ideas in John 8.39f.)

High Christology was not the problem with these opponents; they had not sufficiently balanced the divinity of Christ with a real incarnation.

Eschatology

In the fourth gospel futurist eschatology was present only in very occasional references; John's main intent was to redirect the readers' attention from the problems created by the continued existence of the church, in an era bereft of the Parousia and eyewitness support, to the benefits of living in a Paraclete-inspired community. That is not necessarily to say that John had no need for a future Day of Judgement at the End-Time in his scheme of things, but that it was currently of lesser importance. In 1 John realized eschatology is not really at issue, as neither the delay of the End nor John's solution to this problem are discussed; clearly also both sides in the argument thought they had the support of the Spirit in their church (compare 1 John 4.2–3). Instead he summons up the primitive picture of the End-Time. How do these false teachers relate to conventional eschatology? Clearly they are to be interpreted as the ultimate opposition to the true Christ, the anti-Christ, who was expected before the End.

> *Children it is the last hour; and as you have heard that anti-christ is coming, so now many anti-christs have come; therefore we know that it is the last hour* (1 John 2.18).

The fourth gospel might seem to suggest that the judgement is irrelevant for the believer, who has already passed from death to life; but for 1 John it remains a matter of some concern – as would seem logical in any system which allows of the possibility of post-baptismal sin (e.g. 1 John 5.16). Christians are therefore adjured to remain closely united with Christ ("abide in him"),

> *So that when he appears we may have confidence and not shrink from him in shame at his coming* (2.28).

The Parousia and the judgement are to be borne in mind, particularly in the urgency of the current crisis (2.18). This is not said to make the readers uneasy:

> *that we may have confidence in the day of judgement ... There is no fear in love, but perfect love casts out fear. For fear has to do with punishment* (4.17–18).

This abbreviated passage refers to the perfection of love in the believer; for this to happen suggests a continuing effort in the life of the church, leading up to the End-Time.

The work of the Holy Spirit

Despite the generally accepted importance of the role of the Holy Spirit for the Johannine community, he was strangely absent in places in the fourth gospel, in contexts where one might have expected his presence (especially in chapter 17). The enigma of 1 John is that the focus of divine salvation and continuing presence with the believer is entirely on the Father–Son relationship; the Holy Spirit makes only occasional appearances in 1 John:

> *You have been anointed by the Holy One* (2.20).
> *And by this we know that he abides with us by the Spirit he has given us*

(3.24) (compare 4.13).

By this you know the Spirit of God: every spirit which confesses that Jesus Christ is come in the flesh (4.2).

The Spirit is the witness, because the Spirit is the Truth.

There are three witnesses, the Spirit, the water and the blood (5.8).

Thus his role was restricted to affirm the reality of Christ's Incarnation and the reality of the genuine spiritual experience within Christians.

Such a restriction is hard to explain after the fourth gospel, except in the context of over-extravagant claims for their spirit-led power, being made by those who had withdrawn from the church, with their exuberant prophecy (4.1–4). That the author found this phenomenon difficult to accept, and probably very embarrassing too, is clear from the partial and inadequate solution which he offers in this passage. This would be explicable if his own group thought that they also were Spirit-led. The lack of critical objective criteria in deciding who was right and who was wrong in prophecy led to considerable problems in the early church, as we can see from Matthew 7.15 and *Didache* 11. Tests of behaviour bearing out professed beliefs, or tests of doctrine, as here in 1 John 4.2, were ultimately not enough; and to ban such people from church meetings by some kind of authoritative action was the method of control eventually sought. 1 John's author does not seem to have had such machinery available when he wrote, but it does not seem to have been long before it was developed (see below, p. 286).

Signs of the Church

Sacraments

All that can be said about the sacraments is by inference alone, and that derived from verses much less obviously allusive than are found in the fourth gospel. If baptism was the initiatory rite in this branch of the Johannine community, as would seem inherently plausible, then it can only be understood by implication from related ideas. Baptism would admit to fellowship (1.3), give forgiveness of sins (2.12), and conquest of the devil (2.13); the power of baptism would be enabled through the sacrificial blood of Jesus (1.7, 2.1–2, 4.10). The effect of baptism would be to make one a child of God (3.1, 5.4), through the faith in Jesus as the Son of God, which conquers the world (5.4). It is possible that baptism also involved a ceremony of anointing (2.27), but this may well have been metaphorical only.

Given parallels in the farewell Discourses, it is possible that the references in 1 John to love and abiding in God may well have a eucharistic connotation. Insistence on the reality of the Incarnation in 1 and 2 John would also secure the reality of the communion sacrament, but even so it is unlikely that either the Eucharist or baptism is of other than secondary interest in the section 5.6–8: "He who came by water and blood ..." etc. (where, as we have seen, the main interest is the Incarnation).

Formal structures of the church

The author of 1 John assumes paternalistic authority over the Johannine Christians addressed in 2.1, but does so without claiming any status in the church's ministry entitling him to do so; 2 and 3 John (presuming them to be by the same hand as 1 John) reveal him to be "the Presbyter" (= church elder). Whether he was one presbyter among many or the Presbyter is hard to determine. He certainly does not claim to wield apostolic authority for his injunctions to the community (which would certainly have had an interesting bearing on the discussion of John earlier). His authority in 1 John, such as it is, seems to be based on respect and affection, both of which he has earned from his readers in the past, and on his right to be counted among those who pass on the original authentic teaching, and with whom it is necessary to be in communion (1 John 1.1–3).

In 2 John, where a crisis has been caused by the irruption of false teachers into the community the author addresses, he apparently then has the standing, not only to rule on the position of these false teachers doctrinally –

> Anyone who goes ahead and does not abide in the doctrine of Christ does not have God; he who abides in the doctrine has both the Father and the Son. (2 John 9)

– but also to order that the true Johannine Christians must not hold any communication with them. To receive such bearers of wrong ideas into the house, or to salute them in the street, is to be identified with their evil work (2 John 10–11). 3 John, which is an exasperatingly fragmentary trace of a lost church controversy, centres around church discipline and the authority structure; there is no hint that mistaken Christological doctrine is at stake here. Diotrephes, a self-appointed church leader (at least from the Presbyter's point of view), has apparently applied the ruling of 2 John to itinerant missionaries despatched by the Elder himself. Gaius, to whom 3 John is addressed, will, it is hoped, afford Demetrius and the other Christian missionaries such Christian hospitality as the Elder thinks that they deserve – it is unclear whether Gaius was in a position to be loyal to the Elder, or not.

The Elder postpones a confrontation with Diotrephes on this matter until his own arrival. It is noteworthy that the only criticism made of Diotrephes is his over-zealous application of the powers of excommunication (in itself quite a disciplinary step on the road to authoritarian church government), from debarring travelling preachers of uncertain origin to the banning of those members of his own congregation who welcomed them.

The Elder does not even imply that Diotrephes is guilty of a false doctrinal position; it has been suggested that the position may in fact have been reversed, and to Diotrephes the Elder himself was suspect. If the author of 3 John was unable to impeach Diotrephes for wrong beliefs, it might suggest that in fact Diotrephes held a more conservative position than he did – Diotrephes may even have regarded the author as having dangerously advanced views and have excluded his representatives on those grounds.

As the development of the office of bishop at the turn of the century was largely in order to protect the church from the inroads of heresy, it has been suggested that Diotrephes was an early bishop testing episcopal power (justifiably or not) and excluding the Elder.[13] In the absence of more information, or exact terminology, all such theories must remain what they are – speculative. Some theories are more extreme than others, like the one which sees the Elder as the leader of the semi-Gnostic conventicle operating on the fringes of the Great Church, and being repelled by the Church's representative, Diotrephes.[14]

One neat reconstruction of events in the Johannine community sees the original community, which produced the fourth gospel, subsequently divided by a schism (reflected in 1 John). The smaller part of the community carried the fourth gospel with them to the larger Catholic or Great Church.[15] This Church embraced them and their distinctive doctrine of the pre-existence of Christ; but they lost their identity and had to accept church order as normative. The larger part of the Johannine community (the opponents of 1 John) went on developing an even higher Christology and moved away from orthodox Christianity in an increasingly heretical "Gnos-tic" and "Montanist" (i.e. speculative and charismatic) direction.[16] This theory certainly helps resolve a number of interesting questions. It is notor-iously hard, for example, to find a suitable named second-century group, whose views were identical with those of the false teachers described in 1 and 2 John (even accepting the distortion of them in the Elder's partisan presen-tation). Thus Cerinthus and other former candidates for the position of 1 John's opponents usually had more advanced views than those of 1 John's adversaries. On this theory the opponents' views in 1 John were still in embryo form. Similarly, the spirit-led pretensions of the false teachers could well have developed, given time and the right setting, into those outbursts of enthusiasm and prophecy characteristic of the Montanist movement, which were repeatedly condemned by the Great Church.

Another passage which can now receive a satisfactory exegesis as a result of this theory is the Johannine appendix, chapter 21 in the fourth gospel. This chapter is usually (although not universally) thought to be by a different author from the one who wrote chapters 1 to 20. Chapter 20 had concluded the gospel:

* the disciples saw Jesus;
* they received the Holy Spirit to enable them with their work;
* the purpose of the gospel was summed up in 20.30–31.

Chapter 21, by contrast,

* introduced Jesus again, somewhat clumsily, to unsuspecting disciples;
* the disciples, far from being involved in their mission, were fishing;
* contained differences in Greek vocabulary and style.

The explanation for adding this chapter, before the fourth gospel was publicly issued, runs as follows: chapter 21 belongs to the period after 1 and 2 John, when the smaller, and more orthodox, party from the schism is preparing to join the Great Church, in order to survive. Chapter 21 is a piece of double-edged propaganda:

* to win Petrine enthusiasts to a recognition of the importance of the Johannine founder-figure, the Beloved Disciple, as a witness to Christ who followed without falling, and without needing instructions;

* to gain Johannine Christians' acceptance of Peter's claim to pre-eminence, and of his role in shepherding the church, as Christ-given at the moment of his restoration.

This attractive theory suggests that, during the period when the epistles were written, the Johannine church was moving towards a more rigid system of church authority and discipline. This movement may have been made under the pressure exerted by the breakaway group, with their popular teaching about Christ, on their parent body. The means to resist such pressure was something the Johannine community lacked; although the fourth gospel had supplied it with ammunition to resist Jewish pressure, this was of little use in the current crisis, and the Elder gives the impression of improvising defences. Eventually, rather than capitulate to the false teachers, the remnant of the Johannine community was forced to adopt measures being taken by the Great Church in order to resist the power of unorthodox ideas. These measures involved the appointment and recognition of authorized persons, well able to distinguish true from false in church teaching, and having the power to exclude what was wrong. Eventually each community had to have one such person in authority. If this supposition is right, there is, in the traceable history of the Johannine community, a line of development *from* an anarchic (if close-knit) group, bound to mutual support and brotherhood, as branches of the one vine, committed to and controlled by the love-ethic, *to* a group which had the beginnings of a hierarchical government.

That an internal split in the community may not have happened as late as between the writing of the fourth gospel, chapters 1–20, and the writing of 1 John is possible. There are signs of disunity, or at least of an incipient split in the fourth gospel itself. Despite the claim that Christ's mission was

> *to gather* into one *the children of God* (11.52),

this had not yet happened. Perhaps John stressed unity because it was a problem. For him, unity was important enough to be included in two powerful Christological images – the vine with its branches, and the shepherd with his flock (note 10.16 "one flock"). Most significant is the prominence given to it in Christ's prayer before death in chapter 17. It has been suggested that this is a reference to the Qumran ideal of *yahad*,[17] which conjured up the notion of a united brotherhood (together) separate from the world (alone). This is of course a very sectarian view of things. Chapter 17 welds the unity of the disciples into an overall scheme of the unity of Christ with the Father, and the believers' unity with Christ (17.21). The very fact that John makes it clear that Jesus is praying for the second generation of Christians too (17.20) may suggest that the split had happened there.

Ethics in the community

The fourth gospel is noted for an absence of ethical teaching, relying instead on advice to keep the commandments, and to abide in Christ, to suffice for everyday conduct, which was presumably based on the love-ethic. 1 John is a little more pragmatic, even noting that a mechanism for dealing with sin is required, when ethics break down. The author does not seem to have anything new to add on ethics but, given the relative shortness of his epistle, he does treat the subject as important. He plays with the device of the old/new commandment (1 John 2.7, for instance), which is familiar to us as love of the brethren, and is the basis for eternal life. He returns many times to this and related themes. His only new contributions to the discussion are to hold up the behaviour of Jesus as a model to follow (1 John 2.6), and to suggest generosity and good deeds (1 John 3.17–18). His emphasis on ethics suggests that behaviour was now a matter of some contention within the community, and particularly between it and the breakaway group. Whereas formerly the evangelist could rely on Jewish moral standards (on which his community had largely been reared) to provide the backbone of their conduct, this may no longer have been the case. The breakaway group has already shown in its attitude to the Incarnation that it did not evaluate the human nature of Christ within the mainstream tradition; perhaps it evaluated ordinary human nature outside the accepted norms too.

An unbalanced approach to human nature, or "the flesh" in Biblical terms, tends to propose one of two extremes. Either the discipline will be severe, so that nature will not hamper the soul's salvation (i.e. asceticism, which does not seem to be in view here) or everyday conduct will be irrelevant to salvation, thus opening the way to libertinism or anti-nomianism (i.e. lawlessness). If 1 John's opponents held the latter view, they could not seriously have put these beliefs into practice or 1 John would undoubtedly have contained accusations against them on those grounds.

The writer's method was to offer a critique of their ideas. It would appear that the breakaway group regarded themselves as being sinless, walking in the light, having fellowship with God and knowing him (1 John 1.5–10). To the contrary, the Elder maintained that no one is sinless.[18] Otherwise to send Christ as a propitiation for the sins of the world was a singularly redundant act. Certainly he maintained that his opponents were deceived in all the other points. The dualistic language of the fourth gospel is employed by the author, not only in the realm of light and dark (to distinguish the conduct of the Elder's group from that of their opponents), but also to characterize the two sides as:

* truth and the lie (1.6–10);
* love and hate (2.8–10);
* eternal life and the murder/death associated with Cain.

This means that the sin and failings of his opponents are given a theological significance and in gospel terms they are ranged on the side of evil, and identified with the cosmos.

We have already noticed the unusual prominence given to the love-ethic and behaviour. It was particularly in the area of brotherly love that the author of 1 John found them guilty. This suggested that their claim to know and love God was a lie (1 John 4.20–21). (His opponents would probably have maintained they did love the brethren, but would have defined these as being the right-thinking members of the breakaway group.) It may be that this was not a group poised on the edge of great sins against charity at all; the breakaway group, in the eyes of the author, showed that they failed to love the brethren when they broke away from them. But this view does not cover all evidence.

Loving the brethren involved financial commitment; in 1 John's view some people are more generous in word than in deed. Possibly the opponents in the breakaway group came from richer strata of society, and the poor in 1 John's group were now suffering from the withdrawal of the tangible symbol of love, money, which they had earlier enjoyed – to the author's indignation. 1 John 3.16–18 shows how seriously he takes the situation; he even debases the fourth gospel's teaching of Christ about sacrificial love, and applies it to charity to make his point – generous love is best seen in action.

Apart from meanness with money, other hints about the failings of his opponents may perhaps be seen in the warnings against sensuality and materialism in 1 John 2.15–17. More serious is the limitation to intercessory prayer (1 John 5.15–17), so that effort is not wasted on those deemed to be in mortal sin. This of course raises the speculation as to what was counted as mortal sin in those days. It would probably be a mistake to link this isolated New Testament reference to later church definitions of murder, adultery, etc., and then accuse the breakaway group of committing this kind of lawlessness, any more than it would be fair to accuse them of idolatry on the basis of 1 John 5.21. It is more likely, given the general content of 1 John, that mortal sin is another reference to failure to sustain mutual love among the brethren. So signal a failure to obey God's commands clearly puts one beyond the pale of the community and its love, and beyond God's promise of eternal life.

Conclusions about the Johannine community

Thus, from the epistles of John it is possible to see how the Johannine community continued to evolve. The dangers to unity which threatened to split the church in the evangelist's day became real and schism occurred. This internally caused damage to the church occasioned the Presbyter much pain, particularly because those whom he regarded as renegades did not retreat but attempted to attract more members away from him; this was pioneered by travelling missionaries, who must have been successful in order to have engaged his attention.

The doctrinal and practical dangers to his community ranged from a distorted view of the person and death of Christ, to a failure to take sin and the need for good behaviour seriously enough, the two positions being in all probability linked. In dealing with this problem the Elder found himself in considerable difficulties. His opponents had emerged from his community, may even have been trained by him; their basic views may have coincided therefore – even if the conclusions they drew from those beliefs were rather different. It made it hard to dispute with them on purely Johannine terms, and he retreated to an older and more tested position which threatened them with the consequences of the Last Day on account of the schism.

Part of his difficulty also lay in the fact that both sides had in common not only the body of the Johannine tradition (in the fourth gospel?), but also their beliefs in an exclusive (and therefore mutually excluding) right to the Spirit, as the interpreter of that tradition. The Elder also lacked any kind of authority structure to impose disciplinary measures. Eventually he advocated exclusion and excommunication as the only method of banning wrong teaching by itinerant missionaries (2 John), only to find this a dangerous weapon, for it was turned against himself (3 John).

What was the final outcome for this community, possibly on the edges of the Great Church, which had itself already developed methods of dealing with precisely these problems? It may have lost its distinctive identity, as there is no clear trace of its existence in the writings of the second century; but the gifts and insights which it alone had developed, to give to the church, and to enrich it, were preserved. The distinctive contributions of the Johannine community included theological perception of the real status of the Son of God, before he became man at Bethlehem; the ability of the church to cope with continued existence in history through the evangelist's reappraisal of the events of those formative years; above all they included the appreciation of the role of the Spirit in the continuing life of the church, and not just at the initiation of new members.

CHAPTER 6

The other New Testament writings

A variety of developing situations

The main parts of the New Testament have now been explored. The four gospels, with their distinct characters and purposes, are seen to address and challenge particular types of community. With one of the four gospels, that of John, it is possible for the modern observer to glimpse the story of that community over an extended period. The three letters of John belong in the same collection (or corpus) as the gospel, and probably give an idea of subsequent happenings in the rather inward-looking and meditative community that produced the gospel. And in the case of another gospel, that of Luke, the combination of the gospel with Acts, in a two-volume work, provides the modern reader with a perspective of theology and history that explicitly links the development of the church with the life of Jesus, in a single story.

The other main part of the New Testament (certainly linked to Acts by subject matter) is the collection of the letters of Paul. To concentrate only on the letters where Paul's authorship is best attested (1 Thessalonians, Galatians, 1 Corinthians, 2 Corinthians, Philippians, Philemon and Romans) provides a substantial and significant collection of seven. More can be known from these sources about Paul at first hand than about any other figure of early Christianity. It was remarked at the beginning of the chapter on Paul that attitudes to him are very ambivalent. Some readers are enthusiasts for Paul, like those who preserved his letters; others find him obscure and difficult. But it is clear that in the New Testament he represents a large element out of the books that early Christian writers called "The Apostle" (as distinct from "The Gospel" or "The Lord", that is, the four gospels) and he reveals much about the life of those Christian communities founded or influenced by him.

If the main parts of the New Testament have now been explored, it is necessary to say something about the other writings. The limits set by the canon of the New Testament suggest that what is retained (as opposed to what is discarded and rejected, like Gnostic texts) was regarded by the early church as of great value and kept for a purpose. The rest of the New Testament documents must be listed; three general categories may be used for convenience:

* Apocalyptic texts: Jude, 2 Peter, Revelation of John
* In the tradition of Paul: 2 Thessalonians, Colossians, Ephesians, 1 Timothy, 2 Timothy, Titus
* Theological essays: Hebrews, James, 1 Peter.

Apocalyptic texts

Jude

Roman slave badge; the inscription reads, "Seize me if I should try to escape and send me back to my master". This was the problem Onesimus the runaway slave posed for Paul (according to Philemon).

Jude and 2 Peter will be considered side-by-side because there is clearly a literary relationship between them. It is better to regard Jude as the earlier work, on which 2 Peter depends, for historical, literary, and structural reasons. Jude documents a Palestinian-Christian circle with links to Jesus' family. The work is a sermon in letter form which addresses the particular problem of false teachers (wandering prophets or charismatic figures) in the church. The author's direct appeal ("to you to contend for the faith which was once for all delivered to the saints" – verse 3; see also verses 20–23) is supported by a complex and carefully structured sequence of Old Testament interpretation in the tradition of exegesis found at Qumran. The aim is to demonstrate conclusively that these false teachers, predicted for the last days, do incur divine judgement. The author's standpoint is unselfconsciously eschatological. The use of quotations from 1 Enoch (verses 14–15) and the Testament of Moses (in verse 9, including the ending, which is no longer extant) is also seen to point to a Palestinian context of Jewish Christianity. It is possible that the work could be of quite an early date. The opponents who are denounced do not necessarily have contact with Gnostic doctrines and "the predictions of the apostles of our Lord Jesus Christ" (Jude 17) could refer to the original instructions of the apostles rather than a later legacy remembered in the post-apostolic period.

In what could have been an early atmosphere of heightened eschatology, Jude is concerned with the charismatic prophets and their perversion of divine grace. He takes his stand on the Christian future hope of Christ's coming in mercy to his church, and judgement against those who have seduced and corrupted it by their advocacy of ethical freedom, which raises acute moral issues for a community such as Jude's. Advocates of unrestrained licence, who recognize no moral structures or traditional constraints, must have posed an even greater threat to an early community struggling to survive amid expectations of the end of the world. Just because one is waiting for the end, this does not mean that one should be self-indulgent and have a "final fling" today. The same moral issues of ethical libertinism are raised, in a different and significantly later context, by 2 Peter.

2 Peter

2 Peter makes use of some of the argument from Jude, but the situation is a later development, some distance from Palestinian apocalypticism and problems with the charismatics. 2 Peter has a more Hellenized character and it well illustrates the process of transition from the apostolic to the post-apostolic generation. The author is confronting pagan libertines who wish to rid the church of the embarrassments of eschatological language and

thought, at a time when the expectations of Christ's Second Coming (Parousia) seem to have been disappointed. Among other purposes, 2 Peter is a determined defence of the future hope. Its Hellenistic language is combined with eschatological ideas from sources such as Jude, and the eschatological interpretation and justification are integral to the work.

One of the most surprising features is the account of Christ's Transfiguration at 1.16–18, comparable with the gospel narrative at Mark 9.2–8 and the synoptic parallels. The Transfiguration is often regarded as an anticipation within the life story of Jesus of a Resurrection or Ascension experience. The point in 2 Peter is to sustain the future hope for Christians by an appeal to a gospel tradition (a particular revelation to Peter), and to show how that future hope is essentially founded on Christ. The letter is an apostolic message in a post-apostolic situation, but beyond the sense of apostolic tradition, there is little concern for church structures, set forms, and office-holders. 2 Peter is perhaps most closely related to two works outside the canon, 1 Clement and the Shepherd of Hermas, which came from Rome at the end of the first century.

2 Peter is a genuine letter which begins with the regular pattern of a Christian letter (1.1–15) and ends in the usual way with exhortations (3.11–18a) and, like Jude, with a doxology or expression of praise (3.18b). It was written to a church which was among the recipients of 1 Peter (3.1) and to which one or more of the letters of Paul had been addressed (3.15). It is no "catholic" letter, addressed to the world at large, but a local work for local needs, to confront certain false teachers and their objections to key doctrines and ethics.

2 Peter is also presented in the form of a farewell speech or "testament" of Peter. This form was popular in inter-testamental Judaism as a representation of the last words of Old Testament heroes; it was variously adopted in Christian tradition for words of Jesus (e.g. John 17 or Matthew 25.31–46) and of the apostles (Acts 20.17–34; 2 Timothy). Such testaments had two kinds of contents, and 2 Peter has both: a summing up of ethical admonitions for the future, with eschatological sanctions attached, and a prophetic revelation of the future or an apocalyptic vision of the last days. 2 Peter 1.12–15 uses the kind of language conventional for a farewell speech in describing the occasion for writing; the work has a homily (1.3–11), prophecies (2.1–3; 3.1–4), heavenly revelation (1.16–18), and eschatological exhortations (3.11–15). This is the framework around which is built an apologetic defence of Peter's teaching, against the objections of false teachers. The author uses the device of a testament/letter to communicate the apostle Peter's death-bed prophecies. By these means the apostolic tradition and weight of authority are applied to a crisis which he did not live to see.

The Revelation of John

Revelation is unique in the New Testament in being a full-scale apocalypse. It is alternatively called The Apocalypse of John; the word apocalypse simply means that which is uncovered or revealed. The other full-scale

Plan of *The Book of Revelation*

1.1–3	Introduction as to an apocalyptic work
1.4–8	Introduction as to a circular letter to the Asian churches
1.9–20	John's heavenly vision of Christ as the Son of Man
2, 3	Seven particular letters to seven existing churches (associated with the author) in Asia Minor
4, 5	John's vision of worship in the royal throne-room of heaven Christ as the Lamb receives the sealed book of prophecy
6	Christ opens six of the seven seals: the realities of the present and of recent history (e.g. war and famine) are interpreted as symbols of prophecy
7	Heavenly interlude: the sealing of those who are to be spared the worship by those called to be saints
8, 9	The seventh seal: silence and liturgy six of the seven trumpet blasts portending disasters
10	Interlude: the mighty angel the seven thunders are suppressed the prophet John receives (and inwardly digests) a scroll
11	The contents of this scroll (a flash-back, to interpret past history): the fall of Jerusalem to the Romans (67–70 CE) the model provided by Peter and Paul of apostolic witness to Christ (64–67 CE) The seventh trumpet sounds amid heavenly worship
12, 13	The seventh trumpet heralds the disastrous arrival on earth of the two beasts (13.1, 11) The portent of the woman with the child (12) supplies the context: the diabolical beasts are on earth because the devil was expelled from heaven (12.9); and the expulsion was a consequence of Christ's Incarnation and Resurrection. So the church on earth is persecuted (12.17)
14	The song of the saints in heaven Angelic proclamations of judgement on earth Harvest and winepress as symbols of God's judgement
15	Heavenly interlude, as the seven bowls of wrath are introduced
16	The bowls contain plagues (like the plagues of Egypt at the time of the Exodus) which are the judgement of God's wrath upon the earth (and what the beasts have brought about there)
17	The Roman Empire (particularly the blasphemy of worshipping the emperor as divine) is to be destroyed in God's judgement
18	Warnings of the fall of imperial Rome, and the lamentations of those (merchants and clients) affected by her fall
19	Song of triumph in heaven Anticipation of the marriage of Christ, the Lamb Christ rides forth victorious to the last battle
20	The Millennium (the thousand year reign of Christ and the saints) The final resurgence of the powers of evil The Last Judgement
21.1–22.5	The vision of the heavenly city, New Jerusalem (the church in heaven as the bride of Christ) The new created order – the paradise garden
22.6–20	Final guarantees and solemn warnings, appropriate to an apocalyptic work (see 1.1–3) Christ's Second Coming is imminent
22.21	Ending appropriate to a letter (see 1.4–8)

In the cave of the Apocalypse on the island of Patmos: the traditional site of John's vision is within the railings. On the wall to the left is an icon showing Christ giving messages to the angels of the seven churches (Revelation 1–3), while John has fallen at his feet.

apocalypse in the Bible is Daniel in the Old Testament, but there are also apocalyptic sections in the prophecies of Isaiah, Ezekiel, and Zechariah, and a large number of Jewish or Christian apocalypses outside the canon of the Bible. In Revelation and all these other works there are many ingredients, such as traditional myths and symbols which are reapplied to the current circumstances, and different forms such as prophecies, visions, hymns, and letters. But the whole structure is most completely defined and explained by the conventions of apocalyptic.

These are the aspects of apocalyptic which are most important for Revelation: it is essentially revelatory, and that revelation is made through a framework of narrative. It is unlike the oracle of a prophet because the revelation comes through a mediator who is out of this world (the risen Christ or angelic figures) but who communicates directly to a human recipient (John). What is disclosed is transcendent, beyond this world. The disclosure might be a time sequence (such as linear history), so that at the appropriate moment these realities will appear on earth and so transform events as to bring about a final salvation, or a spatial dimension concerned with the connection between worlds. The new vision is of a key relationship between local happenings and cosmic realities, so that the one is perceived through the other. Such visionary perspectives were applied to a situation of crisis, so as to encourage or console the "righteous" community in its sufferings. But an apocalypse is not only relevant to a time of crisis; in less stressful circumstances it goes on being used in other ways (e.g. to teach moral lessons by extreme example).

The letters to the seven churches (in Revelation 2 and 3) are the part of the apocalypse which identifies it most immediately with the concerns of those named communities in Asia Minor; because they appear to be personal letters, they create the impression of a direct address made to these churches. The seven communities are in one of the areas particularly visited by Paul on his missionary journeys, but these churches now seem to have a relationship not only with one another, but also with the Johannine traditions seen in the fourth gospel and the three letters of John, and above all with the author of Revelation. He has pastoral care over them, but apparently he is now exiled from them on the island of Patmos (1.9). The seven letters follow the pattern of early Christian letters (as seen in Paul's correspondence with its opening and closing formulae). They have very specific, if obscure, references to the characteristics of each church. They are so brief, much shorter than Philemon, that they are unlikely to have been sent but these chapters (2 and 3) set the scene, symbolizing the present realities to which the prophetic visions apply. John, in his solitary exile, imagines himself back with the churches and sharing in their Sunday worship (1.10), when he receives a vision of the risen Christ.

Sociological methods have been used to interpret the data this book gives on the Johannine communities. The best model is thought to be that of a sectarian group, marginalized by the attitudes of society. To some extent this is a reading back from the experience of much more modern groups who have used Revelation, such as Millenarian sects, and accordingly should be

The Lamb of God (1432) by Jan and Hubert van Eyck. The central panel of this altarpiece, from the cathedral of St. Bavon at Ghent in Belgium, represents the glorious vision of the adoration of the Lamb, interpreted from Revelation 5.

The Last Judgement (1516) by Hieronymus Bosch. This central panel from a triptych in the Groeninge-museum at Bruges, Belgium, gives a dramatic representation of Revelation 19–20.

treated with caution. John's community was clearly under stress, not necessarily official persecution by the Roman authorities (for in the first century this was localized and spasmodic, provoked by informers, rather than any regular prosecution), but certainly ostracism and social contempt. The group apparently felt threatened and insecure, and had to contend with religious as well as social stress. This was not only a matter of the externally enforced practice of emperor worship, with social and economic sanctions against those who refused to conform. (Ruler cults were a long-established,

Patmos: a view from the hill near the monastery of St. John. The island was used by the Romans as a penal settlement, to which agitators like the author of the book of Revelation would be banished. The monastery was built in the 11th century CE.

and politically useful device in Asia Minor; in the Roman Empire the East urged the idea out of loyalty and the West reluctantly conformed.) There is also evidence in Revelation for religious stress from internal conflicts, represented in the text by cryptic references to opponents called "the Nicolaitans" (2.6, 15) and "the synagogue of Satan" (2.9).

While there is significant continuity in images and theology between the fourth gospel and Revelation, there is also a surprising difference in the nature of the community. In the gospel it is enclosed and inward-looking, a community of believers apparently liberated from this world and its constraints, but in Revelation the community is not closed (the apocalyptic stereotype of a sect), but instead a group with a very positive sense of world mission. Revelation 7.2–4 speaks of 144,000 who are "sealed" and protected; but this is a symbolic number, modelled on Israel of the Old Testament, whose task is to inspire and lead to salvation a much larger (strictly incalculable) number of people from the whole world (see 7.9ff; 5.9–10; 14.6). A key idea for mission in Revelation is "witness" (which is the same Greek word as "martyrdom"); the visions of chapter 11, which describe the fate of "the two witnesses", indicate how this act of Christian mission and "witnessing" is ultimately effective. "Witness" is therefore the communication of the gospel message in the context of a fundamentally prophetic community.

Witnessing is an activity undertaken in the closest relationship to Christ, on the path from suffering to glory (1.5; 11.8). God's reign is seen as universal in scope, but it works towards its fullest realization through human agencies and representative individuals. The situation is such that acts of witness might entail the completion of that Christian testimony in martyrdom. It is a situation of cosmic confrontation, because the powers of evil ranged against God's purpose for the world are no mere phantoms. The task of Christian prophecy, in part inheriting the Old Testament mantle of the prophet and the negative response he came to expect, is to present the gospel to the world and offer the occasion for repentance and change of heart. The prophetic figure and his community might feel isolated and vulnerable, but the witness speaks with God-given authority and the actions of the group are powerful symbols and a testimony to the world.

However strange and complex the language of Revelation may appear to be, it expresses a number of ideas very clearly:

1 The transcendent power of God as creator, and of Christ as redeemer
2 The relationship of believer through Christ to God in the Spirit
3 The interaction of worship and witness for the church in the world
4 The transitory nature of this age (even in its religious dimension)
5 The element of self-sacrifice inherent in Christian witness
6 The political implications of Christian living
7 The power of a vision of hope, even in a context of suffering

The modern focus of readings of Revelation is on the political and social threat which it encapsulates, and the allied themes of justice, judgement, and

St. John on Patmos is guided by an angel: an illustration from the Douce manuscript of the Apocalypse completed by 1272 CE.

vengeance. The book is a study of power, raising ethical questions about the responses to power at a crisis. Revelation may function as a warning to the complacent within society, or it may have a cathartic effect on the particular community by arousing intense feelings of inflammatory aggressiveness. Or it may be a moral lesson on the victim's desire for vengeance. To decide which function was most appropriate originally may require more evidence about the situation in John's community than can be decoded and derived from the symbolism of the Book of Revelation.

The Pauline tradition

While the seven main letters of Paul in the New Testament are readily identifiable (see p. 292), and there is a general consensus among scholars about their authenticity (subject to some editorial revision), it is another matter with the other letters in the canon associated with Paul. There are arguments about authorship and date. There is no doubt that, in the early church after Paul's death, enthusiastic partisans for Paul saved his writings, edited and interpreted them, and developed some aspects of his theological ideas in new writings. We must look for any clues about authorship and the likely situation to have produced such works; there is no disparagement intended in referring to them as deutero-Pauline, or works in the Pauline tradition.

2 Thessalonians

2 Thessalonians clearly belongs within the tradition of Pauline thought represented in 1 Thessalonians but the problem about their precise relationship is caused by the disagreement between them as to when the expected Second Coming of Christ would take place. The first letter expects this to happen soon (4.13ff; 5.1ff), but the second letter anticipates a delay (2.1–12). It used to be suggested that the situation would be more intelligible if the "second" letter had been sent first; then the "first" letter would display the same terms, but introduce a greater sense of urgency. It is, however, more satisfactory to keep the traditional order and to see the second letter as a commentary upon, and a corrective of, the first from the point of view of a later and changed situation. This fits better with what is known of the development of eschatological thinking within the early Christian communities.

2 Thessalonians should then be regarded as the work of a Christian in the generation after Paul, who is using 1 Thessalonians as a model. It is an attempt within the Pauline tradition to reinterpret and reinforce Paul's theology, to suit the needs of Christians of that later day. The argument works within a structure of church discipline, providing a corrective to irresponsible attitudes. The author tries to correct popular misunderstandings of the original eschatological message; the root of the problem in 2 Thessalonians might well have been an over-enthusiastic response to Paul's

own preaching. It is probable that the original situation in Thessalonica which Paul encountered, and wrote about in the first letter, has now intensified, making the difficulties of this Pauline community even greater. Pagan religious cults posed a major threat to Christianity here, especially when they were conjoined with the politically expedient cults of Rome and the emperor (which were used as a test of loyalty). As can also be seen in Revelation, such threatening circumstances could provoke a response of eschatological enthusiasm among Christians. The vision of Christ's coming at the world's end provided a means of escape from contemporary trials (and perhaps a hope of vengeance).

A primary intention of 2 Thessalonians is to enforce "peace" among the Pauline congregations, by discrediting an "unruly" party of eschatological prophets. The community should not be easily unsettled by some prophecy (2.2) or a false claim to represent the teaching of Paul. The key words repeated in this argument are "lawlessness" (2.3, 7) and "disorderly" (3.6, 11), in contrast to which the author advocates a policy of law and order. The exhortation is to "keep away from any brother who is living . . . not in accord with the tradition that you received from us" (3.6, 14), that is not according to the authentic Pauline tradition as interpreted in this letter. The author condemns a policy of rejecting social commitments, of idleness adopted for eschatological motives while waiting for the end of the world. Such people "are not busy; they are busybodies" (3.11 NIV).

The pastoral letters

It is usual to regard the three letters (1, 2 Timothy, Titus) as a single unit. The label of "The Pastorals" is apt because all three contain instructions and exhortations about the conduct of the pastoral office and leadership in the church. There are instructions on church organization and administration, the appointment of leaders and Christian discipline; and there are exhortations to confess the faith fearlessly, and to keep the boundaries drawn between true and false doctrine, especially in debate with "false teachers". Particular situations are mentioned (Timothy in Ephesus and Titus on Crete), but the instructions given are capable of generalization, and could be intended as types of ministry in general.

Who were Timothy and Titus? Timothy frequently appears in Acts and in Paul's letters as a co-worker, someone who is named as being associated with Paul in the sending of these letters (see Acts 16.1–3 and the openings of 1 Thessalonians, 2 Corinthians, Philippians, Philemon). But Titus is not mentioned in Acts. According to Galatians 2.1, the requirement that he should be circumcised became an issue at Jerusalem because he was a Gentile Christian. In 2 Corinthians 2.13; 7.6, 13 he is named as an assistant of Paul.

The historical situations envisaged in the Pastorals cannot be reconciled with the evidence of Paul's main letters and Acts. There is no time left for them, except by constructing an hypothesis that Paul actually made the trip to Spain, following release from prison in Rome (see Romans 15.24 and 1 Clement 5.7). There would also need to have been time left for further travels in the eastern Mediterranean. Although the Pastorals are called letters, the literary model which is probably closest to the main content is the Mandate or instructions to provincial governors or administrators. 2 Timothy is more personal in tone, resembling a final testament (see 2 Peter). The vocabulary and style belong to a more sophisticated Hellenistic Greek than was used in Paul's main letters, and are comparable with Luke at his least Jewish and most Greek. From these historical and literary arguments it is often concluded that the Pastorals are not by Paul himself, but are intended to keep the Pauline tradition alive after Paul's death.

The tradition of the Pastorals is fundamentally Pauline, but the legacy of Paul is being applied, and the convictions restated, in a changed environment of greater stability, probably at the turn of the century, if not later. An adjustment had been possible, an accommodation of the community's attitude to the world, in a less eschatologically tense atmosphere. The adoption of popular Hellenistic philosophy and ethics (as in 1 Timothy 3.1–7) even suggest the establishment of a Christian "bourgeoisie". The transition to a new situation can be seen in (1) the specific way that doctrine is understood as a deposit of tradition, and (2) the view of the apostle Paul as a figure of authority, at one remove, so that it is the apostle's disciple who guarantees tradition.

The early Christian proclamation (*kerygma*) has become a deposit (*paratheke*). The church is charged with the preservation of the entrusted deposit of tradition (see 1 Timothy 6.20; 2 Timothy 1.12, 14; 2.2). There are several examples in Paul's main letters of statements of faith, quotations which look like the first stages of credal formulae. A later example, more developed structurally if not theologically, is at 1 Timothy 3.16:

> *He was manifested in the flesh, vindicated in the Spirit, seen by angels, preached among the nations, believed on in the world, taken up in glory.*

Even more significantly, it is introduced by phrases which set the context of this statement of faith:

> *the household of God, which is the church of the living God, the pillar and bulwark of the truth. Great indeed, we confess, is the mystery of our religion* [or, mystery of our proper religious observance].

These are the formulae of a developing (?early catholic) church, a constituted order in "the style of what was becoming orthodoxy".[1]

It is difficult to identify precisely the opponents and false teachers who are mentioned repeatedly. The details of beliefs and practices are not discussed because the author is not prepared to debate with them. The language suggests a kind of Gnostic speculation, using the Old Testament, and possibly Judaizing. Jewish regulations of purity, such as food laws, seem to be applied (see 1 Timothy 1.4; 4.7; 6.20; Titus 1.14–15). The theory that the author is opposing Marcion (a Christian heretic of the second century CE), and thereby rescuing the Pauline tradition from the clutches of someone who at that time championed Paul – and very little else of the New Testament

MAP 5 Asia Minor –
the seven churches of
the Revelation.

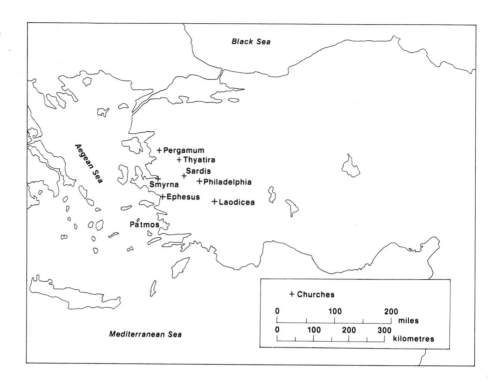

writings – cannot be proved. It is suggested by the exhortation in 1 Timothy
6.20 to "avoid the ... contradictions [antitheses] of what is falsely called
knowledge [*gnosis*]", although Marcion's work *Antitheses* has not survived.
The fact that Marcion rejected the Old Testament, while these false teachers
apparently used it, makes the identification unlikely. The doctrines of the
opponents are summed up in a way similar to the "philosophy" attacked in
Colossians 2.8. But while there is more of a debate with the opponents at
Colossae, in the Pastorals the author simply makes a sharp distinction
between heresy and orthodoxy on the basis of the constituted church. And
the church is exhorted to guard against moral disruptions (either rigorous or
licentious).

> God's firm foundation stands, bearing this seal: "The Lord knows
> those who are his," and "Let every one who names the name of the
> Lord depart from iniquity". (2 Timothy 2.19)

The organization of this church shows a strong sense of hierarchy, with
instructions given for bishops, elders/presbyters, and deacons. The Pastorals
"give us a picture of churches bound together under the overall leadership of
Timothy or Titus, definitely Church-Type churches, yet having also orders
of widows at least [1 Timothy 5.3–16], Sect-Type communities for a few
alongside the churches for everyone."[2] Where ethical obedience is vital
within a structure of authority, this system appears to provide for two
degrees or kinds of obedience (secular and monastic) operating in parallel.

This part of the New Testament lays down precepts for some Christians that not all Christians are expected to follow.

Colossians

A bronze coin from Ephesus (2nd century CE under the emperor Antonius Pius); the design features the temple of Artemis (Diana) – the mother goddess of Ephesus (cf Acts 19.23ff).

The Lycus valley which contains Colossae and the provincial capital of Ephesus on the west coast of Asia Minor are two areas particularly associated with Paul's missionary activities. Yet there are no undisputed letters of Paul written to these centres. It has been claimed both for Colossians and even more for Ephesians that these letters are in the later Pauline tradition, reflecting Paul's ideas but not actually written by him. Taking a clue from the Pastorals, it can be said that these letters were composed to preserve the Pauline apostolic tradition which was then seen to be under threat. In the case of Colossians this threat comes from speculative religious ideas, in a cultic context which makes SYNCRETISTIC use of Jewish regulations and other, possibly pagan, traditions. In these geographical areas it is possible that there was an uneasy coexistence of Johannine and Pauline traditions of Christianity. A major aim of both Colossians and Ephesians is then to reinforce the authority of the Pauline view.

The Colossian church had been established not by Paul but by Epaphras, one of Paul's associates (1.7; 4.12–13). Colossae had been an important centre at the junction of trade routes, but had declined in favour of its neighbours, Hierapolis and in particular the new foundation of Laodicea (4.13, 15–16). The letter gives a picture of a mixed community; in reality or as an ideal they are obedient to the apostolic gospel, living in faith, love, and hope (1.4–5; see 1 Corinthians 13.13).

A major threat is represented by the false teachers with whom the author engages in sharp debate (2.8–23). The foundation of their teaching is undermined; they are confronted with a supreme being infinitely greater than the powers in which they deal; and their ethical regulations are exposed as lacking any binding force. There "philosophy" (2.8) is not the classical teaching of Plato, but religious and philosophical speculations about "the elemental spirits of the universe" (powerful angelic beings or cosmic powers which control the destinies of individual human beings, according to an astrological kind of belief). With this is associated a set of legal demands, regulations for the observance of set days in the calendar, and rules about prohibited foods and drink (2.14, 16, 21). This code of practice is reminiscent of the Jewish Law but does not constitute orthodox Judaism, merely legal elements merged in a mixed cultic syncretism.

Over against this false doctrine (perhaps a caricature of an alternative view) the author sets his affirmation of Jesus Christ as lord of the universe, with all the fulness of deity within his person. The basis of Christian freedom, and liberation from superstitions and tyrannies, is established in the universal scope of what Christ achieved.

He is the image of the invisible God, the first-born of all creation; for in him all things were created, in heaven and on earth, visible and invisible, whether thrones or dominions or principalities or authorities – all things were created through him and for him. He is before all things, and in him all things hold together. He is the head of the body, the church; he is the beginning, the first-born from the dead, that in everything he might be pre-eminent. For in him all the fulness of God was pleased to dwell, and through him to reconcile to himself all things, whether on earth or in heaven, making peace by the blood of his cross. (1.15–20)

This is not the language Paul normally uses to describe Christ, but it could be a hymn that is quoted (as in Philippians 2) or the language of a new situation (or new opponents) that is being imitated. The problem is to establish whether the Colossian "heresy" understated the cosmic significance of Jesus (in the interests of personal salvation), or overstated it (being preoccupied with cosmic forces, or even with a cosmic dimension such as John 1). Certainly there are two main aims in the argument of this passage: to relate Jesus essentially to the cosmic dimension and to relate the cosmic understanding to salvation through "the blood of the cross".

There are hints of contact here with the language of Gnosticism in the way that revelation is experienced. Old Testament ideas from the Wisdom tradition (building on Genesis 1.26f)) are used for indirect revelation through the nature of the God who is essentially invisible. The Old Testament writers saw clearly the danger in looking directly at God. This passage says nothing about Christ's adopting human flesh (Incarnation) as the means of revelation. Christ is a bridge to and from God, not by his Incarnation, but because he essentially exists as a revealer and mediator. There appears to be a tension between verses 15 and 17 as to the precise relationship of Christ to creation, for he is the precursor *and* the principle of coherence in everything. In the background here may well have been some mythology of a Cosmic Man.

1.18 makes a decisive turning-point: "He is the head of the body, the church". The picture is transformed with the mention of the church. This clearly shows a later viewpoint, orientated on the church as the institution of salvation. Christ's creation of the church signifies in itself an act of redemption. It is Christ's activity, as a consequence of his Resurrection, which marks the beginning of an eschatological process of revelation/redemption. The second part of the passage, following the transition from 1.17 to 1.18, concentrates on the task of transforming established ideas about the world (cosmology) into an understanding of the process of salvation (SOTERIOLOGY).

The language of 1.19 is ambiguous: "For in him all the fulness of God was pleased to dwell". Originally this meant that the whole world (possibly the whole range of Gnostic systems) was pleased to find its unity in the "image of God". This phrase underlines the presupposition of this passage about the way of understanding the natural order of the world. But 1.19 can also mean – and for the Pauline tradition must mean – that it is God's decision (his good pleasure) to give pre-eminent status to Christ by allowing all the fulness of

God (total deity) to dwell in him. By these means God achieved the reconciliation of the world to himself, in particular by the peacemaking effect of Christ's blood shed upon the cross. The climax of the argument is thus in the recognition of Christ as the saviour figure, represented by the preaching and life of the church.

This passage presents the belief of the apostolic church, organized according to a logical sequence. Understanding of the natural order of the world (cosmology) leads to an understanding of the process of salvation and redemption. And the church is the significant agency in this, being created as a result of Christ's revelation. In the historical development of Christian doctrine, systematically established in the church's councils, the construction of cosmology (with the formulation of the doctrine of the TRINITARIAN God) preceded the construction of a detailed doctrine of the person of Christ as redeemer (and of his divine and human nature). So the council of Nicea (325 CE), which agreed the structure of relationships in the Godhead, came before the council of Chalcedon (451 CE), which formulated the relationship of human and divine natures within Christ.

Paul as an apostle, however, came to Christianity by a different route and a different logic (to judge from his letters and from Acts). He works by the sequence of faith, and moves from an encounter with the risen Lord, and an experience of redemption in the person and work of Jesus Christ, towards a more systematic statement of how the world must be.

If Paul wrote Colossians, then it must have been as an ageing apostle who had been led to dwell on the mystery of the divine plan of salvation. But it is more likely that it was written by someone in the Pauline tradition, concerned to sustain that tradition and provide a corrective to new theological tendencies which were gaining ground after the apostle's death. Since Timothy is named alongside Paul at 1.1, it has been suggested that he is the actual writer, with authorization from Paul. This could account for differences of language and style from the main letters. But it can only account for the development of theological ideas, the new situation, and the historical problems, if Timothy's commission has been extended beyond Paul's death. This "would represent a transition that would make more intelligible the further development [of the Pauline tradition], perhaps as far as the Pastorals" (Schweizer, p. 24). Such an intermediate theory cannot be proved or disproved. It is likely that in any later "Pauline" text actual Pauline material would be re-used. Thus it can be argued that Colossians depends on the genuine letters of Paul's imprisonment, Philippians and Philemon. For example, from Philippians comes the use of a hymn as a teaching text, and the surprising metaphorical application of "circumcision" (Colossians 2.11ff; Philippians 3.3ff); from Philemon come the names of Paul's co-workers mentioned in Colossians 4.

Relations between Colossians and Ephesians

There are three theories to explain the similarities between these two letters:

1 Both letters are by Paul, written from prison at the same period (to

account for the similarities), but written for contrasting purposes (to explain the differences).

2 Colossians is by Paul; Ephesians depends upon Colossians and is written by a disciple in the tradition of Paul, who only partly understood and certainly modified the material he used. "Ephesians reads like the first commentary on Colossians."[3]

3 Neither letter is by Paul, although both preserve Pauline tradition. In composition and theology Ephesians is one step further removed from Paul than is Colossians. Ephesians is very general in stance and is concerned with the nature of the church as a whole; Colossians is occupied with particular problems in a specific situation and aims "to paint a typical picture of the life of a Christian community."[4]

It is in the third area that the most plausible explanation is to be found.

Parallels between Colossians and Ephesians		
Colossians 1.1–2	Ephesians 1.1–3	Salutation
1.23–29	3.7–9	Paul's ministry
3.12–15	4.2–4	New qualities
3.16–17	5.19–20	Hymns and thanksgiving
3.18–4.1	5.22–6.9	Household codes
4.7–8	6.21–22	Tychicus

Closer attention will show significant differences as well as apparent literary relationships. Some of the relationships may be due to independent use of existing liturgical and ethical traditions. Among the differences are a much more sustained and explicit use of the Old Testament in Ephesians, and some quite subtle shifts in the way shared vocabulary is to be interpreted in both letters. The same Greek word is used at Colossians 1.25 to describe the office of the apostle ("the divine office") and also at Ephesians 3.9 (see 1.10) of God's "plan" for the history of salvation. Again the world "fulness" is used to emphasize the filling of Christ by God in Colossians 2.9, and the filling of the church and all things by Christ in Ephesians 1.23 (in this way Ephesians portrays the cosmic lordship of Christ).

The household codes

At the end of the chapter on Paul, the community rules or household codes were seen as a later development and definition of ethical teaching. The catalogue of virtues and vices (see "new qualities" in the list of parallels above) leads on to detailed illustrations of what obedience to the Lord means in the circumstances of everyday living within the Christian community. The context of baptism was important as the Christian was exhorted to "put on" the new; the catalogue of virtues probably originated in the instruction of candidates before baptism. Paul stresses the need for the new humanity, "the body of Christ", to be exemplified not merely in the virtue of the individual but also in the communal holiness and relationship in unity of the whole congregation.

To this end the model of the extended family or household is used for the community. The Pauline community could naturally be seen, from within, as a growing family, with the apostolic founder Paul himself as a patriarchal figure, the father of the family. The rules which governed the life of the family were built up gradually to take account of the conventions of a mixed and extended family. There was a particular need for such rulings in the absence of the father of the family. This was a more natural and flexible model to use than the rule-books of the *collegia*, the clubs and guilds of Greco-Roman society. In writing within the Pauline tradition, the metaphor of the household is naturally extended both in terms of practical management (the ethics of day-to-day living = the household codes) and in the theological terms of the church as the "household of God". Both of these developments are natural and intelligible in sociological and theological terms; they can be seen readily in Ephesians and Colossians.

The two versions of the household code are found in Colossians 3.18–4.1 and Ephesians 5.22–6.9, with which may be compared 1 Peter 2.13–3.12. Different categories of people in the church community were addressed one after another (e.g. wives/husbands; children/fathers; slaves/masters). In a similar way the Pastoral Epistles focussed on the specific duties of those who held office in the church (1 Timothy 3 and 5; Titus 1). A comparison of the two tables of household duties in Colossians and Ephesians shows that the tersely formulated sentences of Colossians have been extensively elaborated in Ephesians. In this way they are provided with a comprehensive basis in which specifically Christian arguments are much more developed. In the popular philosophy of the Greco-Roman world such instructions were commonplace on the duties of individuals in their respective stations in life. The emphasis was on doing one's duty rather than exercising one's rights (e.g. Seneca, *Epistles* 94.1). In the Jewish synagogues of the Diaspora similar patterns were used for teaching proper conduct in accordance with the Torah (e.g. Philo, *On the Decalogue* 165). It was natural for the Christian communities in turn to adopt such ethical traditions, but also to adapt and develop the exhortations in a Christian way. These codes were seen as instructions which derived their authority "in the Lord". Notice how frequently the expression of Christian motivation occurs even in the brief formulae of Colossians.

In the context of Colossians it is clear that order among the participant members and families of this particular church was felt to guarantee harmony in the community of Christians as a whole (3.12–14). The church family acts as a microcosm for the welfare of society at large. In the same way the vastness of the Roman Empire could be regarded as an harmonious household, provided that the patriarchal authority of Caesar as emperor was acknowledged in each locality. So the codes are needed for the constituent members of each local church cell group, and for the relations within a plurality of such groups (e.g. 4.15). It is also necessary for the Christian way of life to be authenticated in relation to the state. This theme comes at the beginning of the table of household duties in 1 Peter 2.13–17. The classic Pauline statement on this matter is in Romans 13.1–7, where there are no specifically Christian directives. Traditional ethical material has been adopted and given its Christian motivation by the larger context of Paul's letter.

The household codes in Colossians do not provide a brand-new distinctively Christian blueprint for the world; rather they are a Christian acknowledgement of those things which everywhere are judged right and reasonable. See Philippians 4.8:

> *Whatever is true, whatever is honourable, whatever is just, whatever is pure, whatever is lovely, whatever is gracious, if there is any excellence, if there is anything worthy of praise, think about these things.*

It is not an attempt to change the world (e.g. by abolishing slavery), but it is a sober recognition that a Christian should do what was expected of any human being, by acting in a morally responsible way, by not being rebellious, and by imaginatively occupying the position of the inferior. The conviction of this passage is clear, that traditional instructions *do* take on a new meaning and significance, when their fulfilment is understood as an act of obedience to Jesus as Lord. The entire conduct and range of relationships of the believer are seen to be subordinated to the lordship of Christ.

These ethical guidelines are consistent with the social structure and attitudes of the generation after Paul; this was a society which depended on the institution of slavery and saw women as essentially different from and often subordinated to men. Even the theories on which these instructions are based, such as the view of the family in society and the ideal of world harmony, might *now* be discredited. To transport these directives into the social order of today is effectively to alter them in meaning and content. For example, to speak of the subject-status of wives then meant to acknowledge a natural and proper social position; nowadays it is to make a polemical statement with male chauvinist intentions. It might be claimed, however, that the principle of total obedience to Jesus is timeless; but what this entails would have to be worked out anew for each generation and situation.

The household codes in Ephesians consider the same relationships in the same sequence but a detailed theological justification of the marriage relationship is added (5.25–33), together with some scriptural proof-texts (5.31; 6.2–3). In the interests of "good order and to secure your undivided devotion to the Lord" (1 Corinthians 7.35), Paul himself had written to the Corinthians. He expressed his doubts about whether worldly marriage was helpful, or simply a source of anxiety, in relation to the ultimate aim of spiritual union with Christ. In the later situation of Ephesians this spiritual union is itself the model for the marriage relationship, and thus provides a new incentive. The metaphor of the church as the bride of Christ (see Revelation 21.2) is used to express this theological principle. The corporate unity of Christ with his bride is the starting point from which the unity of husband and wife in one flesh is to be interpreted. In a similar way the gospel of John used the theological relationship of Father and Son as the model for the relationship of the community (17.21). In the Ephesian model of Christ and his church, both parties to the marriage have a quasi-independence: Christ's offer of love is made freely, and the church makes a free and willing response. The two parties are distinct, yet in effect bound intimately together in a union which is capable of offering a theological interpretation of the marriage union.

Ephesians: a theological essay

A modern "logo" for the World Council of Churches, a symbol of Christian unity and ecumenism. *Oikoumene* from which derives ecumenism) means the inhabited world; the ship is an early symbol for the Church.

It has recently been argued that Ephesians would be more accurately described not as a personal letter but as a theological essay. It dates from the last quarter of the first century and is a reworking of some of the themes from Colossians. It offers an explanation of Pauline theology and its implications, with particular reference to the nature of the church, salvation history and its future perspective, and the unity which the Holy Spirit brings amid a variety of spiritual gifts. The descriptions, such as that of the church, have a systematic structure; the theological complexity is matched by the expression in long and complex sentences. Considering that Paul knew the church at Ephesus well, it is unlikely that he would have written with only the minimal amount of personal contact implied in this work. Instead, in writing about the church, this author establishes links with a structured universal institution, founded in the past by the apostles (2.20), rather than with any individual congregation. It is probably because of its emphasis on the harmony of a world-wide institution rather than on local characteristics that the work has been used widely as a source of texts for Christian Unity and the Ecumenical Movement. The doctrine of the church is expounded in Ephesians 2 both in an historical perspective and with a sense of development. The church is God's new creation in an eschatological programme inaugurated by the Resurrection of Christ (2.1–10). In the church the promise is fulfilled that the Gentiles will also be incorporated (2.11–19). The church is still growing and evolving within its theological (rather than pragmatic or sociological) definition (2.20–22). This historical and evolutionary process is made concrete in the household of God, which is the body of Christ. It is also an evolution with a sense of mystery, as it proceeds to its ultimate end ("omega point"). It was a modern Roman Catholic scientist and theologian, Teilhard de Chardin, who particularly carried forward this kind of thinking of the cosmic Christ and the process of evolution.

To communicate ideas about the function of the church, and in particular the significance of unity, Ephesians makes use of several vivid images:

* the Bride of Christ (already discussed in relation to marriage under the household codes);
* the Body of Christ;
* Christ as the stone in the building;
* the armour of God.

The Greeks used "body" metaphorically; a sophisticated example comes from Plato's *Timaeus* 32:

Out of the four elements the body of the world was created in harmony and proportion, and therefore having the spirit of friendship; and being at unity with itself was indissoluble by the hand of any other than the creator.

To this can be added the Hebrew presuppositions about the nature of humankind, from Genesis 2.7:

the Lord God formed man of dust from the ground, and breathed into his nostrils the breath of life; and man became a living being.

What is important is the idea of close co-operative unity, achieved from different elements at the initiative of the creator. Ephesians uses the idea of this metaphor to describe the church as the "body" of Christ, developing the thought of 1 Corinthians 12. The solidarity between Christ and the Christian believers is vividly expressed in terms of the unity of action of a single living person (see 1.23; 2.16; 3.6; 4.4, 11–16; 5.23). The church is a corporate totality, an executive "body" which is the recipient of the acts and functions of Christ as its "head". In the words of the fifteenth-century Spanish mystic St Teresa: "Christ has no body now on earth but yours, no hands but yours, no feet but yours."

The image of the church as a building now hardly seems metaphorical, except where church communities have abandoned or never enjoyed the use of special buildings. Of course Ephesians predates any Christian architecture that is known; it comes from the days when Christian communities met in private homes or adopted existing accommodation, at the invitation of a patron. So the theological image goes back to the temple of Israel in the holy city of Jerusalem (by this time destroyed, if 2.14 is an allusion to the sacking of 70 CE).

Behold I am laying in Zion for a foundation a stone, a tested stone, a precious cornerstone. (Isaiah 28.16)

Like the vision of New Jerusalem in Revelation 21, the church in Ephesians 2.20 is "built upon the foundation of the apostles"; Ephesians also mentions the foundation of the prophets, for the Old Testament is part of the continuity of salvation history.

It is natural to think of the apostles as founders of churches and therefore as the "foundation" of the church, but Paul himself was clear that apostolic effort on the foundations would go for nothing, unless it remained true to the foundation which God himself had set, in the work of Jesus Christ (see 1 Corinthians 3.9–15). Early Christian tradition brought together several Old Testament references to "stone", which were seen as fulfilled in Jesus (note especially the three texts in 1 Peter 2.6–8). The central prophecy which confirmed the identification with Jesus was that from Psalm 118.22–23:

The stone which the builders rejected has become the head of the corner. This is the Lord's doing; it is marvellous in our eyes.

Ephesians 2.20–22 bases the historical dependence of the church upon

Christ as the "cornerstone" (the stone which ensures that the building is correctly aligned and built true to the architect's plans). But it is also possible to see the idea of development as the building (the church) grows upward in the person of Christ. The cosmic Christ is represented as the climax of the process, in the "topping out" of the building; for he is the "keystone" of the arch, the last stone in place to secure the whole building.

The final image, that of the armour of God at 6.10–20, occurs in the ethical half rather than the theological half of Ephesians. Although this division is a rough guide to use when examining Paul's letters, it cannot apply rigidly to a theological essay like Ephesians. It has already been noted how the theological image of Christ and his bride is used to decisive effect within the ethical instructions of the household codes. The picture of the

Roman soldiers with weapons and armour, from a 1st century CE bas relief of the emperor's Praetorian bodyguard. Ephesians 6.10–18 refers most immediately to the Roman soldier and his equipment.

well-armed soldier is not only an exhortation to strength and boldness (in striking contrast to the vulnerability of the prisoner); it is also making a theological point, for the armour is God's. Although modelled on Paul's metaphors of soldier and athlete, the essence of this image is the Old Testament picture of God as a mighty warrior, fighting a holy war. Such ideas were much developed at Qumran, as seen in the *Scroll of the War of the Sons of Light against the Sons of Darkness* (1QM), and in the quasi-military discipline of the eschatological community as it prepares for the final battle.

The use of military images is paradoxical in a pacifist community or in the context of the gospel of peace. But the concern is not so much with crusaders in a holy war as with the saints of God who hold their ground even in defeat. The arms described in 6.14–17 are the infantry weapons of the Roman soldier, designed for resistance and defensive solidarity, and to these weapons theological meanings are attached. The word translated "equipment" in 6.15 more commonly means "readiness" or "steadfastness" (these are shoes for standing one's ground). The phrase "whole armour" at 6.11, 13 either refers to the completeness of the equipment, or possibly to its quality and function of impressing. The English word "panoply" is derived from this, and its function can be illustrated by Judas Maccabeus' armour at 1 Maccabees 3.3–4.

The list including "peace", "salvation", "Spirit" shows that it is no catalogue of purely human virtues. These are the gifts of God seen in the context of the Old Testament relationship of covenant with Israel. The same is true of "righteousness" at 6.14; as in the description of the Messiah in Isaiah 11.2–5, this is God's righteousness, right-acting help and salvation. It was God who thus intervened, through Jesus Christ, as Paul defined it in Romans 3.21–31. Ultimately, in the perspective of Ephesians, no one except God will be victorious. Good and evil will not remain locked in conflict for ever. In eschatological imagery the dawn of the new age was imminent, from what had to be the last phase of the present. The task of the Christian in this situation is to take and use God's gifts confidently for the benefit of the whole world. In military terms, the soldier must "keep alert" (6.18), stay awake at his post, and keep watch.

What kind of unity?

The overriding concern in Ephesians for unity in relationship with God may have been influenced by social factors. There is a recognition of the variety in gifts from God and Christian attributes. There may have been continuing disagreements among Christians, and threats from heretical teaching but, although these are mentioned, the lack of specific details, or suggestion of urgent crisis, helps to confirm that here is a discussion of theological principles rather than practicalities. Unity is symbolized in terms of sacraments, baptism, Eucharist and a sacramental understanding of marriage. But this unity does not make identifications between distinct essences or beings by combining different elements into new compounds, with confusion of substances (such as might well happen in the Greek metaphor of the world

The Lycus valley near Colossae. The town of Colossae, to which the Pauline letter was addressed, is now an unexcavated mound of ruins in the Turkish countryside.

Ephesus: the view from the theatre at Ephesus towards the Arcadian Way and the sea.

A 5th century CE mosaic from the baptistery at Albenga in Italy which symbolizes the threefold unity of God: Father, Son and Holy Spirit.

The Taurus mountains in Cilicia, capped with snow in early spring. They mark the south-eastern boundary of the large area of Asia Minor where the Christians addressed in 1 Peter lived.

body, as in Plato's *Timaeus*). There is an effective continuity and solidarity, an organic unity, rather than a uniformity of being, between Christ and the church. The "keystone" or "cornerstone" is not identical with the building. The bridegroom takes a bride; he is not himself both bride and groom. The strengthening power of the Spirit (3.16ff) can be distinguished from the human heart; the body is dependent upon the head (4.15f).

The common feature of all the works in the second section of this chapter is that the community in question had been inspired by Paul. They had inherited a substantial legacy of Pauline tradition and they sought to safe-guard it, and apply their understanding of it quite rigidly in new circum-stances. The result is a considerable intensification of the processes of creative theology. While Paul applied his theology intensely to the present moment as a time of crisis, the new compositions sought to conserve by suggesting a universal applicability and continuing relevance. In this way they institutionalized theology and ethics within a church structure that then had the authority of a man-made organization. One would expect the authority of the household of God to be of a different order from the authority of the apostle who claimed a direct call from the risen Lord.

The opportunity for an elaboration and exposition of theological prin-ciples has been demonstrated especially in Ephesians. This justifies using the label of "theological essay". The same label can be used with equal validity for the remaining works, the third section of this chapter. The real difference is that they represent other traditions than the Pauline.

Theological essays and open letters

The "letter" to the Hebrews

This work ends like a letter, but it does not begin like one. There are none of the opening formulae familiar from the letters of Paul. The association with Paul is merely an uncritical assumption based on little that is stronger than the mention of Timothy at 13.23. Doubts about its Pauline authorship were early and repeatedly expressed. The work as a whole was regarded with suspicion and its place in the canon contested by the Western churches. This was probably due not so much to the absence of proof about apostolic authorship as to the presence within the work of statements ruling out the possibility of a second chance at salvation. If a Christian convert sinned again after baptism, for example by apostasy and renouncing his or her faith in time of persecution, there could be no possibility of a second repentance (see 6.4–6; 10.26f; 12.16f). These texts were applied in a very rigorous way by extremist groups of Christians from the second century onwards. Was this the original intention of the writer? And were more charitable Christians who welcomed any repentant sinner rightly perturbed by such strictures?

Melchizedek and his sacrifice – part of a mosaic from S. Vitale, Ravenna, Italy. Melchizedek the priest-king (Genesis 14.18ff) is a prototype for Christ in the argument of Hebrews.

Abraham ready to sacrifice his only son Isaac at God's command (Genesis 22). Hebrews 11.17–19 uses the episode as prototypes of Christ's sacrifice and resurrection. Miniature from a psalter *c.*1175 CE.

There is certainly a consistency in the writer's argument; his theology is completely integrated with his ethics (unlike the letters of Paul with distinguishable sections on doctrinal and moral questions). The impossibility of any second repentance has its basis in the "once-for-all" nature of the single work of redemption by Christ. This singleness means the perfection of forgiveness of sins. It did not always mean that human actions can make no difference to the result. Ethical strictness is naturally required. This strictness is founded upon consent and obedience to, and total reliance upon, the perfect work of expiation by Christ. This is a gospel which contains the law, a divine grace which accompanies strictness: these are the characteristics of Hebrews where everything is seen to depend on the person and work of Christ.

In the sustained imagery of Hebrews, Christ is represented as a high priest, and the death of Christ is also seen as part of the sacrificial activity of this heavenly priest in the heavenly sanctuary. "When he had made purification for sins, he sat down at the right hand of the Majesty on high" (1.3). Here simple past tenses of the verbs convey the once-for-all nature of this priestly work, and his priestly function is connected as closely as possible with his royal status, as he assumed the royal throne. For this reason Melchizedek, who is both priest and king, is such an important symbol in Hebrews. Melchizedek's activities are illustrated in Genesis 14.18ff; he becomes the prototype for Christ (the Messiah) in Psalm 110 (see especially verse 4) and this Psalm is much quoted in Hebrews. The theology of Hebrews makes the most of this combination of the functions of priest with those of king and Messiah.

It is particularly important in Hebrews to trace the origins of ideas in the text and traditions of the Old Testament. Jewish traditions contributed several striking images of sacrifice for this writer. One which had become very important to Judaism is the *Akedah* (the intention of Abraham to sacrifice his only son Isaac in response to God's command, as described in Genesis 22). It is the most enigmatic of theological ideas, for if Abraham had carried out God's original instruction, he would have destroyed God's purpose for Israel at a stroke. The only really explicit reference to this in the New Testament occurs in Hebrews 11.17–19 (although see also James 2.21). In Hebrews Abraham's offering of Isaac is seen as foreshadowing the offering of Christ as the sacrifice, and Abraham's receiving back of his son foreshadows the Resurrection of Christ.

A whole theological argument can also be built up as an idea is developed out of a chain of Old Testament quotations. Another Psalm which plays a significant role, like Psalm 110, is Psalm 8, as quoted in Hebrews 2.5–9. The context of the quotation is set in 2.5: "For it was not to angels that God subjected the world to come, of which we are speaking". The focus of the argument is the Christian hope. The expectation of the world to come raises the question of who will be in charge. Will it be under the control of angelic beings and powers? The question was answered by the quotation from Psalm 8. At its face value the text suggests that "man" (humankind) will be in charge; this would echo the creation stories in Genesis which stress human responsibility (e.g. Genesis 1.28). In the argument of Hebrews, however, what has been contrasted with the "angels" is not "man" but the "Son" and "Lord". This indicates that Psalm 8.4 is here providing a proof text for the title "Son of Man" (as applied to Jesus in the gospels). Whatever modern scholars want to say about "son of man" as a parallel and equivalent of "man" in this Psalm, there is every indication that the author of Hebrews understood it as Christ.

Two proof texts, from Psalms 8 and 110, are closely associated in the argument. Common to both texts are the ideas of subjection and enthronement. Both are elements in the construction of this author's interpretation of the person and work of Christ. The enthronement of Christ is seen as the vindication of the now-triumphant figure of the Son of Man, just as it is also the climax of the priest-king's work. However, the subjection in Psalm 8 also applies to the humiliation and suffering of Christ, for the "Son of Man" in the gospels is also a suffering figure, associated since the time of the Maccabees (and the book of Daniel) with the collective suffering and martyrdom of

Jewish synagogue observance on the Day of Atonement (Yom Kippur). Key features of the historic rituals of this day of fasting and atoning for sins are used in the argument of Hebrews.

An aureus (a gold coin of 71–75 CE) with a portrait of the young Domitian, later to be an emperor with a reputation for persecution.

God's people. In the distinctively Christian interpretation of Hebrews, the suffering of Christ "was fitting", because there existed a most intimate relationship between the Son of Man (as representative man) and humankind (2.11–12). It is because of this, because Christ so shared humankind's actual situation, that he can be an effective high priest for humankind (2.17–18). The representative character of Christ's work is demonstrated out of the Old Testament, both from the origins of the idea of Son of Man and equally from the expectations of the role of high priest (transformed as priestly Messiah). The work of Christ is described in chapters 8–10 mainly in terms of the activity of the high priest on the Day of Atonement, an annual fast-day of sacrifice and penitence. The author says that historically these actions in terms of the Jewish law have advertised their incompleteness (10.1ff). They take place annually, showing that they need to be repeated constantly, and the high priest has to make an offering for his own sins as well. In an important positive sense, however, they emphasize how essential it is for God to act. In fact, the wrong kind of offering is being made (10.4). A sacrifice was needed which would come in the same category as the sin for which it was made. As sin was a moral revolt against God, what was needed was the offering of a sinless will (10.5–10).

The author is not interested in all the details of the Day of Atonement ceremonies, but four features appear to have been specially important.

1 The sacrifice on this day took place outside the Holy of Holies, so that it was visible to all, and clearly on behalf of all (10.10; 13.12).

2 The high priest then enters the Holy of Holies with the blood, as evidence of the sacrifice offered (9.11–12, 24). The whole gospel story, focussed on the death of Christ, but including the Resurrection (13.20) and the Ascension to heaven, is seen in reference to the Atonement ceremony.

3 The high priest makes prayerful intercession and an act of Atonement in the sanctuary. The single act of Christ (10.14) thereby has an eternal aspect, because its effects last for ever (7.25).

4 Finally, the high priest returns to the public outside (9.28). Sin has been dealt with, but the purpose of this Second Coming is to save those who are eagerly waiting. The results of the act of Atonement are applied in this way.

It is clear that the means of salvation are understood in Hebrews as a sequence of events and not as static phenomena. In this respect too the author is dependent upon the Old Testament model, where salvation is largely understood through history. With the benefit of hindsight, it is realized that the Old Testament processes were prophetic. They are promises that were later fulfilled in the gospel. The central pivot of Hebrews is an extended quotation in chapter 8 from Jeremiah's prophecy of the New Covenant (Jeremiah 31.31–34). The Old Covenant was imperfect and has become obsolete, because the perfect version has been established. Although Christ has been triumphantly effective in the heavenly sanctuary (and his single work is complete), the process of applying the results is not quite complete. It is in this situation that the writer and his community lived. "As it is, we do not yet see everything in subjection to him [the Son of Man]" (2.8). How can this intervening period be characterized? Like the pilgrim people of the Old Testament, this community was conscious that God is eternally active and "on the march with Israel". Their hope for the future, their vision of the world to come, was in terms of a heavenly Jerusalem. "According to Jewish thought, there exists a heavenly city, of which the present earthly Jerusalem is an inferior copy; and ... in the future this heavenly city will in some way be manifested as the Jerusalem of the age to come. This complex dualism is characteristic of apocalyptic; and it is precisely this dualism (and not a Platonic dualism) which appears in Hebrews."[5]

This Christian community, as the church of the last days, could feel privileged in the sense that they had already begun to experience something of the world to come. "You have come to Mount Zion and to the city of the living God, the heavenly Jerusalem" (12.22 – see the whole context of 12.18–24). The pilgrim people of God were within sight of their journey's end. "Not the nature of reality, but the advent of the end is the dominating concern of the writer. For him the eternal world stands essentially in front of us, impending on us as an immediate apocalyptic event, and if he brings in the ideal of its present heavenly circumstance, it is because Jesus has already gone into the world of light as our 'Forerunner' [6.20]. He has placed the anchor of our souls there on the other side of the 'veil'. He atones and intercedes for us there, and our souls are summoned to rise to the full height of their eschatological calling."[6]

What was the nature of this community? The writer and his readers appear confident of salvation, both trusting in what God has done, and being prepared to corroborate it with the proper (legal) human response. In the circumstances of the late first century this was an extremist Christian group, both exclusivist in their view of themselves as heirs to the traditions of Israel, and rigidly puritanical in their expectations of Christian moral behaviour. In both respects it provided a radical contrast to the Pauline church. However, this was not simply a survival of the earliest Jewish Christianity. They were heirs to the Jewish tradition, but were also distanced from the most ortho-dox form of Judaism. That distance might have been created by the Diaspora or Dispersion into Hellenistic culture, or by the fact that the Jerusalem Temple had already fallen to Roman conquest. However this may be, there seems to have been a harking back to the rituals of the Tabernacle in the days of wilderness wandering, rather than an acceptance of the Temple institu-tion. It is reminiscent of the critique of the Temple found in Stephen's speech in Acts 7.44ff.

In a theological essay, or a sustained series of profound meditations, this writer sees a particular Christian interpretation as the perfect fulfilment of previous religious attitudes and practices. One can speculate that the author is worried by a growth of liberal attitudes and an indifference to moral effort among his congregation. By his exploration in depth of what a priestly picture of Christ means, he provides a corrective to theological and moral laxity, setting the heavenly goal firmly before his readers. Such circumstances have called forth a tremendously powerful exposition of these integrated theological themes. In the context of Israel's saving history the symbolism of Jewish sacrifice is pressed to the uttermost. But this theological essay has an intensely practical edge: to quicken an active faith, to promote moral and spiritual earnestness, and to foster a proper dread of the consequences of sin. This practical aim can be summed up by its own description, "my word of exhortation", in 13.22.

The "letter" from James

This work begins like a letter but it does not end like one. It is addressed "to the twelve tribes in the Dispersion" (1.1). But it does not seem to be directed to the Jews of the Diaspora, because there are neither distinctively Jewish matters of content, demonstrations of the techniques of distinctively Jewish exegesis, nor midrashic methods of interpretation. From its contents it appears to be an "open letter', addressed to Christians who regarded themselves as the new Israel ("the Israel of God") living in the wider world. It is intended for the widest application, since it is concerned with the general conduct of Christians in the world and their experiences of everyday life. (Contrast the special situation of persecution that is the concern of 1 Peter.) Of course it is possible for the smallest community or conventicle to presume to represent the concerns of the universe, or to challenge the ways of the world. There are examples of this tendency which we have observed in the gospels of Matthew and John. But in James few traces have been left of the precise nature of the community which produced this author or his work.

The author makes full use of traditional materials from both Jewish and Greek sources of ethical teaching. This dependence is similar to that which we observed in the exhortations and household codes of Ephesians and Colossians. The letter of James uses traditional teaching from Jewish Wisdom literature and from popular collections of Hellenistic philosophy. However, the author selects his material and presents it with a distinctively Christian emphasis. And he is not afraid to refer repeatedly to matters that are on his mind. The result is a quite one-sided statement of the author's position, asserted with a conscious protest against alternative religious developments. The pervasive influence of Christian presuppositions means that it is not possible (as has been suggested) to reconstruct a "Jewish" original merely by deleting the only two specific references to Jesus (1.1; 2.1). The principle by which the work is arranged has mystified many commentators, with the result that many speculative explanations have been proposed. An extreme example is the suggestion that a "Jewish prototype" was in the style of a testament of Jacob, resembling that of Genesis 49. James and Jacob are the same name, and the names of Jacob's sons were thought to be buried in the text and to provide its sequence and structure.

The author is not James the son of Zebedee, as is suggested by a Spanish tradition associated with Santiago de Compostela. The work is not early enough to predate his martyrdom (Acts 12.2). For the same reason the author is unlikely to be James the brother of Jesus who, according to

Josephus, was killed in the early 60s CE. However, the book takes as its patron this second James, called "the Just", who traditionally remained an advocate of strict Jewish-Christian piety to the end of his life. (Hegesippus' legendary account in the second century CE referred to him as a Nazirite, that is, one under strict vows, like Samson or John the Baptist.) The book makes use of the authority of this James, the adopted patron, because James was head of the Jerusalem church and president of the council in Acts 15. The actual author was an otherwise unknown and unnamed "teacher" (3.1), who compiled a pamphlet of ethical guidelines. These series and groupings of sayings deal with the typical rather than the particular. As they concern different categories of people, "it is not possible to construct a single frame into which they will all fit."[7] The text does not apply to any one situation or person, any more than does a set of horoscopes for all signs of the zodiac. What is provided is more like a Christian anthology of predominantly ethical teaching. It can be hard to find a logical continuity within the strings of sayings. However, formal connections do exist, such as an arrangement of sayings linked by Greek "catchwords" (such a device of word association was used in Hebrew as an aid for memorizing the separate oracles of an Old Testament prophet such as Isaiah of Jerusalem).[8]

This collection of teaching under the authority of James has not always met with approval through later centuries. It is widely known that Luther called it an "epistle of straw". The reasons are less well known: "it is flatly against St Paul and all the rest of Scripture in ascribing justification to works"; and compared with other New Testament books "that show you Christ, . . . it has nothing of the nature of the gospel about it" (1522 *Preface to the New Testament and Preface to the Epistles of St. James and St. Jude*). By contrast the response of the nineteenth-century New Testament scholar and preacher Johann Gottfried Herder seems valid: "If the Epistle is 'of straw', then there is within that straw a very hearty, firm, nourishing, but as yet uninterpreted and unthrashed, grain."[9] The section of James which deals with the issues of faith and works, 2.14–26, certainly presupposes the Christian debate on Paul's theology. And a function of the argument here is to provide a theological foundation for the general ethical advice which is characteristic of the letter. In the debate with Paul, however, Paul's positions are caricatured (and misunderstood) in the form of slogans, rather than based on accurate knowledge of his letters and the concepts he used. The most probable explanation of this is that the author is looking back on Paul as a figure in the past. It may well reflect the period of partial eclipse of Paul that occurred at the end of the first century . This is much more likely than that James is responding to vague rumours at the beginning of Paul's missionary activity. The theological principle which the author wishes to assert is that of the Law of freedom as the new law of the well-established Christian community (1.25; 2.12). These are issues which Paul himself also dealt with, as in Romans 8. Nor can James be detached from the gospel as completely as Luther thought. Throughout the work there are many echoes of the sayings of Jesus, as found in the synoptic gospels and particularly in Matthew's Sermon on the Mount.

Martin Luther preaching a sermon. Luther termed the letter of James an "epistle of straw" because it was so different from Paul's writings.

Matthew	5.34–37	James	5.12	Prohibition of oaths
	7.7		1.5; 4.3	Prayer in confidence
	7.24–27		1.22	Put the word into practice
	7.1–2		4.11–12	Do not judge the brother

These are some examples among many. It is tempting to compare the relation between James and Matthew with the reliance of the *Didache* on Matthean traditions.[10] But the situations are not really alike. In James the quotations are not direct ones, but rather echoes or variations upon a theme. There are no attacks on Pharisaic interpreters, so characteristic of Matthew, to be found in James. The attack in James is against the thought of Paul, however parodied; this is not the concern of Matthew. Instead the inclusion of traditional Christian material in James (among other traditional material of Jewish and Greek origin) serves as a reminder that the sayings of Jesus in the synoptic gospels were first collected together by Christians, because of their usefulness in ethical teaching and debate. One can conclude that James is reflecting the general tradition of Christian ethical teaching, rather than depending exclusively on any specific gospel tradition.

Because it is presented straightforwardly as a string of maxims, it is possible to overstate the "simplicity" of James' perspectives, to concentrate on the ethical and to ignore the theological presuppositions. The work is included here among the later theological essays to try and offset this danger. It has been seen that the theological foundation is established in debate by creating an impression of the Pauline position. It is reinforced in a traditional way by echoes of the words of Jesus. The ultimate theological insight is, however, implicit in the view of ethics rather than being made explicit in a doctrinal pronouncement. The underlying principle is that of the imitation of God. It is suggested, for example, in 3.9: "With the tongue we bless the Lord and Father, and with it we curse men, who are made in the likeness of God." Its scope is indicated by the association of ideas within this ethical work.

Humanity is essentially "double-minded" (1.8; 4.8; see 3.8ff), that is, marred by disunity and effective discrimination. The word translated as "double-minded" is not a classical Greek word, and it is used only by James in the New Testament.

James was concerned with metaphysical essences as well as ethical objectives. In contrast to "double-mindedness", the ideal state of humankind is singleness and integrity (1.4; 3.2) from which men and women have fallen into sin. It is entirely consistent with this perspective that James should emphasize the singleness of God, in contrast to the resulting sinful duplicity of humankind (see especially 1.5, 17; 2.19; 4.2).

> *Every good endowment and every perfect gift is from above, coming down from the Father of lights with whom there is no variation or shadow due to change.* (1.17)

A similar message to that which is implicit in this association of ideas in James, namely that humankind should be one and single-minded as God is one, is made explicit in the writings of the Hellenistic Jew of the first century, Philo. It is important to see the application of what is a commonplace of popular ethics, that deceit and cursing are against the good. But the message of James goes deeper. It is human sin which is tearing apart the integrity of God's creation. The tongue, as the instrument of humankind's double-mindedness, is responsible for doctrinal as well as ethical error, for heresy as well as deceit. (See also the quotation from Psalm 34.12–16 in 1 Peter 3.8–12.)

It remains to indicate such clues as can be found to the nature of this community. There is no particular sign of a narrowly enclosed sect. Wealth is obviously recognized as a reality of life, in the repeated contrasts of rich and poor (1.9ff; 2.2ff; 5.1f). References to trade (4.13) and ships and sea-travel (1.6; 3.4; 4.13) may indicate how that wealth is acquired. The language here is at its most stylized and conventional, and may indicate only what is taken for granted in the Roman Empire. However, the special focus, created by the repetition, would seem to reflect the author's real concern about the divide between rich and poor. He senses that most churches concentrate on the advantages of having a wealthy patron and fail to see the dangers of a social schism. In contrast the author emphasizes an active and essentially practical piety of the poor, associated with an opposition to worldliness. It is noteworthy that he cites the prophets (Old Testament or Christian charismatic?) and Job as examples of suffering and perseverance in this way of life (5.10–11).

The meeting of the church community is specifically used as a setting for the contrast between rich and poor (2.2ff). The elders of the church are mentioned at 5.14 in connection with prayer for, and anointing of, the sick; this shows that faith-healing was practised. The power of prayer, particularly by the righteous (5.16), is similarly demonstrated in the rescue of a sinner. In contrast to the rigour of Hebrews about post-baptismal sin and apostasy, there is here a real possibility of the restoration of the sinner (4.8; 5.19f). There is a suggestion of mutual benefit for converter and converted, as the members of the community work to redeem, rather than to exile, the errant one. And so the letters ends very abruptly, but with a sense of immediate concern for matters of belief and practice, within a Christian community that took a large view of the world.

The first letter of "Peter"

The fact that 1 and 2 Peter appear in separate categories points up the difference between them. 1 Peter is from start to finish a letter – not a personal letter like some of Paul's, but an open letter for a general audience. It is addressed to the "chosen and destined . . . exiles of the dispersion" (1.1–2), which should be understood to refer not to Jews but to Christians in the world, in the same way as James 1.1 (see also Hebrews 13.14). These Christians were found over a large area covered by the Roman provinces in Asia Minor to the north and west of the Taurus mountains. The order of listing in 1.1 may actually reflect the reorganization of these eastern provinces by the emperor Vespasian in 72 CE. There may also be a deliberate echo of the place names in Acts 2.9–11: these were the homelands of some of those who heard Peter speak at Pentecost. However, those addressed in this letter are certainly Gentiles (1.18; 2.10 and 3.6 would not be said of Jews). And the area includes what was (formerly) the mission field of Paul.

These Christians are called "exiles" and "(resident) aliens" (1.1, 17; 2.11). The technical terms (*parepidemous* and *paroikous*) could well have a social value, describing the actual situation of Christians who feel estranged and alienated since their conversion to Christianity. They are displaced persons, relocated as residents, or passing through the area. They are not full citizens of the place where they live; as "second-class citizens", people with lesser rights and with special obligations imposed upon them, they may well be blamed for any disturbance of the peace. Of course the terms used may also have a powerful religious symbolism, evoking the Old Testament tradition of Israel's exile and spiritual pilgrimage. "Here we have no lasting city." But the symbolism has added force because of the social realities. "As little as Israel's alien residence in Egypt of Babylon was figurative, so little is that of the Christians in Asia Minor."[11]

Those who already were "second-class citizens" may have been attracted to Christianity because it offered them a more positive identity or a fuller sense of belonging, which was denied to them by society at large. It is also likely that many new Christians found themselves on the margins of society as a direct consequence of their conversion. They needed to know what was the right reaction for Christians to make to this experience of alienation; whether they should emphasize their hope in the future and their belief that as pilgrim people they only belonged in heaven; or whether, rather than face the isolation of an other-world group, they should make compromises with the pagan society around them.

The purpose of the open letter is expressed in 5.12. "I have written briefly to you, exhorting and declaring that this is the true grace of God; stand fast in it." This is a fraternal letter of encouragement, to strengthen the recipients as they face up to sufferings and persecution. The work conveys a sense of urgency, an intensification of the Christian hope, as a result of the situation of persecution. However, unlike Revelation, 1 Peter is not an apocalyptic work full of fantastic imagery and speculation. The hope of the Lord's return is established by understanding what salvation means and how it works (1.10–12). From the suffering of Christ on behalf of sinners, from his work of salvation, one learns what is already possessed and what is to be anticipated as the blessings of salvation (2.2–3). The exhortation is to live up to the fact of redemption and to live for the fulfilment of the promises.

In his history of *The Early Church*, Henry Chadwick explains the rise of official persecution of the Christian communities in these terms:

> *There seemed no necessary reason why the Christians should not also achieve toleration* [like the Jews in the Roman Empire]. *They came into conflict with the State in the first instance by accident, not on any fundamental point of principle . . . The Neronian persecution was*

*confined to Rome and was not due to any sense of deep ideological
conflict between Church and State; it was simply that the emperor had
to blame somebody for the fire [of Rome in 64CE]. Nevertheless it was
a precedent that magistrates had condemned Christians to death
because they were Christians and on no other charge. Probably pressure against the Church continued intermittently, and no doubt many
wavered.*[12]

In a period of incipient, intermittent, and localized persecution it may not be
possible to learn enough from 1 Peter to fix the occasion of this particular
persecution (threatened or experienced). Persecution is repeatedly mentioned in the text (1.6; 3.13–17; 4.12–19; 5.9). It is semi-official or unof-
ficial at the hands of the local pagan population. From the Christian point of
view, the accusations brought against them are false (2.12, 15; 3.14ff;
4.12ff). The Christians are also blamed for non-participation in the secular
way of life and in pagan events (4.3ff). Great suffering is, and will be,
experienced. The Christian must ensure that the pain he or she undergoes is
genuine suffering for Christ's sake, and not a proper punishment for miscon-
duct (2.20; 3.16f; 4.15). There is no case for an anarchist to foment trouble
and then claim the martyr's crown as a reward. It is explained repeatedly
that Christ is the example for this life of suffering and that the sufferings of
Christ are the model for patient endurance (2.18–25; 3.18–22; 4.1f, 13ff).
The situation of a Christian community, under the kind of persecution here
described as inaugurated, leads one to suppose that the lifetime of Peter
himself and his death under Nero have receded into past history.

Traditionally this letter is said to have been written by the apostle Peter
(1.1; 5.1) from Rome (5.13). Most readers identify "Babylon" as a symbolic
name for Rome, here and in Revelation 17–18. If so, it is likely that
Christians borrowed the symbol from the Jews, for whom there was a clear
logic in the idea. Just as the Babylonians were the enemy who destroyed
Israel's Temple for the first time in 587 BCE, so Rome became a second
"Babylon" because the Romans destroyed the Temple for the second time in
70 CE. For this explanation to be valid 1 Peter must have been written after
the fall of Jerusalem. Of course "Babylon" could simply mean "the place of
Israel's exile" and not refer to Rome specifically. Babylon (5.13) would then
be equivalent to "dispersion" (1.1), but again social realities and actual
historical events would reinforce the power of the symbol. It seems most
likely that 1 Peter is a work consciously in the Petrine tradition, written
towards the end of the first century. It could be placed in the troubled reign of
the emperor Domitian, without tying it to a single widespread persecution of
Christians (and Jews?) by Domitian, for which there is disputed evidence.

It is no coincidence that Silvanus is specially mentioned in 5.12, and some
have wished to make him the work's author. Even more to the point is the
fact that he was one of *Paul*'s co-workers (see 1 Thessalonians 1.1;
2 Corinthians 1.19; Acts 15.22ff – Silvanus is the Latin form of the Semitic
Silas). His involvement here (whatever his precise contribution) may help to
explain echoes of Pauline ideas within a work in the Petrine tradition. Such

are the expression "in Christ" at 3.16; 5.10, 14, and the use of "gift" (*charisma*) at 4.10. The letter could be the product of the Roman church which has digested Paul's own letter to them. The presence of Pauline ideas within a letter "in Peter's name" makes this a later New Testament expression of the harmony between Peter and Paul in the service of the gospel (see Galatians 2.7f, and Acts). The opposing tendencies of the Christian mission to Jew and Gentile have been synthesized artificially.

Clement of Rome, writing to the Corinthians, similarly used the idea of harmony produced out of discord, and claimed that it was confirmed by the parallel experience of these two apostles in suffering:

> *Let us set before our eyes* [as examples] *the good Apostles: Peter who through unrighteous jealousy endured not one or two but many labours, and so having borne witness* [by his death] *proceeded to his due place of glory. Through jealousy and strife Paul displayed the prize of endurance; seven times in bonds, driven into exile, stoned, appearing as a herald in both the East and the West he won noble fame for his faith; he taught righteousness to the whole world, and after reaching the limits of the West bore witness before the rulers. Then he passed from the world and went to the holy place, having shown himself the greatest pattern of endurance.*
>
> (Clement of Rome, *First Letter to the Corinthians* 5)

On this theme of the parallel nature of the apostolic witness by Peter and Paul, see also the picture of the two witnesses in Revelation 11.

Various types of traditional material have been identified in 1 Peter, including a liturgy on the themes of the Jewish Passover and a sermon on baptism. In both cases the traditional source would be supplemented with direct references to persecution in the last two chapters. Certainly there are allusions to baptism at 1.3, 23; 2.1–2 and a direct reference (with Old Testament typology) in 3.20ff. As in Paul's letters, baptism is seen as the symbol of salvation and the ground for exhortation to live up to one's initiation. References to Passover are found in the image of the lamb (1.18–19) and the allusions to the text of Exodus (e.g. 1.13 "gird up" = Exodus 12.11; 2.9–10 "royal priesthood, holy nation" = Exodus 19.4ff). The repeated emphasis of suffering is explained from the association of the Greek word *pascho* (= I suffer) with the noun *pascha* (= Passover); but *pascha* does not actually occur in 1 Peter. Although all these images and allusions play a part in the argument of 1 Peter, this does not prove that they are more than imagery and that the work was originally a liturgy or a sermon.

On the other hand, some material from traditional sources is certainly used in 1 Peter. As in James, the ethical material is related to both Hellenistic popular philosophy and to Jewish proverbial wisdom. (Notice also the Old Testament quotation from Psalm 34.12–16 at 3.10–12, and the example of Sarah at 3.6.) The household codes (2.11–3.12) represent a substantial block of traditional material, as in Ephesians and Colossians. The code is developed to apply to officials in the church (5.2–5), as in the Pastoral epistles (1 Timothy 3 and 5). Traditional patterns of ethical instruction are

above, left Israel crossing the Red Sea (from an 18th century CE Ethiopic manuscript): the escape from slavery in Egypt is commemorated annually by the Jewish festival of Passover. Passover is one source of imagery found in 1 Peter.

above, right The Harrowing of Hell depicted in a 15th century CE English alabaster relief from Nottingham. This traditional descent of Christ as Saviour to hell may be alluded to in 1 Peter 3.19; 4.6.

combined with the preaching of the gospel. Christians face up to the problems of suffering in the context of the historic suffering of Christ.

Indeed, 1 Peter itself perhaps creates tradition as well as handing it on. The work offers an isolated instance in the New Testament of what later became an element of Christian dogma. The Apostles' Creed affirms that Christ descended into hell after the crucifixion, and medieval artists dramatically represented Christ's HARROWING OF HELL. These events are seen as a judgement on the world of the dead and a redeeming of the saints of the Old Testament. It can be argued that 1 Peter 3.19; 4.6 provides a New Testament justification for this belief.

1 Peter refers briefly to a church community, its organization (5.2–5), its practice of baptism (3.21), and its use of the greeting, the kiss of love/peace (5.14). The idea of the church as the "house" or "household of God" (2.5; 4.17) was obviously important, most of all because it provided the counterbalance to the sense of "exile" and "alienation" felt by the Christian converts. The Greek words *paroikia* (exile) and *oikos* (house) are clearly contrasted with one another. This way of thinking about the church had a social as well as a theological function, a sense of belonging to one another as they belonged to God.

[1 Peter] *emphasises their communal identity, affirming that sense of belonging (1.2, 10–12; 2.4f); it stresses internal cohesion (1.22) with its concomitant holiness and separation from Gentile behaviour (2.11; 4.2–3) – here the warfare image gives positive meaning to such separation and warns against the temptation to compromise. Distinctiveness, which could become a burden and cause for rejection, is made part of a missionary policy (2.12, 15; 3.15f); for this church there can never be total isolation.*[13]

The previous use of the image of "God's household" has already been noted in Paul's writings and in the Pauline tradition, especially Ephesians. The word "house", like the world "assembly" (church), became increasingly significant in the early history of Christianity. The terms cover both the local meeting or house-church and also the consolidation of several households into a larger communal identity. The singular word is used as a term to cover the universal assembly, the world-wide church, which comprehended within it all the separate groupings, the plural "churches". The various images used (see 2.9–10; 2.17; 2.25 leading to 5.2) are all collective and co-ordinating ideas, to create a sense of belonging to a larger identity. The sense of communal solidarity was thus underlined as a counter to social rootlessness. The household code was used (2.11–3.12; 5.2–5) as an ethical scheme to reinforce internal relationships and solidarity. For the same reason there is a repeated emphasis on submissiveness and "humility" (2.18; 3.1; 5.5–6). This humility is not a self-effacing attitude such as that of Uriah Heep in Charles Dickens' *David Copperfield*, or the classical virtue borrowed from paganism. Instead it is a term adopted to express the solidarity of those who have felt what it is to be humiliated. They have experienced humiliation in social rootlessness and alienation, and in persecution by pagan societies, both of which were the consequences of their Christian confession of faith. As members of God's household, they need no longer be afraid of their situation; but they could live with a vision of the end of domination and oppression.[14]

Conclusion

There can be no simple conclusion to this chapter, beyond the recognition of a broad diversity. There are different kinds of writings, serving a variety of purposes, for a selection of different church communities. But there are some recognizable continuities, as in the use and re-use of traditional apocalyptic ideas, and in the persistence of a tradition of Pauline thought. And there are creative developments, producing theological answers in response to new questions.

CHAPTER 7

Gnosticism: the alternative gospel

Gnosticism a religious way of thought, including a salvation myth set against a dualistic background. Embraced by a large number of people in the ancient world, it is complex, not a clearcut religion with a founder, a code of beliefs and practices, festivals, etc. Its adherents expressed their beliefs in a wide variety of cults, some very difficult for the twentieth-century mind to comprehend. Their Scriptures correspondingly range from the relatively simple to the esoteric. The following account is therefore inevitably open to the charge of over-simplification. All we provide is a starting point; anyone who is interested can go much further.

Gnosticism was also a way of thought which permeated other religions, notably Christianity, where its pervasive influence came to be recognized by some (the "orthodox") as sinister, and it was eventually resisted and repelled. This was not, however, before it had profoundly influenced some of the New Testament authors. A good example is the author of the fourth gospel, who dealt with Gnosticism in his own special way, by shaping his Christology to counter it: Jesus, the divine Revealer, is also clearly portrayed as real flesh and blood, against the Gnostic claim that Christ manifested only an appearance of humanity. The deutero-Pauline authors may well have referred to opponents of Gnostic type in Colossians, Ephesians, and the Pastoral Epistles. Similarly 1 John and Jude tackled the same problem. Opposition to Gnosticism did not prevent these authors from using Gnostic language and ideas, from time to time, e.g. Colossians 1.15, "He is the image of the invisible God, the first-born of all creation."

The great accident – the Gnostic myth

(Note: this is variously told in different systems):

> Once upon a time everything was happy and harmonious. There was in the Light a *Pleroma*, a Fulness, as the collection of divine beings in heaven was called (there were thirty in all, in pairs and groups).
> Then one of the thirty, inaptly called *Sophia*, divine wisdom, had a foolish crisis; she was filled with desire for the Father. This upset the

balance in the Pleroma, and harmony was only restored when the material, lower Sophia, was dumped outside the Pleroma. But this material produced a chain of beings which moved increasingly down and away from the true Light, God. Evil matter came into being, controlled by dark forces. The dark forces included the Zodiac, the planets and the wicked creator of the world himself – the *Demiurge* (God of the Old Testament).

The creation of the world was evil, and it caught up some of the remaining divine sparks which had "fallen" from heaven after Sophia's little mistake had been disposed of, and imprisoned them in matter.

Eventually the Pleroma bestirred itself and set up an organization – despatched a Saviour in later cults – to cope with the plight of these divine sparks, trapped in human beings, and help them escape by providing a route back to their origins and reabsorption.

When all divinity is safely back inside the Pleroma all will be happy and harmonious again.

This diagram is according to the system of Valentinus (a Roman theologian/heresiarch of the mid-second century CE).

KEY TO DIAGRAM
1 The Being (or Aeon) number 30 – Sophia – while outside the Pleroma, produces a lower Sophia (Achamoth). She brings forth: Matter, Soul-element (the Creator comes from this), Spirit. When the Creator makes men from matter and some soul, she adds in the spiritual element, which then has to be rescued. Consequently there are three types of men: Matter only – these cannot be saved; Soul-element included – salvation is tricky, but possible through knowing and copying Jesus; Spiritual element too – salvation is possible by *knowing* Jesus' teaching.
2 Christ and Holy Spirit are produced later, in response to Sophia's crisis (her "little mistake").
3 Saviour Jesus is eventually produced in response to the restored situation. He is regarded as the perfect fruit of the Pleroma.

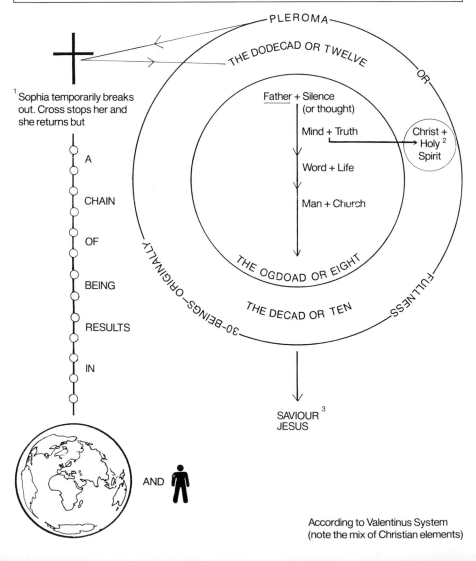

According to Valentinus System
(note the mix of Christian elements)

The divine universe

The Pleroma became encased in a series of protective layers or spheres which the spark must penetrate to rejoin its heavenly origin.

Diagram of the spheres. Knowledge of the route through the spheres and all the passwords and names of guardians had to be memorized by the initiate, for salvation at the tenth sphere. There was of course no question of anything like a Last Judgement preceding the absorption of the individual's spirit into the divine whole.

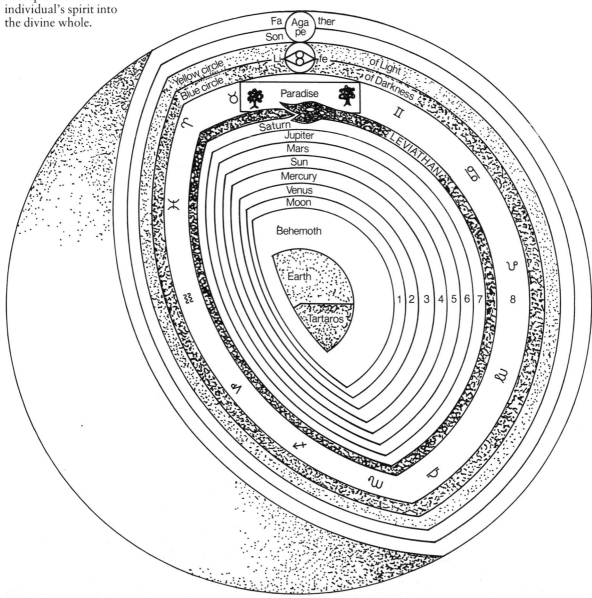

Fundamental ideas of Gnosticism

The following imaginary catechism or questionnaire for intending converts attempts to summarize the basic ideas shared by most Gnostic groups.

Q. What is Gnosticism?

A. It is religious *knowledge* (from the Greek *gnosis*, necessary to salvation).

Q. Who am I?

A. You are a member of the elect to whom this special knowledge from on high will be entrusted.

Q. What is this special knowledge?

A. That you contain a divine spark in your material body. This spark must be liberated to rejoin its parent divinity in heaven.

Q. How did this divine spark get into me?

A. You must understand that Creation is a disaster of cosmic magnitude; it was an accident. Matter should never have been formed, the world never created. In this divine accident some divine sparks became separated off and entrapped in matter. Some human beings contain this spark, most do not.

Q. What must I do to free this captive spark?

A. Join this sect, and become initiated in our ceremonies, the only true way to salvation.

Q. What must I then do?

A. Learn from this sect the way to salvation, the escape route to avoid all the evil powers that will attempt to block the path of your fleeing spirit. We have the map of the universe you must pass through to your heavenly reunion. We alone can teach you what you must learn.

Q. What must I learn?

A. You must know the names of the spheres and their controllers, and you must memorize the passwords for the appropriate ports of entry.

Q. What is my journey's goal?

A. Your goal is to be merged with the divine light.

This "Questionnaire" can be compared with a sequence of religious questions about the meaning of life, such as the following (from Hans Küng's *On Being A Christian*):

> *What can we know? Why is there anything at all? Why not nothing? Where does man come from and where does he go to? Why is the world as it is? What is the ultimate reason and meaning of all reality?*

Gnosticism perceived as a threat

The New Testament writers and the fathers alike viewed Gnosticism with considerable apprehension, presumably because it presented an attractive alternative to Christianity. Potential converts had to be wooed away, and such arguments as the following were employed to demonstrate the wrongness of Gnosticism:

Faith and not knowledge is necessary to salvation

A personal commitment to Christ as Saviour is required, and not the extensive learning of a baffling system. Faith is not capable of measurement and testing; it is much more elusive than "facts" which are learned.

Creation is good

A purposeful act has been performed by a loving creator – not an undesirable disaster brought about by a malicious "Demiurge", as the Gnostics taught.

Dualism

The fundamental type of dualism taught by the Gnostics:

Good	v.	Evil
Light	v.	Darkness
Spirit	v.	Matter
Knowledge	v.	Ignorance

is not acceptable in this thoroughgoing form to a Biblical view of creation, in which matter is not intrinsically evil.

The consequences of this belief in the evil nature of the body were that some Gnostics mortified the flesh and were extremely ascetic, while others adopted libertine excesses, which were followed by the complete breakdown of any recognizable standard of moral or ethical behaviour. It could, however, be said that Gnosticism was much more successful in dealing with the cosmic problem of evil than Christianity, and took the problem of evil far more seriously. A Gnostic would have no problem in explaining earthquakes, famines or genocide. Christians, on the other hand, have found such questions difficult while claiming that the universe was created by a good God.[1]

Christ's nature

The place of Christ is totally undermined by such a system as Gnosticism, which cannot allow the divine to become involved with earthly matter. No Incarnation (God taking flesh) is conceivable. The salvation of the cross proclaimed by preachers is a nonsense, if a divine spirit stands by while a human substitute is put to death. The Son of God must *really* die and not merely *seem* to (as in the *Docetic* [= seeming] idea). Thus, for example, John emphasizes the reality of Christ's birth and death, in response to Gnostic arguments (1.14; 19.34).

Sacraments

Sacraments are similarly exhausted of value when Gnostics cannot accept that material substances can convey the divine presence to men, whereas Christians see water, bread, and wine as channels of God's grace.

Ethics

A positive attitude of obedience to a good God, and an open channel of communication through prayer determines Christians' relationship to the Father. In contrast, Gnostics believed men were separated from the divine by barriers of matter and hostile influences; in such a case obedience is irrelevant.

The origins of Gnosticism

Gnostic influences on the New Testament presuppose Gnosticism as a *pre-Christian phenomenon*, a view radically different from that which used to be held. With the discovery of primary source material the picture changed.

This availability of primary documentation resulted from nineteenth- and twentieth-century archaeological discoveries, particularly in Egypt. The *Corpus Hermeticum*, or Hermetic literature, is a curious body of Greek writing displaying ideas usually accepted as older than the second to third centuries CE when they were written down. The thought expressed in the Hermetic literature, much of it revealed by the Egyptian god of wisdom Thoth, known by the Greek title of Hermes Trismegistos, is a blend of mystical and religious ideas from the Near East and Greek philosophy. The mixture of eastern ideas is known as oriental syncretism. There are plenty of variations within the different writings, but as a broad generalization we can say that they teach knowledge of one good God and a very individualistic brand of piety: each soul looks to its own salvation, and, incidentally, rarely cares for its neighbour. Salvation from this material and evil (?) world was attainable through *gnosis* – knowledge of the God who is life and light and mind (*Nous*) – which could not be achieved by intellectual striving, but through revelation and mystical experience. The *Corpus Hermeticum* represents a halfway position to Gnosticism. The foundation ideas are all there, but much was still to be built upon them.

Usually overshadowed in the popular imagination by archaeological discoveries like the Dead Sea Scrolls, but no less important in its way was the 1946 unearthing of a collection of Gnostic writings at Nag Hammadi in Egypt. Each codex contains several distinct writings in the Greek-influenced Egyptian language of the period called *Coptic*; there are fifty-one writings in all, some stemming from quite varied Gnostic systems. That such a diverse "heretical" library should have to be concealed in a cave at all suggests that it belonged to a community placed under some kind of a threat, but whether it was an external threat related to persecution, or an internal disciplinary

The Nag Hammadi scrolls are important primary sources of evidence for Gnosticism. This is the title page of the Gospel of Thomas.

Thoth was the Egyptian god of wisdom; in Greek guise as Hermes, he gave the information contained in the Hermetic Literature.

threat made by the "orthodox" in purging the church, is not known.

The manuscripts were written *c.*350 CE (dated grain receipts tucked into the binding help to confirm this date). It is thought that the actual composition and translation into Coptic was a century or so earlier. As with the Hermetic literature, indebtedness to Greek philosophical speculation is clearly evident, and there is reliance on Jewish thought too. Some of the writings, forty-one of which were not previously known, exhibit a Gnosticism untainted by Christianity (including, it has been claimed, a wholly independent Redeemer idea – see pie-chart), while others are related to it in varying degrees.

Some of the codices contain books which bear familiar names – the apostles Paul, John, Thomas, Philip, Peter, and James – thought to be an attempt to win confidence for the esoteric information that they offered. Others are known by curious titles, e.g. The Thunder, Perfect Mind, and are not attributed to any named author. Some writings purport to be gospels, of which probably the best known is the gospel of Thomas – "The secret sayings which the living Jesus spoke". This gospel has a questionable relationship to the collections of sayings and teachings of Jesus (such as the reconstructed document "Q"), which are thought to be a source for the synoptic gospels (see p. 22). It also has a distinctly Gnostic theology, and offers private information allowing disciples to know their origin and attain their destiny:

> *Jesus said, "Blessed are the solitary and elect, for you will find the Kingdom. For you are of it, and to it you will return." (49)*
> *Jesus said, "If they say to you, 'Where did you come from?', say to them, 'We come from the light, the place where the light came into being on its own accord' ..." (50)*

The privilege of the hearer/reader in learning this information, which would allow him to forsake his corrupt humanity, is underscored in

> *Jesus said, "It is to those who are worthy of My mysteries that I tell My mysteries." (62)*

(Translation by T.O. Lambdin)

Thus we are now able to read Gnostic writings for ourselves, but it is still difficult to decide how far even the Nag Hammadi documents are related to, or removed from, the New Testament world.

Christian–Gnostic systems appear to have flourished in the second century, drawing opposition from Irenaeus and other writers, when the distinction between what was acceptable to the Christian church and what was not was much less clear than it subsequently became. Gnosticism did not, however, die out with church disapproval; an inspirational teacher called Mani refashioned it, and in its later form of MANICHEISM it travelled widely, even to China. An even longer-lasting group of Gnostics survived into the twentieth century, when most other heresies had vanished years before. The customs and practices of early Gnostic sects are held to have been preserved by the baptizing community of Mandaeans in southern Iraq,

Gnosticism, in the form of the later Manichaean religion, spread along the ancient trade routes as far as China in the east. This is a page from a Manichaean book.

for which there is documentary evidence.

The word "Mandaean" is apparently derived from an older form of word meaning "knowing" or gnostic. The community's supposed veneration for the figure of John the Baptist inevitably led to parallels being drawn with Acts 19.1ff, where Paul encountered at Ephesus some disciples knowing only the baptism of John, and nothing about the Holy Spirit, whereupon Paul administered the baptism of Jesus and the laying on of hands. This view of Mandaeans as spiritual descendants of John is now coming more into question, and the Jewishness of their ancestry is being emphasized. It is

Mani, 3rd century CE, was a religious teacher who combined various existing elements including Gnosticism into a new religion. His death is shown here.

thought that they originated with a Jewish baptismal group in the Jordan area, who came under considerable Gnostic influence at some point. Certainly this community possesses a library of Gnostic books written in a form of Aramaic, which would suggest that their ultimate origin was in Palestine or Syria. The possession of this library proved the group to be a "People of the Book", like Jews and Christians.

The community has priests and ritual as well as scriptures, and these ensure that sacramental procedures of a threefold baptism in "Jordan" (= a pool), and a sacred meal for the dead, are properly carried out; both the washing and the meal are necessary in conjunction with correct *gnosis* to achieve salvation. Correct knowledge includes information on the passwords for moving unscathed at death through the seven planetary spheres, which are inhabited by hostile influences; with the support of the community's rituals, the soul is enabled to reach the divine light.

A pie-chart to show the origins of gnosticism.

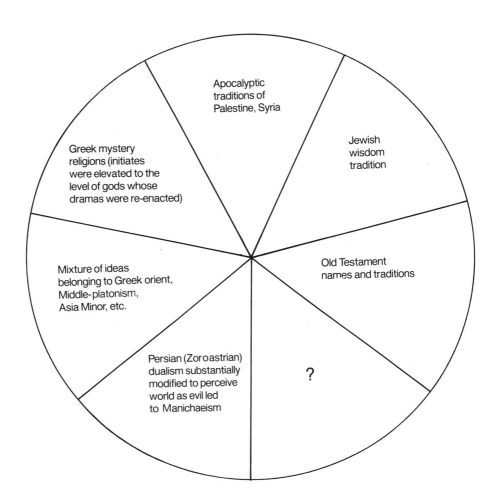

Latter-day Gnostics surviving in Iraq and literary fragments found in Egypt suggest that Gnosticism probably originated in the Fertile Crescent – the lands of the Middle East from Egypt round to Iran–Iraq via Syria. The evidence of the church fathers shows that it spread far round the Mediterranean world, changing and mutating with every new contact. Gnosticism in the form of oriental syncretism may have emerged in recognizable form in the closing centuries before Christ (BCE).

The pie-chart below shows an analysis of the origins of Gnostic material, and indicates its complex past and formation.[2]

Extracts from Gnostic documents

The following selection is taken from *The Nag Hammadi Library* edited by J.M. Robinson.

Exclusive information (*i.e. not accessible to most Christians*)

i *Since you asked that I send you a secret book which was revealed to me and Peter by the Lord, I could not turn you away or gainsay (?) you; but I have written it in the Hebrew alphabet and sent it to you, and you alone. But since you are a minister of the salvation of the saints, endeavor earnestly and take care not to rehearse this text to many – this that the Savior did not wish to tell to all of us, his twelve disciples. But blessed will they be who will be saved through the faith of this discourse.* (The Apocryphon of James, p. 30)

The Nag Hammadi Library, now at Claremont, California.

ii *The teaching (of the Savior) and (the revelation) of the mysteries (and the) things hidden in silence, (all these things which) he taught John (his) disciple.* (*The Apocryphon of John*, p. 99)

iii *These are the secret sayings which the living Jesus spoke and which Didymos Judas Thomas wrote down.*

(*The Gospel of Thomas*, p. 118)

iv *The secret words that the Savior spoke to Judas Thomas which I, even I Mathaias, wrote down – I was walking, listening to them speak with one another.* (*The Book of Thomas the Contender*, p. 188)

Gnostic origins

i *You, together with your offspring, are from the Primeval Father; from Above, out of the imperishable Light, their souls are come. Thus the Authorities cannot approach them because of the Spirit of Truth present within them; and all who have become acquainted with this Way exist deathless in the midst of dying mankind.*

(*The Hypostasis of Archons*, p. 159)

ii *Those who were chosen from an immortal substance . . .*

(*The Apocalypse of Peter*, pp. 344–5)

iii *Jesus said, "If they say to you, 'Where did you come from?', say to them, 'We came from the light, the place where the light came into being on its own accord and established (itself) and became manifest through their image'."* (*The Gospel of Thomas*, p. 123)

iv *Secretly her bridegroom . . . applied . . . a medicine to make her (the soul) see with her mind and perceive her kinsmen and learn about her root, in order that she might cling to her branch from which she had first come forth, in order that she might receive what is hers and renounce (matter).* (*The Authoritative Teaching*, p. 278)

Gnostic destiny

i *His disciples said, "When will You become revealed to us and when shall we see You?" Jesus said, "When you disrobe without being ashamed and take up your garments and place them under your feet like little children and tread on them, then (will you see) the Son of the Living One, and you will not be afraid."* [i.e. when you free yourself from material existence] (*The Gospel of Thomas*, p. 122)

Compare Judas' question to Matthew,

"*We wish to know with what kind of garments we shall be clothed, when we come forth from the corruption of the (flesh)?*"

which merits the reply from the Lord,

"... *Rather, I say to you that you will be blessed when you strip yourselves* ..." (*The Dialogue of the Savior*, p. 237)

ii *For it is necessary that everyone enter the place from whence he came. For each one by his deed and his knowledge will reveal his nature.* (*On the Origin of the World*, p. 179)

iii Paul's description of his heavenly journey in 2 Corinthians 12 proved the basis for one Gnostic book to describe an ascent through the heavenly spheres, each of which opened in turn for him and his escort the Holy Spirit. Interrogation in the seventh heaven leads Paul to claim, "I am going to the place from which I came." He gives "the sign".

> *"And then the (seventh) heaven opened and we went up to the Ogdoad. And I saw the twelve apostles. They greeted me, and we went up to the ninth heaven. I greeted all those who were in the ninth heaven, and we went up to the tenth heaven. And I greeted my fellow spirits."* (*The Apocalypse of Paul*, p. 241)

Thus:

> *He who is to have knowledge in this manner knows where he comes from and where he is going.* (*The Gospel of Truth*, p. 40)

We may compare this with another Gnostic statement, this time as quoted by the church father Clement of Alexandria from a follower of Valentinus, Theodotus:

> *It is not only the washing* [i.e. baptism] *that is liberating, but the knowledge of who we were or where we were placed, whither we hasten, from what we are redeemed, what birth is and what rebirth.* (*Excerpta ex Theodoto* 78.2, translated by R.P. Casey)

Selection for salvation

i *Mankind came to be in three essential types, the spiritual, the psychic, and the material* ... *The spiritual race will receive salvation in every way. The material will receive destruction in every way* ... *The psychic race, since it is in the middle when it is brought forth* ... *is double in its determination for both good and evil* ... *complete escape to those who are good (but the rest) will receive their end suddenly.* (*The Tripartite Tractate*, p. 91)

ii *The Savior said "*... *do not esteem them as men, but regard them as beasts* ... *they are deprived of the kingdom* ... *They will be thrown down to the abyss and be afflicted by the torment of the bitterness of their evil nature."* (*The book of Thomas the Contender*, p. 191)

Jesus' role as Revealer and Docetic Redeemer

i *This is the gospel of the one who is searched for, which [was] revealed to those who are perfect through the mercies of the Father – the hidden mystery, Jesus the Christ. Through it he enlightened those who were in darkness. Out of oblivion he enlightened them, he showed [them] a way. And the way is the truth which he taught them. For this reason error grew angry at him, persecuted him, was distressed at him, [and] was brought to naught. He was nailed to a tree ... [Then] He discovered them in himself, and they discovered Him in themselves, the incomprehensible, inconceivable one, the Father, the perfect one, the one who made the all.* (The Gospel of Truth, p. 38)

ii *The Savior said to me, "He whom you saw on the tree, glad and laughing, this is the living Jesus. But this one into whose hands and feet they drive the nails is his fleshly part, which is the substitute being put to shame."* (The Apocalypse of Peter, p. 344)

Compare this with:

It was another, their father, who drank the gall and the vinegar; it was not I. They struck me with the reed; it was another, Simon, who bore the cross on his shoulder. It was another upon whom they placed the crown of thorns ... And I was laughing at their ignorance. (The Second Treatise of the Great Seth, p. 332)

(Note: There are some Gnostic works where Jesus does not appear.)

New Testament passages heard offkey

i *For the kingdom of heaven is like an ear of grain after it had sprouted in a field. And when it had ripened, it scattered its fruit and again filled the field with ears for another year. You also: hasten to reap an ear of life for yourselves that you may be filled with the Kingdom.* (The Apocryphon of James, p. 34)

ii *He is the shepherd who left behind the ninety-nine sheep which were not lost. He went searching for the one which was lost. He rejoiced when he found it, for ninety-nine is a number which is in the left hand which holds it. But when the one is found, the entire number passes to the right (hand).* (The Gospel of Truth, p. 44)

iii *Jesus said, "Let him who seeks continue seeking until he finds. When he finds he will become troubled, he will be astonished and he will rule over the All ... If those who lead you say to you, 'See the Kingdom is in the sky', then the birds of the sky will precede you".* (The Gospel of Thomas, p. 118)

CHAPTER 8

The ground rule

The need for universal unity is the third and last torment of men.
The Brothers Karamazov, F. Dostoyevsky

The evidence for a variety of early Christian communities has been examined in the literature they produced. It is possible to draw conclusions which polarize the differences between the churches (e.g. Jewish and Gentile Christian introvert and extrovert) and, although some of the variations are quite subtle, the differences certainly cannot be ignored. There is no sign of a universal harmony among the first generations of Christians. A simplicity of Christian unity at the beginning is as much a myth as the straightforward "doctrine-free" picture of the historical Jesus. The reason is the same in both cases: this is what later generations would like to believe, in the teeth of the historical evidence.

The "Basic Christianity" hypothesis

Edwin Hatch delivered the Hibbert Lectures in 1888 on the subject of *The Influence of Greek Ideas on Christianity*.[1] He began by contrasting the Sermon on the Mount with the Nicene Creed. The former "belongs to a world of Syrian peasants, the other to a world of Greek philosophers". The Sermon is concerned with ethics, the Creed with doctrine. "The change in the centre of gravity from conduct to belief is coincident with a transference of Christianity from a Semitic to a Greek soil."[2] This move from ethics to doctrine is seen as a move from "original simplicity" to "later complexity", from individual spontaneity to group associations and assimilation to existing structures.

This theory allowed Christian apologists to reassert the ideal of the "simple gospel" and to detach themselves from the traditional legacies of Greek philosophy. Christianity was allegedly made into the complicated doctrinal structure which it now appears to be by the fathers of the Greek and Latin churches from the second century onward. They were "great admirers of Plato, and accordingly . . . did in outward profession so put on Christ, as that in heart they did not put off Plato".[3] The major problems with this theory are that Christianity did not begin in a vacuum, and that it was quite a complicated phenomenon from the outset. Any investigation of the main texts of the New Testament, seen in relation to the communities which produced them, has to admit the variety and complexity of ideas and practices already found in the first century.

The church's attitude to the world

One of the most significant aspects of early Christianity is the community's view of itself in relation to the world outside. The range of attitudes is indicated by two opposite poles and by a third or compromise position.

1 The attitude of "spiritual exile":
   Being in the world is itself the problem and predicament. Individuals and groups are saved from the world by the processes of religion.

2 The attitude of "covenantal relationship" and "belonging":
   This affirms the essential goodness of the world in both its natural *and* its historical dimensions. This is a "life-affirming" attitude in its fullest sense.[4]

3 The middle position of selective adoption:
   The religious group finds salvation by participating in some but not all aspects of the world around them. They may take up an attitude of imitative involvement in the *timeless* processes of the natural order in the course of their spirituality, but have nothing whatsoever to do with the *time-bound*, historical or political events.

The second attitude is traditionally ascribed to the view inherited from the Old Testament. But even in the earlier books of the Hebrew Bible this is qualified to some extent. The mixed experiences of the wilderness wandering, and of the political situation under judges and kings were influential. The view of God's creation had to accommodate not only human failure but also malign influences. In some parts of later Judaism the view of the world is essentially dualist, with God in the ascendancy. The first attitude can be found among some followers of Christianity, usually because they have been driven to the margins of sectarianism, or into the wilderness, by hostility and persecution but the attitude of the hermit or of desert spirituality may be classified more accurately as within the middle position of those who seek to be in tune with the natural order. All groups, but especially those in the middle ground, are influenced directly by experience of the attitudes which those around the church take.

The two extremes of thought about the mission of the church correspond closely to the polarized attitudes of its members to the world:

1 Its mission is to draw human beings out of a world that is entirely sinful, to experience spiritual transformation within the church (the exile).

2 Its mission is to engage the church, its faith, and its message, in a secular transformation of the world (the covenant).

There is also a third and intermediate way, of integral mission, which takes a more comprehensive, less polarized and divisive view. The present General Secretary of the World Council of Churches, Emilio Castro, has said that "liberation, development, humanisation *and* evangelisation are *all* integral parts of mission ... and cannot be set apart from one another without becoming simply caricatures of what they really are". This gives a clearer sense that (in the Christian view) the mission of God's people means the restoring of a *dialectical* relationship with the world. The church is open to the movement of divine inspiration and relates to the world, so that "the whole work of witness, in word, deed and being, which is mission, becomes, as in the New Testament church, more of a gift exchange set in a context of friendship and genuine caring."[5] As supporting evidence one might cite Luke 7.34 and John 15.13f.

Self-definition and the pressures for unity

Within early Christianity each community was pressed by its experiences to achieve a clearer sense of its own identity in relation to the world around it. In the same way the wider church, as a consolidation of individual communities, needed a clearer description of itself and a greater sense of unity in relation to the world. Moves toward unity could, however, be construed as

Christ as Apollo, with lyre and animals; a marble bust, 4th century CE Byzantine work. Images such as this used within the Christian tradition show the adoption and perpetuation of pagan themes.

Christ as all-powerful (Pantocrator): 12th century CE mural in the church of Panagia Tou Arakou, Lagoudora Monastery, Cyprus.

The Deposition and Rolling away of the Stone, painting by Stanley Spencer (1891–1959).

attempts to achieve uniformity. Not surprisingly, then, pressures towards unity could result in the exclusion of others and the increased polarization of thought and practice.

Identity

A consequence of the search for unity is a division between the "orthodox" and the "heretics". These terms do not represent self-evident definitions, but the view of one group that feels justified in believing that only *they* maintain the true traditions of doctrine or practice. In their eyes, other groups have gone astray and are consequently irredeemable. By repentance these heretics might perhaps have a chance of salvation (but that is not certain). On the other side the "heretics" may be equally confident that only they are heirs to the truth, and that the "orthodox" have compromised themselves.

Orthodoxy and heresy are clearly relative terms. They were used more exactly in the later ages of the church councils, because orthodoxy was then defined in relation to a supposedly representative gathering of the "universal" church. In reference to earlier periods the terms are probably used too readily as an expression of prejudice.

The tendency to polarization can be seen among the early Christians and there were fewer opportunities (or wishes) to compromise. There were different visions of the essentials of the Christian religion, as between Paul and his opponents. Was the new Christian religion in straight continuity with the Jewish revelation, or diametrically in contrast with Judaism? The polarities emerged sharply in the circumstances that produced Galatians. And they are reflected with the benefit of hindsight in the longer perspectives of the account of the Council of Jerusalem in Acts. Distinctive strategies were clearly at work: there were two ways of bringing the Christian mission to the world, two ways of working out the promises represented by the Old Testament traditions.

Christology

There were polarities also in the representations of Christ which the early Christians proclaimed. One Christology emphasized the Ascension of Christ as a triumphant enthronement with God, another emphasized the death of Christ as the sacrificial offering to deal with sin, and propitiate the wrath of God; the Resurrection was then seen as a vindication of Christ, identifying him with the expected figure of Messiah, because resurrection was the sign of the messianic kingdom at the end of the world. For one Christology it was enough that the human figure of God's agent received the seal of approval on his work and was acknowledged by God in his heavenly kingdom. For another it was equally important that Christ came from heaven and went back once more to his heavenly home. For both views the earthly activity and death of Jesus were of vital importance, but the frames in which these were viewed – the sense of what came before and happened afterwards – were in sharp contrast.

Contrasting ways of understanding the person of Christ

Christology (1)	Christology (2)
	Divine Christ with God
	Incarnation
Earthly activity of Jesus	Earthly activity of Jesus
Teaching and miracles	Teaching and miracles
Work seen as vital	Work seen as vital
Passion and death	Passion and death
Death understood as sacrifice	
(dealing with God's anger)	
Christ is vindicated by God	Christ's work approved by God
and revealed as Messiah	Christ received by God in heaven
Resurrection – vital seal of	Ascension – triumphant
God's approval of his Messiah	enthronement in glory
	Christ has returned to his
	position with God

Social environment

There were polarities too in the social structure of Christianity and the circumstances in which the religion was practised. One kind of Christianity worked outwards from an assembly point, the meeting-place of a community with world vision; the church knew no effective boundaries but those of the inhabited world. Another kind of Christianity was produced under very different and hostile circumstances, where the community was embattled or driven to the margins. When its very existence was threatened, the best that the sect could do was to reaffirm its identity as a community and guard its treasure. There could not be a greater contrast between the lifestyles, and the ideals of authority and obedience, of a worldly church on the one hand and a monastic sect on the other.

Elements of unity

The widespread tendency to polarization and diversity persisted throughout the New Testament period. But the existence of some elements of unity can also be recognized within the diversity. These are factors which have the capacity to bind together members of different Christian communities. There are common denominators existing in apparently diverse groups which might provide the basis for a larger structure and even a universal church. The weight of the evidence suggests, however, that it is more accurate to speak of elements of unity in diversity, rather than of diversity within a basic unity. There is more evidence of diversity in the communities of the New Testament.

Christ as a guerilla:
Ospaal poster (1968)
by Alfredo Rostgaard.

The elements of unity are conveniently classified under the headings of practical teaching and ethics; understanding of Christ; and ideas about the church. Just as these are elements which could bind together Christians from different groups, so also these elements are themselves connected to each other. Basic teaching about Christ has ethical implications and also affects the nature of the church.

Practical teaching and ethics

It has been noted how widely Christians made use of a common store of ethical teaching drawn from Jewish wisdom and the popular philosophy of the Greek world. Such traditional borrowing produced patterns of moral exhortation and structured household codes used in many New Testament communities. Much more distinctive to Christianity, but also common in the New Testament documents, is what is called "the love command". This denotes Jesus' answer, in the synoptic gospels, to those who questioned him about the great commandment; it is a double formula of love to God and love to neighbour (see Matthew 22.34–40; Mark 12.28–34; Luke 10.25–28). It has its origin in Jewish summaries of the Law, but the particular emphasis of Jesus' interpretation has become characteristic of Christianity.

Although Paul does not record the teaching of Jesus in detail, he represents love as the power of the new creation which is present and active in the working of the Spirit. The word "love" occurs in every one of the attested letters of Paul (see especially 1 Corinthians 13; 2 Corinthians 5.17; Galatians 2.19–20; Romans 5.5). In the fourth gospel Jesus' command to love is again made explicit, but love is also the principle by which Jesus' own mission was carried out in accordance with God the Father's will. The exposition is to be found in the Farewell Discourses of John 13–17, and summarized in 1 John 4.7–21. The rule of love also has a central place in Colossians (3.14), Ephesians (2.4–7; 4.15–16; 5.2), and 1 Peter (2.17; 4.7–11).

The symbol of love, within the context of an integrated system of ethics and theology, can give spiritual significance to the ideas of sacrifice. The Jewish sacrificial system was superseded in Christianity, and it was also terminated in Judaism by the destruction of the Temple, but the symbol has survived in Christian theology and liturgical practice, because the sacrifices which it represented have been replaced by an individual sacrifice in the death of Jesus. Such a symbol has unifying possibilities. If there is a shared focus of belief and action/response, the symbol unites even if there are variations in the context and manner of its interpretation. In this way the cross has been the international symbol of Christianity.

Christ as the example for Christians to follow is another recurring and unifying element within the New Testament documents. It is demonstrated in the idea of discipleship in Mark's gospel, and developed in the parallel motifs of journeying in Luke–Acts. The disciples follow Jesus who must "accomplish . . . his departure . . . at Jerusalem" (Luke 9.31, 57ff). Likewise the apostles must witness to Jesus "in Jerusalem and in all Judea and Samaria

Christ crowned with thorns, painting by Antonello da Messina (*c.*1430–1479).

and to the end of the earth" (Acts 1.8). Paul can advocate that his Christian converts should imitate him simply because he himself imitates Christ (1 Corinthians 9; Philippians 2, 3, 4).

But while there are unifying elements in these ethical symbols, there were strong differences in degrees of ethical practice and observance among the communities. In this respect the traditions which became "orthodoxy" held the moderate or central ground. Both extreme positions – the wings of ultra-asceticism and of lawlessness – were abandoned in the longer term. This can be seen, for example, when Clement of Alexandria describes the ethical consequences of the Gnostic viewpoints:

> *We may divide all the heresies into two groups.* Either *they teach that one ought to live on the principle that it is a matter of indifference whether one does right or wrong, or they set too ascetic a tone and proclaim the necessity of continence on the ground of opinions which are godless and arise from a hatred of what God has created.*
>
> (*Miscellanies* III, 40)

Understanding of Christ in terms of his death

It is clear that the ethical elements of unity are closely related to, indeed depend upon, theological views about God, Christ, and the world. An important basic element in thinking about Christ, common to many churches, was the emphasis on his suffering and death. This gave rise to various (but related) explanations as to why such suffering was necessary. The more Christians themselves had to suffer for their faith, with the onset of more organized persecution from civic authorities and from Jewish synagogues in the last decades of the first century, the more this suffering was accepted gratefully by them. Christians felt that, in sharing the bitter experiences of Christ's life, they were sharing in the cost of salvation, just as it had been necessary for Christ to identify with human experiences in order to be their saviour. The model of Christ's suffering for the Christian community, and the communal nature of the experiences of humiliation and suffering are both emphasized in 1 Peter. This is a particular meditation on ideas that are widespread in the letters of Paul and in all four gospels.

Understanding of Christ in terms of titles

The pictures of Christ conveyed in the words of the New Testament writings are as varied as the images used by modern artists. The cultural differences between Jew and Greek, or between Roman civil servant and Syrian countryman, can seem as great as between north and south in today's world. It is misguided then to look for elements of unity in the details of these pictures, or to force prototypes such as "Messiah", "Son of God", "Second Adam", "Good Shepherd" into conformity with one another. Each deserves to be understood and appreciated in its own context. But it could be said that Jesus himself is the common denominator, for they are all intended as pictures of him. More than this they are all reverential acknowledgements of his superior status to the mass of humanity, all expressions of obedience to his lordship. Is it then true that another element of unity may have been the recognition of "Jesus as Lord"?

Jesus apparently made a striking impression on those who met him, whether or not they accepted him. Jesus was thought of as a rabbi (teacher), a prophet, perhaps as Jewish Messiah. None of these responses strictly goes beyond human description, yet within one generation Jesus was being described in superhuman terms, and within at the most three generations he was described as one with the Father and God's eternal Word. Thus in Philippians 2, Paul, quoting a hymn, can accord to Christ a place and a rank almost equal to God himself; and in 1 Corinthians 8.6 Paul talks of Christ as the one through whom all things exist, that is, no less than the lord of the universe. This cosmic lordship is even more strongly presented in Colossians and Ephesians, where Christ is agent of creation just as he is agent of redemption. By some extraordinary means, within a generation, a human being is taken to be the agent of creation, God's vice-gerent – if not even more than this.

How did this come about? Was it all implicit in the earliest response and belief, or was there some point in early Christianity at which a massive change occurred? These questions have received various answers. Some say that, when Christianity moved out from the Palestinian/Jewish setting, the Jewish messianic figure (who is strictly a human being) may have been converted into a divine redeemer under Hellenistic influence, because in Greek thought the distinction between divine and human was not sharply made, whereas in Jewish circles this distinction was never compromised. But others say that what happened in Christianity was a development, an unfolding of the implications of what the first eyewitnesses saw in Jesus. This development was predetermined and simply a matter of translation, of saying similar things in different words. There was no dramatic turn, no sudden evolution of a new species.

We can test this by asking what the first Christians are likely to have meant when they said "Jesus is Lord." Does the Greek Christian mean by "Lord" what the Jewish Christian means by "Messiah"? And if it is an equation, is this equation reversible? Even if Jews are more concerned with function and action, and Greeks with the status and nature of things, could one say that ultimately these areas are compatible and complimentary? The word "Lord" is a courtesy title in the Greek world, a polite "Sir" used of any person with authority. In the Roman Empire, when such a title was used of the emperor himself, it also involved the attribution of divine status, because this was implicit in the context of worshipping the emperor. It was also used

A head identified as Christ's – by the Chi-Rho symbol behind it – in a roundel of a Roman mosaic floor at Hinton St. Mary, Dorset. Although this could be an early picture of Christ, its situation on the floor seems irreverent (on a level with pagan images).

as a reverential title for the "guru" or master of a worshipper/initiate in a mystery religion. In the Greek-speaking world there was already a range of meaning, in the spectrum from human to divine, but in any case "Lord" is the antithesis of "slave" or "servant", and indicates an attitude of submission.

In the Greek translation of the Old Testament (the Septuagint), "Lord" is used in place of the name of God (the sacred TETRAGRAMMATON is vocalized as "*adhonai*"). Greek-speaking Christians using the Septuagint were making a theological point ("Jesus is identical with God") which Aramaic-speaking Christians would never have expressed aloud. Yet in Hebrew and Aramaic the words for "lord" could also be used of human lords and masters. It would have been a natural word for Jesus' disciples to use of him, because he impressed them and they respected him as teacher.

It is therefore very difficult to discover with precision what the word "Lord" means in any particular instance. Much depends on the context. It covers the spectrum from human to divine and relates to matters of function ("being in charge") and matters of status ("absolute being"). For a group of people like the Christians, with a strong future hope, there is a merging of present observable realities and future visionary expectations. Christ who will come as judge at the end of time must already have the implicit status of "judge", even in a context in which God alone judges. It might well be said that the inherent flexibility – and actual ambiguity – of the word "Lord" accounts for the frequency of its use, across the range of different Christian communities.

Understanding of Christ in terms of event and story

The common elements of the apostolic preaching about Christ may also have formed a unifying basis of belief. C. H. Dodd compared Pauline preaching (in Romans, 1 Corinthians, Galatians, 1 Thessalonians) with the speeches of Acts (in chapters 2, 3, 4, 5, 10, and 13), and compiled a statement in Pauline terms of the main elements which this church-preaching has in common, set out as follows:

* The prophecies are fulfilled, and the new age is inaugurated by the coming of Christ.
* He was born of Davidic descent.
* He died according to the scriptural prophecies, to deliver men and women out of the present evil age.
* He was buried.
* He rose on the third day, according to scriptural prophecy.
* He is exalted at the right hand of God, as Son of God and Lord of the living and the dead.
* He will come again as Judge and Saviour of men and women.[6]

This summary (and even more the fully documented table) of common elements of preaching is very impressive. But essentially it represents an approach to the evidence from the wrong direction. Such a Pauline summary cannot be read out of any one text from a letter of Paul. It is essentially a synthesis, an attempt to produce coherence and structure out of the emotional reactions and thoughts of the moment produced by a highly original but unsystematic theologian.

Even more significantly, the evidence of the speeches in Acts cannot be regarded simply as the direct record of the apostles' words at the time. It is not even a typical deposit of the early teaching of the Jerusalem church to which Luke had access. Like the speeches of emperors in the historical writings of Tacitus, and like the beginning of the gospel of Luke, this material is the work of a skilled literary craftsman, conveying what he wanted to say in the way he thought it should be said. The Acts preaching is a direct reflection of Lucan theology, but with the perspective of age. It was important to Luke to convey the "traditional" character of preaching and its relationship to Old Testament themes, so that his two-volume work should represent the whole sweep of the history of salvation.

Therefore the compilation of apostolic preaching is not a summary of basic elements, the common denominators of Christian preaching. Instead it is a later consensus, representing the process of harmonizing and desire for unification towards the end of the first century.

Understanding of Christ in terms of future hope

One final element of unity that can be perceived in the early understanding of Christ is the future hope. This can be focussed in the belief that Christ will come again on earth, but this time in triumph rather than in humility, as the all-powerful judge rather than the representative suffering human being. Such future projections are vulnerable to a variety of misunderstandings and reinterpretations, as the evidence of the Thessalonian correspondence shows. For some Christians, the promises of a direct and renewed perception of Christ seemed to have been fulfilled already (at least in part) in the excitement of their new existence as a religious community. For others the crises and local antagonisms made them look for a different order of existence and a complete resolution of their problems. There is a common denominator here, the future dimension of prophecies fulfilled in Christ, the conviction that "the best is yet to be". The Christian position is that, in every crisis and discussion about what still divides, the vision of the Kingdom to come is the overriding consideration.

Ideas about the church

With such an understanding of Christ, looking to the future, it is scarcely surprising that the Christian community generally saw itself as "the community of the last days". In their very existence, however traumatic, they saw a proof of the effect of past events and a guarantee of the future resolution of the world's crises. As a group they existed in the interim, the "in-between times" which linked past and future. It was their duty to face

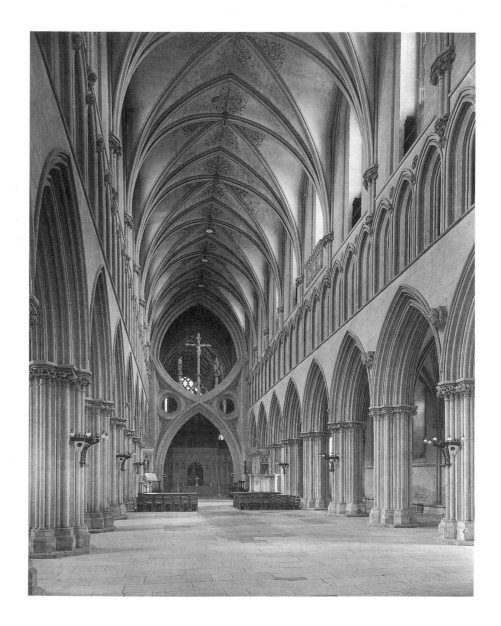

Wells Cathedral, the nave looking east through the striking double-inverted arch topped by a modern rood (crucifixion scene).

the future with confidence, since this was their role in God's purposes. Rudolf Bultmann expressed this unifying element of the early churches in this way:

> *The earliest church presents itself as an eschatological sect within Judaism, distinguished from other sects and trends . . . especially by the fact that it is conscious of being already the called and chosen Congregation of the end of days. Jesus' having come was itself the decisive event through which God called his Congregation [Church].*[7]

Jesus' band of followers and disciples is called the "church" (those who are called and who congregate) in the synoptic gospel tradition in Matthew 16.18f. Here Peter, as leader-to-be, possesses the keys of the Kingdom of Heaven. In other words the congregation forms the porch or the entrance way of God's reign. The church is, according to Luke 12.32, the "little flock" to whom God will give his Kingdom. In fulfilment of eschatological hopes the church members call themselves "the chosen", "the elect", "the saints", "the little ones", and "the poor". Baptism to mark membership, common meals to celebrate fellowship, and consciousness of the presence and power of the Spirit as the gift of the last days, are all taken as signs of the eschatological nature of this congregation. The context is clearly indicated in the unsophisticated language of the prayer in *The Didache*:

> *Remember, Lord, thy church, to deliver it from all evil and to make it perfect in thy love, and gather it together in its holiness from the four winds to thy kingdom which thou has prepared for it. For thine is the power and the glory for ever. Let grace come and let this world pass away. Hosannah to the God of David. If any man be holy, let him come! if any man be not, let him repent: Maranatha [Our Lord! Come!], Amen.* (10.5–6)

The earliest small group of Christians gathered in one place could also naturally call itself "God's household" when the group met in a private house, with the owner of that house frequently seen as "patron" and the apostolic missionary, who called the group together, regarding himself as God's "steward". Each group had its own characteristics and sense of identity. Problems arose when separate groups needed to identify with one another, or when sectarian groups (defined negatively within Judaism) launched out into the world on their own and needed to construct their own positive identity.

One is forced to conclude from the New Testament that the overwhelming evidence is for diversity of outlook, separate developments, and independent identities. Does it necessarily follow that the only model the Bible supplies is then for a loose federation of churches, a pattern for coexistence between independent entities? Certainly by fostering a lively appreciation and acceptance of diversity – if this recognition is accompanied by tolerance and respect for one another's structures and beliefs – it is possible to avoid the dangers of confrontation and schism.

There is New Testament evidence, particularly in the later Pauline traditions, the Pastoral Epistles, and the so-called "Catholic" writings, of attempts to tie churches together in bonds of unity. Unity can be built from the ground-floor. If a local church did not feel threatened in its existence it could be encouraged to join in co-operative activities and discussions. But it is a very different thing if unity is imposed from above by the use of imperialist or universal models of the larger church. There is some New Testament evidence for attempts of the latter kind. The deliberate harmonizing of beliefs and structures, the indications of what has been called "early catholicism", and inter-church reconciliations of traditions and practices, are to be found, for example, in Acts and 1 Peter. There appears to be a similar motivation both here and in the much more extensive attempts to define and impose "orthodoxy" in the second century. The terrors of disunity, negative reactions to the evidence of human differences, have perpetuated managerial solutions of an aggressive and judgemental kind.

The unifying factor of symbols which can embrace and enable diversity by virtue of the shared symbol is also to be found in thinking by and about the early churches. The most telling symbol was that of the twelve apostles. In prophetic fulfilment of Old Testament tradition, these twelve figures were the eschatological leaders of the community of the last days. The leaders of the tribes of Israel gave fair scope for diversity, but later in the New Testament they came to represent the more "imperialist" and exclusivist attitudes of theological control over the universal church. Only upon these foundations could the walls of the true church be built. The collegiate authority of the apostles was then concentrated in one place. This same attitude is displayed by different groups in The Revelation of John and in Ephesians:

> *And in the Spirit he carried me away to a great, high mountain, and showed me the holy city Jerusalem coming down out of heaven from God ... It had a great, high wall, with twelve gates, and at the gates twelve angels, and on the gates the names of the twelve tribes of the sons of Israel were inscribed ... And the wall of the city had twelve foundations, and on them the twelve names of the twelve apostles of the Lamb.* (Revelation 21.10–14)

> *So then you are no longer strangers and sojourners but you are fellow citizens with the saints and members of the household of God, built upon the foundation of the apostles and prophets, Christ Jesus himself being the cornerstone, in whom the whole structure is joined together and grows into a holy temple in the Lord; in whom you also are built into it for a dwelling place of God in the Spirit.* (Ephesians 2.19–22)

Boundaries of belief and practice

Ultimately "unity" seems to be a matter of some groups and their traditions being in the ascendancy, and imposing their will on others who can be coerced, or condemning those who cannot. The major traditions in the New Testament, such as those of Paul, Peter and John, grew in strength, although they might have been confined to certain regions and had their periods of opposition or neglect and relative obscurity. The major church centres, such as Jerusalem at the beginning, Rome, Ephesus, Antioch, and Alexandria, all had a political importance. Traditions were advanced substantially because of strong centres of support in a locality. The strongest base for harmony and ECUMENISM was created by a positive relationship between Pauline and Petrine traditions. The Acts of the Apostles and 1 Peter both demonstrate that the days of confrontation between Peter and Paul were past, or at least passing.

Eventually in the second century unity was imposed and many groups fell away. The arguments to justify the inclusion of a particular writing, or theological tenet, within the scope of orthodoxy were intense and fraught. The main procedures were: the issue of a canon of scripture, the formulation of doctrinal statements, and the establishment of church councils. By these means the church parties in the ascendant could legislate for the beliefs and practices of the "universal" church.

The canon of the New Testament

Some early Christian writings came to be seen as expressing the mind of Christianity, while others remained marginal or were refused authoritative status. The process of determining what should be regarded as authoritative expressions of the faith and what should be rejected extended over the first five centuries of the Christian era, Christian East and Christian West, and beyond the bounds of the Roman Empire at least as far as Edessa.

It is possible to give a summary indication of the pressures to fix the limits of authoritative Christian writings. Essentially there were moves to preserve the structure of church authority that was establishing itself. The first influence has already been discussed in Chapter 7 on the Gnostic gospels. Gnosticism as a movement within Christianity might well have destroyed the authority of the church. It represented claims to private and esoteric

St. Catherine's monastery, Sinai.

sources of revelation by separatist groups with exclusive tendencies. It was the manner of presentation as secret knowledge, as much as or more than the idea that a small religious group possessed its own religious text or revelation, which set the Gnostics apart from those other groups in Christianity who felt themselves more representative of the church at large. Such claims to private sources and private uses of language caused other Christians to state more clearly their own beliefs. In the face of the Gnostic use of religious language there was a new precision in defining doctrines by credal statements, and delimiting the approved authority of religious books by the idea of the canon.

The second influence was Marcion, the son of the bishop of Sinope. Around 144 CE he was expelled from the church at Rome. It was his policy to have nothing to do with those religious writings which did not agree with his own theories. The Old Testament (which for many early Christians was the first or only Bible they had) was rejected by Marcion as unacceptable because of its apparent internal contradictions and opposition to Christian revelation. Any passages in the New Testament documents which echoed the Old Testament (such as the infancy stories in Luke's gospel) were also rejected. Marcion's practice of ideological discrimination and censorship taken to extremes left only a truncated form of Luke and the letters of Paul.

The third influence was a second-century movement called Montanism, which emphasized prophecy and continuing inspiration within the church. There could be no accepting that the first-century gospels constituted any final form of revelation. Montanus and his two female acolytes, in the remote mountain village of Pepuza in Phrygia, claimed that they were now receiving messages to be regarded as the ultimate communication of prophecy. Montanus spoke with authority, regarding himself as Father, Son, and Spirit in person. Montanism illustrated for the remainder of the church the real dangers in allowing claims of direct and private revelations and access to the personal presence of God. There was obviously a direct clash with those forms of church authority which were seeking to establish themselves. The emphasis on prophecy in Montanism stressed the impact of the future in revolutionary terms. No authoritative establishment could afford to be this open to the future, and so the idea of final received revelation was embodied in the canon.

The formulation of doctrinal statements

The formulation of doctrine was not necessarily a retrograde step, and the Greek language in which it was expressed should not be compared unfavourably with Hebrew or the Aramaic of Jesus. It is true that the sophistication and philosophical associations of the Greek language made it particularly suitable for articulating ideas, so the basis of doctrinal formulation is Greek.

If Hebrew stands (in this analogy) for the religious traditions of the past, apparently unreachable on the other side of the language barrier, then Greek may seem to stand for the new language that is sought to communicate with

The Creed of the Council of Nicaea

We believe in one God, the Father almighty, maker of all things visible and invisible; And in one Lord Jesus Christ, the Son of God, begotten from the Father, only-begotten, that is, from the substance of the Father, God from God, light from light, true God from true God, begotten not made, of one substance with the Father, through Whom all things came into being, things in heaven and things on earth, Who because of us men and because of our salvation came down and became incarnate, becoming man, suffered and rose again on the third day, ascended to the heavens, and will come to judge the living and the dead; And in the Holy Spirit. But as for those who say, There was when He was not, and, Before being born He was not, and that He came into existence out of nothing, or who assert that the Son of God is of a different hypostasis or substance, or is created, or is subject to alteration or change – these the Catholic Church anathematizes.

the contemporary world. For Greek is a living language of great flexibility. It is an international language, in touch with a wide range of secular and religious culture, which seems to offer the great advantage of ease of communication. It is also an intellectual language, capable of great refinement, and of using symbolism of great power and depth. The wider opportunities of the Greek world are well indicated in these definitions of Hellenization: "the imposition of Greek culture, the collapse of the Greek city-states and their replacement by a cosmopolis [a world-city], and the breakdown of traditional religions and their incorporation in religious forms and cults capable of universal vision"; "a large groundswell in the rising tide of human destiny, when for the first time this unfolding process, due to sufficient density of population and a sufficiently universal vision of humanity, began to be perceived".

This is the attraction of Greek for the mission of the church that would be universal, and for the precise classification of tenets of belief.

The need for church councils

Many of the major formulations of Christian faith, such as the creed of Nicea, were officially approved at councils of church officials who claimed to represent in some way the larger or the universal church. The credal formulae were constructed for all sorts of church purposes and practical requirements: some were declarations of faith at baptism, or summaries of the essential belief of the church for regular reaffirmation; others were criteria by which outsiders could be judged or "heretics" excluded. However, when such creeds were received and approved by a church council, they were endorsed with the authority of the wider church institution. The primary authority of scripture was reinforced in subsequent generations both by the authority vested in the traditional structures of the universal church, and by the authority of the creeds, which combined the living authority of the church gathered for worship and sacraments with the official approval of the bishops and theologians of the church met for councils on doctrinal issues.

The authority vested in the church councils was a consequence of the authority claimed in the New Testament for the apostles: the twelve disciples traditionally chosen by Jesus himself as the leaders of the congregation of the last days, together with others who were substitutes like Matthias, or recipients of direct revelation like Paul. The authority of the twelve was used as a theological justification by the "orthodox" – probably also as a weapon against other claimants such as Paul. In subsequent generations, when the original apostles and eyewitnesses are no more, some mechanism is needed to preserve for the church such authority as those original disciples of Jesus represented. The nearest equivalent to an apostolic college was the heads of all the churches meeting in council. So the justification of an apostolic succession was employed through the centuries to confer authority on doctrinal and practical issues, down to the Lambeth Conference of Anglican bishops in modern times.

Gatherings of bishops and church leaders are to a greater or lesser extent representative of the church at large. They may believe that they are fully representative of the world-wide church by virtue of a geographical spread or of an unbroken succession from the apostles. In modern times the combination of democracy and theology recognizes its limitations, but it was not always so honestly regarded. The authority of a church council may be further reinforced by a claim to theological supremacy on the part of a particular church leader. This was the case in the Acts of the Apostles with the Council of Jerusalem and the leadership of the Jerusalem apostles, particularly James. There were also subsequently the beginnings of the claim to leadership by Rome as the primary see, or of the succession to Peter as leader of the disciples of Jesus. This claim to primacy has been strongly maintained through the centuries by the Roman Catholic church, which cites the twin authorities of scripture and tradition in support of its own direct authority.

Meetings of the leaders of the church, with authority to take decisions and pronounce doctrinally on behalf of the universal church, were frequently needed in the early centuries of controversy. In the interests of church unity and order they were called upon to decide on issues of doctrine and practice. So, for example, a heretic like Arius was condemned, or the date on which Easter should be celebrated was decided. The frequency – and regularity – of church councils was itself approved, in the decree of the Council of Constance in 1417:

> *for thereby the tangle, the thorns and thistles of heresy, error and schism, are uprooted, distortions corrected, what is inimical to order reformed and the Lord's vineyard brought to its abundant harvest, whereas the neglect of this remedy leads to the spread and nourishment of all these evils we have mentioned, as the memory of the recent past and the contemplation of the present makes abundantly clear.*

In short, there is a lot of work to be done if a world-wide church is to keep itself in order, in accordance with the apostolic authority delegated to it. In modern times, despite the experience of Vatican I and II in the Roman Catholic Church, and the Lambeth Conferences in the Anglican Church, there is a widespread distrust and dislike of decisive meetings and councils. Listening, and the exchange of views, is one thing, telling other people what to do is something else.

Conclusion

This chapter began with a quotation from Hatch, who suggested that Christianity, from pure and simple origins in the New Testament world, deteriorated into complexity on contact with Hellenistic thought. Such charges of an arrogant intellectualization of religion are not uncommonly levelled at theologians and teachers in our own day. In truth it is a long way from the high-flown language of the Councils of the Church to the type of

The domes of the Church of the Holy Sepulchre, Jerusalem in relation to the modern city skyline.

The Heavenly Jerusalem, from the 14th century CE Angers tapestry illustrating the Book of Revelation (21.1–5).

language needed to transmit Christ's message intelligibly to Third World peasants (e.g. the so-called water-buffalo theology). Some people would see such intellectualization of the gospel as has occurred as a deterioration from a pure norm.

Parallel kinds of criticism are made of the growth of the church and its structures, where the intention was to enshrine the gospel and to preserve it. Many students past and present must have toiled on essays set on the famous dictum of Alfred Loisy, the French Modernist theologian: "Jesus proclaimed the coming of the Kingdom and what came was the Church". What relationship does an intricately hierarchical and bureaucratic organization bear to a Galilean preacher and a handful of followers? Cardinal Newman strove to legitimize this relationship by comparing the development of the later church to the growth of the oak-tree from the acorn; others might see a sociologically inevitable emergence of structures for the group; others again the guidance of the Holy Spirit to find the right form for the age.

There are benefits and drawbacks in ritualizing practice and systematizing structures in any religion. It could be said that in Judaism there were brilliant

The pastoral care of a Catholic priest in a Latin-American shanty-town.

The New Jerusalem
(Revelation 21) from
the German 12th
century CE
commentary on the
Apocalypse by Haimo
of Auxerre.

mystics, but no structure for their teachings, and so Jewish mysticism died
away. A similar thing happened to many of the Gnostics, who refused any
structure beyond the system of their beliefs. On the other hand the Christian
churches have tended to hold on determinedly to their structural organization, while at the same time losing much of their vitality. There is a balance to
be achieved between structure and creativity; both are needed for religious
life.

It will have become apparent that the New Testament age cannot be
regarded as any kind of golden age, in which all was basic, simple, normative, united, and agreed. As soon as the "Jesus-Event" had happened –
indeed, while it was in process – different minds and personalities saw,
assessed, evaluated, compared with current expectations, and interpreted
the significance, differently from one another.

Thus there was no golden age from which deterioration could follow. This
is not to lament the lack of original unity, but rather to suggest some reasons
for the diversity. The central events of Christian doctrine – Incarnation,
Passion, Crucifixion, Resurrection, and Ascension – are too complex for one
single view to prevail. Thus tribute is paid to the richness of the gospel
tradition. It is part of the Christian assertion that God gives men freedom.
Human beings are not programmed computers or blind automata. Within
our modern pluralism of society and religion, human freedom must include

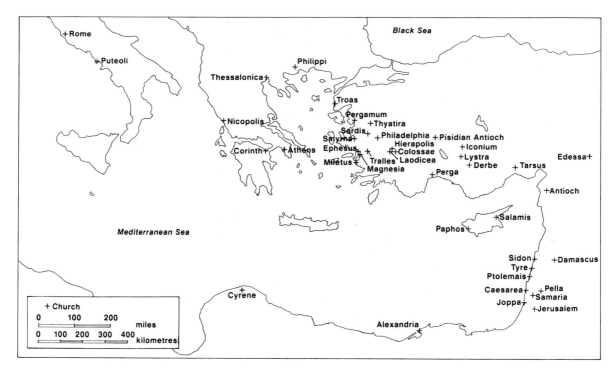

Map showing locations with Church markers (+):

Rome, Puteoli, Philippi, Thessalonica, Troas, Pergamum, Thyatira, Nicopolis, Sardis, Smyrna, Philadelphia, Pisidian Antioch, Hierapilis, Iconium, Corinth, Athens, Ephesus, Colossae, Lystra, Edessa, Miletus, Tralles, Laodicea, Derbe, Tarsus, Magnesia, Perga, Antioch, Salamis, Paphos, Sidon, Damascus, Tyre, Ptolemais, Caesarea, Pella, Cyrene, Joppa, Samaria, Jerusalem, Alexandria.

Black Sea, Mediterranean Sea.

+ Church
0   100   200   miles
0 100 200 300 400 kilometres

MAP 6 Early christian churches established in the 1st century CE.

the right to disagree. Such intellectual freedom must not be abused; it must be seen in a positive and constructive way, and disagreement contained in an atmosphere of mutual love and trust. It does mean, however, that there must be room to tolerate the richness of the gifts brought by a John and a Paul, within the larger Christian church.

The evidence is that, from the start, the important questions of Jesus' identity and authority were answered differently. This difference can be viewed as a positive good for Christian individuals and communities. Faith in Jesus remained central, even if variously interpreted. The consequences of faith, in terms of relationship both to other believers and to the world outside the church, could also be variously defined. It may also be that we have come to see the Christian "hero" figures like Peter and Paul in a different light – less of the stained-glass halo image, more of the hard-pressed church leader deciding important theological questions on the run – sometimes with more success than others.

We have seen that the New Testament writers were not merely scribes writing at divine dictation. Authors of varying backgrounds and attainments were inspired to address the different needs and problems in communities distinguished by social and geographical conditions. There are some signs of underlying unity and continuity, but the influential cultural conditions differed dramatically so that, in addressing these local needs and problems, the writers took the Christian tradition as they had received it, and reinterpreted it for their own day and concern.

Notes

CHAPTER 1
The Marcan prototype

1 *Acts* 12.12, 25; 13.5, 13; 15.37, 39; *Colossians* 4.10; *2 Timothy* 4.11; *Philemon* 24; *1 Peter* 5.13.
2 W. Wrede, *The Messianic Secret*, J.C.G. Greig, 1971. James Clarke, Cambridge/London, p. 131.
3 Frank Kermode, *The Genesis of Secrecy; On the Interpretation of Narrative*, 1979. Harvard, pp. 114, 139.
4 Alan Richardson, *The Miracle Stories of the Gospels*, 1941. SCM Press, London, p. 92.
5 Theodore J. Weeden, Sr, *Mark – Traditions in Conflict*, 1971. Fortress Press, Philadelphia, pp. 162f.
6 C.H. Dodd, *The Parables of the Kingdom*, 1961 (1935). James Nisbet, Fontana Edition, p. 15.
7 C.K. Barrett, *The Holy Spirit and the Gospel Tradition*, 1966 (1947). SPCK, London, p. 125.
8 G.H. Boobyer, "The Eucharistic Interpretation of the Miracles of the Loaves in St. Mark's Gospel", *Journal of Theological Studies* n.s. 3 (1952), p. 171.
9 Ernest Best, *Following Jesus*, 1981. JSNT Supplement 4, JSOT Press, Sheffield, p. 243.
10 R.P. Martin, "A Gospel in Search of a Life-Setting", *Expository Times* 80 (1968–9), pp. 361–4.
11 Klaus Wengst, *Pax Romana and the Peace of Jesus Christ*, 1987. E.T. John Bowden. SCM Press, London, p. 196, n. 14.

CHAPTER 2
Paul and his churches

1 John Chrysostom, quoted from Hubert Richards, *St Paul and his Epistles, a New Introduction*, 1979. Darton Longman and Todd, London.
2 Walter J. Hollenweger, *Conflict in Corinth* 1982. Paulist Press, New York/Ramsey.
3 B. Reicke, *The New Testament Era*, 1969. A & C Black, London, p. 193.
4 Edwin A. Judge, "St Paul and Classical Society", *Jahrbuch für Antike und Christentum 15*, 1972, pp. 20, 25.
5 C.H. Dodd, commentary on *Romans* (Moffatt Series), 1932. Hodder and Stoughton, London.
6 Compare G. Theissen, *The Shadow of the Galilean*, 1987. SCM Press, London, Chapter 5.
7 Klaus Wengst, *Pax Romana and the Peace of Jesus Christ*, 1987. SCM Press, London.
8 See G. Theissen, *The Social Setting of Pauline Christianity*, 1982. T. & T. Clark, Edinburgh; and Wayne Meeks, *The First Urban Christians: The Social World of the Apostle Paul*, 1983. Yale University Press, New Haven.
9 Ronald F. Hock, *The Social Context of Paul's Ministry (Tentmaking and Apostleship)*, 1980. Fortress Press, Philadelphia.
10 Stephen Barton, "Paul and the Cross: A Sociological Approach", *Theology 85* (January 1982), pp. 14ff.

11 R. Bultmann, *Theology of the New Testament*, 1952. SCM Press, London, vol. 1, p. 293.
12 Bengt Holmberg, *Paul and Power – The Structure of Authority in the Primitive Church as Reflected in the Pauline Epistles*, 1978. Fortress Press, Philadelphia, p. 56.
13 Edwin A. Judge, *The Social Pattern of Christian Groups in the First Century*, 1960. London, p. 60.
14 Wayne Meeks, "Since then you would need to go out of the world: Group Boundaries in Pauline Christianity" in T. Ryan (editor), *Critical History and Biblical Faith: New Testament Perspectives*, 1979. Villanova, Pennsylvania, pp. 1–23.
15 C.K. Barrett, *Epistle to the Romans* (Black New Testament Commentaries), 1962. A. & C. Black, London, p. 78.
16 W. Neil, *The Epistles of Paul to the Thessalonians* (Moffatt New Testament Commentary Series), 1950. Hodder and Stoughton, London, p. 196.
17 Samuel Laeuchli, "Prolegomenon to a structural analysis of ancient Christian views of Salvation" in D.F. Winslow (editor), *Disciplina Nostra*, 1979. Philadelphia, p. 148.
18 Ernst Troeltsch, *The Social Teaching of the Christian Churches*, 1931. London/New York, vol. 1, p. 78.

CHAPTER 3
Luke–Acts: the church and the world

1 Paul W. Walaskay, *And So We came to Rome – the Political Perspective of St. Luke*, 1983. CUP, Cambridge.
2 J.A. Bengel, *Gnomon Novi Testamenti* (first published in Latin in 1742), on Acts 28.31.
3 G. Miles and G. Trompf, "Luke and Antiphon: the Theology of Acts 27–28 in the Light of Pagan Beliefs about Divine Retribution, Pollution and Shipwreck", *HTR 69*, 1967, p. 265.
4 Tessa Rajak, *Josephus, the Historian and his Society*, 1983. Duckworth, London, p. 1.
5 Paul S. Minear, *To Heal and To Reveal – The Prophetic Vocation according to Luke*, 1976. Seabury Press, New York, pp. 139, 145–6.
6 See Paul W. Walaskay, *And so we came to Rome – the Political Perspectives of St. Luke*, 1983. CUP, Cambridge, p. 14.
7 Paul W. Walaskay (as note 6) pp. 27f.
8 Paul W. Walaskay (as note 6) p. 14.
9 Robert Maddox, *The Purpose of Luke–Acts*, 1982. T. & T. Clark, Edinburgh, pp. 184f.
10 Robert F. O'Toole SJ, "Luke's Position on Politics and Society in Luke–Acts", in R.J. Cassidy and P.J. Scharper (editors), *Political Issues in Luke–Acts*, 1983. Orbis, New York, p. 8.
11 C.K. Barrett, *Luke the Historian in Recent Study*, 1961. Epworth, London, p. 63.
12 J.M. Creed, *The Gospel according to St. Luke*, 1953. Macmillan, London, p. lxxii.

13 Birger Gerhardsson, *The Good Samaritan – The Good Shepherd?*, 1958. Coniectanea Neotestamentica, Lund/Copenhagen.

14 Raymond E. Brown, *The Birth of the Messiah*, 1977. G. Chapman, London. This is the most comprehensive parallel treatment and commentary.

15 The classic argument for the failure of Acts to understand Paul is: P. Vielhauer, "On the 'Paulinism' of Acts" in L.E. Keck and J.L. Martyn (editors), *Studies in Luke–Acts*, 1968. SPCK, London, pp. 33–50.

16 B. Witherington III, "On the Road with Mary Magdalene, Joanna, Susanna, and Other Disciples – Luke 8.1–3", *ZNW* 70, 1979, p. 244. See also by the same author *Women in the Ministry of Jesus: A Study of Jesus' Attitudes to Women and their Roles as Reflected in his Early Life*. CUP, Cambridge.

CHAPTER 4
The Matthean Church and Judaism

1 Angela Tilby, "Bearing Witness" in *The Way Supplement – Lay Christians: A Variety of Gifts* 60, Autumn 1987, pp. 60–61.

2 Angela Tilby, "Bearing Witness" in *The Way Supplement – Lay Christians: A Variety of Gifts* 60, Autumn 1987, pp. 60–61.

3 Because of the authority of the Pentateuch, an imitation of its five-fold pattern became quite customary in the structuring of for example the book of Psalms, the book of the five scrolls (*Megilloth*: Ruth, Song of Songs, Ecclesiastes, Lamentations, Esther), the history of the Maccabees written by Jason of Cyrene (2 Maccabees 2.23), 1 Enoch, the original *Perekim* that make up *Pirke Aboth*, and Papias' *Expositions of the Lord's Oracles* (perhaps modelled on Matthew). If there are formal parallels of structure between the Pentateuch and Matthew there are obviously differences in content.

4 Benediction 12, as in C.K. Barrett, *The New Testament Background, Selected Documents*. SPCK, London. Translation by F. Gavin.

5 Douglas R.A. Hare, *The Theme of Jewish Persecution of Christians in the Gospel according to St. Matthew*, 1967. CUP, Cambridge, p. 105.

6 John P. Meier in R.E. Brown and J.P. Meier, *Antioch and Rome – New Testament Cradles of Catholic Christianity*, 1983. G. Chapman, London, p. 72.

7 Douglas R.A. Hare, *The Theme of Jewish Persecution of Christians in the Gospel according to St. Matthew*, 1967. CUP, Cambridge, p. 105.

8 Millar Burrows, *The Dead Sea Scrolls*, 1956. London, p. 248.

9 O. Lamar Cope, *Matthew – A Scribe Trained for the Kingdom of Heaven* (CBQ Monographs 5), 1976. CBQ, Washington, p. 10 and n. 36.

10 K. Tagawa, "People and Community in the Gospel of Matthew", *NTS* 16, 1970, p. 151.

11 VII/3 79.19–30; 71.14f.; 75.15ff.; 83.12ff. Schweizer quotes from the German translation of the Berlin group on Coptic–Gnostic writing. In some respects this does not agree with the translation in James M. Robinson (editor), *The Nag Hammadi Library in English*, 1977. E.J. Brill, Leiden. For more detail see Eduard Schweizer,

"Matthew's Church" in G.N. Stanton (editor), *The Interpretation of Matthew*, 1983. SPCK/Fortress Press, London, pp. 143–5. Compare G.N. Stanton on "5 Ezra and Matthean Christianity in the Second Century", *JTS* 28, 1977, pp. 67–83.

12 Raymond E. Brown, *The Birth of the Messiah*, 1977. G. Chapman, London.

13 T.S. Eliot, "The Journey of the Magi".

14 See John M. Court, "Right and Left: The Implications for Matthew 25.31–46", *NTS* 31, 1985, pp. 223–233.

CHAPTER 5
John and the Community Apart

1 Wayne Meeks, "The Man from Heaven in Johannine Sectarianism", *JBL* 91, 1972, p. 70.

2 Other external evidence was used unsuccessfully to suggest that the apostle John was martyred too early on to have written a gospel.

3 John A.T. Robinson, *Redating the New Testament*, 1976. SCM Press, London, chapter IX.

4 See Culpepper in Bibliography.

5 Wayne Meeks, *op. cit.*

6 Such a neat assembly of events has indeed led some people to question whether the Resurrection was really necessary for John, but the neatness of the system is betrayed by the puzzle which Christ's remark to Mary Magdalene represents in the middle of a Resurrection narrative.

7 T. Forestell, cited in Brown's *Johannine Epistles* commentary, p. 79.

8 Curiously although the Day of the Lord was a piece of symbolism that John might well have exploited in connection with Tabernacles, given their intimate connection in Zechariah 9–14, he does not appear to have done so. Perhaps this was because the ideas Zechariah suggested unfortunately fitted better the Palm Sunday Entry and the Cleansing of the Temple, both of which belong to Passover.

9 The offence of the reality of the Incarnation, and the role of the death of Jesus, also have to be borne in mind here in a more widely based exegesis of the passage.

10 Quoted by J.A.T. Robinson in "Priority", p. 74 (but see the discussion too). "For the apostates let there be no hope. And let the arrogant government be speedily uprooted in our days. Let the nosrim and the minim (i.e. the Nazarenes = Christians and the heretics) be destroyed in a moment. And let them be blotted out of the Book of Life and be not inscribed together with the righteous. Blessed art thou, O Lord, who humblest the arrogant." See also p. 196 above.

11 R.E. Brown, *Commentary on the Gospel*, vol. 2, Appendix V.

12 The Greek word is *hilasmos*. For fuller discussions of this word, refer to the commentaries.

13 B.H. Streeter, *The Primitive Church*, 1929. Macmillan, London.

14 E. Kasemann, "Ketzer und Zeuge: zum johanneischen Verfanserproblem", *ZTK* 48, 1951, pp. 292–311.

15 R.E. Brown, *The Community of the Beloved Disciple*, 1979. Doubleday, Geoffrey Chapman.

16 Montanism was an apocalyptic, charismatic, and strictly

disciplined movement in the late second century. Centred on Asia Minor (Phrygia), it was led by the prophet Montanus and two prophetesses. It was joined by one church father, Tertullian and condemned by the rest.

17 R.E. Brown, *Commentary on the Gospel*, vol. 2, p. 777.
18 In fact the Elder did create a problem for himself when he later declared, "No-one who abides in him sins", 1J3.6, cp3.8–9, 5.18. He apparently contradicted himelf. Attempts have been made to explain this in terms of the tension all Christians discover in their lives between "I ought not to sin" in principle, and "I sin" in practice. The latter needs a remedy, the former remains the ideal. It may be more significant to see "does not sin" in 3.9, in the context of 3.10, which again seems to limit the sinning to the failure to love the brother.

CHAPTER 6
The other New Testament writings

1 M. Dibelius and H. Conzelmann, *Commentary on the Pastoral Epistles*, 1972. Hermeneia Series, p. 2.
2 J.C. O'Neill, *Expository Times 99*, 1988, p. 204.
3 E. Lohse, *Commentary on Colossians*, 1971. Hermeneia Series, p. 4.
4 E. Lohse, *Commentary on Colossians*, 1971. Hermeneia Series, p. 181.
5 C.K. Barrett, "The Eschatology of the Epistle to the Hebrews" in W.D. Davies and D. Daube (editors), *The Background of the New Testament and its Eschatology*, 1956. CUP, Cambridge.
6 William Manson, *The Epistle to the Hebrews, An Historical and Theological Reconsideration* (1949 Baird Lecture), 1951. Hodder & Stoughton, London, p. 125.
7 M. Dibelius and H. Greeven, *Commentary on the Epistle of James*, 1976. Hermeneia Series, p. 11.
8 For example the links between 1.4 and 5; 1.12 and 13; 1.26 and 27; 2.12 and 13; 3.17 and 18; 5.9 and 12; 5.13, 16 and 19.
9 *Collected Works*. Berlin 1884, vol. 7, p. 500.
10 Compare Massey H. Shepherd, *Journal of Biblical Literature 75*, 1956, pp. 40–51.
11 John H. Elliott, *A Home for the Homeless*, 1982. SCM Press, London, p. 48.
12 Henry Chadwick, *The Early Church* (Pelican History of the Church, I), 1967, pp. 25–6.
13 Judith M. Lieu, "The Social World of the New Testament", *Epworth Review* 14.3, 1987, p. 51.

14 K. Wengst, *Humility: Solidarity of the Humiliated*, 1988. SCM Press, London. He does not recognize this special association of humility and suffering for the "exiles" in *1 Peter*; they are submissive to the way society regards them. Instead Wengst works with a traditional late Pauline view of the church establishment and a forced attitude of condescension.

CHAPTER 7
Gnosticism: the alternative gospel

1 I am grateful to Professor R.McL. Wilson of St. Andrews, Scotland, for this observation.
2 a Estimates of the percentages for each contribution vary from cult to cult (and from scholar to scholar).
  b Should the blank segment be labelled "Redeemer concept from Christianity"? The question is whether Paul and John understood Christ and his work according to an already existing Gnostic Redeemer ideal or whether later Gnostics lifted from Christianity the idea of a divine Helper.

CHAPTER 8
The ground rule

1 The lectures were published after Hatch's death, edited by A.M. Fairburn, London 1890. The Hibbert Trust was founded in 1847 with anti-Trinitarian aims, to recover the simple gospel.
2 Hatch, see note 1, pp. 1, 2.
3 John Biddle, *Confession of Faith touching the Holy Trinity according to the Scripture*, 1648. London, p. 30.
4 This is based on the threefold typology (exilic, mimetic, and covenantal) for interpreting religious differences, to be found in Merold Westphal's *God, Guilt and Death, An Existential Phenomenology of Religion*, 1984. Bloomington, Indiana University Press.
5 Simon Barrington Ward, "Mission" in *A New Dictionary of Christian Theology*, edited by Alan Richardson and John Bowden, 1983. SCM Press, London, p. 374. For the Biblical references, see Jürgen Moltmann, *The Church in the Power of the Spirit*. SCM Press, London, pp. 115ff.
6 Adapted from p. 28 of *The Apostolic Preaching and its Developments*, 1936. Hodder and Stoughton, London.
7 *Theology of the New Testament* I.42f, 1952. SCM Press, London.

Bibliography

INTRODUCTION

Averil Cameron, 'Neither Male nor Female' *Greece and Rome* 27, 1980, pp. 60–68. An excellent journal article on women in the New Testament world.

Anthony T. Hanson, *The Living Utterances of God – The New Testament Exegesis of the Old*, 1983. Darton Longman & Todd, London. On the interpretation of the Old Testament in the New Testament.

John H. Hayes and Carl R. Holladay, *Biblical Exegesis: A Beginner's Handbook* (second edition), 1987. John Knox Press, Atlanta/1988 SCM Press, London. A clear introductory statement of the critical methods used.

Stephen Neill and Tom Wright, *The Interpretation of the New Testament 1861–1986*, 1988. Oxford University Press. A very readable account of the developments in New Testament scholarship since the middle of the last century.

Calvin J. Roetzel, *The World that Shaped the New Testament*, 1985. John Knox Press, Atlanta/1987 SCM Press, London. A brief guide to the background of the New Testament world.

William H. Stephens, *The New Testament World in Pictures*, 1988. Lutterworth Press, Cambridge. A valuable reference work with mostly black and white pictures illustrating the material remains of everyday life in New Testament times.

Charles H. Talbert, *What Is A Gospel?: The Genre of the Canonical Gospels*, 1977. Fortress Press, Philadelphia/1978 SPCK, London. The case for the gospels as Hellenistic biographies was first presented by this book.

Gerd Theissen, *The Shadow of the Galilean: the Quest of the Historical Jesus in Narrative Form*, 1987. SCM Press, London. An easily readable account of the social, political, economic, and religious environment in which Jesus lived.

CHAPTER 1
The Marcan prototype

Ernest Best, *Following Jesus* (Journal for the Study of the New Testament Supplement Series, 4), 1981. JSOT Press, Sheffield. A detailed study of the theme of discipleship (and its social implications) in Mark.

J.L. Houlden, *Backward into Light: The Passion and Resurrection of Jesus according to Matthew and Mark*, 1987. SCM Press, London. A brief but thought-provoking comparison of the Passion narratives of Mark and Matthew.

Howard C. Kee, *Community of the New Age*, 1977. SCM Press, London. A pioneering work on the social setting of Mark's community.

Burton L. Mack, *A Myth of Innocence*, 1988. Fortress Press, Philadelphia. An extensively argued American view of how Mark's gospel could make social sense as a myth of Christian origins.

Ralph P. Martin, *Mark – Evangelist and Theologian*, 1972. Paternoster Press, Exeter. Redaction Criticism, applied to this gospel, has produced this view on the evangelist.

Willi Marxsen, *Mark the Evangelist – Studies on the Redaction History of the Gospel* [German], 1956. Abingdon Press, Nashville 1969. See above.

Dennis E. Nineham, *The Gospel of St Mark* (Pelican Gospel Commentaries), 1963. Penguin Books, Harmondsworth. A classic commentary, the first based on the RSV, the second on the Greek text.

Vincent Taylor, *The Gospel according to St Mark*, 1959. Macmillan, London/St Martin's Press, New York. See above.

William Telford (editor), *The Interpretation of Mark: Issues in Religion and Theology* 7, 1985. Fortress Press, Philadelphia/SPCK, London. An introduction to the recent scholarship on Mark with a selection of classic essays.

CHAPTER 2
Paul and his churches

Günther Bornkamm, *Paul*, 1971. Hodder and Stoughton, London/Harper and Row, New York. Still the best general introduction, with a theological dimension to the critical questions.

W.D. Davies, *Paul and Rabbinic Judaism – Some Rabbinic Elements in Pauline Theology*, 1948. SPCK, London. Paul seen in relation to Judaism – the classic view.

Robert Jewett, *Dating Paul's Life*, 1979. SCM Press, London. The process of critical "detective" work applied to the dates and chronology of Paul's life.

Johannes Munck, *Paul and the Salvation of Mankind*, 1959. SCM Press, London. An exciting reading of Paul which makes sense of his mission strategy in terms of eschatology.

Jerome Murphy O'Connor, *St Paul's Corinth – Texts and Archaeology* (Good News Studies, vol. 6), 1983. Michael Glazier Inc., Wilmington, Delaware. Documents and data which help to make the social world of ancient Corinth come alive.

Calvin J. Roetzel, *The Letters of Paul – Conversations in Context*, 1975. John Knox Press, Atlanta/1983, SCM Press, London. An introduction to Paul's letters and their contexts.

E.P. Sanders, *Paul and Palestinian Judaism – A Comparison of Patterns of Religion*, 1977. SCM Press, London. Paul seen in relation to Judaism – the new look.

Krister Stendahl, *Paul among Jews and Gentiles*, 1977. SCM Press, London. A polemical view – the real Paul contrasted with Western interpretation from Reformation theology.

Francis Watson, *Paul, Judaism and the Gentiles – A Sociological Approach* (SNTS Monographs 56), 1986. CUP, Cambridge. An important sociological treatment of some large issues.

CHAPTER 3
Luke–Acts: the church and the world

Richard J. Cassidy, *Jesus' Politics and Society: A Study of Luke's Gospel,* 1978. Orbis, New York. Essays on political issues.

Richard J. Cassidy and P.J. Scharper (editors), *Political Issues in Luke–Acts,* 1983. Orbis, New York. Essays on political issues.

Hans Conzelmann, *Acts.* Hermeneia series, Fortress Press, Philadelphia. A commentary on the Greek text.

Martin Dibelius, *Studies in the Acts of the Apostles,* 1956. SCM Press, London. A classic work by the pioneer of Form Criticism.

John Drury, *Tradition and Design in Luke's Gospel,* 1976. Darton Longman and Todd, London. A study of Luke's use of Old Testament techniques of history writing.

Philip F. Esler, *Community and Gospel in Luke–Acts: The Social and Political Motivations of Lucan Theology,* 1987. CUP, Cambridge. A substantial sociological study of the mixed community for which Luke wrote.

Ernest Haenchen, *Acts.* Basil Blackwell, Oxford. A commentary on the Greek text.

Howard Marshall, *Luke.* Paternoster Press, Exeter. A commentary on the Greek text.

Johannes Munck, *Acts,* 1967. Anchor Bible, Doubleday, Garden City, New York. Worth considering on the English text.

Jack T. Sanders, *The Jews in Luke–Acts,* 1987. SCM Press, London. An argument for anti-Semitism on the part of Luke.

C.H. Talbert, *Reading Luke – a Literary and Theological Commentary,* 1982. Crossroad, New York. Worth considering on the English text.

David L. Tiede, *Prophecy and History in Luke–Acts,* 1980. Fortress Press, Philadelphia. A view of Luke's community as Jewish-Christians facing an identity crisis after the destruction of the Jerusalem Temple.

CHAPTER 4
The Matthean Church and Judaism

Francis Wright Beare, *The Gospel according to Matthew – A Commentary,* 1981. Basil Blackwell, Oxford.

G. Bornkamm, G. Barth and H.J. Held, *Tradition and Interpretation in Matthew,* 1963. SCM Press, London. The classic work on Redaction Criticism applied to Matthew.

O. Lamar Cope, *Matthew – A Scribe Trained for the Kingdom of Heaven,* 1976. (CBQ Monographs 5). CBQ, Washington. An investigation of the particular methods by which the Old Testament was interpreted in the gospel.

W.D. Davies, *The Sermon on the Mount.* CUP, Cambridge (an accessible account) or more technical: *The Setting of the Sermon on the Mount,* 1964. CUP, Cambridge. Studies of the Sermon on the Mount.

Terence L. Donaldson, *Jesus on the Mountain – a study in Matthean Theology,* 1985. (JSNT Supplement 8.) JSOT Press, Sheffield. A study of the theology of the mountain setting.

Robert H. Gundry, *Matthew – A Commentary on his Literary and Theological Art,* 1982. Eerdmans, Grand Rapids, Michigan.

Jack Dean Kingsbury, *The Parables of Jesus in Matthew 13,* 1969. SPCK, London. *Matthew: Structure, Christology, Kingdom,* 1976. SPCK, London. *Matthew as Story,* 1986. Fortress Press. A range of books on Matthew which reflect developing concerns in scholarship.

Wayne A. Meeks and Robert L. Wilken, *Jews and Christians in Antioch in the First Four Centuries of the Common Era* (S.B.L. Sources for Biblical Study 13), 1978. Scholars Press, Missoula, Montana. A study of the "social world" of Antioch (out of the S.B.L. and A.A.R. working group).

Daniel Patte, *The Gospel according to Matthew – A Structural Commentary on Matthew's Faith,* 1987. Fortress Press. A commentary on structuralist principles.

Graham N. Stanton, *The Interpretation of Matthew* (Issues in Religion and Theology, 3), 1983. SPCK, London/ Fortress Press, Philadelphia. An introduction to the critical issues in Matthew.

Krister Stendahl, *The School of St. Matthew (revised edition).* An investigation of the particular methods by which the Old Testament was interpreted in the gospel.

CHAPTER 5
John and the Community Apart

C.K. Barrett, *The Gospel according to St. John* (2nd edition), 1978. SPCK, London. A weighty and helpful commentary to those who know some Greek.

C.K. Barrett, *The Gospel of John and Judaism,* 1975. SPCK, London. A brief but specialist book needing careful reading.

R.E. Brown, *The Community of the Beloved Disciple,* 1979. Doubleday, Geoffrey Chapman. A fascinating reconstruction of events in John's church to show the eaglets fighting for the nest.

R.E. Brown, *The Gospel according to John,* vols. 1 and 2, 1966 and 1970. Anchor Bible Series, Doubleday (Geoffrey Chapman in England). A lengthy but readable commentary, the advantage is for those who know no Greek.

R.E. Brown, *The Epistles of John,* 1982. Anchor Bible Series, Doubleday. A lengthy but readable commentary, the advantage is for those who know no Greek.

R.A. Culpepper, *The Johannine School,* 1975. S.B.L. Scholars Press. This examines other contemporary "schools" to provide specifications for the Johannine.

E. Earle Ellis, *The World of St. John,* 1984. Eerdmans. A slim, but useful first book on the fourth gospel.

J.L. Houlden, *A Commentary on the Johannine Epistles,* 1973. A. & C. Black. Briefer than R.E. Brown and on the English text.

J.L. Martyn, *Glimpses into the History of the Johannine Community,* 1979. Paulist Press. J.L. Martyn, *History and Theology in the Fourth Gospel,* 1968, revised

1979. Abingdon. These two see the Johannine community embattled. The fourth gospel was written on two levels: the situation Jesus faced portrayed contemporary problems.

J. Painter, *John: Witness and Theologian*, 1975. SPCK. An excellent introductory guide, simply written.

J.A.T. Robinson, *The Priority of John*, 1985. SCM. A fascinating, lengthy, and one-sided examination of John.

S. Smalley, *John – Evangelist and Interpreter*, 1978. Paternoster. A medium-length, rather conservative, but sensible introductory guide.

D. Moody Smith, *Johannine Christianity*, 1984. University of South Carolina Press. A specialist book to be pondered later.

CHAPTER 6
The other New Testament writings

Jude, 2 Peter
Richard J. Bauckham, *Word Biblical Commentary Vol. 50*, 1983. Word Books, Waco, Texas.

Revelation
John M. Court, *Myth and History in the Book of Revelation*, 1979. SPCK, London/John Knox Press, Atlanta.

E. Schüssler Fiorenza, *The Book of Revelation – Justice and Judgement*. Fortress Press, Philadelphia.

Pastoral Epistles
C.K. Barrett, *New Clarendon Commentary*, 1963. OUP, Oxford.

M. Dibelius and H. Conzelmann, *Hermeneia Commentary*, 1972. Fortress Press, Philadelphia.

E.K. Simpson, *Tyndale Press Commentary on Greek text*, 1954.

Colossians
Mark Kiley, *Colossians as Pseudepigraphy*, 1986. JSOT Press, Sheffield.

E. Lohse, *Hermeneia Commentary*, 1971. Fortress Press, Philadelphia.

E. Schweizer, *EKK Commentary*, 1982. SPCK, London.

Ephesians
M. Barth, *Anchor Bible Commentary* (2 volumes), 1974. Doubleday, Garden City, New York.

Hebrews
C.K. Barrett, "The Eschatology of the Epistle to the Hebrews" in W.D. Davies and D. Daube (editors), *The Background of the New Testament and its Eschatology*, 1956. Cambridge.

F.F. Bruce, *New International Commentary*. Eerdmans, Grand Rapids, Michigan.

James Swetnam, *Jesus and Isaac – A Study of the Epistle to the Hebrews in the Light of the Aqedah*, 1981. Rome.

James
J. Adamson, *New International Commentary*, 1976. Eerdmans, Grand Rapids, Michigan.

M. Dibelius and H. Greeven, *Hermeneia Commentary*, 1976. Fortress Press, Philadelphia.

Sophie Laws, *Black New Testament Commentary*, 1980. A. & C. Black, London.

1 Peter
Ernest Best, *New Century Bible*, 1971. Marshall, Morgan and Scott, London.

F.L. Cross, *1 Peter, a Paschal Liturgy*, 1954. Mowbray, London.

John H. Elliott, *A Home for the Homeless*, 1982. SCM Press, London.

J.N.D. Kelly, *Black New Testament Commentary* (1 and 2 Peter and Jude), 1969. A. & C. Black, London.

CHAPTER 7
Gnosticism: the alternative gospel

James M. Robinson (general editor), *The Nag Hammadi Library*, 1977. E.J. Brill, Leiden. For the actual Gnostic scriptures in English.

Kurt Rudolph (translated and edited by R.McL. Wilson), *Gnosis*, 1983. T. & T. Clark, Edinburgh. For the assessment of the earlier pre-Nag Hammadi generation, there are plenty of books which the student may consult, but in later scholarship this book is the most accessible.

Glossary

APOCALYPSE/APOCALYPTIC (literally "the revelation of things hidden"). Something of the divine plan and organization, normally kept hidden from human beings, is revealed in dramatic events. This revelation is further dramatized and described in the special language and symbolism of a type of literature therefore known as apocalyptic. This is a Jewish type of writing of which the Old Testament book of Daniel is the earliest known example. The origins of apocalyptic writing are associated with the decline of Old Testament prophecy. Often the literature of protest and messages of encouragement were encoded for hard-pressed Jews in these visionary writings or apocalypses.

ATONEMENT The reconciliation (or at-one-ment) brought about between God and human beings, after the covenant relationship has been broken by sin and disobedience. In Judaism reconciliation was achieved by the ritual and sacrifices of an annual Day of Atonement. In Christianity atonement is effected by the death of Christ on the cross.

CATECHISM/CATECHETICAL Knowledge of religion expressed in question and answer form used for the instruction of converts and children.

CODEX/pl. CODICES The earliest form of a book in the sense of pages of vellum or papyrus, folded and stitched together. They were used by Christians as early as the second century CE; earlier "books" were written on long rolls, as the Jewish Torah scrolls are to this day.

CYNIC The name (probably derived from their "dog-like", uncouth habits) for a category of popular philosophers who taught as wandering missionaries in the streets. One of the earliest was Diogenes who reputedly taught from a tub. They went out of their way to defy conventions and show contempt for wealth and luxury.

DIATRIBE A constructed literary form of an imaginary dialogue, with objections being raised by an opponent. Diatribe was a technique of argument used in popular Stoic philosophy and often employed in moral teaching.

DOCETIST Someone who doubted the physical reality of Jesus' birth and death. It was claimed that Jesus only seemed (in Greek *dokein* means to seem) to be a human being, but really remained divine all the time.

DUALISM A system which finds two opposing principles in the universe – good and light versus evil and darkness.

ECUMENICAL From the Greek word for the whole inhabited world, used to describe the world-wide church embracing Jews and Gentiles, or Eastern and Western Christianity (as Ecumenical Councils); or in the twentieth century the movement to unite the separated churches (Ecumenism).

ESCHATOLOGICAL This is concerned with the "Last Days", the period leading up to the Last Judgement and the end of this world/end of time.

EUCHARIST From the Greek word for thanksgiving, one of two words used of Jesus' prayer over the bread and wine at the Last Supper (in the Synoptic Gospels and Paul) and also over the bread and fish at the Great Feeding (in all four gospels). The term came to refer to the whole sacrament of Holy Communion.

FORM CRITICISM This concentrates on the *form* or shape in which separate units of teaching or stories of Jesus were originally told – to make them more memorable or applicable to a Christian community setting – within a tradition that was basically oral.

GNOSTICISM An umbrella term given by scholars to a great variety of quasi-religious groups in the first centuries CE who used syncretistic (mixed) myths and rituals that promised ultimate salvation to initiates. One thing they have in common is the idea that to acquire a certain body of knowledge (gnosis) was essential for salvation. It was a matter of knowledge not faith.

THE GREAT CHURCH Terms such as orthodoxy and heresy are very contentious (and anachronistic) in the study of early church history. This euphemism attempts to describe the majority movement within Christianity at this period.

HARROWING OF HELL A doctrine found in the sixth century CE Apostles' Creed, and a favourite theme in Medieval art, it refers to the defeat of the powers of evil by Christ's descent into hell in the time between his death and resurrection.

JUDAISM The religion of the Jews' emerging from the crucible of their experiences of Exile in Babylon; it was based on the ancestral tribal religion of Israel, but was now centred on the Torah (Law).

THE LAST DAYS An eschatological designation of time, for the end of the created world as we know it, prior to everything being wound up by God.

LITURGY The original Greek word meant a public duty of any kind, but in the Septuagint it referred to the services at the Jerusalem temple. For Christians it means the public worship of the church, the ordered patterns of prayers and readings for those services, or particularly the Eucharist as the chief act of public worship.

MANICHEISM The religious system of the followers of Mani (a Persian of the third century CE) who believed in a rigid dualism between good and evil. Creation was full of particles of light, destined to return to their source when released. So believers were extremely ascetic and regulated their diet to avoid contamination by evil matter.

PAPYRUS/pl. PAPYRI Early form of writing material (origin of the word "paper") made from the dried and pressed stems of the Egyptian papyrus waterplant or reed. Papyrus also gave its name to what was written on it and so early writings (books, love letters, bills and lists) are known collectively as papyri. The survival of this material to the present day was possible in the arid Egyptian climate.

PARACLETE One who comforts/encourages/defends in a court of law/counsels – no one is quite sure what the exact shade of meaning is. It is the Johannine name for the Holy Spirit in his particular role of replacing Jesus both to the believer and as the world's accuser.

PARACLETIC An adjective meaning comforting, encouraging (related to the role of the Paraclete).

PARALLELISM The characteristic structure of Hebrew poetry (as in the Psalms) where two lines together express matching ideas.

PARENESIS A Greek word meaning "exhortation" or "encouragement" which is used for preaching in general, or more particularly ethical teaching presented in a compact and highly structured form.

PAROUSIA The Second Coming or the Reappearance of Christ in glory, expected by Christians at the end of time, heralding the Last Judgement.

PHARISEES (the name may literally mean "the separated ones") a Jewish religious grouping of those who kept the Torah (Law) with great rigour and relevance. They emerged during the late Hasmonean period of the second century BCE to become a weighty party on the Sanhedrin (or supreme Jewish Council). Most of the famous teaching rabbis were Pharisees. The survival of Judaism after the destruction of the Temple in 70 CE was largely due to the Pharisees.

PLATONISM Teaching of the idealist Greek philosopher Plato (427–347 BCE). He believed in two worlds; that the one in which we live is an illusory shadow of the true and real world of ideas. This principle is explained most vividly in the celebrated image of the cave in book 7 of Plato's *Republic*.

POLEMIC Conflict, or more particularly hostile propaganda.

PROOF TEXT A verse or passage from the Old Testament used by New Testament writers to explain and demonstrate why a particular feature of Jesus' life *had* to happen, for example the birth at Bethlehem (Micah 5.2).

RABBI Jewish teacher; more particularly one of the sages of the Pharisees in the first and second centuries CE. The teaching of these rabbis was not collected and published until the end of the second century, long after the books of the New Testament were written.

REDACTION CRITICISM This concentrates on the changes which may have been made to the traditional gospel material by the final editor or redactor, to suit his particular theological purpose.

SACRAMENTS Special signs or tokens of God's grace to the faithful. Two sacraments featured in the gospels, Baptism and Holy Communion, were instituted apparently by Jesus himself. The other five sacraments, as practised in Catholic churches were rites evolved by the Church.

SADDUCEES Their name may mean that they were, or claimed to be, "the righteous ones". Often in rivalry with the Pharisees, they were the priestly, aristocratic, and largely pro-Roman faction in Jewish politics. In religious matters they were ultra-conservative.

SECTARIAN A sect or sub-division of a religious group; such people tend to have their own inward-looking, self-defensive mentality.

SEPTUAGINT A translation of the Hebrew Bible into Greek, made in the second century BCE to help Hellenistic (Greek-speaking) Jews in Alexandria. Traditionally it was the work of 70 (Latin – septuaginta) elders. The Jews made other Greek translations not least because the early Christians adopted the Septuagint.

SOPHIST The Greek word means a wise man, a professional teacher. It comes to denote an "alternative" philosopher whose art is to ask awkward questions, and rely on the innate skills of human wisdom. Socrates in Athens of the fifth century BCE would not have called himself a sophist but behaved rather like one.

SOTERIOLOGY The study of ideas about salvation and the role of a saviour or redeemer.

STOIC A follower of the school of moral philosophy founded by Zeno at the beginning of the third century BCE. Stoics believed that the duty of man was to follow Reason and the Natural Law, and to suppress emotion. A belief of head rather than heart, Stoicism advocated the virtues of humanity and tolerance, and the appropriateness of suicide as a last resort.

STRUCTURALISM A modern way of analyzing language, literary texts, or myths, in terms either of the surface patterns of meaning or of the underlying principles and relationships/contrasts of fundamental ideas.

SYNAGOGUE Meeting place (literally); where the local Jews met to study Torah (Law) and for daily prayer. Synagogues appeared before the destruction of the Temple in 70 CE; the origin of the synagogue may date to the Babylonian Exile (587–535/458 BCE), but actual buildings are hard to trace before the New Testament period. What is certain is that the existence of synagogues enabled Judaism to survive the catastrophe of 70 CE.

SYNCRETISM A mixture of religious ideas from various sources.

SYNOPTIC GOSPELS These are the gospels of Matthew, Mark and Luke, which are regarded as having a literary relationship with each other, because they share common material and a similar order. A favoured explanation is that Matthew and Luke are both expanded versions of Mark. In the past these three gospels were thought to belong together, sharing the same view of Jesus and clearly distinct from the Fourth Gospel, John.

TETRAGRAMMATON Literally "the four letters", in Hebrew YHWH, that is a prominent name for God in the Old Testament. In older English translations of the Bible it was rendered as Jehovah, but is now reckoned by scholars to be Yahweh. It was the sacred name for God, so holy that by Jesus' time it was blasphemous even to utter it (except for the High Priest in the Temple on one day in the year).

THEOPHANY A display of him/herself by a god or goddess to the believer.

TRINITARIAN Related to an understanding of God as three distinct persons in the one single Godhead.

ZEALOT A person believing that direct action to dispose of the Roman occupation through terrorism was a religious duty for a Jew. The name comes from the religious "zeal" exclusively directed to Israel's God. "Cananean" in Aramaic means the same as "Zealot" (see Mark 3.19; Matthew 10.4). The Romans called such people "sicarii" (men with daggers).

Index